HOW CHILDREN UNDERSTAND WAR AND PEACE

This book is dedicated to the memory of Yitzhak Rabin, who was assassinated in the midst of his effort to bring peace to the Middle East.

HOW CHILDREN UNDERSTAND WAR AND PEACE

A Call for International Peace Education

Amiram Raviv

Louis Oppenheimer

Daniel Bar-Tal

Editors

Jossey-Bass Publishers
San Francisco

Jossey-Bass books and products are available through most bookstores. To contact Jossey-Bass directly, call (888) 378-2537, fax to (800) 605-2665, or visit our website at www.josseybass.com.

Substantial discounts on bulk quantities of Jossey-Bass books are available to corporations, professional associations, and other organizations. For details and discount information, contact the special sales department at Jossey-Bass.

 Manufactured in the United States of America on Lyons Falls Turin Book. This paper is acid-free and 100 percent totally chlorine-free.

Library of Congress Cataloging-in-Publication Data

How children understand war and peace : a call for international peace education / Amiram Raviv, Louis Oppenheimer, and Daniel Bar-Tal, editors. — 1st ed.
    p. cm.
Includes bibliographical references and index.
ISBN 0-7879-4169-7 (acid-free paper)
    1. Peace—Study and teaching. 2. Children and peace. I. Raviv, Amiram. II. Oppenheimer, Louis. III. Bar-Tal, Daniel.
JZ5534 .H69 1999
303.6'6—dc21D

          98-40154

FIRST EDITION

HB Printing 10 9 8 7 6 5 4 3 2 1

CONTENTS

PART THREE
Learning in Schools

PREFACE

ALL THREE OF US KNOW from personal experience what peace, conflict, and war are. We all are Israelis, though one of us is also Dutch, and we participated in some of the Israeli-Arab wars. We also followed, with hope and active support, the beginning of the peace process in the Middle East, heralded by the arrival of Egyptian president Anwar Sadat in Jerusalem in November 1977, and years later we continue to support the Oslo accords, which attempted to resolve peacefully the protracted conflict between Israeli Jews and Palestinians.

We believe that violent conflicts and wars are hideous reflections of the darker aspects of human nature, and all efforts should be made to stop human beings from engaging in intergroup violence and warfare. The present book expresses our concerns and, we hope, constitutes a small contribution to the stated aspiration. This book is based on the assumption that people as group members engage in conflict and war on the basis of beliefs they hold. Individuals need justifications, rationales, and explanations as a basis for their violent actions. Their beliefs about peace, conflict, and war are part of this epistemic basis. Hypothetically, if human beings were to believe that wars should not take place under any circumstances, being evil and immoral, their occurrence would probably be reduced. In contrast, however, human beings have believed throughout centuries of civilization that various situations justify war and that there are goals which sanctify certain means. Therefore, it is important to learn how people view peace, conflict, and war, since this knowledge may determine to a great extent humanity's well-being. Knowledge about peace, conflict, and war is acquired during childhood and applied to the understanding of interpersonal and intergroup relations. This early learning is often the foundation upon which new beliefs and perceptions are formed. Thus, it is of great importance to study the kinds of beliefs children form about peace, conflict, and war; the changes which take place in the course of their development; and the factors influencing their acquisition and modification of this knowledge.

We recognize that society's active and intentional efforts may strengthen views which are instrumental in peacekeeping and peace building around the world. Schools may play an important role in these efforts, since children and adolescents are required to attend these educational institutions, which provide experience and knowledge relevant to the understanding of peace, conflict, and war.

The assumptions we have elaborated here led us to compile a volume presenting attempts made in various parts of the world to study children's and adolescents' beliefs about peace, conflict, and war. We hope that it contributes to the understanding of how these beliefs are formed and that this may help to create conditions and develop interventions which foster beliefs facilitating the peaceful resolution of conflicts and prevent the outbreak of intergroup violence.

Through the years, psychologists, applying psychological knowledge, contributed greatly to warfare by developing the means to wage psychological wars. It is time for psychologists to find ways to make some active contribution to strengthening peace in the world.

AMIRAM RAVIV
LOUIS OPPENHEIMER
DANIEL BAR-TAL

INTRODUCTION

UNDERSTANDING PEACE, CONFLICT, AND WAR

Louis Oppenheimer, University of Amsterdam;
Daniel Bar-Tal, Tel Aviv University;
and Amiram Raviv, Tel Aviv University

The world cannot just be explained, it must be grasped
and understood as well. It is not enough to impose one's
own words on it, but one must also listen to the polyphony
of often contradictory messages the world sends out and try
to penetrate their meaning. It is not enough to describe, in scien-
tific terms, the mechanics of things and events; their spirit must
be personally perceived and experienced. [One] cannot merely
follow the timetable we have set for our influence on the world;
we must also honor and respect the infinitely more complex
timetable the world has set for itself. That timetable is the sum
of the thousands of independent timetables of an infinite
number of natural, historical and human actions.

—Václav Havel, 1996, p. 209

AT THE ONSET OF THE PROCESS which led to the realization of the present volume, we had not read this excerpt from one of President Václav Havel's speeches. In spite of this, we were convinced that to discuss the

I

way in which children and adolescents in our societies come to understand peace, conflict, and war, and the consequences of conflict and war on their emotional, cognitive, and behavioral functioning, would require a broad and open approach—an approach which would include diversity of theoretical conceptions, empirical methods, and applied interventions without imposing a priori constraints.

Why Study Children's and Adolescents' Understanding of Peace, Conflict, and War?

Knowledge about the developmental course of children's and adolescents' understanding of peace and war is scarce. While information is available dealing with their understanding of war as a manifestation of violence and peace defined as the absence or negation of war (negative peace), little is known about the acquisition of knowledge about peace defined in terms of harmony, cooperation, and coexistence (positive peace; cf. Galtung, 1985) and about conflict and war as consequences of mutually affective conflicts between groups and nations.

A variety of arguments can be presented for the importance of studying the content and developmental course of the understanding of peace and war. First, war and conflict will to a large extent determine for some time to come the well-being of people wherever they live on our earth, because "the sources of conflict and war are pervasive and deep" (Boutros-Ghali, 1992, p. 2). That is, "the development of a peace culture is not easy in any circumstances . . . in which conflict has developed a long history and become part of the culture" (Gillett, 1994, p. 20). According to the United Nations report, "The Impact of Armed Conflict on Children" (Machel, 1996), "thirty major armed conflicts raged in different locations around the world" in 1995 (p. 1) and because of changes in "patterns and characteristics of contemporary armed conflict . . . the [risk] for children has considerably increased" (p. 5) and the "proportion of war victims who are civilians has leaped dramatically from 5 percent to over 90 percent" in recent decades (p. 6). This situation highlights the importance of finding means which may support the effort to achieve a culture of peace or "peace building" (Boutros-Ghali, 1992). Peace building involves every activity by which structures are identified and supported which "will tend to strengthen and solidify peace in order to avoid a relapse into conflict" (Boutros-Ghali, 1992, p. 10) or which "will tend to consolidate peace and advance a sense of confidence and well-being" (p. 32).

We believe that the study of the developmental course by which children and adolescents come to understand concepts such as peace, conflict, and war, as well as the role of societal and individual variables in the development of this understanding, constitutes an important contributive activity for the process of peace building for two reasons. First, it will enhance our knowledge about how children and adolescents understand these concepts and what kind of meaning they ascribe to them. Second, because knowledge serves as an important basis for attitudes and behavior, these insights can be used to explain attitudes toward, cognitive reasoning about, and behavior in situations of peace, conflict, and war (see, for example, Bar-Tal, in press). The latter is especially important because knowledge that is acquired during childhood and adolescence serves as a basis for adult understanding. Experiences which shape early understanding may be crucial for the way the world is perceived in adulthood.

The second argument concerns the insight that the development of any concept is a constructive process and is based on "seeing, hearing, and remembering" which make use of stimulus information depending on circumstances (Neisser, 1967, p. 10). Consequently, the contents and structure of children's and adolescents' understanding of peace, conflict, and war are shaped by developmental factors, external sources of information, and experience within sociocultural structures or settings (Neisser's "circumstances" or nation-state societies; Oppenheimer, 1995, 1996b). According to Valsiner (1988), the sociocultural structure, in the sense of a collective entity, is "learned by the children in the context of their *whole* experience within their environments, rather than merely in settings where adults explicitly teach the children" (p. 292; e.g., Elias, 1939). The internalization of values, norms, and attitudes inherent in the generally shared sociocultural structure will result in "personal sociocultural structures." Because internalization processes are dependent on each child's internalized knowledge structures, these processes will take place in personal and unique ways. The personal sociocultural structure, then, is the product of "co-constructivism" in which the child and the environment participate actively. Norms, values, and attitudes "will come to be similar in the children's age cohort by way of being shared collectively" (Valsiner, 1988, p. 293). Hence, commonalties in images or knowledge schemas concerning peace, conflict, and war are socially negotiated to become interpersonally meaningful. It is the personal sociocultural structure and the knowledge schemas inherent in such a general structure, for example, Piaget's "accommodative schemas" (Piaget, 1981; Chapman, 1988), which regulate and monitor behavior, affections, and thought. In addition and as was noted previously, the shared sociocultural structure or the view of the world as shaped in childhood and adolescence to a large part determines adult perspectives.

One of the goals of developmental psychology is to trace commonalties, for instance, in conceptual and behavioral development. From these commonalties inferences can be made about the norms and values inherent in the sociocultural structure which are considered interpersonally meaningful and which will be amplified by the individuals functioning in this structure (cf. Goody, 1991). When different sociocultural structures are compared (for instance, with regard to the understanding of peace, conflict, and war), inferences can be made about the culture-universal and culture-specific processes and determinants of this knowledge.

Finally, we believe that the study of children's and adolescents' understanding of peace, conflict, and war contributes to efforts aiming at the attainment of a culture of peace. Because socialization and education are fundamental processes in such efforts, detailed knowledge is required about the prerequisites for children's and adolescents' learning and development of the underlying principles necessary for endurable peace. The lack of such knowledge may be a major cause of the limited effectiveness of peace education programs (cf. Oppenheimer, 1989, 1995; Vriens, Chapter One of this volume). Education toward a culture of peace, however, is not an easy undertaking. Peace is considered a "second-order" concept *derived* from the "first-order" concept of war (Lourenço, Chapter Four of this volume), a passive concept which makes it extremely difficult to formulate *activities* which relate to peace. Whereas children have no problems when asked to "play war," a total lack of activity and blank stares are observed when children or even adults are asked to "play peace."

Hence, the central purpose of peace education may well be the generation of ideas and programs to *activate* the concept of peace (Oppenheimer, 1996b) and simultaneously to change the romantic images of war and heroism. Such socialization and education may be realized by sharing meaningful knowledge involving, for example, the conviction that cooperation (peaceful coexistence) is more valuable than conflict or war. Thus, socialization and educational processes should be directed to reciprocal understanding, respect, and tolerance (cooperation and coexistence) within the immediate setting with younger children, more elaborate social settings with older children, and sociocultural and global settings with adolescents. For instance, according to Piaget (1948/1980), the task of the educator is "to mold a spiritual tool in the mind of the child—not a new habit, or even a new belief, but rather a new method and tool that will permit him to understand and to find his way" (p. 135). For Piaget the essential target of the educational process is for children to discover by "lived-in experience" the nature of the "conflicts of reciprocity and the same misunderstandings of all social intercourse." In addition, following the organization of social life among the students, the educational process should be extended "in the direction of international exchanges or even of study groups that have international problems as their object" (p. 141). These *active* educational processes, which have the stimulation and promotion of international life as their targets, will result in real changes in the personal and shared general sociocultural structure and, hence, in the emergence of a culture of peace. To achieve this goal, it is indispensable to have information about the meanings children and adolescents attach to peace, conflict, and war.

With these reasons in mind, it is thus not surprising that social and behavioral scientists have devoted much time and effort to trying to understand the causes of wars and conflicts (cf. Auvinen, 1997; Galtung, 1996), the management and resolution of conflicts (cf. Ayres, 1997; Bar-Tal, Kruglanski, & Klar, 1989; Bloomfield, 1995; Bonta, 1996; Mor, 1997), and the essence of peace (cf. Howell & Willis, 1989). Since individuals or groups ultimately initiate conflict, the outbreak of war, and the negotiation of peace, some of these efforts have been directed toward studying the psychological basis of human behavior. This research trend has included, over the last three decades, studies which have attempted to investigate how children and adolescents understand war, conflict, and peace (for a review, see Hakvoort, 1996; Hakvoort & Oppenheimer, 1998) and how these events affect their psychological functioning (cf. Leavitt & Fox, 1993).

The study of both the understanding of and acquisition of knowledge about peace, conflict, and war has been conducted from very different theoretical perspectives. In the next section, these theoretical perspectives, their conceptions, and their contributions will be succinctly discussed.

The Acquisition of Understanding: Theoretical Perspectives and Conceptions

Phenomena like peace and war deal with relationships among and between people, groups, and nations and involve a continuous sequence of interactions in which perspectives are either shared or ignored, and actions and reactions are coordinated (cf. Galtung, 1996). Peace and war can be defined as social phenomena and viewed as an integral part of a child's social world and experience. From this point of view, children's and adolescents' understanding of and reasoning about peace and war as well as developmental changes in this understanding are considered to be part of their social knowledge.

The development of social knowledge can be studied from different angles. In particular, with regard to the development of knowledge about peace, conflict, and war, four different approaches are relevant. These theoretical conceptions involve the cognitive-developmental, social learning, socialization, and ecological approaches. Within the cognitive-developmental or "organismic" approach (Piaget, 1952; cf. Hetherington & Parks, 1993), the development of knowledge and understanding is the result of interactions between the maturing individual and the environment; the child is perceived as actively seeking information and new experiences (cf. Chapman, 1988; Durkin, 1995; Flavell, 1963). Piaget accords social factors a prominent status in his explanation of the development of (social) knowledge. To become a "decentered epistemological subject" (Piaget, 1970, p. 361), interactions and social coordination between individuals are prerequisites (Durkin, 1995, p. 15; see also Chapman, 1988, pp. 336–340). Children adapt to their environment by assimilating new information and experiences to fit existing knowledge structures. If this is not possible, the existing knowledge structure has to be reorganized or accommodated to adapt to the new information. Development is then characterized by increasingly complex reorganizations and interrelations of mental structures to more advanced levels of cognitive functioning as the child matures (Chapman, 1988). The successive levels present different modes of cognitive organization and structure and reflect different ways of understanding the world. These changes in the *structure of thinking* (operational knowledge) have profound effects on the *contents* of knowledge as individuals mature. Consequently, age-related changes in the understanding of peace, war, and conflict are expected.

In contrast to the cognitive-developmental approach, the social learning approach perceives the child as relatively passive and molded by environmental factors which modify behavior. The behavioral perspective on learning, in which learning is seen as a continuous process over the life span supported by classical and operant conditioning processes, also includes imitation. Studies based on this perspective, for instance, have focused on the positive and negative aspects of television as a common source of models for children. According to this theory, children are selective about whom and what behaviors they imitate. Contemporary versions of social learning theory have included the role of cognitive factors in their accounts of learning (cf. Bandura, 1989).

Because cognitive structures emerge and change as a result of interactions with the environment, the development of social understanding thus depends on sociocultural factors. Understanding is then formed or given meaning by social influences, including potent agents of socialization such as parents, media, and schools. Socialization focuses on the processes whereby an individual's standards, skills, motives, attitudes, and behaviors are influenced to conform to those regarded as desirable and appropriate for his or her present or future role in society (Hetherington & Morris, 1978). Socializing agents not only provide information about the world but also actively try to mold children's perceptions, attitudes, and behaviors (Bar-Tal & Saxe, 1990). Certain groups and organizations within society, such as the family, school, and political parties, play key roles in socialization. Parents, siblings, peers, and teachers spend a great deal of their time communicating values and directing and modifying children's behavior. The socialization approach, hence, focuses on the intergenerational transfer of particular values and norms rather than on behavior modification in general as a consequence of learning.

Because "social agents *share* scales of social values by virtue of living in a common culture" (Chapman, 1988, p. 182, italics ours), children are not perceived as passive receivers of input but are thought to actively seek, organize, and use social information, which in part is acknowledged in contemporary cognitive-learning models. In addition, children either directly or indirectly experience various events which affect the way they understand peace, war, and conflict. Different sociocultural contexts are characterized by differences in the content of socialization processes (for example, values and norms), in opportunities to seek information, and in social and interpersonal events (Oppenheimer, 1996a, 1996b). Consequently, in spite of similarities in developmental processes, we expect differences in the perceptions and understanding of peace, war, and conflict across different sociocultural contexts.

Finally, during development societal organizations, such as the family, school, and political parties, will exert different influences. When children mature they will come into contact with a progressively larger number of different societal organizations and institutions. The ecological approach stresses the importance of understanding the relationships between the developing child and environmental systems such as the family, school, community, and culture. In this model, development involves the interplay between changing children and their changing relationships with different ecological (societal) systems. The children's subjective experience and understanding of the environment are important aspects of this perspective (cf. Bronfenbrenner, 1979, 1988; Valsiner, 1988; Vygotsky, 1978). For instance, in some sociocultural contexts but not others, schools play a particular and important role in the socialization of children's and adolescents' understanding of political knowledge (political socialization; cf. Löfgren, 1995). First, a number of study topics in the curricula contain contents which are directly concerned with these issues (Burns, 1995). Second, schools, by means of various interventions and extracurricular activities, may actively attempt to influence children's and adolescents' understanding of the government, national and international policy, and loyalty to the state (cf. Brock-Utne, 1994a, 1994b). However, research has suggested that the impact of these socialization processes is differentially related to the home background of the child and the nature of the relationship between the child and school. Consequently, schools may either directly or indirectly affect children's and adolescents' beliefs about peace, war, and conflict or not affect them at all. Finally, since school is itself a social system, it provides interpersonal and intergroup experiences which have an impact on how these concepts are understood.

It is obvious from the preceding discussion that each of the theoretical approaches can be applied to different contexts: the direct environment (the family, the peer group, and the school) and the indirect environment (the media, books, and so on). Each of these contexts will offer opportunities to experience, either directly or indirectly, situations of peaceful coexistence, conflict, and war, while distinctions should be made between knowledge acquired within the family, peer, and school settings and their interrelations as well as from the media (cultural variables) and direct experience. For instance, learning from indirect experiences could involve the acquisition of insights into the nature of interpersonal, intergroup, or international relations; learning from direct experiences may depend on factors such as the child's role within interpersonal and intragroup relationships (the extent of his or her participation), its intensity, its duration, and the reactions of the environment (Rafman, Canfield, Barbas, & Kaczorowski, 1996, 1997).

The theoretical approaches which have been discussed all perceive knowledge about peace, conflict, and war—like any other knowledge—to be based on personal constructions which are codetermined by a multitude of individual and environmental variables. While this knowledge may be shared by cohorts within sociocultural contexts, it is subjective knowledge which is directly related to the experiences of individuals and their level of operational thinking. This knowledge is always subject to changes as a result of a changing understanding of the world and relative to the knowledge of others. Hence, knowledge of peace, conflict, and war is considered to be changeable and dynamic.

Finally, as was discussed previously, our knowledge, or the way we understand our environment and our interpersonal and intergroup relationships (our accommodative schemes), regulates our attitudes and affective reactions toward peace and war and, by monitoring our emotions and behaviors, has behavioral implications.

The above discussion points toward interrelationships among the different theoretical approaches. However, in the literature on the development of knowledge and understanding about peace, conflict, and war, little intertheory discussion is present. For instance, a Piagetian cognitive-developmental framework is present in the research by Cooper (1965) and Ålvik (1968). In agreement with Piaget's theory, both authors assumed that to comprehend the relationships between actions (the causes and effects of peace and war), an understanding of the reciprocal nature of relationships among events was necessary. Whereas Cooper (1965) used this Piagetian framework to explain and understand the findings of his study, Ålvik (1968) explicitly tested this hypothesis by assessing children's ability to use reciprocal reasoning with Piagetian tasks (p. 190). With respect to the concept of peace, Ålvik (1968) did not find a clear relationship between the understanding of reciprocity and the development of positive conceptions of peace involving active intergroup interactions (for example, cooperation or negotiation). According to Ålvik, children's ability to better use reciprocal reasoning did not result in more sophisticated perceptions of peace, because the children were too well informed about the concrete aspects of peace through the mass media. With the concept of war, young children emphasized concrete visual cues (physical objects of war), while older children referred more frequently to the physical events and consequences of war and offered negative evaluations of war activities. Conceptions pointing to wars or conflicts as mutually effective interactions between nations were not present.

The socialization model for development has been used in studies by Haavelsrud (1970) and Rosell (1968). These authors made use of socialization principles within a political context; they focused on processes which affect an individual's political attitudes and behaviors and adapt the individual to his or her present or future role in a "democratic" society. In particular, the influence of social and political environments (the sociocultural structure) on children's understanding of peace and war is emphasized rather than cognitive maturity (the cognitive-developmental model). For example, Rosell (1968) explained the dominant emphasis on war activities among eight-year-olds and the increase of concerns dealing with the negative consequences of war among eleven- and fourteen-year-olds by "age socialization" (p. 271). In other words, the social environment does not expect young children to reflect on the consequences of war. Similarly, children's understanding of peace as the negation of war (negative peace) was explained by the strong emphasis on a negative peace (the termination or absence of war) by society as well as by the media. In a similar vein, Dinklage and Ziller (1989) studied influences of the social environment on children's understanding of peace and war. They noted that in different sociocultural contexts (United States and Germany), children photographed different scenes to express their ideas about peace and war. Dinklage and Ziller concluded that in the two cultural settings, different meanings were attached to the concepts of peace and war.

As can be noted from this short overview, to date the major emphasis in the study of children's and adolescents' understanding of and knowledge acquisition with respect to peace, conflict, and war has been on the cognitive-developmental model, embedded in social contexts (culture). This situation will additionally be emphasized when we review the available accumulated knowledge about the development of this knowledge and understanding.

State of the Art

Over the last three decades, two distinct research waves have been present with respect to children's and adolescents' understanding of peace and war. During the 1960s and 1970s, a "first wave" of studies was conducted which had as its focus developmental changes in children's understanding of peace and war. The studies involved primarily Western European countries (Cooper, 1965: England; Haavelsrud, 1970: Germany; Mercer, 1974: Scotland; Rosell, 1968: Sweden; Ålvik, 1968: Norway). Only Cooper's study included Japanese children and adolescents. In addition, this study set an example for the type of questionnaire which would be used in later studies (at least some questions were identical). While an interview procedure was most often used with the younger children (five- to seven-year-olds), a pencil-and-paper procedure was often employed with the older children. Only Ålvik (1968) used interviews with all his subjects (eight- to twelve-year-olds).

The findings of the studies in the first wave with younger children (cf. Cooper, 1965; Rosell, 1968; Ålvik, 1968) demonstrated that from the age of six onward, children developed clear conceptions of peace and war, and that the understanding of war developmentally precedes the understanding of peace. With younger children, peace was primarily characterized by social activities (playing together, being kind to one another) and negation of war. This type of conceptualization of peace increased until approximately the age of twelve and was also frequently observed with Swedish (Rosell, 1968) and Japanese (Cooper, 1965) adolescents. During late adolescence, more abstract conceptions involving international issues such as processes toward integration, reconciliation, and bilateral cooperation (positive peace) became evident. In spite of these findings, the expected positive relation between age and these more abstract issues was only observed with adolescents from West Berlin (Haavelsrud, 1970). In general, these studies showed that children and adolescents were well acquainted with the concrete aspects of peace. The characteristic of "peace of mind" was mentioned most frequently by English adolescents (Cooper, 1965).

War was predominantly characterized by concrete aspects such as objects of and participants in war and war activities. As the children matured they mentioned more often negative consequences of war (for example, destruction) in relation to negative emotions (for example, pain and sorrow). A few gender differences were reported in the understanding of war. English girls as well as girls from West Berlin mentioned war activities more often then objects of war, which were mentioned more often by the boys. Swedish girls associated war with the consequences of war more frequently than boys did.

During the 1980s and 1990s, a second wave of studies concerning children's and adolescents' understanding of peace and war was conducted in Western Europe in The Netherlands and West Germany (Hakvoort & Oppenheimer, 1993; Van Kempen, Peek, & Vriens, 1986; Dinklage & Ziller, 1989; Falk & Selg, 1982) and in Eastern Europe in East Germany and Rumania (Von Jacob & Schmidt, 1988; Cretu, 1988), as well as in Israel (Spielmann, 1986), Australia (Hall, 1993; Rodd, 1985), and Canada and the United States (McCreary & Palmer, 1991; Covell, Rose-Krasnor, & Fletcher, 1994). Various investigators (cf. Covell et al., 1994; Hakvoort & Oppenheimer, 1993; Hall, 1993) again based their questions on Cooper's questionnaire (1965); others constructed their own questionnaire (cf. McCreary & Palmer, 1991). Whereas the pencil-and-paper procedure was most frequently used, other methods were also used, including interviews, written essays, drawings, and photo-communication.

Several studies from the second wave confirmed the results of studies from the first wave. Young children were again observed to conceptualize war developmentally prior to peace (cf. Covell et al., 1994; Falk & Selg, 1982; Hakvoort & Oppenheimer, 1993; Von Jacob & Schmidt, 1988; Van Kempen et al., 1986). The dominant themes related to peace involved harmony (perceived as harmony in nature), social relationships (for example, friendship and happiness), the absence of quarrels, the negation of war, and a calm and tranquil environment. The Israeli children and adolescents in Spielmann's study (1986) also mentioned freedom of travel and security. In accordance with the first-wave studies, the second-wave studies showed that it was not until adolescence that ideas about reconciliation (international and positive contributions to peace) appeared in conceptualizations of peace. Evidence for a positive relation between these ideas and age was only found with Australian children and adolescents (Hall, 1993). Indications of age-related changes in conceptions of peace were also found by Hakvoort and Oppenheimer (1993) and Spielmann (1986). Ideas about equality, mutual respect, and the absence of discrimination were almost exclusively mentioned by adolescents. Contrary to the studies in the first wave, gender differences in the understanding of peace were reported in the second-wave studies. With younger girls, peace was understood in terms of social relationships and meaning (Falk & Selg, 1982) and was frequently perceived within the context of the immediate social environment (Hakvoort & Oppenheimer, 1993). Boys, on the other hand, understood peace more frequently in terms of disarmament (as a strategy to attain peace).

With regard to the concept of war, the findings of the studies from the first wave were replicated. In children's definitions of war, identical themes were observed relating to concrete aspects of war such as objects of war and war activities. Concerns about the negative consequences of war, as well as negative evaluations of war, became more frequent as the children grew older. Girls understood war more frequently in terms of negative emotions, while boys mentioned concrete aspects of war more frequently (Falk & Selg, 1982; Von Jacob & Schmidt, 1988). In agreement with the gender differences observed for the understanding of peace, Hakvoort and Oppenheimer (1993) observed that girls perceived war in terms of quarrels between friends (referring to the immediate social environment) more often than boys. Dutch boys did not relate war to their immediate social environment but rather referred to conflicts between distant nations. (For a more extensive review of the literature, see Hakvoort & Oppenheimer, 1998.)

The Present Volume

As we noted at the beginning of this Introduction, the purpose of this volume is to offer an overview of contemporary insights, accumulated research, and conceptual explanations which may shed light on how children and adolescents in our societies come to understand peace, conflict, and war. For this purpose we opted for a diversity of theoretical conceptions and empirical methods. Although various studies dealing with these issues have already been published, this volume is unique in that it attempts to provide a coherent, systematic analysis of available knowledge by presenting different conceptions and methods in a complementary way.

In addition, the chapters in this volume present a host of new information and empirical data from different international perspectives. As a consequence, culture-universal and culture-specific factors are illuminated. The different conceptions and methods are in part a result of the different disciplinary approaches to the topic. The chapters are written by developmental, social, educational, and clinical psychologists, as well as educational scientists. Because of the complementary nature of the chapters, they provide the added value of an interdisciplinary approach to the study of children's and adolescents' understanding of peace, conflict, and war. The different disciplinary approaches also lead to different levels of analysis with respect to the developmental course for this understanding. The role of the immediate environment (the family, school, and peer group—the micro level) is included, as well as the roles of social institutions, society, and culture (the macro level). As a consequence, the chapters include both descriptive and prescriptive orientations, or a combination of both. When the different dimensions presented in this volume are perceived to be complementary, we offer a variety of suggestions for more sophisticated and interdisciplinary measurement techniques and methods for future studies.

The book is organized in three sections which focus on different perspectives adopted in the study of children's and adolescents' understanding of peace, conflict, and war: (1) developmental perspectives, (2) approaches involving processes of socialization and the contribution of experience, and (3) the role and impact of the educational system and learning in school.

Developmental Perspectives

The first section of the book deals with developmental perspectives in the study of children's and adolescents' understanding of peace, conflict, and war. These perspectives are characterized by a variety of approaches which are primarily informed by Piagetian developmental theory. Of crucial importance within this theoretical approach is the idea that the developing individual stands central. Instead of perceiving development from the perspective of the social environment (the adults' perspective), development is studied from the perspective of the child. As a consequence, the expectations of the social environment, which includes parents, teachers, and the school, may not correspond to the thoughts, understanding, and experience of the child. When such a lack of correspondence lies at the basis of our approach toward children, the effectiveness and efficiency of the approach may be questioned. This is exactly the central tenet of Lennart Vriens in Chapter One. Vriens assumes that peace education has almost entirely been shaped by the concern of adults for their world: the way they perceive threats and problems with respect to peace and war has been directly transformed into the subjects of peace education curricula without taking into account whether children perceive the same threats and problems in an identical way. As a consequence, peace education programs rarely make use of or include children's own experiences of conflict and violence. In his chapter, Vriens offers an extensive review of the differences between adults' and children's thinking about the damage caused to children by real war experiences, children's knowledge about peace and war, their fears about nuclear disasters, and their understanding of peace and war in relation to everyday experiences. The consequences for peace education are emphasized.

Changes in the organization and structure of thought as a function of age relate directly to the way the developing individual perceives interpersonal relationships and moral values. In Chapter Two, Ilse Hakvoort and Louis Oppenheimer present the results of a longitudinal, time-sequential study of Dutch children's and adolescents' understanding of peace and war. The guiding hypotheses of this study were (1) that peace is primarily understood as the negation of war (negative peace) and that during adolescence peace will become perceived as a process toward integration and peaceful coexistence (positive peace); (2) that the understanding of peace and war will change from being concrete (materially related) to abstract (norm-related); and (3) that developmental changes in the understanding of interpersonal relationships underlie changes in the understanding of peace and war. The third hypothesis includes the assumption that a prior understanding of the mutually interdependent and affective nature of the opinions of different individuals is required to understand peace as consisting of dynamic reciprocal relationships between nations and war as consisting of a disturbance in these relationships. On the basis of their findings, the authors develop a theoretical model in which the understanding of peace and war is embedded within a social-cognitive, developmental framework defined by the development of interpersonal understanding.

A somewhat different approach, though one which also involves interpersonal relationships, is adopted by Robert Ziller, Dahlie Moriarty, and Stephen Phillips. In Chapter Three, Ziller, Moriarty, and Phillips assume that children's images of peace and war mirror their personality and, in particular, their nonprejudiced views of relationships between themselves and others. The way children perceive their relationships with others is characterized by a "universal orientation" which postulates that children use a perception of similarity rather than difference between the self and others. On the basis of this universal orientation, photos of destruction and human suffering are predicted to be perceived as more characteristic of war than photos of war objects such as tanks, planes, and soldiers. In addition, this orientation is thought to be subject to intervention. For instance, showing a slide show of photographs from the book *The Family of Man,* in which the commonality of life events such as birth, childhood, joy, love, suffering, and death is emphasized among diverse people, strengthens the universal orientation.

Since contemporary sociocultural structures (societies) are basically warlike (Bjerstedt, 1993), Orlando Lourenço assumes that war, as a true, real, and unfortunate "institution," is a first-order phenomenon. Peace, on the other hand, is generally reduced to the negation of war (the absence of war) or the "not-being" of warlike attitudes and, hence, is a derived or second-order phenomenon. In Chapter Four, Lourenço constructs an argument leading to the conclusion that to develop positive conceptions of peace, peace education should be related to justice education. In the first section of his chapter, he presents the argument that any effort to make children become aware that peace is a positive process (one involving social harmony, interpersonal understanding, cooperation, and a desire for justice) is a moral injunction equal to Kohlberg's ethic of justice and Gilligan's ethic of care. In the second section, facts are presented from different social and psychological domains to show that war is considered to be a first-order, affirmative, and active phenomenon. Peace is then reduced to a second-order, negative, and reactive process. This section is followed by the presentation of findings with regard to Portuguese children's understanding of peace, war, and strategies to attain peace which illustrate the asymmetry of peace and war. In the final section, the conclusions are presented.

Socialization and Experience

The second section of this volume focuses on the social context in which children understand phenomena like peace, war, and conflict. In these chapters, attention is given to the role of socializing agents such as parents, media, and schools, as well as to the way in which social experiences shape the development of this understanding. The effects of differences in these variables across societies are discussed in several chapters in terms of cross-cultural differences in the understanding (meaning) of peace, war, and conflict.

According to Katherine Covell (Chapter Five), concepts of peace and war are socialized as a joint function of direct and indirect experiences and the contexts in which those experiences occur. In this chapter, Covell examines the impact of sociocultural contexts as socialization frameworks which set beliefs about, and attitudes toward, peace and war. Because the children and adolescents in Covell's study are not directly experiencing war or conflicts, their understanding of peace and war should be related to the prevailing ideologies, values, and attitudes of the sociocultural context in which they are being reared. This hypothesis is tested by comparing the ideas about and attitudes toward peace and war of children and adolescents raised in Canada and the United States. While the sociocultural contexts of both countries are similar in many respects, important differences include a strong ethic of multiculturalism in Canada which discourages the overt political socialization and training in patriotism which is characteristic of the value placed on assimilation within the U.S. educational system. Furthermore, in contrast to the military interventionist approach of the United States, Canada's focus has been on peacekeeping and backroom diplomacy. On the basis of these differences in the socialization framework presented in the two sociocultural contexts, differences in the way children and adolescents think about peace and war are expected.

The outcome of political socialization can also be examined by studying loyalties and identities at different national and international levels. Political socialization involves the processes by which children and adolescents come to understand political knowledge and develop their attitudes toward particular political systems. As was noted previously, their understanding of peace, war, conflict, and related issues such as life and death and right and wrong is a product of internal, cognitive variables and the external contexts in which individuals mature. With this basic assumption in mind, Raija-Leena Punamäki sets out in Chapter Six to analyze how children's understanding of peace, conflict, and war develops under different political and military conditions. According to Punamäki, understanding of peace and war takes place within the context of a society fighting against somebody and for something. Understanding and knowledge, however, also develop in relation to the level of children's cognitive-emotional development. Hence, insights into the way children at different levels of development perceive peace and war, as well as their emotional reactions to war experiences and their ability to cope with them, are of crucial importance to understanding the developmental course of children's and adolescents' understanding of peace, conflict, and war. In this chapter, the separate and integrated contributions of societal, or national, and individual determinants in children's attempts to understand peace and war are studied. Empirical examples of Israeli and Palestinian children's attitudes toward peace, war, and the enemy are presented within three different military settings.

To obtain insights into changes in the understanding of peace and war as a consequence of contextual changes, Frances McLernon and Ed Cairns report in Chapter Seven on a series of studies dealing with North Irish adolescents' understanding of peace and war prior to and following the Irish Republican Army (IRA) cease-fire, as well as immediately after the ending of the cease-fire. McLernon and Cairns explicitly place their study within the context of previous studies because of the need for comparison; they examine the differences and similarities in the understanding of peace by children living in different war conditions (for example, North Irish children versus Israeli children), as compared with that of children living in peaceful societies. Similarly, they compare the understanding of war by North Irish children with that of children living in peaceful societies. In addition to these comparisons, the studies reported in this chapter are unique in that information is presented which deals with the direct contribution of a societal change (the IRA cease-fire) on the way in which children think about peace, war, and conflict.

In Chapter Eight, Amiram Raviv, Daniel Bar-Tal, Leah Koren-Silvershatz, and Alona Raviv report on a study in which Israeli children's understanding of peace and war, as well as of approaches to stop conflicts, prevent wars, and maintain peace, are assessed at two different moments in recent history: during a relatively peaceful period in Israel and during the Gulf War. The authors focus on two different aspects which may contribute to the development of this understanding: receiving information about an event and experiencing it. Using the assumption that the experience of war and warlike events will have a profound effect on the way children and adolescents think about peace, war, and conflict, along with empirical data from their study, the authors discuss a conceptual framework that includes experience as a basis for the representation of knowledge.

In Chapter Nine, Solveig Hägglund embeds the development of the understanding of peace, war, and conflict in the early everyday experiences of children, for example, friendship and antagonism. According to Hägglund, there is ample evidence that the experiences of being friends, having friends, and friendship relate to the understanding of peace, whereas losing friends, being enemies, and antagonism relate to the understanding of war. When children mature, the friendship-antagonism dimension is replaced by a more complex understanding of peace and war which includes abstract and universal norms. On the basis of this process, Hägglund assumes that the meaning attached to friendship and antagonism in childhood constitutes a basis for a more complex and mature understanding of peace and war, respectively. Because the meaning of peace and war is collectively structured in a sociocultural context, differences between sociocultural contexts will lead to differences in the meanings attached to friendship and antagonism and, hence, in the understanding of peace and war. These assumptions are discussed by means of the theory of social representations and are empirically illustrated by the data from a Dutch-Swedish comparative study and an ongoing study on Swedish children's perceptions of rules for social responsibility in the classroom setting.

To date, in most research involving the developmental course of children's understanding of peace, war, and conflict, this understanding has been used as a dependent variable in examining the influence of sociocultural variables such as violence on this developmental process. In Chapter Ten, Michael Van Slyck, Marilyn Stern, and Salman Elbedour reverse this order and examine the way adolescents' attitudes toward conflict and violence may affect other social aspects, such as their attitudes and behavior toward others. The authors report on a series of studies in which components of adolescents' attitudes toward conflict are assessed—as a self-reported conflict response tendency or a stereotype response tendency toward other cultural groups—and the relationship of these variables to factors such as mental health status, personality traits, and amenability to conflict intervention. The findings are discussed within the theoretical framework developed by the authors, which suggests that acquiring "positive" (prosocial) attitudes and behaviors toward conflict is developmentally appropriate and that the acquisition of such attitudes and behaviors will have a positive impact on attitudes and behaviors in other aspects of the adolescent's life.

Learning in Schools

Schools may directly affect children's and adolescents' beliefs about peace, war, and conflict through curricular topics, such as transfer of information about the government, national and international policy, and loyalty to the state, and extracurricular activities, such as interventions and conflict-resolution programs.

In Chapter Eleven, Kathy Bickmore argues that conflict-resolution programs are often started in school because the school's adult leadership sees problems with violence and "cooperation" among students. Different types of conflict-resolution programs for public schools are discussed with respect to their underlying theories and the ways such opportunities do and do not fit comfortably in the social and curricular contexts of the regular school program. In general, conflict-resolution programs involve a pullout of a selected group of pupils for special training workshops, followed by deployment of these students to help peers manage interpersonal conflicts in a few well-bounded contexts. Conflict-resolution programs concern peer "monitoring" and compliance with school behavioral codes, as well as democratic education, youth leadership, and the politics of peacemaking. In addition to designated conflict-resolution programs, Bickmore discusses other important ways in which conflict is addressed (and denied) in schools. These involve, among others, the conditions under which students practice managing conflict and using conflict resolution in the context of regular curricular activities and what they learn about themselves as managers of conflict in extracurricular activities such as democratic education within student councils or student leadership programs. According to Bickmore, by keeping the "peace" and avoiding conflict in daily school activities, lower-status students, in particular, may be denied an opportunity to develop conflict-resolution skills which may not be available outside school.

In Chapter Twelve, Patricia Avery, David Johnson, Roger Johnson, and James Mitchell adopt the position that conflict is a necessary and vital part of living in a multicultural, pluralistic democracy. The way in which people deal with controversial public issues and approach interpersonal conflict is thought to be directly linked to the quality of the sociocultural structure and civic discourse within this structure. Because school is one of the primary socializing agents for young people, it plays an important role in structuring students' experiences and helping them to interpret their experiences with both academic and interpersonal conflict. In two sections, the authors offer an in-depth review of research on the school as a context for teaching and learning about conflict. The first section focuses on the macro- and micro-level barriers to exploring conflict in the classroom. The macro-level barriers include institutional norms and sociocultural contexts; the micro-level barriers include the teachers' beliefs and values and the students' cognitive, social, and psychological development. In the second section, a description is given of research-based methods for structuring academic controversy and interpreting interpersonal conflict in the classroom.

The role of peers in conflict management has not received much attention to date. In Chapter Thirteen, Robin Hall states that the study of peer mediation in schools is a relatively new phenomenon. Hall offers a summary of the characteristics of peer mediation programs, gives outlines of their historical development, and reviews the empirical research on their effects and effectiveness. On the basis of this summary, different approaches to learning about conflict management are discerned through peer mediation programs. Evaluations of the outcomes of these programs are discussed in terms of the observed effects on the mediators, the disputants, discipline, and the school and classroom climate. The characteristics of successful programs are reviewed and suggestions for further research are offered.

The subject of the final chapter returns to the contents of the first chapter by Lennart Vriens. In Chapter Fourteen, Ian Harris outlines the history of peace education, which has shifted from focusing on a global interstate system which caused wars, slaughter, and suffering at the beginning of this century, to dealing with conflict resolution within the context of international forms of violence. The approach of the global interstate system had as its purpose to cause students to think of themselves as compassionate global citizens who could identify with people struggling for peace throughout the world. The conflict-resolution approach focuses on mediation and communication skills and promotes empathy and problem-solving skills; its purpose is to educate children toward peaceful familial and friendship relations. In addition to these two major forms of peace education, peace education programs exist which deal with violence prevention (for example, domestic violence and sexual assault) and which promote building a more positive future (for example, through human rights education and environmental studies). Consequently, contemporary peace education appears to focus on the three complementary processes of peacemaking, peacekeeping, and peace building by applying insights from the field of peace research to all levels of schooling.

○

This book aims to be a source for any student of the development of the understanding of peace, conflict, and war and the processes and variables involved in this development. We have opted for a variety of complementary theoretical perspectives and conceptualizations, as well as empirical methods and applied interventions. It is clear that the understanding of peace, conflict, and war is subjective, relative, and subject to change; is in part shared by societies; and has affective and behavioral consequences. The attainment of a culture of peace does not imply that conflicts have to be abolished, the more so since conflicts are dynamic sources for change within individual development, as well as in the history of society. Rather it is the way in which conflicts are solved which makes the difference between peace and war. Hence we are condemned to live with violent conflicts and wars as long as individuals, groups, and nations perceive war as a solution for conflicts. More than hitherto has been the case, individuals and societies have to learn and understand the costs and the meaning of war, how to resolve conflicts peacefully, and how to maintain peace. Such knowledge and understanding are extremely important and children should acquire them from as early an age as possible. Therefore, we should do everything possible to actively influence the understanding of peace, conflict, and war in order to make the world a better place to live in. This book is a contribution to such a goal.

REFERENCES

Ålvik, T. (1968). The development of views on conflict, war and peace among school children. *Journal of Peace Research, 5,* 171–195.

Auvinen, J. (1997). Political conflict in less developed countries 1981–89. *Journal of Peace Research, 34,* 177–195.

Ayres, R. W. (1997). Mediating international conflicts: Is image change necessary? *Journal of Peace Research, 34,* 431–448.

Bandura, A. (1989). Human agency in social cognitive theory. *American Psychologist, 44,* 1175–1184.

Bar-Tal, D. (in press). *Societal beliefs of ethos: Social psychological analysis of a society.* Thousand Oaks, CA: Sage.

Bar-Tal, D., Kruglanski, A., & Klar, Y. (1989). Conflict termination: An epistemological analysis of international cases. *Political Psychology, 10,* 233–255.

Bar-Tal, D., & Saxe, L. (1990). Acquisition of political knowledge: A social psychological analysis. In O. Ichilov (Ed.), *Political socialization, citizenship education and democracy* (pp. 116–133). New York: Teachers College Press.

Bjerstedt, Å. (1993). *Peace education: Global perspectives.* Stockholm: Almqvist & Wiksell International.

Bloomfield, D. (1995). Towards complementarity in conflict management: Resolution and settlement in Northern Ireland. *Journal of Peace Research, 32,* 151–164.

Bonta, B. D. (1996). Conflict resolution among peaceful societies: The culture of peacefulness. *Journal of Peace Research, 33,* 403–420.

Boutros-Ghali, B. (1992). *An agenda for peace: Preventive diplomacy, peacemaking and peace-keeping.* New York: United Nations.

Brock-Utne, B. (1994a). Creating change through adult education: Suggestions for two priority areas. In P. Beckman and F. D'Amico (Eds.), *Women, gender and world politics: Perspectives, policies and prospects* (pp. 175–187). New York: Bergin & Garvey.

Brock-Utne, B. (1994b). The distinction between education about peace and development and value-centered education intended to promote them. In D. Ray (Ed.), *Education for human rights: An international perspective* (pp. 55–83). Paris: UNESCO, International Bureau of Education

Bronfenbrenner, U. (1979). *The ecology of human development: Experiences of nature and design.* Cambridge, MA: Harvard University Press.

Bronfenbrenner, U. (1988). Interacting systems in human development. Research paradigms: Present and future. In N. Bolger, A. Caspi, G. Downey, & M. Moorehouse (Eds.), *Persons in context: Developmental processes* (pp. 25–49). Cambridge: Cambridge University Press.

Burns, R. (1995). Peace education, the representation of participants and the presentation of conflict through school textbooks. In H. Löfgren (Ed.), *Peace education and human development* (pp. 76–98). Malmö, Sweden: University of Lund, School of Education.

Chapman, M. (1988). *Constructive evolution: Origins and development of Piaget's thought.* Cambridge: Cambridge University Press.

Cooper, P. (1965). The development of the concept of war. *Journal of Peace Research, 2,* 1–17.

Covell, K., Rose-Krasnor. L., & Fletcher, K. (1994). Age differences in understanding peace, war, and conflict resolution. *International Journal of Behavioral Development, 17,* 717–737.

Cretu, T. (1988). Peace and its most obvious meanings in preschool children's drawings. *Revue Roumaine des Sciences Sociales—Serie de Psychologie, 32,* 97–99.

Dinklage, R. I., & Ziller, R. C. (1989). Explicating conflict through photocommunication. *Journal of Conflict Resolution, 33,* 309–317.

Durkin, K. (1995). *Developmental social psychology.* Cambridge, MA: Blackwell.

Elias, N. (1939). *Über den Prozess der Zivilisation. Vol. 2: Wandlungen der Gesellschaft, Entwurf zu einer Theorie der Zivilisation.* Basel: Verlag Haus zum Falken.

Falk, A., & Selg, H. (1982). Die Begriffe "Krieg" und "Frieden" in der Vorstellung von Kindern und Jugenlichen [The concept of war and peace in the minds of children and youths]. *Psychologie in Erziehung und Unterricht, 29,* 353–358.

Flavell, J. H. (1963). *The developmental psychology of Jean Piaget.* New York: Van Nostrand Reinhold.

Galtung, J. (1985). Twenty-five years of peace research: Ten challenges and some responses. *Journal of Peace Research, 22,* 145–157.

Galtung, J. (1996). *Peace by peaceful means: Peace and conflict, development and civilization.* London: Sage.

Gillett, N. (1994). "An agenda for peace" and the role of peace education. *Peace, Environment and Education, 5,* 3–23.

Goody, E. (1991). The learning of prosocial behaviour in small-scale egalitarian societies: An anthropological view. In R. A. Hinde & J. Groebel (Eds.), *Cooperation and prosocial behaviour* (pp. 106–128). Cambridge: Cambridge University Press.

Haavelsrud, M. (1970). View on war and peace among students in West Berlin public schools. *Journal of Peace Research, 7,* 99–120.

Hakvoort, I. (1996). *Conceptualizations of peace and war from childhood through adolescence.* Unpublished doctoral dissertation, University of Amsterdam.

Hakvoort, I., & Oppenheimer, L. (1993). Children and adolescents' conceptions of peace, war, and strategies to attain peace: A Dutch case study. *Journal of Peace Research, 30,* 65–77.

Hakvoort, I., & Oppenheimer, L. (1998). Understanding peace and war: A review of developmental psychology research. *Developmental Review, 18,* 353–389.

Hall, R. (1993). How children think and feel about war and peace: An Australian study. *Journal of Peace Research, 30,* 181–196.

Havel, V. (1996). *Toward a civil society.* Prague: Lidové Noviny.

Hetherington, E. M., & Morris, W. N. (1978). The family and primary groups. In W. H. Holtzman (Ed.), *Introductory psychology in depth: Developmental topics.* New York: HarperCollins.

Hetherington, E. M., & Parks, R. D. (1993). *Child psychology: A contemporary viewpoint.* New York: McGraw-Hill.

Howell, S., &. Willis, R. (Eds.). (1989). *Societies at peace: Anthropological perspectives.* London: Routledge.

Leavitt, L. A., & Fox, N. A. (1993). *The psychological effects of war and violence on children.* Hillsdale, NJ: Erlbaum.

Löfgren, H. (Ed.). (1995). *Peace education and human development.* Malmö, Sweden: University of Lund, School of Education.

Machel, G. (1996). *The impact of armed conflict on children.* (Report of the Expert of the Secretary-General A/RES/48/157). New York: United Nations.

McCreary, J. A., & Palmer, L. L. (1991). Adolescent perspective of ways of thinking and believing that promote peace. *Adolescence, 26,* 849–855.

Mercer, G. (1974). Adolescent views of war and peace. *Journal of Peace Research, 11,* 247–249.

Mor, B. D. (1997). Peace initiatives and public opinion: The domestic context of conflict resolution. *Journal of Peace Research, 34,* 197–216.

Neisser, U. (1967). *Cognitive psychology.* Englewood Cliffs, NJ: Appleton-Century-Crofts.

Oppenheimer, L. (1989). *The international centre for peace in the Middle East: An impact study.* Report for the Dutch Organization for International Developmental Cooperation (NOVIB). Amsterdam: University of Amsterdam.

Oppenheimer, L. (1995). Peace, but what about societal constraints? *Peace and Conflict: Journal of Peace Psychology, 1,* 383–397.

Oppenheimer, L. (1996a). Developmental processes in socio-cultural contexts: The need for multidisciplinary cooperation. *The Polish Quarterly of Developmental Psychology, 2,* 169–180.

Oppenheimer, L. (1996b). War as an institution, but what about peace?: Developmental perspectives. *International Journal of Behavioral Development, 19,* 201–218.

Piaget, J. (1980). The right to education in the present world. In J. Piaget, *To understand is to invent: The future of education* (pp. 128–142). Harmondsworth, England: Penguin Books. (Original work published 1948.)

Piaget, J. (1952). *The origins of intelligence in children.* Madison, CT: International Universities Press.

Piaget, J. (1970). *Biology and knowledge.* Edinburgh: Edinburgh University Press.

Piaget, J. (1981). *Intelligence and affectivity.* Palo Alto, CA: Annual Reviews.

Rafman, S., Canfield, J., Barbas, J., & Kaczorowski, J. (1996). Disrupted moral order: A conceptual framework for differentiating reactions to loss and trauma. *International Journal of Behavioral Development, 19,* 817–830.

Rafman, S., Canfield, J., Barbas, J., & Kaczorowski, J. (1997). Children's representations of parental loss due to war. *International Journal of Behavioral Development, 20,* 163–178.

Rodd, J. (1985). Preschool children's understanding of war. *Early Child Development and Care, 22,* 109–121.

Rosell, L. (1968). Children's view of war and peace. *Journal of Peace Research, 5,* 268–276.

Spielmann, M. (1986). If peace comes . . . Future expectations of Israeli children and youth. *Journal of Peace Research, 28,* 231–235.

Valsiner, J. (1988). Ontogeny of co-construction of culture within socially organized environmental settings. In J. Valsiner (Ed.), *Child development within culturally structured environments: Social co-construction and environmental guidance in development* (Vol. 2, pp. 283–297). Norwood, NJ: Ablex.

Van Kempen, M., Peek, T., & Vriens, L. (1986). *Vrede en oorlog als kinderprobleem* [Peace and war as problems of children]. Unpublished research report. Utrecht, The Netherlands: Rijksuniversiteit Utrecht.

Von Jacob, A., & Schmidt, H.-D. (1988). Die Konzeptualisierung von "Krieg" und "Frieden" bei sechs-bis zwölf-järigen Kindern in der DDR [Conceptualization of "war" and "peace": Six- to twelve-year-old children in the DDR]. *Zeitschrift für Psychologie, 196,* 265–277.

Vygotsky, L. S. (1978). *Thought and language.* Cambridge, MA: MIT Press.

PART ONE

DEVELOPMENTAL PERSPECTIVES

CHILDREN, WAR, AND PEACE

A REVIEW OF FIFTY YEARS OF RESEARCH
FROM THE PERSPECTIVE OF A BALANCED
CONCEPT OF PEACE EDUCATION

Lennart Vriens, Utrecht University

ALTHOUGH WAR HAS ALWAYS BEEN PART of human history, peace education is an invention of modern times. Many cultures had their peace activists and propagators, but mostly, peace as a political issue was not connected with education as a matter of personal development. Religion offered the idea of inner peace, but this ideal could easily be combined with the duty to defend your own country, or worse, to fight in just wars.

The Alternative of Peace Education

Peace education became possible when the German philosopher of the Enlightenment, Immanuel Kant, in his manuscript *Zum ewigen Frieden* (1795), made it clear that war is not a natural or divine disaster, but a product of human action. Since then, peace has become part of the ideals of the democratic development and improvement of the world. These ideals had a two-way influence on the development of peace education. First, they justified the great liberation movements of the nineteenth and

I would like to acknowledge the assistance of Jo Hilhorst and Mark Goudkamp in the preparation of the English text.

twentieth centuries (Blankendaal, 1980; Grossi, 1994). Of these, liberalism and socialism became the most important, but anarchism, feminism, internationalism, and pacifism have also had an influence. Second, they were an important incentive for the educational reform movements of the twentieth century. The peace movement contained many teachers who, inspired by the movement's ideals, zealously advocated a less nationalistic and less warlike teaching of history for international contacts, the introduction of Esperanto as the global language, and the propagation of the League of Nations. They also objected to war toys and to certain songs, books, and movies. Furthermore, some teachers tried to realize their ideas about peace and social change by changing the educational system. They often had contacts with the peace movement and argued that better education with more respect for children and their natural development would create a new human being who would be able to abolish war and create a just world. They were inspired by the political and pedagogical ideas of the Russian writer and prophet Tolstoy (Jochheim, 1977, pp. 97–109; Vriens, 1987, pp. 100–110).

The First World War caused trauma for the peace movement. The socialists in Germany and France betrayed their peace ideals and accorded the war budget. The laborers did not choose their comrades; they chose their national armies and marched to die in the trenches. After the Great War, there was a new wave of educational optimism in which peace ideas still played an important part, but World War II put an end both to pacifism and to the rather naive concepts of peace. In the 1950s, peace education was even suspected of being a secret Communist undermining of our Western democracies.

In the 1960s and 1970s, new concepts of peace education were developed. This development got an important stimulus from the famous passage in the preamble of the United Nations Educational, Scientific, and Cultural Organization (UNESCO): "Since wars begin in the minds of people, it is in the minds of people that the defenses of peace have to be built" (Ter Steeg, 1969, p. 66). Most projects tried to translate the concepts and theories of the new discipline of peace research into educational programs. Peace education was merely seen as an introduction to knowledge about war and peace, with the hope that youngsters would use this information as a basis for choosing peace. So the pupils got information about the Cold War and the arms race, as well as controversial issues like Cuba, the nature of conflict, social justice, open and structural violence, nonviolent resistance, and so on.

In the 1980s, peace education became a rather important issue "on the back of the peace movement" (Maasen, 1996, p. 129). Although most projects had a wider scope than the peace movement, they had to defend themselves against being identified with the peace movement or, more accurately, with the common narrow perception of the peace movement as a nuclear disarmament movement. Looking back at that time, this was not a coincidence. The end of the Cold War in 1989 not only caused the collapse of the peace movement as a mass organization; it also caused a serious setback for peace education.

If we try to evaluate this brief history of peace education, we first have to note that peace education must be interpreted as a part of modern optimism. But its special message is that we must not forget the humane part of the Enlightenment's optimistic idea that people have the capacity and the responsibility to create a truly humane world for everybody.

However, when we look back at the concepts and the practical initiatives of peace education, we have to conclude that most of them have been dominated by a one-sided orientation. Peace education got its shape from the idea of peace as a wished future, but it failed to recognize the dialectical nature of the educational process. Only some projects included the child's own world and the problems of peace within the child's world in their scope. As a consequence, most peace educators have primarily seen the younger generation as a "tool" for creating a future peace without realizing that children are humans who have the right to make their own choices. This was, in essence, an instrumentalist view of the possibilities of education. Instead we need a more balanced concept of peace education.

A Balanced Concept of Peace Education

A balanced or dialectical concept of peace education takes both the ideal of peace in the future and the child's present everyday life into account. It interprets its task neither primarily in terms of creating peace nor through an overoptimistic view of the possibilities of the next generation to shape a peaceful future. In this concept, peace education cannot claim to achieve peace directly. Instead, peace education acts in an indirect way. Its aim is to make young people *conscious of their own responsibility* for peace. But ultimately, youngsters have to arrive at their own point of view about their situation and their influence on and contribution to the peace process, at both the personal and structural levels. The contribution of peace education to the peace process is (1) that it confronts young people with the responsibility they share with others for the preservation of the world and a humane future for its inhabitants and (2) that it encourages them to accept this responsibility and to realize it in a creative way in their own lives.

In this way, peace education has to start as early in life as possible. The basis of peace education lies in early childhood, in particular in the domain of norms and values. Very young children can already experience the way that people orient themselves to a peaceful attitude. If educators of young children do not choose basic values and norms of peace like trust, critical solidarity, nonviolence, and cooperation, it will be more difficult to start peace education later in schools and other educational institutions. In that case, children will have to find their own orientation in different or even competing educational systems. The way the family deals with the information given by the mass media will also play an important part.

Peace education can take a more cognitive approach in the schools. It can present knowledge and insights about the complex processes which are either obstacles to, or supportive of, peace. However, peace education as an explicit confrontation with the peace problem cannot orient itself exclusively toward peace as a goal; it also has to reckon with the perspectives of children. But most peace education projects lack such a balanced strategy, because of either a strong goal orientation or a lack of empirical knowledge about children's lives and their perspectives about war and peace. Yet even in situations without war, children have a lot of knowledge about war and peace. They know from television that worldwide conflicts belong to everyday life, but at the same time they are often taught that conflicts are not allowed. In school they learn that human beings have been struggling with war and peace for centuries. They experience power, violence, and injustice daily, but they are also taught that use of their own power is seldom allowed. War toys as models for the cultural expression of violence are readily available and are given to children as presents. Children therefore learn to accept war as part of daily life. Still, they hear about the pain, destruction, and death caused by the use of weapons in war. Although awareness of suffering and death is kept away from their world as much as possible, information about it reaches them through history lessons, television programs, computer games, and so on. And, in threatening situations, they often have very good intuition about their parents' anxieties.

A balanced concept of peace education integrates the perspectives of young people with their future responsibility for peace. But what exactly do we know about children's and youngsters' knowledge of war and peace and their interpretations of the peace problem? And what do we know about the development of these perspectives and interpretations? In this chapter I want to look for answers to these questions by means of an examination of fifty years of studies about children, war, and peace.

Studies About Children and the Problem of War and Peace

When the bombs fell on Hiroshima and Nagasaki in August 1945, only a few people realized that this was the beginning of a new and dangerous era in human history. Still fewer recognized that this nuclear technology would also influence the everyday world of many people in the 1970s and 1980s, including children. And hardly anybody foresaw the many worldwide conflicts and "small" wars which would damage so many children, be it as victims, as "soldiers," or as daily spectators via television.

In the more than fifty years since the war, we have seen a growing number of studies on children, war, and peace. However, a careful global examination of the results of these studies is not very easy to make. First of all, there has been much more research on children and war than on children and peace. Second, projects carried out in different countries are often difficult to compare because of the vast differences in research methods and in the ages and the sociocultural and socioeconomic backgrounds of the children. There is also much variation in the nature of the questions and the interpretations of the responses. Often researchers do not know about other researchers' work, which prevents them from building a body of knowledge.

Yet we can create some order in this abundance of information. A careful examination of a variety of these studies suggests that, at least in the culture of Western Europe and North America, there is a tendency for adults to construct their studies on the basis of their own concerns. Generally speaking, this concern leads to three types of research: research on children in a situation of violence and political conflict, research on the influence of nuclear threat on children, and research on children's conceptions of war and peace. We can show this tendency by dividing the post–World War II era into roughly five periods, 1945–1955, 1960–1970, 1970–1979, 1980–1988, and post-1989, and by connecting the dominant images of war and peace of each period with the different types of research.

Between 1945 and 1955: Overcoming World War II

The period from 1945 to 1955 was dominated by World War II. Peace was identified with overcoming that war and with the creation of the United Nations as a new world order in which the peoples of the Earth would live peacefully together. The only concept of peace education at that time was the promotion of international understanding between youngsters of different countries, but after the division of Western and Eastern Europe it did not have much influence. International exchange with the other side became suspect. This may explain why only one study about children's conceptions about war and peace was found. In 1951, Piaget and Weil published an article about the possibilities of peace education in relation to the development of children's ideas about their homeland and about other countries.

Before 1955, nuclear armament was hardly seen as a peace problem. Most people tended to see these new weapons as a guarantee of peace because of their deterrent potential. There were no studies about children and nuclear armament.

Most studies about children, war, and peace were exclusively focused on war damage as the most important threat to the child's world. Two months after the end of the war, a first study of the psychological problems of displaced persons was published by an inter-Allied psychological study group (United Nations Relief and Rehabilitation Administration, 1945). Another World War II problem was that of surviving Jewish children. In 1946 the Union Oeuvres de Secours aux Enfants wrote a report about the children of Buchenwald. Jouhay and Shentoub (1949) published a book about the consequences of the war on children's mental development. They examined the development of a number of French Jewish children who had been heavily affected by the war and concluded that a new stabilization was needed through a kind of reeducation. In the same year, the Central Commission on Children and War reported about these problems to an international congress on mental health in New York (Central Commission on Children and War, 1948). In a more journalistic way, Dorothy Macardle (1949) wrote about the consequences of war for youth in different European countries. She described such problems as the nazification of youth, the consequences of living in an occupied country, and destructive persecution. Her book also showed that after the war the problems were not over immediately. There were many reasons to care about hunger, fugitive children, stolen children who had to find their identity, and children who did not trust the world anymore. Brosse (1949, 1950) reported to UNESCO about children as victims of the war in Europe. All these reports led to the conclusion that children should be protected in situations of war and that this protection is the task of international organizations.

In the Netherlands, Langeveld (1952) and Perquin (1953) pointed out that Dutch youth, especially the so-called mass youth, developed socially unacceptable behavior, a development which was called social and moral disintegration. The origin of this development was seen as World War II, which disturbed social life, norms and values, and authority. The alarming message of these reports even bothered Dutch politicians. Clinical studies were done in Finland by Donner (1947) about children as victims of the "Winter War" of 1939, and by Carey-Trefzer (1949) in England and by Janis (1951) about the stresses of an air war.

But in 1952, Baumert concluded in large-scale sociographic research that German youngsters were no longer war victims. Even the German fugitive children did not differ significantly from the "authentic" German children. However, this conclusion did not include special groups of children. Frankenstein (1954) reported serious problems among the illegitimate children of foreign soldiers in Germany, especially when they were easy to recognize because of their different color. Nevertheless, after 1955 hardly any child psychologist connected the identity of youth to World War II or to experiences with other conflicts.

From 1960 to 1970: Nuclear Fear and the Development of a Scientific Peace Concept

The first half of the 1960s was dominated by the Cold War. The rivalry between West and East led to a nuclear arms race and severe political confrontations. The crises over Berlin in 1961 and Cuba in 1962 made people aware of the dangers of this development and stimulated the politicians toward a détente which would last until the middle of the 1970s. As a consequence, we see growing prestige for the new discipline of peace research and a revival of the idea of peace education. This situation produced a number of new studies about children, war, and peace. And again it would appear that there is a parallel between political problems and what is researched in the world of children.

Children and Conflict Situations

Although the post–World War II era had many armed conflicts, some studies were still made about the influence of this war on children. Lunder (1963) did a comparative study about juvenile criminality in thirteen countries after the two world wars. But just like Roskamp's study (1969) of the identity problems of students who were born in the war, this was more a fundamental study than a current topic. Brandt (1964) concluded that in Germany there were no significant differences between the children of German fugitives and *einheimische* (original) Germans.

A new topic within this type of research came from the American psychiatrist Robert Lifton (1967). Apparently inspired by the studies on nuclear fear between 1962 and 1965, he published a study on survivors of Hiroshima. This theme would become a persistent issue in peace education.

Children and Nuclear Fear

In the first half of the 1960s, there was something like an outburst of studies on children and the fear of nuclear weapons. It is easy to see the parallel between adults' anxieties and the intentions of the child studies. The first studies, in the early 1960s, by Escalona (1962) and Schwebel (1963, 1965) were directly related to the crises in Cuba and Berlin. They reported that the fear of a nuclear disaster had become part of the youngsters' world image and self-perception. Schwebel conducted his study during the Berlin crisis of 1961. Schwebel (1965) asked about three thousand children between the ages of nine and sixteen the following questions:

1. Do I think there is going to be a war?
2. Do I care? Why?
3. What do I think about fallout shelters? (pp. 211–212).

Schwebel found that half of the students expected a war to come, 95 percent of the students said that they cared about war, and 50 percent of the students were positive and 50 percent negative about fallout shelters. He connected his results with a concept of mental health: "Wars, hot or cold, like depressions, unemployment, poverty, give rise to social problems that are incontrovertibly related to individual behavior. They influence morality and hence interpersonal relations; they shake security and thus shape perceptions of the social scheme and expectations for the future. . . . An insecure world is bound to take its toll of health" (p. 219).

Escalona conducted her first study just after the Cuban crisis of 1962 with 311 children and adolescents between the ages of ten and seventeen. Although she wanted to elaborate a child development theory which would teach us how children would be able to learn to live with the problems of war and peace and their fears about nuclear armament, she took care not to direct the youngsters to the issue of the threat of nuclear war. In her research she did not use the words *war*, *nuclear war*, or *peace* but opted for a more open strategy. She asked the children to imagine the near future, including their own position:

Think about the world as it may be around ten years from now:

1. What are the ways in which it would be different from today?
2. How would you like it to be different?
3. If you had three wishes, what would they be?

In spite of the fact that Escalona did not refer to war, 70 percent of her respondents referred to war and peace in their answers. Of the children who mentioned war, 35 percent considered the outbreak of war possible and some of them thought it was likely. Although she knew that her results could not be generalized, she offered the hypothesis that uncertainty about the future has a destructive influence on the development of children and the process of identity formation among adolescents. Further, she concluded that children of different ages have their own defense mechanisms to protect themselves from fear and to feel safe. She connected these insights with advice for parents and professional educators.

These pioneer studies of Schwebel and Escalona were followed by studies by Darr (1963), Escalona (1963a, 1963b, 1965), and Wrightsman (1964). In 1965 Elder presented a summary of these studies, which were not continued. During the thaw period, the war problem was not dominated by nuclear threat anymore.

Conceptions of War and Peace

In the wake of the new discipline, peace studies, which wanted to discover the origins of war and the conditions for peace, researchers became more interested in the development of the child's knowledge and perceptions of war and peace. In 1965 Cooper offered a comprehensive research study in which he compared an English group of 300 children between the ages of five and sixteen with a Japanese group of 120 children between the ages of seven and fourteen. He used interview techniques for the younger children and questionnaires for the children seven years old and older. His findings suggest that children have verbal associations with the concepts of war and peace by the age of six. From eight on they construct images of war and peace for themselves. In the beginning, war is a scuffle or a large-scale quarrel, which is strongly connected with concrete aspects of war, like weapons. When children reach about the age of eleven, they are capable of seeing the social and political elements of war, motives of countries, justifications, and consequences. This is related to cognitive development, which enables them to have a better understanding of space and time and a growing insight into motives for war. Because of their developmental background, older children tend to value war less negatively than younger ones. Cooper also found that thirteen-year-olds can consider a nuclear war in the future but do not see the implications for themselves. Cooper's research concentrated on children's conceptualization of war, but their ideas about peace were also questioned. English children hardly connected the peace concept with political ideas about international relationships, political negotiations, and so on. The most dominant ideas were harmony and social activities, inner peace and silence.

Cooper's methods, especially his questionnaire, were also used in other studies, which confirmed his main results. Ålvik (1968a, 1968b) found that Norwegian children had more knowledge about war than peace, that this knowledge was on a concrete level (fighting, killing, weapons), and that they believed that peace was not an objective to pursue. Rosell (1968) stated that until the ages of eleven or twelve, children have a negative peace concept: peace is a situation without a war. Haavelsrud (1970a) and Targ (1970) offered us the same impression and saw a growing pessimism about humanity and its intentions as the child grows older. Haavelsrud (1970b) found that children and adolescents in West Berlin became more and more pessimistic about war and tended to become less idealistic as they obtained knowledge about war and the justification for it. Targ found the same growing pessimism about the possibility of a coming annihilating war together with a more "realistic" vision of the war parties: there are good and bad countries and our country belongs to the good ones. Yet the research left some questions. Torney, Anderson, and Targ (1969) found that preadults' conceptions of war in different countries differ. Youngsters in England, Germany, and Japan tended to show an increasing idea of the negative effects of war, while Norwegian preadults showed a decreasing tendency. There were also differences in the influence of socialization agents like family, friends, school, mass media, and religion. These findings led to a number of further research studies in the early 1970s.

In the 1960s, we see the first initiatives to develop projects of peace education. These projects oriented themselves to the concepts of peace research. Although studies about children's conceptions might have been of interest to these projects, they apparently had no real influence. Generally speaking, the projects were goal-oriented and did not integrate insights about the development of children and youngsters. And even though many of the administrators of those projects told their pupils about armaments and the Cold War, they did not refer to the studies of Escalona and Schwebel.

Between 1970 and 1979: War Victims and Further Studies About Concept Development and Nuclear Victims

Looking back at the 1970s from the perspective of the problem of war and peace, we see a number of competing tendencies. The first was the continuation of the détente in the Cold War, but after the end of the Vietnam War in 1975 new weapons like the neutron bomb put pressure on this situation. Although a growing peace movement tried to find new ways to achieve disarmament, a new arms race between East and West developed and would be "justified" by the Russian invasion of Afghanistan at the end of the decade. At the same time, on almost every continent greater or smaller conflicts created many victims, including children. And finally, somehow the spirit of the "revolution" of the 1960s supported initiatives for social change. In this context new peace education projects got the chance to develop more systematic concepts about how to influence the younger generation toward the building of peace. They derived their ideas from peace research; from general theories about political socialization; from revolutionary ideas about education in the Third World, especially from Paulo Freire; and from basic pedagogical and didactic ideas about good education. In some projects we also saw the first recognition of the need to consider the child's own world as an indispensable element of peace education.

Studies About War Victims

In a world with many armed conflicts, there were many studies about children who were confronted with a real war, general studies about children as war victims (Clavel, 1970; Hulot, 1978; Freedman, 1978), and studies about their reactions to wartime stress (Kruglanski & Shulman, 1974), separation from their parents (Hansburg, 1972), or absence of the father (Dahl, McCubbin, Hamilton, & Gary, 1979). Baider and Rosenfeld (1974) claimed that children's reactions are influenced directly by their parents' behavior. This seems to be in line with the World War II studies of Anna Freud and Dorothy Burlingham (1943) in England: if children are not directly confronted with aggressive war behavior, they can manage rather extreme situations. They are more damaged by emotional tension caused by separation from their parents or the anxious behavior of their direct relatives than by the situation as such. "Objective" security is not the same as experienced security. Situations are traumatic for children if and because they are traumatic for their parents.

But in most conflicts this separation cannot be made. Most war situations are very traumatic both for children and their parents, and their influence can linger for a long time. Robin Burns (1985), for example, reported in the middle of the 1980s that Australian teachers were seriously shocked by the very dramatic artistic reproductions of war by Vietnamese fugitive children and the vehemence of the feelings of fugitive children from Cyprus and Lebanon.

Besides these general studies, we see many reports about children in current war situations, for instance, in Palestine (Saudi, 1970), South Vietnam (Assemblée Internationale, 1975), Israel (De Shalit, 1970; Marberg

& Susz, 1972; Milgram & Milgram, 1978, Milgram, 1976), and Northern Ireland (Fraser, 1972, 1974; Jahoda & Harrison, 1975; Morrow, 1979). The studies of Morris Fraser, who reported on children in the religious and ethnic conflict in Northern Ireland, had some influence on the idea of peace education in Western Europe. On one hand, he came to the same conclusion as Freud and Burlingham about the influence of parents on children's judgment of situations; on the other hand, he saw that children experienced hate caused by violence and offered suggestions to overcome both hate and prejudice by reconciliation and a common educational system for both Protestants and Roman Catholics.

In the 1970s, there also was a revival of attention to the influence of World War II on children. Carlsmith (1973) reported on the influence of separation on the personality development of boys, Merlier and Rimbaud (1975) asked children to tell about the occupation and liberation of France, and Robinson (1979) did research on late effects of the Nazi occupation on children who survived persecution. Langeveld (1976) wrote about the personal therapeutic methods he had developed in the 1950s to help some seriously damaged children find new possibilities for a positive future. Henry and Hillel (1976) published research on the children of the SS, who may also be seen as war victims like the children of Holocaust survivors (Phillips, 1978).

At that time, hardly any of these studies had an influence on the theory and practice of peace education. The historical lessons of these studies were not easy to connect to the peace problems of the 1970s. However, there were two exceptions. First, we see a growing number of publications about the effects of the atomic bombs which fell on Hiroshima and Nagasaki. Studies by Hamadate (1971), Belsky (1973), Kobayashi (1973), Masuma (1975), and Nagai (1979) told about the Japanese experiences in World War II. These studies, which often included the effects of the bomb on children, became a strong incentive to a concept of peace education as a warning about the risks of nuclear armament. Japanese peace educators transferred the experiences of Hiroshima survivors into lessons and offered materials to colleagues in international peace organizations like the International Peace Research Organization and the World Council for Curriculum and Instruction. Famous contributions to the concept of peace education as nuclear disarmament education were the books *Unforgettable Fire* (Japan Broadcasting Corporation, 1977), a testimony with pictures and text of Hiroshima survivors, and *Cries for Peace* (Youth Division of Soka Gakkai, 1978) in which Japanese victims of World War II told about their experiences. Second, at the end of the 1970s, the television movie *Holocaust* generated studies about children's and youngsters' reactions to

the fate of the Jews in World War II. Many of these studies drew pedagogical conclusions about what children should learn about this historical disaster.

Conceptions of Peace and War

In the first half of this decade a number of studies were done on the topic
of young people's conceptions of war and peace. Most of these studies got
their inspiration and methodology from the earlier research of Cooper
and Haavelsrud. Bursterman (1973) reported on a study in the United
States and Japan on children's and adolescents' conceptions of peace. She
asked youngsters aged seven to twenty-one (1) what the word *peace*
meant to them, (2) who was a peaceful person, and (3) how we could get
peace in our own town, state, nation, or the world; she then offered a
description and interpretation of the answers. Her conclusions were in
line with the earlier findings: peace is a vague concept in the minds of
most people, and it is not usually included in the behavioral goals of education. A study by Mercell (1974) reported that adolescents' notions
about peace hardly changed between the ages of twelve and seventeen.
Only "signs of a slowly emerging belief that peace may be achieved
through active promotion and international cooperation, such as direct
attacks on what are seen as the underlying causes of war—like poverty
and over-population," were found (p. 247). This study seems to be in line
with the ideas of so-called critical peace research, which stressed the
importance of these underlying causes of war. But when the peace research
discussion stopped, these studies also came to an end.

Haavelsrud was challenged by the finding of Torney et al. (1969) that
youngsters' conceptions of war in different countries differ and that the
sources for their conceptions also differ. Together with colleagues in the
United States and Canada, he conducted seven identical studies of high
school students in Seattle (Haavelsrud, 1970a; Simmons, 1974), Vancouver (Haavelsrud, 1971), New York (Haavelsrud, 1975), and Houston
(Canning, 1977). The Seattle studies found that white suburban youngsters tend to identify more with symbols of peace and environments of
peace, whereas urbanites more often express the ideas that war can be
avoided and that it is immoral. For both groups, the mass media, especially television, are the primary sources of orientation toward war and
peace. The New York study suggested that the family offers the most
important influence on believing that war can be prevented. But mass media
have the strongest impact on the concept of war and peace. The Houston
research found that religion can play an important part in learning about

international conflicts. For the Catholic pupils, the father was a very important source of political socialization. Finally, in the Vancouver study, Haavelsrud described some important differences between young people's concepts of war and the causes of war on one hand and of peace, prevention of war, human nature, the avoidability of war, and the immorality of war on the other hand. Children mainly get their peace concepts at home and their war ideas and values from the mass media. For tenth to twelfth graders, textbooks are a useful source of information about war concepts, but religion has a greater impact on their orientations toward peace and human nature. However, it is difficult to interpret the differences in the results of these studies.

Challenging for peace education were the studies of Hollander (1971) and Howard Tolley (1973), who combined a study about children's conceptions of war (Hollander) with their ideas about a current war. Tolley described extensively how 2,677 children built up their opinion of the Cold War, the H-bomb, and the Vietnam War. Much attention was paid to the last topic, which is understandable when we realize that in the early 1970s, American involvement in this war was under vehement discussion. Hollander did not investigate peace concepts but looked for sources of information about war in general and the Vietnam War specifically.

At the end of the 1970s, Volmerg and Stehr (1978) added a new element to the discussion about children, war, and peace. They pointed out that opinions about security, threat, and conflict originate in *Alltagser-fahrungen* (everyday experiences) in early childhood learning about power, threat, and the power hierarchy. When children are confronted with new situations, they try to project familiar knowledge onto this new condition. This everyday experience, which is partly shaped by education, leads to acceptance of various attitudes associated with the arms race: everyone wants power so you can't take risks, if one party develops a new weapon the other will develop a better one, never trust people because it's dangerous, and so on.

From 1980 to 1988: The Dominance of Nuclear Fear

After 1979, the political landscape of war and peace was dominated for about ten years by two opinions. The first, which was dominant in the governments of almost every North Atlantic Treaty Organization country, stressed the necessity of developing new weapons in order to defend Western security. This opinion led to a new Cold War and a nuclear arms race between East and West. Contrary to this opinion, a growing peace movement propagated a step-by-step strategy toward disarmament. A first step was seen as a necessary strategy toward building up mutual trust between the rival parties as a condition for peace. In this situation we see an outburst of publications about children, war, and peace.

Children and Nuclear Fear

The main issue of the peace movement in the 1980s was the fear of nuclear annihilation of the human race. A great many researchers thought that the same anxiety could be proved to exist in children. Like Escalona and Schwebel in the 1960s, they pointed out that war, peace, and armament had become part of the world image of children and youth. Bachman (1983) reported an enormous growth in the percentage of students who were worried about a nuclear war. In 1975, 7 percent of the students were bothered about the future; in 1980, more than 30 percent of the students were. A study by Kramer, Kalick, and Milburn (1983) suggested that the expectation of a nuclear war had become widespread and that a majority of adults thought that it would not be possible to survive a nuclear war. In America especially, the studies of Mack (1982a, 1982b), Beardsley and Mack (1982, 1983), Chivian and Snow (1983), and Chivian and Goodman (1984) received much attention. They used open-ended questions about nuclear war, nuclear power, nuclear weapons, civil defense, and so on. Mack, a psychiatrist with Harvard Medical School, stated that a large percentage of American children were sharply aware of the danger of an atomic war. In 1983, together with Chivian and others (Chivian et al., 1985), he interviewed Russian students. The researchers concluded that these young Russians were at least as caring about the future as American youngsters and that they were generally better informed about the consequences of the use of nuclear weapons. Schwebel (1982) and Escalona (1982) updated their old studies and were supported by Friedman (1984); Lifton (1983); Verdon-Roe (1983); Gould, Berger Gould, and Eden (1984); Goldenring and Doctor (1985); and Van Hoorn (1986) in America.

The propagation of these results became a prominent task of the International Physicians for the Prevention of Nuclear War, which interpreted anxiety about nuclear weapons as a problem of mental health. The group invited researchers all over the world to copy the investigations of Goldenring and Doctor in order to compare the problems of children and youngsters in as many countries as possible. In those years we see many studies like these in Austria (Oppolzer, 1985), Canada (Sommers, Goldberg, Levinson, Ross, & LaCombe, 1984; Hargraves, 1984), Finland (Solantaus, 1983; Solantaus, Rimpela, & Taipale, 1984; Solantaus, 1986),

The Netherlands (Van Dellen & Ten Hoorn, 1981; Van IJzendoorn, 1986), Sweden (Holmborg & Bergstroem, 1984), and West Germany (Büttner, 1982). It seems likely that this list of research on the fear of nuclear armamant is far from complete. In 1986, however, after an overview of the main research on this topic, Barbara Tizard (1984, 1986) concluded that in the Western world, more of the same research would not add new knowledge and insights. There was a need for further interpretative data and not for gathering new information. She pointed to hypotheses about differences in ages and differences between boys and girls, and to the interpretation of differences in terms of the development of the child. In her opinion, the real problem was not mental health, but education, or how to assist young people to become aware of the problems that threaten their future, and how to encourage them to take part in solving these problems. At the Ninth Annual Scientific Meeting of the International Society for Political Psychology, held in Amsterdam in 1986, most of the questionnaire research was criticized for having no theory. The development of a theory about children and war and peace was seen as an urgent condition for better research.

Through the end of the Cold War in 1987 and the collapse of the Eastern bloc as a political unity, the peace movement dwindled and so did these studies. Although there was only partial nuclear disarmament, fear of these weapons was no longer either a political or a pedagogical issue.

Children's Conceptions of War and Peace

Because of the general attention to the nuclear fear issue, studies about children's conceptions of war and peace did not have a great influence on the discussion of peace education. Yet, maybe because they had to reflect their position in the nuclear debate, these studies had a great creative potential for peace education options. Most studies used other techniques than those used in the studies of this issue in the 1960s and 1970s. Falk and Selg (1982) were the only researchers who used a questionnaire from the age of eight on; information about younger children was obtained in interviews. Other researchers got their information from drawings (Engel, 1984; Maasen, Peek, & Vriens, 1984; Van Kempen, Peek, & Vriens, 1986; Coles, 1986; Cretu, 1988), writing (Engel, 1984; Van Kempen et al., 1986), different kinds of interviews (Rodd, 1985; Van Kempen et al., 1986; Coles, 1986), free association (Von Jacob & Schmidt, 1988), photo-communication (Dinklage & Ziller, 1989), and so on. Although hardly any of these studies refer to Volmerg and Stehr (1978), it looks as if they were inspired by Volmerg and Stehr's suggestion to broaden the idea of knowledge about war and peace from a cognitive to a more holistic approach, embedding children's concepts into their everyday world.

Some of these studies also offered a sharp methodological critique on the studies on nuclear fear. Robert Coles (1986) stated that adults often project their fears on children and that his own research results differed from the questionnaire outcomes. Using his own qualitative approach, he found nuclear fear only among children in the higher social classes whose parents were highly involved in the peace movement (p. 276). Lower-class children also thought about physical annihilation but by hunger and starvation. Van Kempen et al. (1986) and Vriens (1987) criticized the "educative" nature of the questionnaires used: if the children were not anxious about nuclear armament before answering the questions, they had hardly any chance to be in the same mood afterward (Van Kempen et al., 1986, p. 28; Vriens, 1987, p. 256). They offered an alternative qualitative approach based on phenomenological methodology, developing an elaborated description of the interpretations and conceptions of war and peace by children from six to twelve years old within the context of their own life-world. In this approach the researchers tried to step aside from adult meanings and presuppositions in favor of taking the child's own experiences and utterances seriously. In accordance with the triangulation principle for qualitative research, they used different forms of information: the children's creative products like essays about the future and drawings of war and peace, open interviews with small groups of children, and interviews with the children's educators.

Following are the main conclusions of this research. First, children have their own interpretations of peace and war, and most of them are somehow integrated into the children's world. Second, children between the ages of six and twelve go through three consecutive stages in determining their position on the subject of war and peace. For six- and seven-year-olds, the notions of peace and war are relatively difficult to understand. This situation changes rapidly from the age of seven onward; children develop more and more elaborated ideas about peace and war. At this stage the differences between boys and girls grow. Generally speaking, boys have a positive attitude toward war from the age of seven or eight on, whereas girls are quite outspoken against war and in favor of peace. From the age of about eleven, another change takes place. From then on nuclear weapons become part of the children's concept of the world. This causes boys to reconsider their positive attitude and strengthens a more critical position in relation to war. This shift is sometimes connected with a cynical evaluation of the intentions of politicians. A third conclusion was that there are a number of substantial differences in perceptions between boys and girls, which can help in understanding their different judgments about war and peace. For example, girls tend to identify mainly with the victims of a war situation and the caring aspects of life, while boys show a tendency to identify with the soldier and war technology. These orientations create almost totally separated worlds, a fact that is hardly ever recognized in peace education. Finally, the researchers reported that they did not find massive fear of a nuclear disaster, although nearly 25 percent of the children over ten who participated in the project were somehow concerned about the future.

Children in Conflict Situations

During the 1980s, studies were still being done on children in conflict areas like Northern Ireland (Harbison & Harbison, 1980; Harbison, 1983), Palestine (Birnstingl, Rose, & Zinkin, 1982), and Israel and Palestine (Punamäki, 1982). Rosenblatt (1983) reported discussions with children of Northern Ireland, Lebanon, Israel, Cambodia, and Vietnam. Studies by Osada (1980) and Yamaguchi (1983) of the experiences of children who survived the bomb in Nagasaki or Hiroshima were about real war damage with children, but they could also be interpreted in support of the studies of nuclear fear. Woods (1980) and Van Zwan (1987) wrote about a "new" problem, that of the child as soldier. Like the studies of nuclear fear, these projects offered information in the context of a political message: everybody should know the absolute madness of war and its consequences for the coming generation.

After 1989: Looking for Integration

After the short peace euphoria of 1989 and 1990 which ended with the Gulf War of 1990, the problem of war and peace changed thoroughly. The Cold War was over, leaving a splintered world in which nationalism, racism, anti-Semitism, xenophobia, and neo-Fascism, together with a number of violent conflicts all over the planet, dominate the news. Peace educators have to look for new orientations, because all material must be updated and cleaned of elements of the Cold War and nuclear armament. This situation also has meant the end of the studies of nuclear fear, which have lost their function in both the political and the pedagogical debate.

Children in Conflict Situations

The end of the Cold War has led to a new interest in studies on the damaging effects on children of war and war-connected violence. There are enormous problems for children in these situations. Because of their vulnerability, children are the main victims of these conflicts. They are easy targets and are often misused by war parties to break the resistance of their opponents. Children are used as soldiers for the political aspirations of others. When they can escape the violence, they suffer from being separated from their parents, their home, and their country.

This serious situation for so many children in different conflict regions has been the source of two types of studies. The first type consists of case studies about children in situations of violence, as in Cambodia, Palestine, Somalia, or Bosnia. These studies can be interpreted as political documents which are helpful to justify the efforts of UN and nongovernmental organizations, like Defence for Children International, to implement the UN Convention of the Rights of the Child more effectively. This includes the ratification of this convention, the creation of "zones of peace" for children in conflict situations, and campaigns against land mines, of which children are the main victims, and child soldiers. The same can be said about more general publications on children in armed conflict (Machel, 1996).

The second type of study has concentrated on helping children to cope with the stresses of war and the treatment of war-related traumas. Psychologists and social workers offer assistance in coping with living in host countries, and psychotherapists offer help in overcoming the stresses of different war experiences. Macksoud (1993) and United Nations High Commissioner for Refugees (1994) offer a description of the main problems of children and strategies for parents and teachers in "normal" situations and in situations with severe or extreme stress reactions. Here, too, we see a tendency for UN organizations like the United Nations Children's Fund (UNICEF) and UNHCR to organize the exchange of professional help. They are supported by organizations which work in the interest of the child, like Defence for Children International, Amnesty International, and the International Dialogues Foundation.

Conceptions of War and Peace

In the studies of children's conceptions of war and peace, we also see a tendency toward coordination and standardization. According to Hakvoort (1996, p. 18), most studies of the 1990s (McCreary & Palmer, 1991; Hakvoort & Oppenheimer, 1993; Covell, Rose-Krasnor, & Fletcher, 1994) were based partly on the questionnaire approach of the studies in the 1960s by Cooper (1965), Rosell (1968), and Haavelsrud (1970a) and partly on other methods, like interview techniques. Peace and war are clearly recognized as concepts in the social development of children, so developmental psychologists support their findings with social and cognitive developmental psychology. Hakvoort (1996) and Hägglund (1996) add at least three important new elements to existing research: they combine questionnaire studies with qualitative analyses of structured interviews with children, they offer a longitudinal approach, and they develop a cross-cultural comparison between Dutch and Swedish adolescents. Other cross-cultural studies using their method have been done in Northern Ireland, India, South Africa, and Australia (Hägglund, Hakvoort, & Oppenheimer, 1995). According to Hakvoort (1996, p. 138), this will help to discriminate the general characteristics of young people's sociocognitive development from culture-specific elements. But she also concludes that the development of conceptions of peace and war is affected by a multitude of variables, which means that a lot of work still has to be done.

Conclusion

A balanced concept of peace education primarily consists of a dialogue between educators and children about the global problems which are our shared responsibility. Such a dialogue must be part of a "peace in practice" process, which means that it must be based on mutual respect and basic trust in the future. But peace education as a dialogue needs more than an attitude; the dialogue cannot be held without information and skills. It is the task of the educator to help children and youngsters to gather, understand, and interpret this information by developing the necessary knowledge and skills. This can be done both spontaneously and systematically.

But what does our study of fifty years of research on children, war, and peace tell us about the possibilities of this type of peace education? Will it be possible to bridge the difference between the perspectives of adults and youngsters? Can these studies tell us what the best strategy is to direct young people to accept peace building as their co-responsibility? In my opinion it is impossible to find such straight, practical answers. This overview shows too many differences between the studies, in the youngsters who are the subject of the research, in circumstances, in the aims and methods of research, and in the positions of the researchers. Yet we can draw some general conclusions.

First, peace education is an extremely difficult task in war and postwar situations. Almost all studies of children in conflict show how deeply damaging war and violence are in the lives of young people, even when they are not physically harmed and show only "normal" reactions. When children are living in war circumstances or have problems which are caused by a war situation, peace education has to start with as much restoration of normal life conditions as possible. This is not only restoration in a material or physical sense; it is also a matter of mental recovery. Children have to overcome their sorrow by mourning, utterance of anger, and integration of the experience of violence in a way that is not self-destructive. This is an extremely hard and often time-consuming task. After this, educators can try to help them to orient themselves toward the new positive possibilities of overcoming enmity and toward taking co-responsibility for peace. In this situation it can be helpful to offer children peace heroes to identify with as an alternative to their past war indoctrination (Dasberg, 1994, p. 7).

Second, peace education is no easy task in more peaceful circumstances either. Studies of the development of children's conceptions of peace and war suggest that for most children these concepts are difficult to integrate into their world vision in a realistic way. In our culture, wars are constantly presented by the media, although mostly without any explanation or background information. Other "educational" influences like war toys shape boys' appreciation of war games and war techniques in an uncritical way at an early age. On the other hand, peace is hardly an issue to be presented in the news and it seems to be an implicit subject in the schools. Most studies suggest that at the age of about ten or eleven, children become interested in what is going on in the world. They also form ideas about the political dimensions of the problem of war and peace. It is important for peace education to answer that need for information with a good introduction to the concepts of war and peace and to their challenge and context.

A third conclusion is that our distinction of three different types of research gives us a better idea of the relationship between the concerns of adults and what they are describing as children's problems. Our study suggests that when adults are concerned by peace problems or war threat, they tend to focus the research they do on children, war, and peace on these problems. These studies are then used to justify a concept of peace education which has to be a remedy for these perceived problems. This is obvious when we look at the studies of children and nuclear fear in the early 1960s and the first half of the 1980s. These studies can hardly be understood without knowledge of, first, the crises in Berlin and Cuba in 1961 and 1962 and, second, the struggle over further nuclear armament or disarmament between the political leaders of the 1980s and a strong opposing peace movement. Especially in the 1980s, researchers used their findings about children's fear of a nuclear disaster as an argument to support the peace movement. Since some of these studies were methodologically weak and prejudiced, we can question how much the results really mirrored the concerns of the children and how much they mirrored the concerns of the adult researchers.

Of course, this does not mean that adults' and children's concerns about war and peace cannot coincide, nor that research on children cannot start from adults' concerns. But researchers have the obligation either to show that both concerns are parallel or to explain how much their own concerns influence their results for the children. In the studies of children in situations of armed conflict, we see many similarities between traumatizing effects on young and older victims. But most studies make it clear that children are more vulnerable to violence because they are weaker and more dependent than adults. Even where children seem to be more adaptive, for instance, in the case of child soldiers, we see this vulnerability as soon as these children get out of their "protected" environment.

The studies on children's conceptions of war and peace have tried to overcome the possibility of bias by the researcher by standardizing their research methods, like the studies in the early 1970s, or by adding their use of the researcher's subjectivity to the discussion, like the studies in the 1980s. Studies in the 1990s have tried to integrate the best aspects of the different approaches.

A last conclusion is that generally speaking, studies of children's conceptions of war and peace are very important for the realization of a balanced peace education strategy. The studies of the 1980s and 1990s can especially help us here. The former gave us a good idea about the complexity of children's construction of the world and the integration of peace and war in their world vision. After these studies, naive concepts of peace education as "just teach peace!" are no longer possible. The studies of children's conceptions of peace and war in the 1990s confirm and diversify the results of the 1980s. Some of these studies have a longitudinal and cross-cultural approach, which in the long run can give peace educators a better idea of the limitations and possible successes of their attempts to influence the ability of the younger generation to find a peace-promoting position in their own future situation. An integrative approach to situations in which children are seriously damaged by war and violence may help us to overcome illusions which are too optimistic.

After this review I want to make one remark. Research has a better potential to tell us what should *not* be done than what to do. This means that it can offer us valuable insights into the chances and limits of children's ability to conceptualize and understand the problems of war and peace in connection with their age, development, and circumstances. Peace educators will have to accept the limits which research has found. It is no use confronting children with information which they cannot understand because of limitations in their cognitive or emotional development. For instance, young children have not yet developed adequate social-cognitive structures to understand the necessarily complex information which is needed for a good political conception of war problems. When a child has been seriously damaged by war violence, it is a waste to offer a conceptual analysis of the conflict as a good basis for an orientation to the possibilities of peace and to expect the child to accept her or his own responsibility.

Research cannot tell us what peace education should be. Possibilities are not necessities. If research tells us that it is possible to teach children in detail about violent actions in war, this does not mean that we *should* teach children about this violence in detail. Peace educators have their own responsibility to decide what to do with the information, knowing that children have a limited ability to grasp problems of life and death at the global level. However, for a balanced concept of peace education, this can be a good starting point for a serious dialogue.

REFERENCES

Ålvik, T. (1968a). The development of views on conflict, war and peace among school children. *Journal of Peace Research, 5,* 171–195.

Ålvik, T. (1968b). The problem of anxiety in connection with investigations concerning children's conception of war and peace. *Scandinavian Journal of Educational Research,* pp. 215–233.

Assemblée Internationale pour le Pensement des Blessures de Guerre et pour la Reconstruction du Vietnam. (1975). *Les orphelins de guerre au Sud-Vietnam.* Paris: Huynh Vietnam, Fraternité Vietnam.

Bachman, J. G. (1983). American high school seniors view the military: 1976–1982. *Armed Forces and Society, 10,* 86–104.

Baider, L., & Rosenfeld, E. (1974). Effects of parental fears on children in wartime. *Social Casework, 55,* 497–503.

Baumert, G. (1952). *Jugend der Nachkriegszeit. Lebensverhältnisse und Reaktionsweisen.* Darmstadt, Germany: Gemeindestudie des Instituts für Sozialwissenschaftliche Forschung; Monographie.

Beardsley, W., & Mack, J. (1982). The impact on children and adolescents of nuclear developments. In R. Rogers (Ed.), *Psychosocial aspects of nuclear development, Task Force Report 20* (pp. 64–93). Washington, DC: American Psychiatric Association.

Beardsley, W. E., & Mack, J. E. (1983). Adolescents and the threat of nuclear war: The evolution of a perspective. *Yale Journal of Biology and Medicine, 56,* 79–91.

Belsky, J. J. (1973). The health of atomic bomb survivors: A decade of examinations in a fixed population. *Yale Journal of Biology and Medicine, 46,* 284–296.

Birnstingl, M., Rose, S., & Zinkin. P. (1982). *After the bombing and the massacres: The condition of Palestinian people in the camps of South Lebanon. Report of a visit for peace in Lebanon and Israel.* Unpublished manuscript.

Blankendaal, T. M. (1980). *Vredesbeweging en vredesopvoeding: Nederland 1870–1940. Deel 1.* Haren: Polemologisch Instituut, Rijksuniversiteit Groningen.

Brandt, U. (1964). *Flüchtlingskinder.* Serie Wissenschaftliche Jugendkunde H 6. Munich: Johann Ambrosius Barth.

Brosse, T. (1949). *L'enfance victime de la guerre: Une étude de la situation européenne* (Publication No. 461). Paris: United Nations Educational, Scientific, and Cultural Organization.

Brosse, T. (1950). *War-handicapped children: Report of the European situation.* (Publication No. 439). Paris: United Nations Educational, Scientific, and Cultural Organization.

Burns, R. (1985). Peace education: Is it responding sufficiently to children's fears of the future? *Australian Journal of Early Childhood, 10* (4), 16–23.

Bursterman, J. P. (1973). Let's listen to our children and youth. In G. Henderson (Ed.), *Education for peace: Focus on mankind.* Washington, DC: ASCO Yearbook.

Büttner, C. (1982). *Kriegsangst bei Kinder.* Munich: Kösel.

Canning, W. S. (1977). *Channels of communication in the formation of Catholic and non-Catholic students' orientations towards war and peace.* Unpublished doctoral dissertation, East Texas State University, Commerce.

Carey-Trefzer, C. J. (1949). The results of a clinical study of war damaged children who attended the Child Guidance Clinic, the Hospital for Sick Children, Great Ormond Street, London. *Journal of Mental Science, 95,* 535–559.

Carlsmith, L. (1973). Some personality characteristics of boys separated from their fathers during World War II. *Win, 1,* 466–477.

Central Commission on Children and War (1948). *Report of the Central Commission on Children and War to the International Congress on Mental Health.* New York.

Chivian, E., & Goodman. J. (1984, Winter). *What Soviet children are saying about nuclear war.* IPPNW Report. Boston: International Physicians for the Prevention of Nuclear War.

Chivian, E., Mack, J. E., Waletzky, J., Lazaroff, C., Doctor, R., & Goldenring, J. M. (1985). Soviet children and the threat of nuclear war. *American Journal of Orthopsychiatry, 55,* 484–502.

Chivian, E., & Snow, R. M. (1983). *There's a nuclear war going on inside me: What children are saying about nuclear war.* Videotape of classroom discussions. Boston: International Physicians for the Prevention of Nuclear War.

Clavel, B. (1970). *Le maccacre des innocents*. Paris: Editions Robert Lafftont.

Coles, R. (1986). *The moral life of children*. New York: Grove/Atlantic.

Cooper, P. (1965). The development of the concept of war. *Journal of Peace Research, 3,* 1–18.

Covell, K., Rose-Krasnor, L., & Fletcher, K. (1994). Age differences in understanding peace, war, and conflict resolution. *International Journal of Behavioral Development, 17,* 717–737.

Cretu, T. (1988). Peace and its most obvious meanings in preschool children's drawings. *Revue Roumaine des Sciences Sociales—Serie de Psychologie, 32,* 97–99.

Dahl, B., McCubbin, B., Hamilton, E., & Gary, R. (1979). War-induced father absence: Comparing the adjustment of children in reunited and reconstituted families. *International Journal of Sociology of the Family, 6,* 99–108.

Darr, J. W. (1963). The impact of the nuclear threat on children. *American Journal of Orthopsychiatry, 33,* 203–204.

Dasberg, L. (1994). Kinderen en geweld. De antwoorden van de volwassen omgeving in historisch-pedagogisch perspectief. *Tijdschrift voor vredesopvoeding, 9* (2), 5–8.

De Shalit, J. (1970). Children and war. In A. Jarus et al. (Eds.), *Children and families in Israel* (pp. 164–179). Newark, NJ: Gordon & Breach.

Dinklage, R. I., & Ziller, R. C. (1989). Explicating conflict through photocommunication. *Journal of Conflict Resolution, 33,* 309–317.

Donner, S. (1947). Unsere Kinder und der Krieg. Finnlands Kinder im Winterkriege 1939–1940. Eine psychologisch-psychiatrische Studie. *Acta Psychiatrie Neurologie* (Suppl. 47), 274–285.

Elder, J. H. (1965). A summary of research on the reactions of children to nuclear war. *American Journal of Orthopsychiatry, 35,* 120–123.

Engel, B. (1984). Between feeling and fact: Listening to children. *Harvard Educational Review, 54,* 283–303.

Escalona, S. K. (1962). *Children and the threat of nuclear war*. New York: Child Study Association.

Escalona, S. (1963a). Children's awareness of the threat of war: Some developmental implications. *American Journal of Orthopsychiatry, 33,* 204–205.

Escalona, S. (1963b). Children's responses to the nuclear war threat. *Children, 4,* 137–142.

Escalona, S. (1965). Children and the threat of nuclear war. In M. Schwebel (Ed.), *Behavioral science and human survival* (pp. 201–209). Palo Alto, CA: Behavorial Sciences Press.

Escalona, S. (1982). Growing up with the threat of nuclear war: Some indirect effects on personality development. *American Journal of Orthopsychiatry, 52,* 600–607.

Falk, A., & Selg, H. (1982). Die Begriffe "Krieg" und "Frieden" in der Vorstellung vond Kinderen und Jugendlichen. *Psychologie in Erziehung und Unterricht, 29,* 353–358.

Frankenstein, L. (1954). *Soldatenkinder: Die uneheliche Kinder ausländischer Soldaten mit besonderer Berücksichtigung der Mischlinge.* Munich: Wilhelm Steinebach.

Fraser, R. M. (1972). At school during guerilla war. *Special Education, 2,* 61.

Fraser, M. (1974). *Children in conflict.* Harmondsworth, England: Penguin Books.

Freedman, A. M. (1978). Children under fire. In *Psychopathology of children and youth: Cross-cultural perspective* (pp. 187–199). Paris: Congresreport.

Freud, A., & Burlingham, D. (1943). *War and children.* New York: Medical War Books.

Friedman, B. (1984). Preschoolers' awareness of the nuclear threat. *California Association for the Education of Young Children Newsletter, 12,* 2.

Goldenring, J., & Doctor, K. (1985). Californian adolescents' concern about the threat of nuclear war. In T. Solantaus, E. Chivian, & S. Chivian (Eds.), *Impact of the threat of war on children and adolescents. Proceedings of an International Research Symposium, Helsinki, Finland.* Boston: International Physicians for the Prevention of Nuclear War.

Gould, J. B., Berger Gould, B., & Eden, E. (1984, December). *The threat of war in the minds of junior high school students in the U.S.A.* Paper presented at the symposium "The Psychological Effect of the Nuclear Threat on Children: Strategies for Action." University of California, Berkeley.

Grossi, V. (1994). *Le pacifisme européen 1889–1914.* Brussels: Bruyant.

Haavelsrud, M. (1970a). *Seminal agents in the acquisition of international orientations.* Unpublished doctoral dissertation, University of Washington, Seattle.

Haavelsrud, M. (1970b). Views on war and peace among students in West Berlin public schools. *Journal of Peace Research, 7,* 99–120.

Haavelsrud, M. (1971). *Learning resources in the formation of international orientations.* Paper presented at the National Convention of the Association for Educational Communications and Technology, Philadelphia.

Haavelsrud, M. (1975). *Perceptions about source utility in communications about war and peace among students in New York and Oslo.* Unpublished report.

Hägglund, S. (1996). Developing concepts of peace and war: Aspects of gender and culture. *Peabody Journal of Education, 71,* 29–41.

Hägglund, S., Hakvoort, I., & Oppenheimer, L. (Eds.). (1995). *Research on children and peace: International perspectives.* (Report No. 1996:04). Göteborg, Sweden: Göteborg University.

Hakvoort, I. (1996). *Conceptualization of peace and war from childhood through adolescence: A social-cognitive developmental approach.* Unpublished thesis, University of Amsterdam.

Hakvoort, I., & Oppenheimer, L. (1993). Children and adolescents' conceptions of peace, war and strategies to attain peace: A Dutch case study. *Journal of Peace Research, 30,* 65–77.

Hamadate, K. (1971). *Collective evacuation of schoolchildren.* Tokyo: Taihei-Shuppansha (The Violence of War, 4).

Hansburg, H. G. (1972). Separation problems of displaced children. In R. S. Parker (Ed.), *The emotional stress of war, violence and peace.* Pittsburgh, PA: Stanwix House.

Harbison, J. (Ed.). (1983). *Children of the trouble: Children in Northern Ireland.* Belfast: Stranmillis College.

Harbison, J., & Harbison, J. (Eds.). (1980). *A society under stress: Children and young people in Northern Ireland.* North Shepton Mallet, England: Open Books.

Hargraves, S. L. (1984). *Psychological impact of nuclear developments on youth: A local study.* Unpublished thesis, Simon Fraser University, Burnaby, Canada.

Henry, C., & Hillel, M. (1976). *Children of the SS.* London: Hutchinson.

Hollander, N. (1971). *Adolescents' perceptions of sources of orientations to war.* Unpublished doctoral dissertation, University of Washington, Seattle.

Holmborg, P. O., & Bergstroem, A. (1984, June). *A survey of attitudes of Swedish adolescents towards nuclear war.* Paper presented at Fourth Congress of International Physicians for the Prevention of Nuclear War, Helsinki, Finland.

Hulot, N. (1978). *Ces enfants qui souffrent.* Paris: Pac. Editions.

Jahoda, G., & Harrison, S. (1975). Belfast children: Some effects of a conflict environment. *Irish Journal of Psychology, 3,* 1–19.

Janis, I. L. (1951). *Air war and emotional stress: Psychological studies of bombing and civilian defense.* New York: McGraw-Hill.

Japan Broadcasting Corporation (NHK) (Ed.). (1977). *Unforgettable Fire. Pictures drawn by atomic bomb survivors.* New York: Pantheon Books.

Jochheim, G. (1977). *Antimilitaristische Aktionstheorie, Soziale Revolution und soziale Verteidigung. Zur Entwicklung der Gewaltfreiheitstheorie in der europäischen antimilitaristischen en sozialistischen Bewegung 1890–1940, unter besonderer Berücksichtigung der Niederlande.* Frankfurt am Main: Haag und Herchen.

Jouhay, E., & Shentoub, V. (1949). *L'évolution de la mentalité de l'enfant pendant la guerre.* Neuchâtel: Delachaux et Niestlé.

Kant, I. (1795). *Zum ewigen Frieden: Ein philosophischer Entwurf.* Kaliningrad, Russia: Friedrich Nicolovius.

Kobayashi, F. (1973). *Children lived through war: A record of a schoolteacher.* Tokyo: Hatonomori Shobou.

Kramer, B. M., Kalick, S. M., & Milburn, M. A. (1983). Attitudes towards nuclear weapons and nuclear war, 1945–1982. *Journal of Social Issues, 39,* 501–530.

Kruglanski, A. W., & Shulman, S. (1974). Children's psychological reactions to wartime stress. *Journal of Personal and Social Psychology, 30,* 24–30.

Langeveld, M. J. (1952). *Maatschappelijke verwildering der jeugd. Rapport betreffende het onderzoek naar de geestelijke gesteldheid van de massajeugd; samengesteld in opdracht van het Ministerie van onderwijs, kunsten en wetenschappen.* Den Haag: Staatsuitgeverij.

Langeveld, M. J. (1976). *Gunstige verwerking van ongunstige ervaringen in de levensgeschiedenis o.a. bij oorlogskinderen. Enige aspecten van de klinisch pedagogische benaderingswijze in onderzoek en behandeling.* Amsterdam: Noord-Hollandsche Uitgevers Maatschappij.

Lifton, R. J. (1967). *Death in life: Survivors of Hiroshima.* New York: Random House.

Lifton, R. J. (1983, September 20). *Implications of the arms race upon children. Presented before the U.S. House of Representatives, Select Committee on Children, Youth and Families.* Washington, DC: U.S. Congressional Report.

Lunder, W. A. (1963). *War and delinquency: An analysis of juvenile delinquency in thirteen nations in World War I and World War II.* Ames, IA: Art Press.

Maasen, J. (1996). Peace education on the back of the peace movement: Some shared problems. In R. J. Burns & R. Aspeslagh (Eds.), *Three decades of peace education around the world: An anthology* (pp. 129–140). New York: Garland.

Maasen, J., Peek, T., & Vriens, L. (1984). *"Dat noem ik geen oorlog meer." Kinderen praten en tekenen over oorlog en vrede.* Utrecht, The Netherlands: Vredesopbouw.

Macardle, D. (1949). *Children of Europe. A study of the children of liberated countries: Their wartime experiences, their reactions and their needs, with a note on Germany.* London: Gollancz.

Machel, G. (1996). *Impact of armed conflict on children.* New York: United Nations Children's Fund & United Nations Department of Public Information.

Mack, J. E. (1982a, April). Psychological effects of the nuclear arms race. *Bulletin of the Atomic Scientists.*

Mack, J. E. (1982b). The perception of U.S.-Soviet intentions and other psychological dimensions of the nuclear arms race. *American Journal of Orthopsychiatry, 52,* 590–599.

Macksoud, M. (1993). *Helping children cope with the stresses of war: A manual for parents and teachers.* New York: United Nations Children's Fund.

Marberg, H. M., & Susz, E. (1972). Development of a kibbutz girl who lost her father at the age of two years. *Acta Paedopsychiatrica, 39* (3), 59–66.

Masuma, S. (1975). *Children in the war: A record of two navy juveniles.* Kobunsa: Koujin-sha.

McCreary J. A., & Palmer, L. L. (1991). Adolescence perspective of ways of thinking and believing that promote peace. *Adolescence, 26,* 849–855.

Mercell, G. (1974). Adolescent views of war and peace: Another look. *Journal of Peace Research, 11,* 247–249.

Merlier, O., & Rimbaud, C. (Eds.). (1975). *La drôle de guerre: L'occupation, la libération racontées par des enfants.* Paris: Julliard.

Milgram, N. A. (1976). Psychological stress and adjustment in time of war and peace: The Israeli experience as presented in two conferences. *Israeli Annals of Psychiatry and Related Disciplines, 16,* 327–338.

Milgram, R. M., & Milgram, N. A. (1978). The effect of the Yom Kippur War on anxiety levels in Israeli children. *Journal of Psychology, 94,* 107–113.

Morrow, M. E. R. (1979). The function of playgroups in Northern Ireland. In E. F. Purcell (Ed.), *Psychopathology of children and youth: A cross-cultural perspective. Report of a conference* (pp. 181–185). New York: Josiah Macy Jr. Foundation

Nagai, T. (Ed.). (1979). *Living beneath the atomic cloud: The testimony of the children of Nagasaki.* Tokyo: Chuou-Shuppansha.

Oppolzer, A. (1985). *The impact of nuclear war among young Austrian people.* Paper presented at the Fifth Congress, International Physicians for the Prevention of War, Budapest, Hungary.

Osada, A. (Ed.). (1980). *Children of Hiroshima.* Basingstoke, England: Taylor & Francis; Committee for "Children of Hiroshima."

Perquin, N. (1953). *Moderne jeugd op weg naar volwassenheid. Onderzoek in opdracht van het Ministerie van onderwijs, kunsten en wetenschappen; Rapport van het Mgr. Hoogveldinstituut te Nijmegen.* Den Haag: Staatsuitgeverij.

Phillips, R. E. (1978). Impact of Nazi Holocaust on children of survivors. *American Journal of Psychotherapy, 32,* 370–378.

Piaget, J., & Weil, A. M. (1951). The development in children of the idea of the homeland and of relations with other countries. *International Social Sciences Bulletin, 3,* 561–578.

Punamäki, R.-L. (1982). Childhood in the shadow of war: A psychological study on the attitudes and emotional life of Israeli and Palestinian children. *Current Research on Peace and Violence, 5,* 26–41.

Robinson, S. (1979). Late effects of persecution in persons who—as children or young adolescents—survived the Nazi occupation in Europe. *Israeli Annals of Psychiatry and Related Disciplines, 17*, 209–214.

Rodd, J. (1985). Preschool children's understanding of war. *Early Child Development and Care, 22*, 109–121.

Rosell, L. (1968). Children's views on war and peace. *Journal of Peace Research, 5*, 268–276.

Rosenblatt, R. (1983). *Children of war.* New York: Anchor Books.

Roskamp, H. (1969). On identity conflicts of students born in World War II. *Psyche, 23*, 754–761.

Saudi, M. (Ed.). (1970). *In time of war, children testify. Drawings of Palestinian children.* Beirut: Mawakaf.

Schwebel, M. (1963). Studies of children's reactions to the atomic threat. *American Journal of Orthopsychiatry, 33*, 202–203.

Schwebel, M. (1965). Nuclear Cold War: Student opinion and professional responsibility. In M. Schwebel (Ed.), *Behavioral science and human behavior.* Palo Alto, CA: Behavioral Science Press.

Schwebel, M. (1982). Effects of the nuclear threat on children and teenagers: Implications for professionals. *American Journal of Orthopsychiatry, 52*, 608–618.

Simmons, J. R. (1974). *Sources of political socialization to international conflict: Influences of the mass media, family, peer group, school, and religion on adolescents' orientations towards war and peace.* Unpublished dissertation, University of Washington, Seattle.

Solantaus, T. (1983). Children and the threat of nuclear war. In M. Kahnert, D. Pitt, & I. Taipale (Eds.), *Children and war: Proceedings of symposium at Siuntio Baths, Finland 24.3–27.3, 1983.* Kirjapaino, Finland: Oy Gummerus Ab, Jyväskylä.

Solantaus, T. (1986). Adolescence and the nuclear threat in Finland. In B. Berger Gould, S. Moon, & J. Van Hoorn (Eds.), *Growing up scared? The psychological effect of the nuclear threat on children.* Berkeley, CA: Open Books.

Solantaus, T., Rimpela, M., & Taipale, V. (1984). The threat of war in the minds of 12- to 18-year-olds in Finland. *Lancet, 1* (1), 784–785.

Sommers, F., Goldberg, S., Levinson, D., Ross, C., & LaCombe, S. (1984, June 4–9). *Children's mental health and the threat of nuclear war: A Canadian pilot study.* Paper presented at the Fourth Congress, International Physicians for the Prevention of Nuclear War, Helsinki, Finland.

Targ, H. (1970). Children's developing orientations to international politics. *Journal of Peace Research, 7*, 70–97.

Ter Steeg, L. (1969). Het godsdienstonderwijs en de vrede. In M. Albinski et al., *Vrede in vakken.* Roermond: Romen.

Tizard, B. (1984). Problematic aspects of nuclear education. *Harvard Educational Review, 54* (3), 271–281.

Tizard, B. (1986). The impact of the nuclear threat on children's development. In M. Richards & P. Light (Eds.), *Children of social worlds: Development in a social context.* Cambridge: Polity Press, pp. 236–256.

Tolley, H. (1973). *Children and war.* New York: Teachers College Press.

Torney, J. V., Anderson, L. F., & Targ, H. (1969). A review of existing and needed research on the development of international orientations during childhood and adolescence. In J. M. Becker (Ed.), *An examination of objectives, needs and priorities in international education in U.S. secondary and elementary schools.* Washington, DC: U.S. Office of Education.

United Nations High Commissioner for Refugees. (1994). *Refugee children. Guidelines on protection and care.* Geneva: UNHCR.

Union O.S.E. (1946). *Les enfants de Buchenwald.* Geneva: Union Oeuvres de Secours aux Enfants.

United Nations Relief and Rehabilitation Administration, European Office. (1945). *Psychological problems of displaced persons. A report prepared for the welfare division of the European regional office of the UNRRA by the Inter-Allied Psychological Study Group.* London: UNRRA European Office.

Van Dellen, P., & Ten Hoorn, H. (1981). Voorlichting en beeldvorming. Hoe denken leerlingen over oorlog en kernwapens en hoe reageren zij op angstaanjagende informatie? In H. B. Gerritsma (Ed.), *Aspecten van mondiale vorming; een greep uit de literatuur.* Groningen, The Netherlands: Polemologisch Instituut.

Van Hoorn, J. (1986). Facing the nuclear threat: Comparisons of adolescents and adults. In B. Berger Gould, S. Moon, & J. Van Hoorn (Eds.), *Growing up scared? The psychological effect of the nuclear threat on children.* Berkely, CA: Open Books.

Van IJzendoorn, M. H. (1986). Morele argumentatie en bezorgdheid over kernbewapening: Enkele empirische studies onder jongeren. *Pedagogische Studiën, 63* (1), 1–13.

Van Kempen, M., Peek, T., & Vriens, L. (1986). *Vrede en oorlog als kinderprobleem.* (Research Report). Utrecht University, Utrecht, The Netherlands: Utrecht University, Faculty of Education.

Van Zwan, E. (1987). Kindersoldaten. *Intermediair, 23,* 9–11.

Verdon-Roe, V. (1983, January). Growing up in the nuclear age: What the children can tell us. *East West Journal,* pp. 24–31.

Volmerg, U., & Stehr, U. (1978). *Sicherheitspolitik als Thema der Erwachsenenbildung.* Frankfurt am Main, Germany: Fischer.

Von Jacob, A., & Schmidt, H.-D. (1988). Die Konzeptualisierung von "Krieg" und "Frieden" bei sechs-bis zwölfjärigen Kindern in der DDR. *Zeitschrift für Psychologie, 196,* 265–277.

Vriens, L. J. A. (1987). *Pedagogiek tussen vrees en vrede: Een pedagogische theorie over vredesopvoeding* [Pedagogy between fear and peace: A pedagogical theory of peace education]. (Thesis, Utrecht University). Antwerp, Belgium: Internationale Vredesinformatiedienst.

Wrightsman, L. S. (1964). Parental attitudes and behaviors as determinants of children's responses to the threat of nuclear war. *Vita Humana, 3–4* (7), 178–185.

Woods, D. (1980, April 15). Children bearing military arms. *Friends Journal,* Geneva, pp. 12–14.

Yamaguchi, Y. (1983). Children of Hiroshima and Nagasaki. In M. Kahnert, D. Pitt, & I. Taipale (Eds.), *Children and war: Proceedings of symposium at Siuntio Baths, Finland* (pp. 24.3–27.3). Kirjapaino, Finland: Oy Gummerus Ab Jyväskylä.

Youth Division of Soka Gakkai (Ed.). (1978). *Cries for Peace: Experiences of Japanese victims of World War II.* Tokyo: The Japan Times, Ltd.

2

I KNOW WHAT
YOU ARE THINKING

THE ROLE-TAKING ABILITY AND
UNDERSTANDING OF PEACE AND WAR

Ilse Hakvoort and Louis Oppenheimer,
University of Amsterdam

CHILDREN'S AND ADOLESCENTS' UNDERSTANDING of and reasoning about peace and war as well as developmental changes in this understanding are considered to be part of their social knowledge (see Chapters Four, Five, and Eight in this volume). Hence, peace and war are defined as social phenomena and viewed as an integral part of children's social world and experience.

Within the field of social-cognitive research, a number of stage theories exist which focus on abilities of interpersonal inference and an understanding of social phenomena. In particular, studies dealing with the development of the ability to place oneself in the position of others and infer their feelings and thoughts (the role- or perspective-taking ability) and its relationship with cognitive development and social behavior stand central in social-cognitive research (cf. Shantz, 1975, 1983). The most detailed developmental model for social role taking during childhood and adolescence was formulated by Selman (1980). In this model, the maturing individual is thought to progress in understanding the feelings, attitudes, and opinions of others and the mutually affective nature of such perspectives with regard to one's own and others' thinking, feeling, and so on. We perceive the course by which children come to understand the social world and the development of the role-taking ability, in particular, to be fundamental in their understanding of peace and war. Transitions toward higher levels of role taking and the increasing ability to coordinate different points of view are hypothesized to be conditional for qualitative changes in children's and adolescents' understanding of these concepts.

According to Selman (1980), young children are characterized by an inability to differentiate between their own perspective and those of others (stage 0: the egocentric viewpoint). Based on this inability, young children understand peace and war only from their own personal perspective. Associations with peace and war are concrete, visible, and materially oriented and are predominantly described in static situation-related terms. Between the ages of five and nine, the inability to differentiate between perspectives is replaced by an awareness that others have perspectives which may differ from the child's own (stage 1: social-informational role taking). Because children tend to focus on one perspective relative to another rather than on the mutual relationships among perspectives (that is, coordination), the perspectives are still unrelated. Children are able to recognize personal relationships, permitting peace to be understood as being friends and war as having quarrels.

Between the ages of seven and twelve, a shift toward self-reflective role taking (stage 2: self-reflection) takes place. Self-reflective role taking is defined by the understanding that individuals in interactions are aware of the perspective of others and that this awareness influences their own and others' views of each other. The attainment of self-reflective role taking is presumed to be conditional for the understanding of peace as a result of cooperation based on psychological processes between groups or nations. The understanding of the reciprocal nature of interpersonal relationships (stage 3: mutual role taking) emerges between the ages of ten and fifteen. This understanding permits children to take a position outside a two-person interaction and to view the interaction from a third person's perspective. In particular, the development of mutual role taking enables children to distinguish between different nation-related points of view, to coordinate different points of view, and to understand the mutual role of groups or nations in conflict situations as well as in bilateral collaborations. Hence, mutual role taking is assumed to be a developmental prerequisite for the ability to perceive peace or strategies to attain peace involving general human attitudes such as mutual respect, equality, and the acceptance of different points of view.

The last stage in this developmental sequence refers to social and conventional system role taking (stage 4). This type of role taking, also called interdependent role taking, leads to the realization that there is no complete understanding and that particular social conventions are compromises based on democratic processes. This realization will be related to the understanding that political decisions relate to a variety of different points of view within pluralistic societies and lead to the inclusion of universal human rights and values in definitions of peace. Conflicts are then understood to be present within and between complex systems.

In summary, prompted by the development of interpersonal understanding as well as by age, the understanding of peace and war is thought to shift from concrete, observable events to more abstract conceptions, for example, ideas about tolerance and acceptance as well as universal rights (see Hakvoort & Oppenheimer, 1993). The differentiation between thinking of peace in terms of the absence or negation of war (negative peace) or in terms of a dynamic, interactive process (positive peace) is not expected to emerge prior to adolescence. Besides the hypothesized changes along the dimensions of concrete-abstract reasoning and negative-positive conceptions of peace, a change is also expected from egocentric "self-oriented" conceptions (those related to the immediate environment) to conceptions based on cooperation and democratic compromises between larger groups and nations (those related to the world in general).

In this chapter, a study is reported in which special attention is given to the concept of peace by explicitly involving children's and adolescents' ideas about strategies to attain peace. We assume that an exploration of the developmental course for conceptions of peace, war, and strategies to attain peace during childhood and adolescence contributes to the formulation of a comprehensive developmental, theoretical framework for these phenomena. To date, this area of research has been theoretically underdeveloped.

The Study

In this study, a time-sequential, longitudinal design was used involving three successive assessments (1991–92, 1992–93, and 1993–94). This design combines a cross-sectional and longitudinal design and offers control facilities for unconfounded cohort effects as well as repeated-measurement effects (Baltes, Reese, & Nesselroade, 1977). The use of such a design permitted the study of developmental trajectories over longer age periods. At the first assessment, 216 Dutch children and adolescents between the ages of six and sixteen participated. Five age cohorts were formed: age ranges from six to eight years of age (n = 44: 23 boys, 21 girls), eight to ten years of age (n = 41: 21 boys, 20 girls), ten to twelve years of age (n = 51: 26 boys, 25 girls), twelve to fourteen years of age

(n = 39: 20 boys, 19 girls), and fourteen to sixteen years of age (n = 41: 19 boys, 22 girls). A total of 203 children and adolescents participated in all three assessments. During the last assessment the participants were between eight and eighteen years of age. The sample was selected from elementary schools (ages six to twelve) and secondary schools (ages twelve to eighteen) serving middle-class urban neighborhoods.

All children and adolescents were interviewed by means of a semi-structured interview with fixed open-ended questions. An interview procedure was opted for because it could be used with all age groups and because we expected that interviews rather than other methods would offer more meaningful data and insights about the participants' real understanding of peace, war, and strategies to attain peace. The questions in the semistructured interview were grouped into six clusters which appeal to different aspects of peace and war (see Hakvoort, 1996a, 1996b). To assess the development of children's and adolescents' role-taking ability, three of Selman's role-taking tasks (1980) were administered at each of the three successive assessments.

Verbatim transcriptions of the recorded interviews were used to systematically transform and aggregate the raw data into categories. The responses to all questions were reduced into their thematic units, which were assigned to different sets of nominal categories for peace (Table 2.1) and war (Table 2.2; cf. Hakvoort, 1996b).

Two general rules for categorization of the thematic units were used. First, to prevent verbal ability from biasing the assessment, each category in a participant's response was coded only once (that is, dichotomous decisions were made for each thematic unit: users versus nonusers, 1 or 0). Second, because each response was divided into its thematic units, more than one thematic unit could be identified and, hence, classified into the predefined categories. On the response level, the sets of categories for each question could be defined as exhaustive but not exclusive. Each thematic unit was assigned to only one category; categories were considered to be mutually exclusive. When subjects responded to a particular question with "I do not know," an exception to the second categorization rule (that more than one thematic component could be identified) was made. When this thematic unit was identified, it was not possible to identify any other theme.

The responses to the role-taking tasks were scored in accordance with Selman's criteria (1980). The three role-taking tasks were coded separately, resulting in three scores which offered information about each participant's level of role taking for each task (level 0, 1, 2, 3, or 4). The average scores over the three tasks were also calculated to obtain an overall index for children's role-taking ability.

Table 2.1. Nominal Categories for Peace and Strategies to Attain Peace.

Category 0		Missing
Category 1		War-related
Category 2	a	Religion
	b	Material-related
		Nature and pollution
Category 3	i	Positive emotions at an individual level
	g	Positive emotions at a global level
Category 4	i	Negation of war at an individual level
	g	Negation of war at a global level
Category 5	a	Disarmament
	[b	Sharing]
Category 6		Human attitudes
Category 7		Universal rights

Note: *The category between brackets (category 5b) is only applicable with the strategies.*

Table 2.2. Nominal Categories for War.

Category 0		Missing
Category 1		Peace-related
Category 2		Weapons and soldiers
Category 3		Quarrel, row
Category 4		War activities
Category 5		Human aspects of war
Category 6		Consequences of war
	a	Negative consequences of war
	b	Positive consequences of war
Category 7		Negative emotions
Category 8		Conflict
	a	A row between national leaders or nations, without referring to mutuality
	b	Mutual character of fights is emphasized
Category 9		Qualitative evaluation of war

To attain an accurate and reliable coding procedure, an unambiguous coding system was developed and systematically recorded in a coding manual. Further, a variety of analyses were used to assess different aspects of the reliability of the coding process. In particular, the accuracy with which themes were identified—that is, the so-called process of unitizing (see Holsti, 1969, p. 136; Krippendorff, 1980, p. 57)—were studied, as well as the consistency of the classification of selected themes to the nominal categories (cf. Guetzkow, 1950; Montgomery & Crittenden, 1977). For all analyses, "substantial" and "almost perfect" statistics (reliability coefficients) were obtained (cf. Hakvoort, 1996b).

Results

For the analysis of the categorical variables, multivariate frequency or contingency tables were employed (cf. Hagenaars, 1990; Wickens, 1989). To analyze systematic interactions between the independent variables age, gender, and a category, two- and three-way contingency tables (age[5] x gender[2] x category[2]) were constructed. When a category was used by less than 10 percent of the total sample, this contingency table was excluded from further analysis. The remaining contingency tables were analyzed by statistical tests based on the assumption of an underlying chi-square distribution (chi-square and hierarchical loglinear analyses; cf. Hagenaars, 1990; Wickens, 1989).

The findings of this study confirmed the results of previous studies which had shown that at a young age children have already developed an understanding of the concepts of peace and war. With the exception of one child at the first assessment, all six- to eight-year-olds understood the concept of war and were able to describe aspects of war. The absence of clear developmental changes in the understanding of war from this age onward suggests that major developmental changes in the understanding of war occur prior to the age of six. To test this assumption, additional research needs to be conducted in which preschool ages are also included (cf. Rodd, 1985). For the understanding and verbalization of the concept of peace, major developmental changes were evident between the ages of six and ten. It was not until the age of nine that nearly all of the Dutch children showed a full understanding of peace. When we compare this finding with those reported in the majority of studies conducted in other countries (cf. Cooper, 1965; Hall, 1993; Rosell, 1968; Ålvik, 1968), the understanding of peace by Dutch children appears to proceed more slowly than elsewhere. This finding, however, replicates and confirms findings of earlier studies with Dutch children (Hakvoort, 1989; Van Kempen, Peek, & Vriens, 1986).

In spite of this replication, differences exist with respect to gender-related developmental processes. Whereas Hakvoort and Oppenheimer (1993) reported that seven- to nine-year-old girls understand peace earlier than their male peers, our present findings show that it is the boys who developmentally precede the girls in their understanding of peace. At the first assessment, more six- to eight-year-old boys (74 percent) than girls (43 percent) understood the concept of peace. One year later, in the second assessment, this gender difference had disappeared. This reversal in gender-related developmental order may be the result of either measurement errors in one of the studies or cohort effects (the study by Hakvoort and Oppenheimer [1993] was conducted in 1989 [Hakvoort, 1989]; the present study was conducted from 1991 to 1994). Whatever the reason, these findings prevent us from concluding unequivocally that boys understand peace developmentally earlier than girls.

The Concept of Peace

The thematic components in the responses to the free-association and definition questions (that is, children's understanding of peace) were systematically coded into the eleven categories shown in Table 2.1. Children's understanding of peace showed that from the age of eight, most children already perceived peace as involving the negation of war at a global level (category 4g), with "the absence of war" and "the absence of shooting" as general thematic components. Children who did not show this type of understanding of peace (children younger than eight) did not understand peace at all or were not able to verbalize it. From the moment when children come to understand peace, it is understood foremost as the absence or negation of war. Our findings suggested that the emergence of the concept of peace is paralleled by the understanding of peace in terms of negative peace (the negation of war).

A second dominant theme which could be discerned in children's understanding of peace was the negation of war at an individual level (category 4i), which is defined by thematic components such as the absence of fights or the absence of quarrels with friends. Reasoning about peace as the negation of war at an individual level was not systematically related to age. This finding could be explained by the relatively large proportion of participants who used this thematic component in their reasoning about peace. Between the ages of eight and eighteen, the percentages ranged from 46 to 73 percent. The lower percentages for the youngest children were caused by the number of children who did not understand peace. As with negation of war at a global level, only with the youngest children were developmental changes evident for the understanding of peace as the absence of quarrels. With the development of an understanding of peace, ideas about this individual level emerged. Of interest is the finding that girls mentioned this individual level more often than boys (this difference tended to significance).

Third, the understanding of peace as a positive emotion (category 3i— for example, being friends or kind to each other) was saliently present. From the age of seven, more than half of the participants in each age group included positive emotions in their understanding of peace. This type of understanding followed an identical developmental pattern as the understanding of peace as the negation of war at individual and global levels. When children came to understand peace, positive emotions were described. With progressing age, however, positive emotions were included less frequently in the understanding of peace. All the other categories in Table 2.1 were mentioned infrequently (that is, between 0.5 percent and 11 percent of the total number of responses).

Strategies to Attain Peace

Strategies to attain peace were assessed by requesting children and adolescents to formulate ways in which peace could be attained or maintained from different social positions. The social positions consisted of one unspecified position and three specified positions. For the categorization of the responses to these questions, one subcategory which referred to "sharing" (category 5b) was added to the set of nominal categories (see Table 2.2). Sharing was perceived as a separate category involving themes such as the importance of sharing goods with poor people and taking care of Third World countries.

When the children and adolescents in this study reasoned about strategies to attain peace from an unspecified social position (that is, the first strategy question), thematic components belonging to the negation of war at global and individual levels (categories 4g and 4i) and positive emotions at an individual level (category 3i) again constituted more than 10 percent of the participants' total number of responses. Positive emotions at the individual level, however, were thought to be considerably less adequate as strategies to attain peace than as aspects of peace (for example, in the associations to peace). It was foremost the younger children who mentioned these themes in their strategies.

In strategies from specified positions (the national and international positions), both the use of the individual emotional category and negation of war at an individual level were further reduced. Whereas peace remained primarily related to the absence and termination of wars and the absence of international conflicts (negation of war at a global level), the negation of interpersonal conflicts (negation of war at the individual level) and the promotion of interindividual positive emotions came to play a less important role. Fewer than 10 percent of all participants considered that these aspects of peace contributed to the attainment of peace from specified social positions. The participants understood that different social positions require different levels of reasoning. For the older children and adolescents, "making friends" and "making other people happy" were no longer considered to be adequate strategies for national and international leaders to attain peace. "Stopping or preventing quarrels," which was more frequently present in strategies from the unspecified social position, was also rarely observed when it was formulated from specified positions. It was primarily the six- to twelve-year-olds who considered "ending a quarrel between yourself and a friend" or "forgetting that there was any quarrel" to be an effective strategy to attain peace.

The inclusion of questions which required participants to formulate strategies to attain peace from different social positions resulted in findings not yet reported elsewhere. When compared with free-association and definition questions, the formulation of strategies resulted in a considerably larger repertoire of different themes. The presence of themes like nature and pollution, positive emotions at a global level, disarmament, and sharing pointed to a considerably more sophisticated understanding of peace than had hitherto been observed.

Concerns with the protection of nature and taking care of pollution became evident in strategies to attain peace from the position of a national or international leader. These concerns were not observed in the responses to the free-association and definition questions, nor in the strategies from the unspecified position. Though the proportion of the responses including these concerns was small, it is important to note that these issues became important when specified positions had to be taken into account in the attainment of peace. No effects for age and gender were found over the repeated assessments.

Positive emotions at a global level (category 3g), referring to international meetings, economic and commercial relations, and a United Europe, were most frequently observed with the oldest adolescents. The absence of clear age-related differences may be due to recurrent fluctuations in the use of this type of understanding of peace. From its appearance at approximately the age of ten, this type of understanding is used with changing emphasis by the different age groups at different assessments; the highest frequency was present with the fourteen- to sixteen-year-olds. While for this age group the effect for age tended toward significance, no corresponding increase in the use of this category was observed with younger age groups (the use of this category increased too slowly over the repeated assessments). We speculatively assume that during the three-year assessment period, particular events took place in the adolescents' social or school environment which affected their ideas about strategies to attain peace. For instance, because the adolescents were recruited from identical grades from secondary schools, a topic like the European Union may have been part of their history or geographic curricula and may have been discussed in detail at approximately the same period for this age group.

Although disarmament was observed at the last assessment in strategies from the unspecified social position, it was more frequently observed in strategies from specified positions. An identical pattern was found for the category of "sharing." No age and gender effects could be examined.

Strategies from an unspecified social position also included themes involving equality, desegregation, tolerance, and respect between people (category 6: human attitudes). The presence of human attitudes in the understanding of peace was unambiguously and systematically age-related. From the age of ten, peace was progressively understood to involve mutual respect and tolerance toward one another and among peoples. Before the age of ten, human attitudes were hardly present. In the strategies from the position of national and international leaders, human attitudes were even more frequently mentioned. Significant effects for age were also present for all assessments. The increase in proportion from the first to the third assessment for age group 2 (from eight to ten years of age to ten to twelve years of age) was considerable. For the third age group (from ten to twelve years of age to twelve to fourteen years of age), this increase was even larger. We hesitate to explain this difference in terms of a birth-cohort effect. It seems more plausible and valid to consider this increase to be an effect of the repeated-measurement procedure employed in this study. At the time of the third assessment, the ages of the children in age group 2 ranged from ten to twelve, an age period which is often characterized by important developmental changes in children's cognitive and social-cognitive abilities. Consequently, the possibility should not be neglected that compared with other age periods, children between the ages of eight and twelve profit more efficiently from the learning situation presented by the repeated-measurement procedure. The strong increase in the observed use of human attitudes in the strategies can then be considered a measurement bias.

In the strategies to attain international peace and maintain peace in The Netherlands, increases were also observed in the use of themes like the presence and continuation of free elections, the necessity of democracy, and freedom of the press and speech (category 7: universal rights). An age-related increase was present when strategies included universal rights. For instance, the use of "just societal systems" did not occur before the age of ten; from the age of ten on, universal rights became part of strategies, and it was only after the age of twelve that an increase was observed in the understanding and use of universal rights.

The Concept of War

To assess the understanding of war, one free-association question and two definition questions were used. The thematic components in the responses to these three questions were categorized in an identical set of twelve categories (ten major categories and two subcategories; see Table 2.2).

Children's and adolescents' understanding of war is best described by concrete aspects of war such as war activities (category 4), objects of war (category 2), and negative consequences of war (category 6a). Negative consequences concerned "destroyed houses," "graveyards," and "burying the dead." Because these negative consequences closely parallel the war images presented by the media (for example, in the news on television and in pictures in newspapers), we agree with Ålvik (1968) that these consequences represent the tangible aspects of war. The use of these tangible aspects of war varied with the different age groups and questions. Nevertheless, their presence in children's and adolescents' understanding of war was consistent. Other themes such as quarrels (category 3), negative emotions (category 7), peace-related issues (category 1), and the understanding of the nonmutual (category 8a) and mutual (category 8b) nature of conflicts attained the > 10 percent requirement for some of the questions. For example, quarrels were mentioned more often when participants had to define war to a five-year-old child; the understanding of conflicts as nonmutual or mutual events was only observed in definitions of war offered to peers. Of particular interest was the finding that aspects of peace were also mentioned in the free-association responses (for example, "thinking about peace" and "war goes together with peace"). In an earlier study, Hakvoort and Oppenheimer (1993) concluded that the understanding of peace was directly related to war (the negation of war). They argued, however, that the reverse (war defined by the negation of peace) was not necessarily implied. In spite of this assumption, some participants in the present study spontaneously referred to peace when expressing ideas about war. The relative proportions for such responses in each separate age group were too small to detect any age or gender effects.

As with the understanding of peace, a gender difference was present in reasoning about war on the individual level (interpersonal conflicts). More girls than boys included "quarrels" in their free-association and definition responses. In addition, in their definitions six-year-old boys characterized war by the activities of war more often than girls did. This finding parallels the variation observed in reasoning about peace in terms of the negation of war at a global level, where boys more frequently refer to the absence of war than girls do.

Role Taking and the Understanding of Peace and War

To be able to embed the study in our theoretical framework (the social-cognitive approach), it was essential to examine whether particular levels of interpersonal understanding (role taking) would be indicative of children's and adolescents' understanding of peace and war. Because the free-association, definition, and strategy questions resulted in the use of fairly identical sets of categories, we collapsed the response ranges for the seven questions (one free-association, two definition, and four strategy questions). For the actual understanding of war, the response ranges of the three questions about war were collapsed.

To test the relationship between the development of role taking and the understanding of peace and war, the role-taking scores and the scores per category (0 [no reference or use] or 1 [reference or use]) were included in the analyses. Because the effect of age was significant for both developments, age (measured at an interval scale) was included as covariate in all analyses (the effects of age were controlled).

Role Taking and the Understanding of Peace

With age as covariable, a significant difference was present between children's and adolescents' role-taking ability and the use of positive emotions at a global level. Children who did not understand the reciprocal affective nature of points of view and were not able to form coordinated chains of perspective (stage 2, self-reflective role taking), were not able to understand peace in terms of positive emotions at a global level. When self-reflective role taking emerged, the use of positive emotions such as friendly relations between nations or the European Union appeared and increased.

The use of human attitudes such as respect, tolerance, and desegregation was also significantly related to levels of interpersonal understanding. Only after children understood that each individual was aware of the other's point of view and that this awareness was reciprocal (stage 2) did the use of human attitudes in reasoning about peace become evident. With the attainment of the third level of role-taking development (stage 3, the ability to adopt a third-person perspective), an additional increase in reasoning about human attitudes was observed. A comparison of the proportions of participants mentioning aspects of universal rights (category 7) at different levels of role taking demonstrated that the use of this category was only observed after stage-3 role taking was acquired.

These findings warranted the conclusion that age-related changes in the understanding of peace are structurally related to children's and adolescents' understanding of interpersonal relationships. That is, a relationship between the development of the role-taking ability and the way children reason about peace and strategies to attain peace was present when the effects of age were controlled.

Role Taking and the Understanding of War

Several trends were observed for the relation between role taking and the understanding of war, but no unequivocal relationship between these developments was evident. The observed effects for levels of role taking suggested a relationship between children at stage 2 and the understanding of war as nonmutual or mutual conflict. For war as nonmutual conflict (category 8a), interactions with the role-taking ability were evident at the second and third assessment (with age as covariate). The proportions of children referring to war as nonmutual conflict increased only after they attained stage-2 reasoning in role taking. For war as mutual conflict (category 8b), interactions with children's role-taking ability could only be demonstrated at the first and third assessments. While the younger children (those at stage-1 reasoning in role taking) hardly evidenced any understanding of the mutuality of conflicts, a slight increase in this understanding was observed in correspondence with the development of role-taking ability. In addition, qualitative evaluations of war appeared to be affected by the ability to adapt a third-person perspective (stage-3 role taking). Theoretically, it was argued that to understand war as bilateral or multinational conflict children should understand the reciprocity between perspectives (stage-2 role taking), and further increases were expected with the understanding of the mutual nature of interpersonal relationships (stage 3). Our findings did not unequivocally confirm this assumption. To do so, additional research is definitely required.

Discussion

In the general discussions about the meaning of peace (cf. Brock-Utne, 1989; Galtung, 1964, 1969, 1985), a distinction is made between a negative and positive dimension of peace. *Negative peace* is defined by the absence of "direct violence" (negation of war). *Positive peace* is defined by dynamic, interactive processes (cooperative patterns) which aim at the collaboration between groups and nations, as well as by the absence of "indirect violence," for example, structural violence in society (Galtung, 1996). A distinction is also made between unorganized and organized violence. *Unorganized violence* is mostly shown by individuals on the micro level (within the direct environment or on the individual level); *organized violence* is observed on the macro level (the global level; cf. Brock-Utne, 1989, p. 47, table). Based on these distinctions in the definition of peace, the findings of the present study can be summarized in an age-by-peace matrix (see Table 2.3).

All children and adolescents between the ages of six and eighteen who understand the concept of peace show this understanding of peace as the

Table 2.3. Summarized Integration of the Understanding of Peace in Relation to the Understanding of Interpersonal Relationships.

Age	IpU	Negative Peace Concept		Positive Peace Concept	
		Individual Level	Global Level	Individual Level	Global Level
12–18	3				Universal rights
10–18	2/3			Human attitudes	
	2				Positive emotions
					Sharing
			Disarmament		Nature and pollution
6–18	1	Absence of quarrels	Absence of war	Positive emotions	

Note: *IpU = level of interpersonal understanding.*

absence of quarrels (with negative peace defined by the absence of unorganized violence) and peace as the absence of war (with negative peace
defined by the absence of organized violence). When participants discuss
peace along the positive dimension, they refer to social activities in the
immediate environment (for example, being friends or being nice to each
other). While it is difficult to view these social activities as processes which
reduce structural violence, they do involve cooperation between individuals. This type of understanding is here considered to be a precursor to
understanding positive peace as a dynamic, interactive process.

The understanding that peace also involves disarmament, taking care of
nature and pollution, sharing, and positive emotions at a global level is not
characteristic for any particular age. Nevertheless, no references to these
issues are found in children's free associations and definitions. We speculatively argue from a theoretical perspective that understanding the role of
disarmament, sharing, and so on requires inferential skills, or higher levels
of interpersonal understanding. For instance, to include disarmament as an
activity within a strategy to attain peace, some understanding must be present that actions such as "throwing away all weapons" or "closing weapons
depots" have to be mutual and collective to be effective in attaining peace.
Similarly, we assume that the inclusion of themes such as taking care of
nature and pollution, as well as sharing, require an awareness and understanding of inequality or asymmetry in situations: a polluted environment
or lack of food will harm people and may lead to violence. When we look
at human attitudes—mentioned by participants older than ten years—some
participants emphasize that segregation (the absence of respect and tolerance between people) should be resolved to attain or maintain peace, while
others emphasize that conditions should be created for respect and tolerance to develop. Because the absence of these human attitudes can be said
to "reduce the quality of life" (Brock-Utne, 1989, p. 47), these attitudes are
definitely part of the definition of positive peace. The final step in the developmental sequence for positive peace deals with the inclusion of universal
rights, such as democratic processes and free elections.

To integrate and embed the findings concerning children's and adolescents' understanding of peace in a broader developmental framework, the
relationship with the development of role taking will be discussed. The
relationship between the development of interpersonal understanding and
peace is present when the effects of age are controlled. This finding war-
rants the conclusion that age-related changes in the understanding of
peace are structurally related to the understanding of interpersonal relationships. Based on this finding, the age-by-peace matrix in Table 2.3 also
includes the levels of role-taking development.

Gender-related differences in the understanding of peace are present most saliently when the questions are considered separately and in the instances when peace is understood in terms of negation of war at the global and individual levels. When the responses to free-association, definition, and strategy questions are collapsed, no structural gender differences are present. In the associations with and definitions of peace, as well as the strategies to attain peace from the unspecified social position, male participants understand peace to involve the negation of war at the global level more often than female participants do. Girls, on the other hand, understand peace to relate to the absence of conflicts at the individual level more often than boys do. The tendency to give a higher emphasis to the negation of war at the individual level by female participants is also present with the strategy questions from the specified social positions. Boys express a greater concern about the pollution of the environment.

Only part of our theoretically formulated expectations involving systematic age-related changes in the understanding of peace were confirmed. First, we expected that the understanding of peace would change from a concrete, material understanding to a more abstract, norm-related understanding. No unequivocal evidence for such a shift from childhood through adolescence was present. That is, early childhood understanding of peace is not replaced by a different adolescent understanding later. The dominant thematic components of young children's understanding of peace are also present in adolescents' reasoning. New and more abstract ideas about peace are added to existing knowledge, and understanding and reasoning about peace become more varied and complex as children mature.

Second, we expected that the differentiation between peace defined by the absence of war (negative peace) and peace defined by dynamic interactive processes (positive peace) would not occur before adolescence. When we strictly adhere to the definition of positive peace as consisting of dynamic interactive processes, our hypothesis is confirmed. The inclusion of dynamic interactive processes dealing with tolerance and respect between countries, groups of people, and individuals, as well as those dealing with democracy, only emerge from the onset of adolescence. However, during childhood peace is already related to collaborative and cooperative processes between countries (positive emotions at a global level). In addition, an understanding of peace through positive social activities on the individual level (for example, friendships), as well as through caring for others (sharing) and the environment (addressing nature and pollution), cannot be merely rejected and considered to be aspects of negative peace. From a developmental perspective, we tend to interpret these positive social connotations as precursory (childhood) conceptions of positive peace. That is, during childhood an understanding of "positive peace" is already present, although it is developmentally constrained to or defined by the immediate interpersonal environment. With the development of social knowledge, and interpersonal understanding (role taking) in particular, we assume these early conceptions of positive peace to be generalized to wider national and international contexts.

Third, an age-related change was expected from egocentric, self-oriented perspectives (those related to the immediate environment) to decentered, outward-oriented perspectives (a global perspective related to interactive processes within national and international contexts). Our findings show that all children and adolescents use both perspectives in their reasoning about peace (for example, positive emotions or negation of war at an individual level and negation of war at a global level). The global perspectives of the younger children, however, are not characterized by the interactive processes discussed previously. These processes emerge only during adolescence.

Contrary to our expectations, no clear evidence was present for age-related changes in children's and adolescents' understanding of war. When children mature, concrete aspects of war are and remain predominant themes in their reasoning about war (see Table 2.4). We believe that this finding was due to the limited set of questions about the understanding of war, an assumption which is corroborated by our findings for the understanding of peace. The major age-related changes in understanding peace were observed in the reasoning about strategies to attain peace. Consequently, we suggest that to assess children's and adolescents' understanding of war properly, free-association and definition questions are not sufficient. Additional questions should be formulated, for example, questions about causes which may harm peace or cause war (see Chapter Eight in this volume). Despite this procedural limitation, indications were present that the understanding of the mutual nature of war was age-related. The number of participants who showed this type of understanding, however, remained small.

Table 2.4. Summarized Integration for the Understanding of War.

Age	Concept of War	
	Individual Level	Global Level
		Qualitative evaluation Mutual nature of conflicts Nonmutual nature of conflicts
6–18	Negative emotions Quarrels	Activities of war; objects of war; negative consequences

REFERENCES

Ålvik, T. (1968). The development of views on conflict, war and peace among school children. *Journal of Peace Research, 5,* 171–195.

Baltes, P. B., Reese, H. W., & Nesselroade, J. R. (1977). *Life-span developmental psychology: Introduction to research methods.* Belmont, CA: Wadsworth.

Brock-Utne, B. (1989). *Feminist perspectives on peace and peace education.* New York: Pergamon Press.

Cooper, P. (1965). The development of the concept of war. *Journal of Peace Research, 2,* 1–17.

Galtung, J. (1964). Editorial. *Journal of Peace Research, 1,* 1–4.

Galtung, J. (1969). Violence, peace and peace research. *Journal of Peace Research, 6,* 167–191.

Galtung, J. (1985). Twenty-five years of peace research: Ten challenges and some responses. *Journal of Peace Research, 22,* 142–158.

Galtung, J. (1996). *Peace by peaceful means: Peace and conflict, development and civilization.* London: Sage.

Guetzkow, H. (1950). Unitizing and categorizing problems in coding qualitative data. *Journal of Clinical Psychology, 6,* 47–58.

Hagenaars, J. A. (1990). *Categorical longitudinal data: Loglinear, panel, trend, and cohort analysis.* Thousand Oaks, CA: Sage.

Hakvoort, I. (1989). Children and adolescents about peace. Unpublished master's thesis, University of Amsterdam, Amsterdam.

Hakvoort, I. (1996a). Children's conceptions of peace and war: A longitudinal study. *Peace and Conflict: Journal of Peace Psychology, 2,* 1–15.

Hakvoort, I. (1996b). Conceptualizations of peace and war from childhood through adolescence. Unpublished doctoral dissertation, University of Amsterdam, Amsterdam.

Hakvoort, I., & Oppenheimer, L. (1993). Children and adolescents' conceptions of peace, war and strategies to attain peace: A Dutch case study. *Journal of Peace Research, 30,* 65–77.

Hall, R. (1993). How children think and feel about war and peace: An Australian study. *Journal of Peace Research, 30,* 181–196.

Holsti, O. R. (1969). *Content analysis for the social sciences and humanities.* Reading, MA: Addison-Wesley.

Krippendorff, K. (1980). *Content analysis: An introduction to its methodology.* Thousand Oaks, CA: Sage.

Montgomery, A. C., & Crittenden, K. S. (1977). Improving coding reliability for open-ended questions. *Public Opinion Quarterly, 41,* 235–243.

Rodd, J. (1985). Preschool children's understanding of war. *Early Child Development and Care, 22,* 109–121.

Rosell, L. (1968). Children's view of war and peace. *Journal of Peace Research,* *5,* 268–276.

Selman, R. L. (1980). *The growth of interpersonal understanding: Developmental and clinical analysis.* Orlando: Academic Press.

Shantz, C. U. (1975). The development of social cognition. In E. M. Hetherington (Ed.), *Review of child development research* (Vol. 5, pp. 257–323). Chicago: University of Chicago Press.

Shantz, C. U. (1983). Social cognition. In J. H. Flavell & E. Markman (Eds.), *Handbook of child psychology: Cognitive development* (Vol. 3, pp. 495–555). New York: Wiley.

Van Kempen, M., Peek, T., & Vriens, L. (1986). *Vrede en oorlog als kinderprobleem* [Peace and war as problems of children]. Unpublished research report. Utrecht, The Netherlands: Rijksuniversiteit Utrecht.

Wickens, T. D. (1989). *Multiway contingency tables analysis for the social sciences.* Hillsdale, NJ: Erlbaum.

3

THE PEACE PERSONALITY

Robert C. Ziller, Dahlie S. Moriarty, and Stephen T. Phillips,
University of Florida

If you can see yourself in the eyes of others,
then whom can you harm?

—Gautama Buddha

THE IMPLICIT HYPOTHESIS in this quotation attributed to Buddha is that persons who are predisposed to attend to similarities (rather than differences) between themselves and others may be expected to be more empathic and less hostile under a variety of interpersonal conditions including conflict and war. Persons who are similarly oriented are more capable of identifying with the other or of unilaterally reversing roles with the other to the extent that they experience the emotional responses of the other in the observed circumstances. In contrast, those who would harm others avoid personal, emotional responses by dehumanizing the other (Jersey, 1987). Buddha's hypothesis will be tested here by relating a measure of the tolerant personality, or universal orientation (see Phillips & Ziller, 1997), to American students' responses to "real" and "romanticized" photographs of the Gulf War. The real photographs of war depict death, destruction, and suffering largely, but not exclusively, concerning Iraqi soldiers and civilians. A romanticized photograph of war avoids evoking empathy toward the opponent; instead it promotes the image of war as an exhilarating, adventurous campaign without a hint of its horrors with regard to both ourselves and others. Finally, a pilot study of empathy and peace induction is described which involves an exhibition of photographs from *The Family of Man* (Steichen, 1955).

The Peace Personality

The pathway to the peace personality begins with selectively attending to similarities rather than differences between the self and others, leading to the concept of oneness or universal orientation. Universal orientation, in turn, is associated with a general empathy or identification with others. This involves the recognition that apparent differences among humans are distractions which can block the recognition and appreciation of our commonality, including the joys of life and the continuous struggle for survival. Similarity orientation, then, is associated with universal orientation, which in turn is associated with a general empathic response to others, deriving, in part, from a recognition of the homologous nature of humankind.

It is proposed, then, that if the inclusiveness of the humankind category is recognized, this awareness is accompanied by an appreciative regard for the feelings of the other. Indeed, under these conditions, the emotional dispositions of the self and other are closely associated; the joys and sorrows of each are experienced by the other. Thus, each is less likely to harm the other because harm to the other is reflexive, if for no other reason than, as Gandhi noted, violence to others is violence to yourself, which prevents self-realization (Naess, 1958). The peace personality initiates and creates a peace environment by nonverbally communicating the perception of similarity between self and other. Henceforth, this proclivity to orient toward similarities between the self and others, which leads to a general empathic response and broadly inclusive self-other categories, will be referred to as universal orientation, the personality of peace. The concept derives from Buddhist writings (see Smith, 1958) concerning the experience of oneness. Oneness is operationally defined as the dismissal of all distinctions, but particularly any distinction between self and other. More positively, it is the total acceptance of others, as we will emphasize. Perceptions of differences are eschewed and the dichotomy of self and other is avoided by ceasing to evaluate: "Do not seek after truth, merely cease to hold opinions" (Smith, 1958, p. 152).

Various social science investigators and theorists have considered the implications of an integration between self and others similar to Bakan's communion modality (1966). An integrated self-other perspective is discussed in relation to a sense of oneness in the development of empathy

(Hoffman, 1976), heightened awareness of the strengths and weaknesses of others and a reduction in denigration and potential conflict (Deutsch, 1990), and greater acceptance of divergent views and a reduction in splitting others into simple good-evil and we-they categories (Optow, 1990). Furthermore, an interdependent construal of self in relation to others (Markus & Kitayama, 1991) results in a sense of connectedness, oneness, or relatedness. Similar to the conceptualization of "including others in the self" (Aron, Aron, Tudor, & Nelson, 1991), self-other integration is characterized by cognitive representations of self and other containing common elements or occupying overlapping regions of a cognitive matrix, access to which follows similar pathways.

Most recently, Phillips and Ziller (1997) introduced the concept of "nonprejudice," which derives from an orientation toward self-other similarities, an avoidance of self-other distinctions, an orientation toward oneness, a nonevaluative posture regarding others, and an inclusive rather than exclusive perception concerning self and other. The evolving measure was the Universal Orientation Scale (Ziller, 1987). In the present context, it will be referred to as the peace personality. It is hypothesized that the peace personality will tend to be more empathic with regard to images of war depicting the suffering of "the enemy" because this personality will identify with everyone. Or more directly, from Gandhi (Naess, 1958), the universally oriented personality recognizes that violence against anyone is violence against oneself.

Images of the Meaning of War

In an earlier study of children's images of the meaning of war (Dinklage & Ziller, 1989), children in Germany submitted more photographs depicting destruction, and children in the United States submitted more photographs indicating their relative isolation from war, including photographs which can be interpreted as presenting a romanticized view of war (such as a photograph submitted by one eighth grader which showed a child dressed in a camouflage uniform pointing a pistol at the prostrate form of another child). In the current study, this distinction between real and romanticized images of war was studied by collecting fifty-one photographs within the context of the Gulf War. A description of the photographs is included in Exhibit 3.1. The numbers of the "real" photographs are in bold (the numbers indicate the order in which the slides were shown in the experiment proper).

Fifty-one black-and-white photographs of war were collected from a wide selection of news magazines and journals, along with several books

Exhibit 3.1. Images of War.

1. General Schwarzkopf in a parade with West Point cadets.
2. Iraqi prisoners of war four abreast with their hands above their heads.
3. American helicopter hovering over the flight deck of an aircraft carrier.
4. Saddam Hussein in a field uniform on the phone.
5. Two rows of Iraqi war dead wrapped in white linen being mourned by their relatives.
6. Several U.S. soldiers with bayonets in place moving cautiously through an Iraqi-held city.
7. Map of the Iraqi campaign.
8. Arab soldier who has lost his forearms and is in a hospital being visited by a Saudi officer.
9. The general of the U.S. Army and the chief of staff addressing the press.
10. Arab women on a pistol-shooting range.
11. About fifteen U.S. soldiers in combat dress carrying the flag and disembarking from a large helicopter.
12. A portrait of General Schwarzkopf.
13. U.S. military funeral amid white crosses on gravestones. The casket is carried by six pallbearers followed by the escorted widow.
14. The signing of the war treaty observed by about fifty members of the victorious army.
15. Two Arab women assembling prosthetics for soldiers who have lost their limbs in war.
16. A parade of U.S. soldiers in combat uniforms carrying the flag.
17. An Iraqi soldier whose feet have been burned off by a napalm bomb.
18. Arab civilians (mostly women with their faces covered) in the aftermath of a bombing raid.
19. An Oriental boy seven to ten years of age learning to operate a machine gun.
20. Combat-ready U.S. soldiers marching in closed ranks.
21. A U.S. soldier in front of a pile of sandbags smiling and wearing a Santa Claus hat.
22. A photo opportunity for U.S. troops, who are pointing their weapons at the imaginary Iraqi enemy.
23. Two seriously wounded U.S. soldiers being transported to a hospital by helicopter.
24. Two U.S. soldiers in a forward machine-gun post, one of whom is peering through binoculars.
25. A woman (not from the United States) with a wounded or dying man lying across her lap.
26. An enormous U.S. tank moving across the desert with a crewman in the port.
27. A bombed-out Arab mosque.
28. An Arab mother and baby lying dead side by side in the street.
29. A very large U.S. cannon firing at night at a distant target.
30. U.S. soldiers patrolling the streets of Kuwait while other soldiers are riding through on a Humvee with a mounted machine gun.
31. A bombed-out Iraqi building amid ruins.

Exhibit 3.1. Images of War, Cont'd.

32. U.S. soldiers smiling about crudely fashioned street signs in Kuwait indicating the distance in miles to Indiana and other states.
33. U.S. soldiers in combat with weapons in the ready position who appear to have just been fired upon.
34. Silhouette of a U.S. tank at sunset with a soldier with binoculars peering out of the top turret.
35. Arab child sitting as the sole survivor in the ruins of a bombed-out building.
36. Dead Iraqi soldier alone in a barren area.
37. Platoons of U.S. combat troops disembarking from several large helicopters.
38. Two U.S. soldiers supporting a third wounded soldier toward further medical aid.
39. U.S. soldiers in combat crawling in the sand and peering toward a shell bursting some distance forward.
40. U.S. battleship firing its guns toward the enemy.
41. An Arab civilian hospital war scene showing an area crowded with wounded civilians being attended by relatives and staff.
42. U.S. combat soldiers in the desert looking at a photograph of a young woman in a bathing suit.
43. An enemy soldier reaching out toward a dead comrade.
44. A U.S. soldier viewing a mass grave where fifty or more noncombatants have been massacred.
45. U.S. soldiers peering over the edge of a trench with weapons pointing toward the unseen enemy.
46. A group of Iraqi soldiers surrendering.
47. Iraqi oil wells aflame while a group of U.S. engineers attempts to control the fire.
48. The Vietnam War Memorial with flowers, flags, and mementos strewn before it.
49. An Iraqi tank in flames.
50. U.S. combat troops disembarking from a large aircraft.
51. A wounded U.S. soldier receiving first aid.

concerning the Gulf War but including some photographs depicting various aspects of the Vietnam War and the war in Bosnia. The main focus of the photographs, however, was on the Gulf War, because this war occurred when the participants in the study were between the ages of twelve and fourteen, and it was presumed to be the most pertinent with regard to their perceptions of war.

While the photographs included in the collection were selected in order to capture a variety of views of war, the selection was guided by our earlier study of children's images of war (Dinklage & Ziller, 1989), which had suggested that the images could be arranged in two categories: real and romanticized images of war. The real images of war include death, destruction, and suffering, whereas the romanticized images, or mythical images in Barthes's terms (1957; see Vera & Nathans, 1983), depict power values and induce national pride in a studied campaign to modify popular attitudes. In order to justify recourse to war, the romanticized images of war included in this study are designed to distract and direct attention away from the harsh realities of war. The "real" and "romanticized" categorization of the photographs was determined by four raters, who were provided with the definitions of "real" and "romanticized" as described here. Consensus was unanimous regarding all fifty-one photographs.

Method

Participants

The participants in the study were ninety first- and second-year students from the University of Florida who volunteered for the study and received class credit for completing the requirement of participation in an experiment.

Procedure

The study was conducted in two sessions separated by four weeks. In the first session the participants completed the Universal Orientation Scale (Ziller, 1987; Phillips & Ziller, 1997). In the second session the participants responded to the series of war photographs. The sessions were conducted independent of each other in that no references were made to the other study.

UNIVERSAL ORIENTATION SCALE. The Universal Orientation Scale (UOS) consists of twenty verbal items (see Exhibit 3.2). Responses to the statements were selected from a five-point scale ranging from 1 (Does not describe me well) to 5 (Describes me very well). Eight of the items were reverse-scored. The internal reliability coefficient (Cronbach's alpha) was .76, and a six-week test-retest reliability check was .75. Phillips and Ziller (1997) report that the correlation between the UOS and social desirability was not significant. The UOS correlated significantly but negatively with Dogmatism and Modern Racism and positively with the Davis measure of empathy (Davis, 1983). It was also shown that the UOS is associated with being less evaluative of others and preferring heterogeneous to homogeneous group composition (Phillips & Ziller, 1997). Construct validity studies of the instrument conclude that the UOS is a valid measure of nonprejudice or tolerance or, even more generally, of the peace personality.

Exhibit 3.2. Universal Orientation Scale.

1. The similarities between males and females are greater than the differences.
2. I tend to value similarities over differences when I meet someone.
3. At one level of thinking we are all of a kind.
4. I can understand almost anyone because I'm a little like everyone.
5. Little differences among people mean a lot.
6. I can see myself fitting into many groups.
7. There is potential for good and evil in all of us.
8. When I look into the eyes of others I see myself.
9. I could never get accustomed to living in another country.
10. When I first meet someone I tend to notice differences between myself and the other person.
11. "Between" describes my position with regard to groups better than do "in" and "out."
12. The same spirit dwells in everyone.
13. Older persons are very different than I am.
14. I can tell a great deal about people by knowing their gender.
15. There is a certain beauty in everyone.
16. I can tell a great deal about a person by knowing his or her age.
17. Men and woman will never totally understand each other because of their inborn differences.
18. Everyone in the world is very much alike because in the end we all die.
19. I have difficulty relating to persons who are much younger than I am.
20. When I meet someone I tend to notice similarities between myself and the other person.

THE MEANING OF WAR. The directions for showing and responding to the slides were as follows:

> Today you will view a series of slides depicting various aspects of the Gulf War involving primarily the United States and Iraq. Each slide will be shown for six seconds followed by a fifteen-second pause which will permit you to record your feelings associated with that slide. After viewing each slide try to examine how the slide made you feel rather than what you thought about it or how you evaluated the slide. [These are essentially the directions used by Bradley and Lang (1994) to measure emotion in response to photographs, where the responses were made on a nine-point scale graphically illustrated by a mannequin.] For example, look at your response sheet. Line 1 represents two feelings regarding the first slide. The first response is to be made by placing an "X" on one of the nine points on the pictorial scale.
>
> Now look at the board. The two figures on the left represent the two ends of the scale, ranging from "very upset" to "not at all upset."

> For example, if you do not feel upset at all, place an "X" through the figure on the right. This corresponds to the ninth position on the scale. If you feel extremely upset, place a large "X" through the figure on the extreme left. [Show this.] Any response between "not at all upset" and "very upset" is to be made somewhere along this nine-point scale.
>
> Now we will show each of the fifty-one slides depicting facets of the Gulf War. Each slide will be shown for six seconds, followed by a fifteen-second pause while you record your feelings with regard to that specified image of the war. Before each slide is shown, I will give the signal "Slide 1," and so on, and the image will immediately follow when the blank screen appears for fifteen seconds. All right, let's begin.

Following this phase of the study, which was designed to review all the slides before rating them in the main part of the study, the second phase of the study commenced:

> Now we will show the slides a second time. This time record your responses to each of the slides on a seven-point scale. The number on the scale represents how much the image represents your concept of war or what war signifies to you. Each slide will be shown for six seconds. Then you will have six seconds to record your rating on the seven-point scale, where 1 on the scale is "not at all" what war means to you, and 7 on the scale is "a great deal" like what war means to you.

Results

A correlation analysis involving ratings of emotional arousal upon viewing the photographs and evaluation of the same photographs as to how well they depicted war resulted in a correlation of .33 ($n = 40$, $p < .04$) with regard to the "real" war photographs, but the correlation was not statistically significant regarding the "romanticized" photographs ($r = .25$, $n = 40$, $p < .12$). The ratings of the real war photographs appeared to possess a strong emotional component; the ratings of the romanticized photographs of war did not. These results may be interpreted as validating the two categories of war photographs.

Correlation analyses between the UOS and the real versus the romanticized photographs of war resulted in $r = .39$, $n = 40$, $p < .01$ regarding the real category of war photographs and $r = .01$, $n = 40$, n.s. regarding the romanticized photographs. Greater universal orientation was associated with greater responsiveness to the photographs of war depicting death, destruction, and suffering. An analysis of variance was also conducted with the same variable. The results are shown in Table 3.1.

Table 3.1. Universal Orientation Means for Dependent Measures,
Realistic War Images, and Romanticized War Images.

	Universal Orientation Means	
	High	Low
Realistic images	149.95$_A$	129.05$_B$
Romanticized images	108.45$_C$	104.50$_C$

Note: *Means with different subscripts*
significantly differ from each other (t = 2.02, p < .05).

The main effects with regard to high and low universal orientation and real versus romanticized photographs of war were both statistically significant. Those scoring higher on the UOS tended to view all the photographs as more representative of war. In addition, all the participants rated the real war photographs as more representative of war from their perspective.

The most important result, however, is that while there was essentially no difference in the rating of the romanticized photographs of war for persons with high and low universal orientation (108.45 versus 104.50), the difference between highs and lows with regard to the real photographs of war was statistically significant (149.95 versus 129.00, $t = 2.01$, $p < .05$). Those who were most universally oriented perceived the photographs depicting death, destruction, and suffering as the most defining photographs of war. It should be underscored that most of the photographs focused on the suffering of Iraqis.

Discussion

We began with the hypothesis that universally oriented persons are loath to harm others because they tend to identify with a wide variety of others and vicariously share their pain. Universally oriented persons may be described as empathic in general. They describe themselves as connected to a greater variety of others, show a preference for heterogeneously composed groups rather than homogeneous groups, are less evaluative with regard to others, and may be described as more tolerant or even nonprejudiced (Phillips & Ziller, 1997). Here, it has been shown that they recognize the stark realities of war (death, destruction, and suffering among all humankind, with whom they identify). It was shown that universally oriented persons show a more intense emotional response to the harsh realities of war because they are not detached observers but rather are personally involved by virtue of their identification, empathy, and responsiveness to others. They "see themselves in the eyes of others" and in the suffering of all others.

Thus, under conditions of war, it may be anticipated that the leaders of the warring factions will avoid giving the public access to photographs depicting death, destruction, and suffering (the reality of war) but will promote the publication of photographs which describe a mythical, almost aseptic, war, war at a distance, war in the abstract. These mythical photographs of war tend to support the in-group over the out-group and to avoid engendering empathy for all those who are suffering as a consequence of the war, including opponents as well as constituents. The mythical, sanitized, and romanticized photographs of war render war "politically correct." They are propaganda designed to manipulate the attitude of the public with regard to war and to support the use of violence in conflict resolution. To those who would avoid humanizing their opponent in a conflict, the universally oriented person (the peace personality) represents a potential obstacle in the war effort or even a potential enemy.

For the universally oriented person, compassion transcends the us-versus-them categories. If one believes in "oneness," that is, the unity of all humankind, then whom can you harm? Or, indeed, who will harm you? Against whom will you wage war? This leads inexorably to a proposal for peace: increase the percentage of universally oriented persons by avoiding the viewing of romanticized action photographs of war and substituting photographs from The Family of Man (Steichen, 1955) which depict the common life experiences of all humankind from the womb to the tomb, including childhood play, friendship, love, marriage, work, sorrow, happiness, illness, aging, and death.

Indeed, this strategy may have been used during the Vietnam War, when a single photograph raised the level of awareness among Americans with regard to the realities of war and also induced universal orientation; it is a photograph of a Vietnamese girl, about nine years of age, whose clothes have been burned off by a napalm bomb. She is shown fleeing up a dirt road and crying out in fear and pain. Buddha's question might well have been the nonverbal caption of this photograph, which was permanently etched in the mind of anyone who was exposed to it if only for a fleeting second. A similar approach may have been employed by Iraq in the recent United Nations–Iraq conflict concerning armed inspection procedures. At a critical juncture, Iraq held a ceremony in memory of the many women and children who were killed when their shelter was bombed, having been mistaken for an ammunition storage area.

Education for Peace

The experiment described here, along with the image of the Vietnamese child of war and that of the Iraqi women and children who were bombed by mistake, suggests the potential for a pictorial induction of a peace offensive. More specifically, it is proposed that persons who examine a series of photographs designed to portray the commonality of human experience will manifest greater universal orientation and concurrently will manifest alternatives to conflict resolution other than the use of aggression or violence.

A pilot study of this proposition was conducted in which forty-five college students studied forty slides of photographs from Steichen's classic exhibition and book, *The Family of Man,* and a control group of forty college students studied forty slides depicting the meaning of war which had been used in the previous experiment. Following the slide display, both groups completed the Universal Orientation Scale. The results showed that persons who viewed the *Family of Man* photographs as opposed to the war photographs were more universally oriented.

Peace induction or nonhostile induction through photographic depiction of the universal plight of humankind can be effective. But the induction probably will not endure without repeated antiwar inoculations and peace-promoting actions on a daily schedule, an action peace prayer, if you will. This educational approach is probably most effective if the person is his or her own omnipresent teacher and peace is the daily teaching objective, using the World Wide Web as a "blackboard."

Again, the photographs from *The Family of Man* show the fundamental common experiences of life among all the people of the Earth. These include the Earth we share, birth, the family, children playing, friendship, love, reproduction, work, music, dancing, education, food gathering and preparation, conflict, despair, poverty, joy, abundance, illness, death, spiritualism, and continuity. Against this background, the distracting small differences among Earth's people fade and there remains the beautiful and simple reality of life shared by humankind.

Epilogue

The central concepts employed throughout this chapter concern universal orientation, the peace personality, nonprejudice, and oneness. There is an apparent underlying idealistic perspective inherent in these ideas. It is proposed, however, that idealism is the philosophical foundation for life as a social system in which each living member's fate affects, in interaction, every other member's fate. It is this premise that led Gandhi to the proposition that violence to anyone is violence to oneself, although the same conclusion may be reached if the Hindu assumption is accepted that God is in everyone.

These idealistic social assumptions oppose the human proclivity for personal satisfaction as the primary consideration, for exclusive rather than inclusive categories of persons, for evaluations between the self and others, and for the tendency to establish a personal identity by orienting oneself toward self-other differences. Idealism is at the basis of all social controls, which are the sine qua non of group life, even if idealism is somewhat self-deceptive in that it does not adequately acknowledge human egocentrism. Perhaps, however, this idealism is most effective when the self-deception is acknowledged; it is then under our control, because we understand the underlying purpose of self-deception in this cause, to moralize for commonality in order to maximize the common good.

REFERENCES

Aron, A., Aron, E. N., Tudor, M., & Nelson, G. (1991). Close relationships as including other in the self. *Journal of Personality and Social Psychology, 60*, 241–253.

Bakan, D. (1966). *The duality of human existence.* Boston: Beacon Press.

Barthes, R. (1957). *Mythologies.* Paris: Le Sevil.

Bradley, M. M., & Lang, P. J. (1994). Measuring emotion: The self-assessment manikin and the semantic differential. *Journal of Behavior Therapy and Experimental Psychiatry, 25*, 49–59.

Davis, M. H. (1983). Measuring individual differences in empathy: Evidence for a multidimensional approach. *Journal of Personality and Social Psychology, 44*, 113–126.

Deutsch, M. (1990). Psychological roots of moral exclusion. *Journal of Social Issues, 46*, 21–25.

Dinklage, R., & Ziller, R. C. (1989). Images of war and peace among German and American children. *Journal of Conflict Resolution, 33*, 309–317.

Hoffman, M. L. (1976). Empathy, role-taking, guilt, and development of altruistic motives. In T. Likona (Ed.), *Moral development and behavior* (pp. 124–143). Austin, TX: Holt, Rinehart and Winston.

Jersey, B. (1987). *Faces of the enemy.* Berkeley, CA: Catticus Corporation.

Markus, H., & Kitayama, S. (1991). Culture and the self: Implications for cognition, emotion, and motivation. *Psychological Review, 98*, 224–253.

Naess, A. (1958). A systemization of Gandhian ethics of conflict resolution. *Journal of Conflict Resolution, 2*, 140–155.

Optow, S. (1990). Moral exclusion and injustice: An introduction. *Journal of Social Issues, 46,* 1–20.

Phillips, S., & Ziller, R. C. (1997). Toward theory and measure of non-prejudice. *Journal of Personality and Social Psychology, 72,* 50–71.

Smith, H. (1958). *Religions of man.* New York: HarperCollins.

Steichen, E. (1955). *The family of man.* New York: Museum of Modern Art.

Vera, H., & Nathans, S. (1983). On the real and make-believe. *Social Forces, 35,* 37–47.

Ziller, R. C. (1987). *The Universal Orientation Scales.* (Available from Department of Psychology, University of Florida, P.O. Box 112250, Gainesville, FL 32611.)

4

TOWARD A POSITIVE
CONCEPTION OF PEACE

Orlando Lourenço, University of Lisbon

IN THE SEVENTEENTH CENTURY, the philosopher Spinoza claimed that peace is not the mere absence of war, but a virtue that comes from the vigor of one's soul and mind. After three centuries, however, the heroes of peace, who many times are assassinated by their own followers (for example, Mohandas Gandhi and Yitzhak Rabin), "look pale beside the heroes of war" (Gillet, 1994, p. 21).

Although peace remains one of the greatest aspirations of humankind, what we see around us is a culture or even an institution of conflict and war (see Oppenheimer, 1996). As recently pointed out by Scott Sleek (1996, p. 1), the Cold War ended only to usher in a period of smaller, but far bloodier, fighting in the Balkans, Africa, and parts of the old Soviet Union. Ethnic and religious hatreds escalated out of control, with Hutus and Tutsis slaughtering each other in Rwanda; Croats, Muslims, and Serbs in murderous battle in Bosnia; and religious and ideological radicals launching ferocious attacks in Israel, Palestine, Liberia, and other countries. In other words, however much we talk about peace, it is war that is apparent, pervasive, and omnipresent (I will return later to this point).

I want to thank all the children and all my students who made the two empirical studies reported in this chapter possible. I also thank Ann Sanson, Armando Machado, Louis Oppenheimer, and anonymous reviewers for their valuable comments and suggestions on earlier versions of this chapter.

Aware that this culture of conflict and war constitutes an unjust, dangerous, and pernicious context for children's global development and for people's well-being and health (see Cairns, 1987; Punamäki, 1996), psychologists are now beginning to be actively involved in the construction of a culture of peace (see Galtung, 1985; Oppenheimer, 1996).

The development of a peace culture is not easy. First, war and conflict have a long history and have become part of our culture (see Hinde, 1991). As a result, any attempt to promote a culture of peace is likely to be countered by the existing war-oriented social institutions and to fail even before it has been initiated. Second, although several studies have been carried out by political psychologists and social psychologists to investigate the psychological causes of war, conflict, and violence (Cairns, 1996; Pruitt & Rubin, 1986), psychological research on conflict and war tends to be focused on the negative effects of political violence on children. But, as noted by Cairns (1994, p. 674), "We cannot simply continue to reveal the terrible things political violence is doing to children [and] we must do something to try to understand the underlying causes of political conflict," such as poverty and social exclusion (see also Brock-Utne, 1985). The importance of pointing to such causes in the transformation of a culture of war into a culture of peace becomes clear as soon as we realize that no remedy is effective when one looks at the symptoms of a disease while ignoring the underlying causes.

Third, although embedding children's understanding of peace within a solid theoretical perspective has been done by some early investigators (e.g., Piaget, 1934/1989) and has recently been done by others (e.g., Hakvoort & Oppenheimer, 1993), psychological studies on children's ideas about peace and war tend to be descriptive and often lack a clear theoretical framework. As a result, it is likely that, for instance, those who are concerned with peace education in schools resort to strategies that are theoretically ungrounded and that may lead to what was not intended at the outset (but see Deutsch, 1993, for a contrary example). Therefore, as noted by Cairns (1994, p. 674), "We need work of a more theoretical nature."

Fourth, mounting evidence shows that when children think of peace they are more likely to conceive of it as a reactive manifestation against war (that is, negative peace) rather than as a proactive and positive process involving interpersonal understanding, integration of different voices, and cooperation among people and nations (that is, positive peace; see Ålvik, 1968; Hakvoort & Oppenheimer, 1993; Lourenço, 1996). Given that the idea of positive peace is quintessential to peace, the development of a culture of peace has to face and change children's, and for that matter many adults', pervasive tendency to think of peace in terms of negation of war rather than in terms of a positive process irreducible to the absence of conflict and violence.

Finally, everyday experience reveals that we fall easily into the inconsistency fallacy. On the one hand, we are always preaching peace and arguing against conflict, violence, and war. On the other hand, we act and react aggressively and egocentrically. This discrepancy between reasoning and acting peacefully shows that the development of a peace culture will partly remain as an idea and a dream. But, in a certain way, dreams also contribute to changing things and society.

In this chapter I argue for a positive conception of peace. The chapter is divided into four sections. First, I argue that there is much to be gained if peace education and development are viewed in terms of a basic moral injunction incorporating both Kohlberg's ethic of justice (to respect others' rights; Kohlberg, 1984) and Gilligan's ethic of care (to be sensitive to others in need; Gilligan, 1982). Second, I present some facts and realities that show how we regard war and conflict as a first-order, affirmative, and active phenomenon and reduce peace to a second-order, negative, and reactive process. Third, I illustrate the asymmetry in our conceptions of peace and war by means of two empirical studies on Portuguese children's ideas of peace, war, and strategies to attain peace. Finally, I discuss some of the developmental-educational implications of the peace education conception stressed in this chapter.

Peace Education as a Basic Moral Injunction

Does it make any sense to think of an unjust and yet peaceful world? Responses to this question can certainly vary, but throughout several parts of this chapter I argue that the idea of a peaceful and yet unjust world makes little if any sense. For that reason, this section revolves around the idea of peace education as a basic moral injunction; that is, an education that assumes that the many aspects of peace, such as cooperation, coexistence, interpersonal understanding, mutual respect, and conflict resolution (see Covell, Rose-Krasnor, & Fletcher, 1994; Hakvoort & Oppenheimer, 1993), are subsumed to a great extent under what moral development researchers call the two basic moral injunctions: "not to treat others unfairly and not to turn away from someone in need" (Gilligan & Wiggins, 1987, p. 281; see also Kohlberg, Boyd, & Levine, 1990).

In this vein, to claim a moral-developmental basis for peace education is to acknowledge that peace education (and research) can also be framed in other theoretical terms, such as interpersonal understanding (Hakvoort, 1996) or cooperative learning (Deutsch, 1993). It also acknowledges that a peaceful world is not in reach as soon as peace education is viewed as a basic moral injunction. In fact, although the consistency between moral cognition and moral action increases with moral development (McNamee, 1978), people often do not do what they think should be done (see Blasi, 1980). Everyone knows of good ideas (and dreams) that were subverted as soon as they began to be implemented, but this is not a reason to give them up. Moreover, to think of a peaceful and yet unjust world would appear to be more discrepant and ungrounded than to embrace ideals or moral injunctions whose practicality is problematic.

As I have no empirical data to present in this section, my position should be seen as speculative. My conviction, however, is that there is much to be gained when the development of peace education is regarded as a basic moral injunction, one that incorporates Kohlberg's ethic of justice and Gilligan's ethic of care. Seen from such an angle, peace education (and research) gains a clear *theoretical* basis because it can be related to moral development in general and to justice and caring development in particular. In addition to assigning a clear telos to peace education, relating peace education to sociomoral development may help us to analyze, for example, how a comprehensive or advanced understanding of peace and war is developmentally associated with high levels of respect for others' rights and sensitivity to others' needs. Furthermore, looking for a conceptual focus to frame peace education (and research) also agrees with the invitation from the Committee for the Psychological Study of Peace, addressed to psychologists from diverse nations and cultures, to "develop the theoretical foundations of the culture of peace" (Wessells, 1994, p. 2).

When peace education is framed in terms of justice and caring, it acquires a *moral* emphasis and tone. The development of peace education begins to be seen not only as a desired and good achievement but as a desirable and right thing to do. Even if Kohlberg's and Gilligan's theories can be criticized (see Modgil & Modgil, 1985), their implications for peace education remain key because, as alluded to earlier, the idea of a peaceful though immoral world seems incoherent and aberrant. In addition, when the development of peace education is considered to be a moral injunction linked to Kohlberg's ethic of rights and Gilligan's ethic of responsibility, one becomes aware that peace is a *multidimensional* concept and reality because it appeals to several elements such as coexistence, cooperation, mutual respect, justice, and caring. In the process, peace psychologists are reminded that they have to work with other professionals, such as philosophers, sociologists, anthropologists, historians, and politicians. For example, peace psychologists are likely to exchange ideas with philosophers who are concerned with definitions of rightness and wrongness or with sociologists who are interested in groups' aspirations, needs, and values.

Relating peace education to Kohlberg's theory of moral development and Gilligan's claims for caring development enables us to pursue, at least conceptually, recent theoretical and empirical efforts to embed children's conceptions about peace and war in a *developmental* perspective, namely Selman's interpersonal understanding approach (1980; see Hakvoort & Oppenheimer, 1993). Given that Kohlberg claimed that interpersonal understanding is a necessary though not sufficient condition for moral development, the idea of relating peace education to moral concepts is relatively close to the idea of associating peace education with concepts of interpersonal understanding. Furthermore, information about children's and adolescents' understanding of war, conflict, and peace is crucial to the design of peace education programs and the definition of universal and contextual developmental prerequisites for peace building (see Covell et al., 1994; Oppenheimer, 1996).

Viewing the development of peace education as a basic moral injunction also has *methodological* or procedural advantages. Some well-known procedures used to promote moral development, such as discussion of hypothetical or real-life moral dilemmas, cooperative learning, nonviolent conflict resolution, and the construction of just communities or moral atmospheres (see, for instance, Deutsch, 1993; Power, Kohlberg, & Higgins, 1989), may be and are already being used in conflict resolution and peace education (see Wahlström, 1988). Of course, one may think that there is a considerable difference between reasoning and acting morally and that such a discrepancy runs against a Kohlbergian perspective of peace education. Without denying such vulnerability, it should be noted that in addition to valuing subjects' moral cognition, Kohlberg's model also emphasized the importance of living in just communities. Furthermore, his idea that as moral development proceeds there is a greater consistency between action and cognition has also received empirical support (Kohlberg & Candee, 1984).

Thinking of peace or peace education and development as a basic moral injunction helps us not to lose sight of the *underlying causes* of peace, violence, and war. For instance, we are more likely to see poverty, social exclusion, and injustice as direct causes of violence and conflict, and justice and caring as means to promote and foster peace development (Brock-Utne, 1985). In fact, if justice is an attitude that seeks to integrate the concern for both respect and benevolence (Kohlberg et al., 1990) and the first virtue of social systems (Rawls, 1971), then a just world seems to be a necessary condition for a peaceful world. In addition, we are likely to reject as simplistic the idea that peace and war lie in people's hearts (as was said in a statement by the United Nations Educational, Scientific, and Cultural Organization) and also less likely to fall into the psychologist fallacy, the trap of believing that psychology has all the answers for eradicating conflict and violence from the Earth and promoting peace around the world.

Finally, conceiving of peace and peace education and development in terms of a basic moral injunction is a means of moving away from a negative to a positive conception of peace, from peace as the mere negation of war—a second-order phenomenon and a "not-being"—to peace as an affirmative, complex, and dynamic process, a first-order reality and a "true being." Once peace education is linked to both caring and justice, it is seen not as the absence of war and war-related activities and consequences but as a complex process involving interpersonal understanding (see Chapter Two of this volume), coordination of perspectives (Piaget, 1934/1989), cooperative learning and nonviolent conflict resolution (Deutsch, 1993), and respect for the rights of other people, cultures, groups, and nations (Kohlberg, 1984).

Peace and War as Asymmetrical Realities

Although the idea of peace as a proactive, positive phenomenon involving interpersonal understanding, social harmony, cooperation, and nonviolent conflict resolution is desirable from an ideal viewpoint, it is the idea of peace as the negation of war and a reactive reality that pervades culture, minds, and even most of the peace- and war-oriented research. The focus on violence, war, and war-related matters is pervasive when compared with the emphasis given to harmony, tolerance, and peace-related issues. My conviction is that a culture of positive peace entails a reversal of this state of affairs.

In what follows I present various facts, features, and findings that show that whereas war and conflict are considered to be first-order, salient, and important phenomena, peace and harmony are generally viewed as second-order and insignificant matters (see Lourenço, 1996). For example, *Collier's Encyclopedia* (1990, Vol. 18) devotes more than thirty pages to war and war-related matters and ignores the concept of peace. Similarly, what we see daily in the media, particularly on television, are reports on violence, conflict, and war—the negative. Reports on peace, harmony, and prosociality—the positive—are rare. News about peace is generally news of cease-fires and peacekeeping troops, thus news that refers to peace but is worded in terms of war or war-related activities.

A culture of war to the detriment of peace is also visible in the asymmetrical way we treat the heroes of peace and the heroes of war. Society generally does not view peacemakers with the same awe and reverence that it affords warriors. Furthermore, there exists a long list of peaceful leaders killed by followers who felt that the leaders had become peaceful and conciliatory toward "enemies" and opponents. The recent assassination of Israeli prime minister Yitzhak Rabin is an illustrative case.

This prevalence of the idea of violence, conflict, and the negative to the detriment of the idea of harmony, shared perspectives, and the positive is also found in psychological research. For instance, what is more apparent in moral development studies is the violation paradigm, not the adherence one. That is, when investigators do research on moral development and behavior, they prefer to use situations and dilemmas that involve transgressions instead of adherences (see Turiel, 1983). Kant (1930) himself conceived of negative or moral duties as perfect, and of positive or prosocial duties only as imperfect.

Moral researchers, however, are not alone in attributing more weight to the negative and transgressions than to the positive and adherences. In a series of studies on children's orientation to what Fuller (1969) called the morality of duty (attributing more blame for misdeeds than credit for good behavior) and the morality of aspiration (giving more credit for good action than blame for misbehavior), I found that children at five, seven, and nine years of age generally commit the "fundamental-education error" (Lourenço, 1994): when asked to choose between sanctioning a positive and a negative act related to moral, prosocial, and academic domains, children state that people do not have to be praised for doing what they should do, but they should always be blamed or even punished for misbehavior. Peace-war researchers also tend to exhibit this negative bias: they generally give more attention to war issues than to peace matters. For instance, studies on the effects of war, conflict, and violence are overabundant compared with studies on the effects of living in peace and harmony (see Hobfoll et al., 1991). It seems that peace researchers assume that peace consequences are negligible outcomes and, hence, that their attention should be directed to the outcomes of conflict and war.

For all these reasons, it is not surprising that children's minds are often filled more with ideas of war and violence than with ideas of peace and harmony, and more with ideas of negative peace than with ideas of positive peace. For example, in a study involving 101 children and adolescents between the ages of eight and sixteen, Hakvoort and Oppenheimer (1993) found that children's understanding of war comes before their knowledge of peace, and that peace, defined by the absence of quarrels and war or war-related matters (negative peace), precedes developmentally the idea of peace as a positive process, entailing talk, dialogue, reason, prosocial intervention, negotiation, compromise, and cooperation. This finding constitutes additional evidence for my claim that war tends to be regarded as a first-order phenomenon, whereas peace is simply a second-order reality. In the next section, I further illustrate the asymmetry of conceptions of peace and war by means of two studies on Portuguese children's ideas about peace, war, and strategies to attain peace.

Children's Ideas of Peace and War: A Portuguese Example

In my first study (Lourenço, 1996), I had two main goals: first, to collect some data on Portuguese children's understanding of peace, war, and strategies to attain peace such that cross-cultural comparisons with a Dutch-Swedish ongoing research program could be made (see Hägglund, Hakvoort, & Oppenheimer, 1996), and second, to examine whether some of children's ideas of peace (for example, as the absence of war or as a desirable situation) would have conceptual counterparts in their ideas about war (for example, as the negation of peace or as an undesirable situation).

Sixty children from three age groups participated in the study: twenty five- to six-year-olds; twenty eight- to nine-year-olds; and twenty ten- to twelve-year-olds. All children were white and came predominantly from middle-class families. We used a semistructured interview partly based on previous studies on children's understanding of peace and war (Hakvoort & Oppenheimer, 1993; Rosell, 1968). The interview included the nine following standard questions (follow-up questions were used whenever the children's answers were unclear):

1. Can you explain to me what war is to you? (to define war)

2. Can you tell me why people make war? (causes of war)

3. Can you tell me who makes war? (knowledge about war)

4. Can you tell me what happens in a country at war? (consequences of war)

5. If you want to explain what peace is to one of your friends, what would you say? (to define peace)

6. Do you think that peace is better than war? Why? (to conceive of peace as the absence of war or as a positively defined process)

7. How could people live in peace with one another? (strategies to achieve peace)

8. If you were the "boss" in a country at war, what would you do to make peace? (strategies to attain peace, national level)

9. Now you are the "boss" of the world. What would you do to make peace? (strategies to attain peace, international level)

The answers were classified on the basis of previous studies on children's conceptions about peace, war, and strategies to attain peace (e.g., Hakvoort & Oppenheimer, 1993) and on children's development of interpersonal understanding and negotiation strategies (Selman, 1980). The answers were also analyzed with categories derived empirically from the present study. Agreement between two independent coders ranged from 82 to 95 percent. All the results that will be indicated from now on are statistically significant.

Children's conceptions about peace and war revealed the following patterns. First, by the age of five to six, the children have acquired fairly well defined ideas about peace and war. In fact, all children gave "reasonable" definitions of war (for example, "a physical event in which there are soldiers, weapons, and killing"), and the majority of them were able to present "acceptable" definitions of peace (for example, "an absence of war, a state of stillness, or a desirable situation"). Second, with increasing age, Portuguese children's definitions of peace and war became more complex and composite ("War is when there is no peace, when there are enemies, and when people fight for political reasons") and less linked to concrete and material characteristics, such as shooting, killing, fighting, destroying, and violence. Third, the results showed that children at all ages tended to regard war as a first-order phenomenon, an event that exists in itself ("War is shooting, weapons, and fighting"), whereas peace was viewed mainly as a second-order reality, an event that is more the negation of war or conflict than an active state of affairs ("Peace is when there is no war").

Several pieces of evidence substantiate the just-mentioned asymmetry. First, the percentage of responses appealing to the idea of peace as a mere state of stillness or the absence of war (34.8, 46.2, and 41.1 percent for younger, intermediate, and older children, respectively) had no correspondence in children's idea of war as the negation or absence of peace (0, 0, and 7.1 percent). Second, the concept of war as an undesirable event ("War is an awful thing because it kills people") among the three age groups (38.1, 32, and 35.7 percent) appeared more often than the corresponding concept of peace as a desirable or good situation (7.8, 11.5, and

5.9 percent). Third, in this study there were six five- to six-year-olds who were incapable of defining peace, whereas all the children were able to define war.

The idea of peace as a second-order phenomenon is well documented in the children's reasons for their preference for peace over war. As Table 4.1 shows, children at all ages primarily based their preference for peace over war on negative peace-oriented reasons ("Peace is better than war because there is no war and people aren't killed"), not on positive peace-oriented reasons ("Peace is better than war because we are friends"). In other words, children mainly mentioned that they preferred peace to war because peace avoids the consequences of war (negative peace), not because it brings about positive outcomes and results (positive peace).

Children's strategies to achieve peace were classified in one of the three following categories: *prescriptive strategies,* if children appealed to positive action or activity ("To live in peace, people should talk to and play with one another"); *proscriptive strategies,* if they referred to strategies that involved more omission and passivity than action or activity ("To live in peace, people should not fight with one another"); and *mixed strategies,* if they mentioned both prescriptive or positive peace-oriented strategies and proscriptive or negative peace-oriented strategies. Children at all ages were more likely to mention negative peace-oriented strategies than either positive peace-oriented or mixed-orientation strategies.

Consistent with previous studies on children's and adolescents' understanding of peace and war (e.g., Ålvik, 1968; Covell et al., 1994; Hakvoort & Oppenheimer, 1993), the preceding findings show that Portuguese children are more likely to think of peace as a second-order phenomenon reducible to the absence of war than as a first-order process entailing positive dimensions such as cooperation, negotiation, and a desire for justice. Given that in this study children were asked to define war before defining

Table 4.1. Frequency of Children's Reasons for
Preferring Peace to War, by Age Group.

Type of Reason	5–6 Years	8–9 Years	10–12 Years
Negative peace-oriented	9 (45)	9 (45)	12 (60)
Positive peace-oriented	5 (25)	5 (25)	4 (20)
Mixed-orientation	1 (5)	5 (25)	3 (15)
Not classifiable	5 (25)	1 (5)	1 (5)

Note: N = 20 *for each age group. Numbers in parentheses are percentages.*

peace, one might think that the asymmetry in their war-peace conceptions was primarily a methodological artifact. My second study was carried out in a way that controlled for this possibility.

The second study used a between-subjects design. Ninety-six children at two age levels were interviewed: forty-eight seven- to eight-year-olds and forty-eight eleven- to twelve-year-olds. In each age group, which had equal numbers of boys and girls, half the children were confronted with peace-oriented questions and the other half with war-oriented questions. I used a semistructured interview that focused on the following standard questions: (1) definitions of peace and war, (2) consequences of peace and war, (3) people responsible for peace and war, (4) reasons for the existence of peace and war, (5) symbols of peace and war, (6) strategies to maintain peace between nations living in peace or to stop war in nations at war, and (7) reasons to prefer peace to war. This last question was identical in both groups. Follow-up questions were used when children's answers were unclear. For questions 1, 2, and 3, the children's answers were classified into more than one category. For the remaining questions, the categories were exclusive. Agreement between two coders ranged from 85 to 95 percent.

As in the first study, the responses appealing to the idea of peace as the negation of war and to the idea of war as an affirmative process were frequent in younger children (58.3 percent and 87.5 percent to define peace and war, respectively) and older children (83.3 percent and 50 percent). Older children were more likely than younger ones to define peace as the negation of war, although this result was not statistically significant. In contrast, younger children were more likely than older ones to define war in terms of physical and concrete characteristics. In addition, the idea of war as the negation or absence of peace never appeared among the seven- to eight-year-olds' responses and appeared only three times among the eleven- to twelve-year-olds' responses (see Table 4.2). Given that the idea of war as a bad thing to do was more frequent than the corresponding idea of peace as a good thing to do in both younger and older children, it seems that these Portuguese children are more sensitive to war than to peace.

There is not enough space to present in detail all of the results of this second study. In general terms, however, they showed that children's ideas of war as a first-order phenomenon and peace as a second-order phenomenon that our first study found were not due to the effect of the order of the questions. For instance, whereas many children in both age groups mentioned the absence of war as one of the consequences of living in peace, no child indicated the absence of peace as a consequence of the existence of war. Children also viewed bad people as responsible for war more often than they viewed good people as responsible for peace.

Table 4.2. Children's Definitions of Peace and War, by Age Group.

To Define Peace	7–8 Years	11–12 Years
Good thing to do	3 (9.68)	3 (6.98)
Negation of war	14 (45.16)	20 (46.52)
Being friends	13 (41.94)	13 (30.23)
Positive emotional state	0	5 (11.62)
Human attitudes	1 (3.22)	2 (4.65)

To Define War	7–8 Years	11–12 Years
Bad thing to do	7 (24.13)	13 (32.5)
War-oriented matters	21 (72.42)	12 (30)
Disagreement	1 (3.45)	11 (27.5)
Restoration of justice	0	1 (2.5)
Absence of peace	0	3 (7.5)

Note: N = 24 *for each age group; because categories were not exclusive, their total number could be greater than 24. Numbers in parentheses are percentages.*

The prevalence of the idea of war as a first-order reality and of peace as a second-order phenomenon is well documented in the children's reasons for the existence of both peace and war (see Table 4.3). Whereas most children mentioned egocentric or war-oriented reasons for the existence of war ("to get power," "to take advantage," "retaliating or doing harm"), only one out of the forty-eight older children gave a social or peace-oriented reason ("People make war because they want to live in peace and improve others' well-being"). An analysis of the data in Table 4.3 shows that even when children thought of reasons for people's desire to live in peace, absence-of-war motives or negative peace reasons were more frequent than positive peace reasons.

The prevalence of the idea of negative peace was also found in the strategies mentioned by children to either maintain peace or stop war. With respect to the former, in both younger and older children negatively oriented strategies, such as aggressive intervention and unilateral stopping of war, were more likely than positively oriented strategies, such as prosocial intervention, negotiation, talk, and reason. With respect to strategies to stop war, both younger and older children were also more likely to indicate negative or absence-of-war strategies than positive or beyond-absence-of-war strategies, such as removing the causes of war, negotiation, and compromise. As to the children's reasons for preferring peace to war,

Table 4.3. Frequency of Children's Reasons for the
Existence of Peace and War, by Age Group.

Peace	7–8 Years	11–12 Years
Negative peace reasons	16 (66.6)	10 (41.6)
Positive peace reasons	3 (12.5)	4 (16.8)
Mixed reasons	4 (16.7)	10 (41.6)
Not classifiable	1 (4.2)	0
War	7–8 Years	11–12 Years
War-oriented reasons	21 (87.5)	17 (70.8)
Peace-oriented reasons	0	1 (4.2)
Mixed reasons	1 (4.2)	3 (12.5)
Not classifiable	2 (8.3)	3 (12.5)

Note: N = 24 for each age group. Numbers in parentheses are percentages.

negative peace-oriented reasons were also more frequent than either positive peace-oriented reasons or mixed-orientation reasons.

In summary, the results of this second study show again that Portuguese children's ideas of war are more prevalent than their ideas of peace and that they think of peace more in terms of a negative and second-order phenomenon than in terms of a positive and first-order reality. Studies mentioned earlier (e.g., Covell et al., 1994; Hakvoort & Oppenheimer, 1993) indicate that Portuguese children are not alone regarding this asymmetry in the understanding of peace and war.

Developmental and Educational Implications of Peace Education as a Basic Moral Injunction

I want to return now to the idea of peace education as a basic moral injunction and ask what follows, developmentally and educationally, from such a conception of peace and peace education. I only point to some implications. In addition, educational and developmental implications appear intertwined at times.

A first educational implication is that peace education appears not only as worthwhile but also as imperative and mandatory. That is, when it is conceptualized in terms of a basic moral injunction, peace education appears not only as a responsibility of schools and peace organizations but also as a moral responsibility of society in general and of each of its members in particular (see also Boutros-Ghali, 1992). A second implication is that peace education has two clear and overarching developmental goals: to develop children's respect for others' rights and to develop their empathy toward others in need. In addition, everybody accepts the idea that in terms of educational goals, the more we know exactly where we want to arrive, the more likely we are to be effective educators.

A third educational implication is that such a conception of peace education may help us to avoid what Kohlberg (1984) would have called the "bag of virtues" approach to the development of peace education. That is, by valuing certain behaviors and attitudes without paying due attention to their underlying sociomoral reasons, peace education may end up being less peace-oriented than it appears at first. For instance, cooperation with others for the purpose of waging war is a form of cooperation that is not cooperation at all, because it is neither reversible (it cannot be maintained if places are traded) nor universalizable (it cannot be applied to all circumstances; see also Mueller, 1991). It seems, then, that peace education framed in terms of caring and moral respect for others' needs and rights encompasses the several faces of peace (coexistence, cooperation, mutual respect, conflict resolution, and so on), with the additional advantage of looking at them structurally and developmentally, that is, without forgetting that such behaviors and attitudes can express distinct and qualitatively different forms of justice and caring.

When peace education is framed in terms of sociomoral-developmental goals, a constructivist approach to peace education is likely to appear and to be stressed (see DeVries & Zan, 1994). That is, children's and adolescents' peace reasoning and attitudes are viewed not so much as a result of social transmission but as a result of their actions, operations, and interactions with the physical and social environment. Moreover, if Piaget (1972, p. 24) is correct when he states that "to understand is to invent, or to reconstruct by reinventing," then there are implications in terms of the educational methods used in the development of peace education. For instance, it would follow that discussions of peace dilemmas and the establishment of a moral atmosphere in the classroom should be emphasized, and the teaching of apparently peaceful behaviors and attitudes in a relatively authoritarian context should be de-emphasized (see also Deutsch, 1993).

When a developmental, sociomoral conception of peace education is adopted, we are also less likely to fall into some fallacies that can pave the road leading to a culture of peace (see also Bjerstedt, 1993). Here, I emphasize only four, the inconsistency fallacy, the psychologist fallacy, the educationist fallacy, and the peace activist fallacy. We commit the inconsistency fallacy whenever we speak in favor of and discourse upon peace and tolerance, while at the same time we act and behave egocentrically. We fall into the psychologist fallacy when we believe that psychology in general, or peace-oriented research in particular, will find complete answers for understanding the existence of war, eradicating conflict from the Earth, and promoting peace across cultures and minds. We fall prey to the educationist fallacy when we think that peace education programs in schools constitute a sufficient condition to replace a culture of war with a culture of peace. Finally, we commit the peace activist fallacy when in our otherwise sincere and permanent appeals to peace and peace slogans we forget the underlying causes and conditions that lead directly to violence, conflict, and war (see Galtung, 1985).

A final implication follows from such a sociomoral conception of peace education. When the main purpose of peace education is to develop children's competence in respecting others' rights and being sensitive to others' needs and concerns, the idea of positive, not negative, peace appears more worthwhile, both educationally and developmentally.

As alluded to earlier, such a conception of peace education may also have its vulnerabilities: running the risk of overvaluing reasoning to the detriment of behavior (Bandura, 1991) and not giving due attention to some aspects of the peace concept (see Deutsch, 1993; Hakvoort & Oppenheimer, 1993). In my opinion, however, framing peace education and development in terms of a moral injunction incorporating Kohlberg's ethic of justice and Gilligan's ethic of caring should not be seen as completely at variance with other conceptions and approaches, some of which are addressed in this volume (see Chapters Two and Fourteen). More than this, such a conception of peace education and development would help to foster not only peace research and education but also a culture of positive peace. As Joseph Rotblat, the 1995 Nobel peace laureate, noted in a recent visit to Portugal, it is absolutely mandatory that we generate a new statement and commitment that can replace the old Roman perspective on peace and war. Instead of being concerned with attaining peace through continuing preparation for war, we (as individuals, groups, and nations) should adopt a new formula and attitude: to be prepared for peace if we want to live in a peaceful world.

Final Words

Throughout this chapter, I have argued that the idea of positive peace as a first-order and affirmative process involving integration, cooperation, and coexistence, rather than as the absence or negation of war, is of paramount importance for the construction and development of a culture of peace. In the first section, I defended the proposition that there is much to be gained if peace education is framed in terms of a moral injunction incorporating both the Kohlbergian ethic of justice (to treat others fairly) and the Gilliganian ethic of care (to be sensitive to others in need). In the second section, I referred to diverse social features of our times that show how our cultures and minds are more responsive to conflict, war, and the negative than to peace, social harmony, and the positive. The two studies reported on in the third section also reveal that Portuguese children's understanding of peace, war, and strategies to stop war and attain peace are guided by ideas of negative peace more than positive peace. Finally, I discussed some educational and developmental implications of the conception of peace referred to previously. One of them is that peace should be contemplated directly. Accordingly, I have suggested that when peace education is framed in terms of a moral injunction appealing to respect for others' rights and sensitivity to their needs, there is more room for positive than negative peace.

REFERENCES

Ålvik, T. (1968). The development of views on conflict, war and peace among school children. *Journal of Peace Research, 5,* 171–195.

Bandura, A. (1991). Social cognitive theory of moral thought and action. In W. Kurtines & J. Gewirtz (Eds.), *Handbook of moral development. Vol. 1: Theory.* Hillsdale, NJ: Erlbaum.

Bjerstedt, Å. (Ed.). (1993). *Peace education: Global perspectives.* Stockholm: Almqvist and Wiksell International.

Blasi, A. (1980). Bridging moral cognition and moral action: A critical review of the literature. *Psychological Bulletin, 88,* 1–45.

Boutros-Ghali, B. (1992). *An agenda for peace: Preventive diplomacy, peacemaking and peacekeeping.* New York: United Nations.

Brock-Utne, B. (1985). *Educating for peace.* Oxford, England: Pergamon Press.

Cairns, E. (1987). *Caught in crossfire: Children and the Northern Ireland conflict.* Belfast, Northern Ireland: Appletree.

Cairns, E. (1994). Children and political violence: An overview. *International Journal of Behavioral Development, 17,* 669–674.

Cairns, E. (1996). *Children and political violence.* Oxford, England: Blackwell.

Collier's Encyclopedia. (1990). New York: Macmillan.

Covell, K., Rose-Krasnor, L., & Fletcher, K. (1994). Age differences in understanding peace, war, and conflict resolution. *International Journal of Behavioral Development, 17,* 717–737.

Deutsch, M. (1993). Educating for a peaceful world. *American Psychologist, 48,* 510–517.

DeVries, R., & Zan, B. (1994). *Moral classrooms, moral children: Creating a constructivist atmosphere in early education.* New York: Teachers College Press.

Fuller, L. (1969). *The morality of law* (2nd ed.). New Haven, CT: Yale University Press.

Galtung, J. (1985). Twenty-five years of peace research: Ten challenges and some responses. *Journal of Peace Research, 6,* 167–191.

Gillet, N. (1994). An agenda for peace and the role of peace education. *Peace, Environment and Education, 5,* 3–23.

Gilligan, C. (1982). *In a different voice: Psychological theory and women's development.* Cambridge, MA: Harvard University Press.

Gilligan, C., & Wiggins, G. (1987). The two origins of morality in early childhood relationships. In S. Lamb and J. Kagan (Eds.), *The emergence of morality in young children.* Chicago: University of Chicago Press.

Hägglund, S., Hakvoort, I., & Oppenheimer, L. (Eds.). (1996). *Research on children and peace: International perspectives.* Göteborg, Sweden: Göteborg University, Department of Education and Educational Research.

Hakvoort, I. (1996). *Conceptualization of peace and war from childhood through adolescence: A social-cognitive approach.* Amsterdam: University of Amsterdam.

Hakvoort, I., & Oppenheimer, L. (1993). Children and adolescents' conceptions of peace, war, and strategies to attain peace: A Dutch case study. *Journal of Peace Research, 30,* 65–77.

Hinde, R. (Ed.). (1991). *The institution of war.* London: Macmillan.

Hobfoll, S., et al. (Eds.). (1991). War-related stress: Addressing the stress of war and other traumatic events. *American Psychologist, 46,* 848–855.

Kant, I. (1930). *Lectures on ethics* (trans.). London: Methuen. (Original work delivered 1780–1781)

Kohlberg, L. (1984). *Essays on moral development: The psychology of moral development* (Vol. 2). San Francisco: HarperCollins.

Kohlberg, L., Boyd, D., & Levine, C. (1990). The return of stage 6: Its principle and moral point of view. In T. Wren (Ed.), *The moral domain.* Cambridge, MA: MIT Press.

Kohlberg, L., & Candee, D. (1984). The relationship of moral judgment to moral action. In W. Kurtines & J. Gewirtz (Eds.), *Morality, moral behavior and development.* New York: Wiley.

Lourenço, O. (1994). Portuguese children's judgments of moral, prosocial, and academic norms: Duty or aspiration? *International Journal of Behavioral Development, 17,* 367–381.

Lourenço, O. (1996). Research on children and peace: A Portuguese example. In S. Hägglund, I. Hakvoort, & L. Oppenheimer (Eds.), *Research on children and peace: International perspectives*. Göteborg, Sweden: Göteborg University, Department of Education and Educational Research.

McNamee, S. (1978). Moral behavior, moral development and motivation. *Journal of Moral Education, 7,* 27–32.

Modgil, S., & Modgil, C. (Eds.). (1985). *Lawrence Kohlberg: Consensus and controversy*. Bristol, PA: Falmer Press.

Mueller, J. (1991). War: Natural, but necessary. In R. Hinde (Ed.), *The institution of war*. London: Macmillan.

Oppenheimer, L. (1996). War as an institution, but what about peace? Developmental perspectives. *International Journal of Behavioral Development, 19,* 201–218.

Piaget, J. (1972). *Où va l'éducation*. Paris: Denöel/Gonthier.

Piaget, J. (1989). Is an education for peace possible? *The Genetic Epistemologist, 17,* 6–9 (Original work published 1934)

Power, C., Kohlberg, L., & Higgins, A. (1989). *Lawrence Kohlberg's approach to moral education*. New York: Columbia University Press.

Pruitt, D., & Rubin, J. (1986). *Social conflict: Escalation, stalemate and settlement*. New York: Random House.

Punamäki, R.-L. (1996). Can ideological commitment protect children's psychosocial well-being in situations of political violence? *Child Development, 67,* 55–69.

Rawls, J. (1971). *A theory of justice*. Cambridge, MA: Harvard University Press.

Rosell, L. (1968). Children's views of war and peace. *Journal of Peace Research, 5,* 268–276.

Selman, R. (1980). *The growth of interpersonal understanding: Developmental and clinical analyses*. New York: Academic Press.

Sleek, S. (1996). Psychologists build a culture of peace. *American Psychological Association Monitor, 27* (1).

Turiel, E. (1983). *The development of social knowledge: Morality and convention*. Cambridge: Cambridge University Press.

Wahlström, R. (1988). Educating preschool children for shared responsibility and peace: Notes from a peace education project in Finland. *Reprints and Miniprints* (Malmö, Sweden: School of Education), *590,* 2–8.

Wessells, M. (1994). Report of the Committee for the Psychological Study of Peace. *Newsletter of the Committee for the Psychological Study of Peace of the International Union of Psychological Science (IUPsyS), 2,* 1.

PART TWO

SOCIALIZATION AND EXPERIENCE

5

CULTURAL SOCIALIZATION AND CONCEPTIONS OF WAR AND PEACE

A CROSS-NATIONAL COMPARISON

Katherine Covell, University College of Cape Breton

ONE OF THE MORE INTRIGUING FINDINGS in the literature is that the impact of war on children is not uniformly negative. Diverse responses to war may in part be accounted for by the child's personal or family characteristics. However, in this chapter, I will argue that responses to war are mediated by cultural ideology which, through political socialization, affords different concepts of war. The everyday experiences children have are directly related to the prevailing ideologies, values, and attitudes of the culture in which they are reared. Children's interpretations of experiences and media information, their schooling, and the pressures upon them for sex-stereotyped behavior are affected by their sociocultural contexts. The focus of this chapter is the impact of cultural ideology on political socialization and concepts of war among U.S. and Canadian children, children who are not directly experiencing war. Using Bronfenbrenner's ecological model of development (1979) as the theoretical framework, cultural values will be compared, and the empirical literature on children's and adolescents' concepts of war will be assessed in terms of political socialization, schools, television, and gender role expectations. First, the link between socialization and social concept formation will be described briefly.

Socialization and Social Concepts

There is a difference between the development of an understanding of physical concepts, for example, the explosion of bombs, and the development of an understanding of social concepts, for example, the nature of political violence. Concept formation about the physical world generally depends on age or cognitive level. The learning of social concepts, in contrast, is affected by the sociocultural context in which the learning occurs. Since social information tends to be ambiguous (Rose-Krasnor, 1988), divergent views of social reality will result from culturally divergent socialization.

Concepts of war and peace contain both physical and social attributes. The physical attributes of war—for example, the fact that it involves weapons, death, and destruction—are understood increasingly with age (e.g., Ålvik, 1968; Covell, Rose-Krasnor, & Fletcher, 1994), as is children's understanding of peace (e.g., Hakvoort & Oppenheimer, 1993). However, whether war is understood as glorious, necessary, good, exciting, right, or evil is less dependent on age than on political socialization.

Political Socialization

Political socialization blends with cultural background; it describes the process by which children acquire their basic political knowledge, values, and attitudes and learn to be effective members of their (political) society. The family plays a very weak role in the political socialization of children (Dyck, 1996; Gallatin, 1980) compared with schools (e.g., Banks & Roker, 1994; Palonsky, 1987) and the mass media (e.g., Furnham & Stacey, 1991; Gallatin, 1980). Schools and the mass media are the major transmitters of the overriding cultural beliefs and values of the society in which the child is raised. The socialization of war concepts by the school and the media may be understood best within Bronfenbrenner's ecological systems theory (Bronfenbrenner, 1979; see also Chapter Nine of this volume).

Bronfenbrenner (1979) describes how interactions among social structures affect development. The ecology of development is presented as a dynamic and interactive "set of Russian dolls" (p. 3) in which the parent-child dyad is nested within a microsystem defined as social activities, roles, and relationships directly experienced by the individual. The microsystem in turn is nested within a mesosystem. The mesosystem comprises interrelations between two or more settings in which the individual actively participates, for example, home and school. Mesosystems are nested within exosystems: these consist of social settings which affect what happens in the meso- and microsystems, for example, mass media, community resources, and the educational system. The most encompassing is the macrosystem, which contains the beliefs and ideologies of the society, constituting a pervasive set of values around which the society is organized.

Social concept formation will be influenced by all these systems. Because there is reciprocal influence among the systems, concepts of war will reflect the totality of the child's socialization. The political socialization of children in their microsystems (any direct socialization environment) is affected by and interacts with what is happening in other systems or environments: the school, the community, and the society. For example, the school curriculum and the child's classroom experiences are affected by societal goals for education, community resources, and the family situation.

The least explicated socialization influence and the focus of this chapter is the child's macrosystem—the blueprint of the society in which the child is raised and a powerful, albeit indirect, influence. Macrosystem values shape the attitudes and behaviors of the members of the society as well as the interpretation of social information or social experience, including concepts of war. As Cairns and Dawes (1996) noted, war occurs and is understood in particular social contexts.

There are many indications in the literature that the social context of war affects children's responses to war. For example, the political organization of South Africa is reflected in its children's interpretations of the political violence they experience (Liddell, Kemp, & Moema, 1993). Low levels of anxiety among Israeli kibbutzim children are thought to result from community values and the confidence placed in the Israeli army (Ziv & Israel, 1973). Israeli children's attitudes toward war reflect their cultural heritage (Punamäki, 1996), as did English children's interpretations of British and Japanese war involvement (Cooper, 1965). The mechanism by which the social context or macrosystem exerts its influence is political socialization. To illustrate the effects of the macrosystem, I will now turn to an examination of the agents of political socialization and their impact on concepts of war and peace within two nations: Canada and the United States.

The Macrosystems of Canada and the United States

Whereas the North American cultures are similar in many respects, there are important differences between the political culture of Canada and the United States which create different macrosystems. Three macrosystem variables provide different political socialization: differences between the two nations in their policies toward ethnic minorities, the relative value they place on individualism, and the emphasis they place on international policy.

Canada has an official policy of multiculturalism, which means that ethnic minorities are encouraged to maintain their traditional cultures. Immigrants are expected to retain their ethnic identity, customs, and traditional values and are given state support, including financial support, to do so (Fleras & Elliott, 1992). In contrast, although there has recently been some lessening of its strong attempts at acculturation, generally the United States tries to assimilate its ethnic minorities and immigrants into a defined and dominant culture (Lipset, 1990). This contrast is usually defined in terms of the mosaic (Canada) and the melting pot (United States). Second, the United States is a more individualistic culture than Canada. Individualistic cultures tend to show more aggressive responses to conflict resolution at both individual and societal levels (Durkin, 1995). A comparison of the annual number of murders with handguns clearly illustrates the difference at the individual level: 8,915 in the United States, 8 in Canada (Dorgan, 1995). Third, the focus of international policy is on peacekeeping in Canada and on military interventionism in the United States. Since the Second World War, U.S. international policy has been characterized by military intervention in response to conflicts, whereas during the same period, Canada's role in international relations has primarily been that of peacemaker. Canada has focused on compromise through UN involvement in conflicts, backroom diplomatic efforts to reduce the militancy of U.S. foreign policy, and provision of assistance to the Third World as a means of reducing one potential cause of warfare (Dyck, 1993). The impact of these contrasting values is seen in the way children and adolescents are socialized directly and the way they interpret social information. A comparative examination of schooling and television in the two cultures will exemplify the macrosystem's effect on the concepts of war and peace.

Schools

The values of the macrosystem are realized through schooling. Although they are transmitting the values of the macrosystem, schools also have a major impact on the experiences, beliefs, and values of the developing child by affecting how the microsystem and mesosystem operate. Because schools reflect the beliefs of the society in which they reside, they tend to be relatively homogeneous in the way they function within a given society. Overall, despite provincial variations, Canadian schools reflect the macrosystem ethic of multiculturalism and the value of ethnic diversity

(Fleras & Elliottt, 1992). This makes difficult the development of any sense of national identity and nationalism. Further obstacles to the promotion of a sense of Canadian identity are seen in Quebec nationalism (promotion of a separate Quebec), First Nations self-determination (promotion of Native sovereignty or independence), and regionalism (promotion of strong provinces).

Although it embraces multiculturalism, Canada officially comprises two founding nations, French and English. The province of Quebec is home to most French Canadians, many of whom wish a separate identity from English Canada. In many Quebec schools, children are socialized to be French rather than Canadian; the fleur-de-lis replaces the Canadian maple leaf, and "Gens de Pays" replaces "O Canada." French Canadians in Quebec are taught different Canadian history and current political issues than are English Canadians (Dyck, 1996). The First Nations people's wish for self-determination has grown from a history of well-intended but ill-fated attempts to acculturate aboriginal children into white culture (Johnson & Cremo, 1995). Over the past two decades, tribal awareness has grown and is now celebrated. In Native-run day-care centers and schools, children are taught to be proud of their Native heritage rather than their identity as Canadians. Finally, with the exception of federal financial support to promote multicultural education (Friesen, 1995), educational policy in Canada is under provincial jurisdiction. The provinces characteristically reject a strong central Canadian government in favor of provincial power and a focus on issues of provincial rather than federal importance. Issues emphasized in school curricula then tend to be of regional or provincial relevance rather than of national importance (Dyck, 1996).

In summary, the Canadian school system reflects the culture's pluralistic values as well as the historic tensions between the French and English cultures, and it promotes heritage issues. Its overarching political socialization, rather than being nationalistic, is restricted to global concerns such as environmentalism. Nationalism and patriotism are missing from the Canadian school agenda. Typically, Canadian children and adolescents have little knowledge of their government and little reason for national pride (Pammett, 1971).

Compared with their U.S. peers, Canadian children know relatively little about their political system or their political leaders and are more likely to know who the U.S. president is than the Canadian prime minister (Pammett, 1971). Not surprisingly, the current state of Canadian political education has been described as deficient (Dyck, 1996). The focus in schools on multiculturalism and ethnic diversity encourages awareness of differing social and political perspectives. The lack of formal teaching about government and politics in schools promotes ignorance and cynicism about political leaders rather than admiration or respect (Covell, Rose-Krasnor, Fletcher, & Owen, 1992). And the lack of a nationalistic spirit makes it unlikely that a Canadian prime minister would receive the support, legitimacy, or hero status accorded the U.S. president.

The value placed on political knowledge and patriotism in the U.S. school system stands in sharp contrast to that in Canadian schools. Although there is significant local control of public education throughout the United States, it is also the case that across the country, much of the content of the curriculum, particularly in social studies, is designed specifically to teach children about U.S. politics (Palonsky, 1987; Wayne, MacKenzie, O'Brien, & Cole, 1995). Schools socialize through patriotic rituals: reciting the Pledge of Allegiance (learned long before it is understood), saluting the flag, recognizing national holidays, and singing patriotic songs. By the second grade, children are familiar with national symbols such as the flag, the national anthem, and George Washington and have some knowledge of the structure of government. Prior to the scandals of 1998, studies showed that children identified the president as being good, wise, and among their favorite people (Wayne et al., 1995). Such political socialization not only promotes positive perceptions of government and country but also allows for a strong national identity and patriotism. The latter was exemplified during the Persian Gulf War, when many U.S. schoolchildren wrote letters to American soldiers and decorated their school buildings with yellow ribbons.

Television

Like schools, the media exist within the exosystem, reflect the values of the macrosystem, and in turn influence the child's micro- and mesosystems through the provision of information. Television is one of the most potent and widespread sources of information for North American children.

In contrast to their experiences at school, Canadian and U.S. children receive very similar information through television. For children in both countries, as in other countries, television is the major source of information about war (Hakvoort & Oppenheimer, 1993; Hargraves, 1986). However, since that information is largely social in nature, the cultural ideology (macrosystem) will give it meaning by affecting how it is presented and interpreted. Information about war on television is compressed to fit time slots, and it focuses on images and impressions which are usually designed to shape the views of its public. War news can be presented in a biased manner which is designed to mobilize public support, justify action, and evaluate positively the outcomes of action. Liebes's explication (1992) of Israeli televised coverage of the Palestinian uprising on the West Bank and in Gaza (the Intifada) provides a clear example here. The Arabs primarily were presented in conflict-related roles: blocking roads, burning tires, and throwing Molotov cocktails. The Israelis were presented primarily as forces of law and order reacting to the violent initiations of the Palestinians, and as victims of war's devastation. Similarly, U.S. television's presentation of military action in Grenada and Libya suggested that the United States was the necessary force of law and order, able to end wars quickly and successfully (cf. Roscoe, Stevenson, & Yacobozzi, 1988).

In North America, the Persian Gulf War was presented like a video game, reinforced with bloodless terminology (Covell et al., 1994; Roscoe et al., 1988). Commentators described "surgical strikes" and "collateral damage" as viewers watched images of eerily beautiful bombers flying in the moonlight. When victims were shown or described, they were American. The implicit message to North American children was that war is a game which the United States wins.

Symbolic representations, mostly through television, provide social realities in areas where there is little direct experience (Bandura, 1986). The less direct experience children have with war, the more powerful television's potential is in shaping their war concepts. Television information, however, is not simply accepted; it is interpreted (Bandura, 1986). Concepts of war and peace for North American children, then, will be molded by their interpretation of the televised images of war which they see. The standards used for interpretation depend on macrosystem variables. Cooper (1965) suggested that the information presented passes through a "patriotic filter" which distorts the (already biased) information. Some information is admitted, some distorted. Patriotism allows the division of players into "us" and "them"—the "good guys" and the "bad guys." As Cooper (1965) explained, this division has a hostile function: the "bad guys" are immoral, cowardly, and treacherous, whereas the "good guys" are justified and patriotic. As Liebes (1992) described, the viewer is led to commit the fundamental attribution error. The "bad guys" are acting in accord with their dispositions; they are initiating violence, or war, because they are violent. We "good guys," on the other hand, are acting in response to the demands of the situation, stopping the violence and protecting the people. Our motivations, then, are prosocial rather than aggressive and therefore are more likely to be evaluated positively (Rule & Nesdale, 1976).

U.S. children, since they are socialized for patriotism and usually are members of the "good guys" (for example, in presentations of war in

Libya, Panama, or Grenada), must be expected to interpret the war information presented on television differently from Canadian children. Support for military intervention is facilitated by patriotism and by the positive character of U.S. children's perception of the U.S. political system fostered by schools (cf. Wayne et al., 1995).

In Canada, children's interpretations of what they see on television will be affected by the multicultural educational policy, which not only discourages patriotic nationalism but also promotes acceptance of a diversity of viewpoints. This makes it more difficult to differentiate the "good guys" from the "bad guys." Indeed, strong group identity and ideological commitment may be necessary precursors to negative evaluations of an enemy. Thus Canadian children are expected to hold less positive attitudes toward military intervention and war than their U.S. peers. Further, when Canadian children do receive different information about war from television (or in schools), that information centers on Canada's role as a peacekeeper or on peacekeeping-related problems such as those which were experienced in Somalia. We might then expect Canadian children's beliefs about war or Canada's role in war to be centered on Canada as peacekeeper.

In an empirical assessment of the effects of the macrosystem on attitudes toward war, I compared the attitudes toward war of samples of Canadian and U.S. adolescents (Covell, 1996). The study took place in early 1993, after the Persian Gulf War had ended but during a period when there was daily graphic television coverage of conflicts in Bosnia, South Africa, and Haiti and of the disintegration of the Soviet Union. The roles which had been played by the United States and Canada during the Gulf War were characteristically interventionist and negotiating, respectively. The study consisted of 106 U.S. and 148 Canadian adolescents from twelve to fifteen years of age. They were sampled from U.S. and Canadian schools within five miles of the Canada-U.S. border. The adolescents on both sides of the border received the same television stations and were comparable in general resources, neighborhoods, and socioeconomic status. The questionnaire was based on one used by Roscoe et al. (1988). It comprised a number of questions about war, peace, and the inclusion of women in the military.

The major findings in the cross-national comparisons were consistent with the macrosystem differences between the two nations. American adolescents held more patriotic and positive attitudes toward war and their country's involvement in war. Compared with the Canadian adolescents, the U.S. adolescents were more likely to believe that their country could win a war, that their president's war-related reports were honest, that military intervention was appropriate, and that war could be good. The Canadian adolescents were significantly less trusting of their prime minister and were unlikely to believe Canada capable of winning a war. Canadian adolescents, consistent with Canada's emphasis on peacekeeping, tended to describe war and the role of the military in terms of protective and defensive functions. In contrast, U.S. adolescents were more likely to describe war's purpose as the promotion of rights and freedoms, the military's function as that of killing, and war's end as being brought about by death or poverty rather than the compromise or surrender suggested by the Canadian adolescents.

The data obtained support the idea that a country whose macrosystem has a relative emphasis on nationalism, interventionist policies, and militaristic solutions socializes concepts of war which are different from those socialized in a nation whose macrosystem publicizes as virtues its peacekeeping status and pluralism. The data also support the idea that schools, which directly reflect the values of the macrosystem, are more powerful in shaping attitudes toward war than is television, whose presentations are interpreted by macrosystem values.

Gender Role Socialization

Macrosystems and their media also affect gender role socialization. The question of relevance here centers on the effects of the macrosystem on gender role socialization as it affects war attitudes. There are neither theoretical nor empirical reasons to suppose that the macrosystem differences between Canada and the United States affect gender role socialization. Historically, both have endorsed differential socialization of males and females. Currently both countries are in a period of transition toward more egalitarian socialization of male and female children.

It has been suggested (Gilligan, 1982) that females are less accepting of aggression, including war, because they are socialized to have greater concern for the well-being of others. Males, on the other hand, who are socialized to be concerned with rules and abstract principles of justice and to be aggressive, are expected to be supportive of war. Gilligan's theoretical predictions received some support in earlier studies in which females were found to focus more than males on the emotional and human aspects of war (e.g., Cooper, 1965; Zur & Morrison, 1989). The continued existence of gender differences in attitudes toward war remains unclear.

There have been significant changes at the macrosystem level in both the United States and Canada with regard to expectations of appropriate behaviors for females. Over the past decade, there has been decreasing differential socialization of children in both countries (Lytton & Romney, 1991). Although males for the most part continue to be socialized in the traditional manner, North Americans no longer discourage displays of aggressive, or traditionally masculine, behavior among their female children. The impact of this change on attitudes and behavior is seen in a number of areas. A lessening of gender differences in attitudes toward aggression is seen in recent studies of children's spontaneous narratives. Unlike those conducted in the 1980s (Libby & Aries, 1989; Peirce & Edwards, 1988), recent studies find no sex differences in the number of narratives with aggressive or violent content (e.g., Farver & Frosch, 1996). Studies of aggressive behavior show that there has been a significant escalation in the number of females committing violent crimes (Calhoun, Jurgens, & Chen, 1993; "Female Teens Turning to Crime," 1995). The media no longer restrict their images of females to traditional homemaker roles (e.g., Belknap & Leonard, 1991). And in schools across North America, females increasingly are treated and are performing the same as their male peers (e.g., Allaire & Campbell, 1994).

Growing equality between the sexes in North America, particularly with regard to military participation, also might lessen gender differences in attitudes toward war. Historically only males were socialized to be aggressive and prepared for combat (cf. Stevenson, Roscoe, & Kennedy, 1988). In contemporary society, as evidenced in the Persian Gulf War, females also can be expected to take combat roles (Schroeder, Gaier, & Holdnack, 1993). Females' participation in the military has increased in numbers as well; Canada experienced a 9 percent increase from 1990 to 1995 ("Women in Management," 1996). Nonetheless, macrosystem variables such as beliefs about women's equality exert their effects slowly over time. North Americans are now in a transitional period. For example, although women are shown leaving for war alongside males, they are rarely shown in combat or as military experts in interviews (Jackson, 1992).

Consistent with the concept of a transitional period are the recent data on sex differences. Whereas some recent researchers have observed sex differences in concepts of war (e.g., Hakvoort & Oppenheimer, 1991) or general attitudes to war (Roscoe et al., 1988), there is also evidence that sex differences are not as readily apparent as with earlier cohorts. No sex differences have been found in political socialization (Fratczak-Rudnicka, 1991), in understanding of war and peace (e.g., Covell et al., 1994), in behavioral responses to war (e.g., Rahav & Ronen, 1994), or in beliefs about justifications for war (Roscoe et al., 1988). Inconsistent findings in the recent literature may reflect methodologies; however, it seems more likely that what is reflected is the transition in macrosystem values for gender socialization.

The impact of changing macrosystems with regard to gender socialization is exemplified well in statements made by adolescents in a recent cross-national comparison of war attitudes (Covell, 1996). As described previously, in a partial replication of the Roscoe et al. (1988) study, attitudes toward warfare were compared for Canadian and U.S. school students whose average age was thirteen. Overall, in analyses of the quantitative data, sex differences were obtained which were consistent with those of previous studies (e.g., Cooper, 1965; Roscoe et al., 1988; Schroeder et al., 1993), as well as with the theoretical predictions of Gilligan (1982). Compared with their female peers, males from both countries were more accepting and supportive of war. However, the qualitative data, the responses to questions about female involvement in the military, indicated a confusion between older gender stereotypes and the more recent value placed on equality. When asked whether girls should be allowed equal participation in the military, most adolescents agreed. Typical of the responses of female students was that they must be allowed equal military involvement because "we're strong and just as good." However, few females expressed a desire for military involvement for themselves, and few subjects seemed clear on what females in the military did. Some descriptions given about what people in wars do reflected old gender stereotypes: (girls) "type the telegrams and wash the weapons," (boys) "kill people, drink beer, and kill more people." Other descriptions appeared to be clear exemplars of confusion created by the transition in macrosystem values about appropriate roles for women, for example, (girls in wars) "fight, kill, and break their nails" and "cook, fix clothing, and destroy enemies" (Covell, 1996).

A transition in values is also apparent in Gingras's study (1993) of Canadian women in the military. Contradictory pressures were reported: these included pressures to be pacifistic associated with one brand of feminism and pressures to overconform to aggressivity in order to gain acceptance and be "as good as the boys" associated with another. Such contradictory pressures reflect well the inherent contradictions of current North American macrosystems in regard to the appropriate values and behaviors for females.

In summary, although the empirical data on sex differences have some inconsistency, overall, studies suggest that whereas there may still be gender differences in attitudes toward war, these are perhaps not as great as with previous cohorts. We might anticipate a continued lessening of the gap between females' and males' concepts of war and peace as the macro-system's move to equality becomes more entrenched in socialization and daily life.

Conclusion and Implications

In the absence of further cross-national comparisons, one must be cautious about generalizations. Nonetheless, the Covell (1996) research described here, whose findings support the idea that macrosystem values shape concepts of war, does overcome the methodological shortcomings common to many studies of the cultural effects of political attitudes (see Furnham & Gunter, 1983; Furnham & Stacey, 1991).

The research findings described here show that in the absence of direct experience with war, children's and adolescents' attitudes toward war and corollary attitudes toward peace are shaped by political socialization which reflects the culture's macrosystem. A culture's ideology about war provides the societal blueprint within which the child learns about war; it designs the nature of social institutions (schools and media) and social activities in the exosystem. In turn, the child's classroom experiences and social understanding reflect societal values.

The discussion in this chapter provides a basis upon which researchers can build. Further research is needed to identify conditions in which political socialization may be less powerful, the impact of competing subcultures (for example, nations which have major religious divisions rather than the political hegemony of the United States), and the relative impact of political socialization where there is also significant direct experience with war.

The demonstration of macrosystem effects and the comparison of war concepts between U.S. and Canadian children raise an interesting moral or pragmatic issue. The issue centers on the potential costs and benefits of socializing children to positively evaluate military interventions. On the one hand, it seems morally repugnant to socialize children to idolize government leaders, to be patriotic, and to perceive war as necessary if not good. Such socialization does not presage world peace. Political attitudes are the best predictors of political behavior (Furnham & Stacey, 1991). On the other hand, such socialization may well have a protective function for children living in war zones in that it justifies and gives positive meaning to the violence which surrounds them. Informed consideration of this issue might best take place after further study of the impact of official multiculturalism on attitudes toward war. Perhaps a comparison between the United States and Australia, whose policy of multiculturalism is most similar to that of Canada, would be helpful.

Finally, it must be noted that Bronfenbrenner's ecological model not only emphasizes the importance of the macrosystem in the child's development but also allows for multidirectional interaction between systems. Social change can be initiated at any level. Peace education in the classroom has the potential to have an impact on all other levels from the most proximal (the child's daily experiences) to the most distal (cultural values). Ultimately a peaceful world is the preferred context for development. Increased understanding of the link between culture, socialization, and acceptance of war can be used to promote conditions which are optimal for the development and stability of peace.

REFERENCES

Allaire, L., & Campbell, J. A. (1994). The girls are way ahead of the boys in Quebec schools. *Inroads, 3,* 108–114.

Ålvik, T. (1968). The development of views on conflict, war, and peace among school children. *Journal of Peace Research, 5,* 171–198.

Bandura, A. (1986). *Social foundations of thought and action.* Englewood Cliffs, NJ: Prentice Hall.

Banks, M. H., & Roker, D. (1994). The political socialization of youth: Exploring the influence of school experience. *Journal of Adolescence, 17,* 3–15.

Belknap, P., & Leonard, W. M. (1991). A conceptual replication and extension of Erving Goffman's study of gender advertisements. *Sex Roles, 25,* 103–117.

Bronfenbrenner, U. (1979). *The ecology of human development: Experiments by nature and design.* Cambridge, MA: Harvard University Press.

Cairns, E., & Dawes, A. (1996). Children: Ethnic and political violence— A commentary. *Child Development, 67,* 129–139.

Calhoun, G., Jurgens, J., & Chen, F. (1993). The neophyte female delinquent: A review of the literature. *Adolescence, 28* (110), 461–471.

Cooper, P. (1965). The development of the concept of war. *Journal of Peace Research, 2,* 1–17.

Covell, K. (1996). Adolescents' attitudes toward international conflict: A cross-national comparison. *International Journal of Behavioral Development, 19* (4), 871–883.

Covell, K., Rose-Krasnor, L., & Fletcher, K. A. (1994). Age differences in understanding peace, war, and conflict resolution. *International Journal of Behavioral Development, 17,* 717–737.

Covell, K., Rose-Krasnor, L., Fletcher, K., & Owen, F. (1992, August). "Like being homeless in your heart": Children's understanding of war. Paper presented to the American Psychological Association, Washington, DC.

Dorgan, C. A. (1995). *Gale country and world rankings reporter.* New York: International Thompson.

Durkin, K. (1995). *Developmental social psychology.* Cambridge, MA: Blackwell.

Dyck, R. (1993). *Canadian politics.* Scarborough, Canada: Nelson Canada.

Dyck, R. (1996). *Canadian politics: Critical approaches* (2nd ed.). Toronto: Nelson Canada.

Farver, J. M., & Frosch, D. L. (1996). L.A. stories: Aggression in preschoolers' spontaneous narratives after the riots of 1992. *Child Development, 67* (1), 19–32.

Female teens turning to crime at twice the rate of young males. (1995, August 12). *The Toronto Star,* p. C4.

Fleras, A., & Elliott, J. L. (1992). *The challenge of diversity: Multiculturalism in Canada.* Scarborough, Canada: Nelson Canada.

Fratczak-Rudnicka, B. (1991). Political socialization and gender. *Politics and the Individual, 1* (2), 1–12.

Friesen, J. W. (1995). Multicultural education as a component of formal socialization. In K. Covell (Ed.), *Readings in child development* (pp. 172–184). Toronto: Nelson Canada.

Furnham, A., & Gunter, B. (1983). Political knowledge and awareness in adolescence. *Journal of Adolescence, 6,* 373–385.

Furnham, A., & Stacey, B. (1991). *Young people's understanding of society.* London: Routledge.

Gallatin, J. (1980). Political thinking in adolescence. In J. Adelson (Ed.), *Handbook of adolescent psychology* (pp. 344–382). New York: Wiley.

Gilligan, C. (1982). *In a different voice: Psychological theory and women's development.* Cambridge, MA: Harvard University Press.

Gingras, F. P. (1993). Gender differences in the attitudes of the military towards world peace, nuclear disarmament, and related issues. Paper presented at the 65th Annual Meeting of the Canadian Political Science Association, Ottawa.

Hakvoort, I., & Oppenheimer, L. (1991). Understanding peace, war and strategies to attain peace during childhood, preadolescence and adolescence: A social cognitive approach. Unpublished paper, Department of Psychology, University of Amsterdam, The Netherlands.

Hakvoort, I., & Oppenheimer, L. (1993). Children and adolescents' conceptions of peace, war and strategies to attain peace: A Dutch case study. *Journal of Peace Research, 30* (1), 65–77.

Hargraves, S. (1986). The nuclear anxieties of youth: A partial replication of the Beardslee/Mack (1982) study in Burnaby, British Columbia. *Peace Research, 18* (2), 46–65.

Jackson, R. (1992). Young adolescents' understanding of war. Unpublished thesis, Brock University, St. Catharines, Canada.

Johnson, N., & Cremo, E. (1995). Socialization and the Native family. In K. Covell (Ed.), *Readings in child development* (pp. 159–171). Toronto: Nelson Canada.

Libby, M., & Aries, E. (1989). Gender differences in preschool children's narrative fantasy. *Psychology of Women Quarterly, 13,* 293–306.

Liddell, C., Kemp, J., & Moema, M. (1993). The young lions: South African children and youth in political struggle. In L. A. Leavitt & N. A. Fox (Eds.), *The psychological effects of war and violence* (pp. 199–214). Hillsdale, NJ: Erlbaum.

Liebes, T. (1992). Television, parents, and the political socialization of children. *Teachers College Record, 94* (1), 73–86.

Lipset, S. M. (1990). *Continental Divide.* New York: Routledge.

Lytton, H., & Romney, D. M. (1991). Parents' differential socialization of girls and boys: A meta-analysis. *Psychological Bulletin, 109,* 267–296.

Palonsky, S. B. (1987). Political socialization in elementary schools. *Elementary School Journal, 87,* 493–505.

Pammett, J. H. (1971). The development of political orientations in Canadian school children. *Canadian Journal of Political Science, 4* (1), 132–140.

Peirce, K., & Edwards, E. (1988). Children's construction of fantasy stories: Gender differences in conflict resolution strategies. *Sex Roles, 18* (7), 393–404.

Punamäki, R.-L. (1996). Can ideological commitment protect children's psychosocial well-being in situations of political violence? *Child Development, 67,* 55–69.

Rahav, G., & Ronen, T. (1994). Children's perceptions of their behavior problems during the Gulf War. *Anxiety, Stress, and Coping: An International Journal, 7* (3), 241–252.

Roscoe, B., Stevenson, B., & Yacobozzi, B. (1988). Conventional warfare and U.S. military involvement in Latin America: Early adolescents' views. *Adolescence, 23* (90), 357–372.

Rose-Krasnor, L. (1988). Social cognition. In T. D. Yawkey & J. E. Johnson (Eds.), *Integrative processes and socialization* (pp. 79–95). Hillsdale, NJ: Erlbaum.

Rule, B. G., & Nesdale, A. R. (1976). Moral judgement of aggressive behaviour. In R. G. Green & E. O'Neal (Eds.), *Perspectives on aggression* (pp. 37–60). New York: Academic Press.

Schroeder, D. F., Gaier, E. L., & Holdnack, J. A. (1993). Middle adolescents' views of war and American military involvement in the Persian Gulf. *Adolescence, 28* (112), 951–962.

Stevenson, B. W., Roscoe, B., & Kennedy, D. (1988). Perceptions of conventional warfare: Late adolescents' views. *Adolescence, 23,* 613–627.

Wayne, S. J., MacKenzie, G. C., O'Brien, D. M., & Cole, R. L. (1995). *The politics of American government.* New York: St. Martin's Press.

Women in management. (1996). *Newsletter of the Women in Management Program, 6* (3). London, Canada: University of Western Ontario.

Ziv, A., & Israel, R. (1973). Effects of bombardment on the manifest anxiety level of children living in kibbutzim. *Journal of Consulting and Clinical Psychology, 40,* 287–291.

Zur, O., & Morrison, A. (1989). Gender and war: Reexamining attitudes. *American Journal of Orthopsychiatry, 59* (4), 528–533.

6

CONCEPT FORMATION
OF WAR AND PEACE

A MEETING POINT BETWEEN CHILD DEVELOPMENT
AND A POLITICALLY VIOLENT SOCIETY

Raija-Leena Punamäki, University of Helsinki

HUMAN BEINGS HAVE ALWAYS STRIVED to make sense of the conflicting and painful issue of war and peace. According to a Greek myth, during the romance between Ares, the god of war, and Aphrodite, the goddess of love, children named Phobos, Demos, Harmonia, and Eros were born. The myth conceptualizes the liaison between war and peace, breeding both negative consequences (fear and horror) and positive ones (unity and passion).

Understanding and solving conflicting issues is crucial in child development. The conceptualization of good and bad, right and wrong, life and death, and war and peace changes according to maturation, instruction, and social change. As children grow and enjoy wise guidance, their understanding develops from concrete to abstract, from specific to general, and from atomistic to comprehensive accounts. The ability to reason with respect to the causes and consequences of war and the means of attaining peace is especially salient for children living in war and political violence; consequently their concept formation may involve unique elements, relations, and contradictions. In this chapter I analyze the special characteristics of concept formation among children living in a society at war and discuss how conceptualization develops when children themselves are victims of political violence.

The crucial question relates to the ways by which an atmosphere of war and violence finds its way into concept formation. Accordingly, I present the approaches of sociocultural, cognitive, psychoanalytic, and learning theories to analyze concept formation. Each of the major theories can contribute to an understanding of how children go about making sense of their lives in peaceful and violent societies.

I start by discussing some aspects of sociocultural theory which delineate how children incorporate their cultural heritage and social wisdom into their concept formation. I continue by discussing the cognitive theory controversy over whether concept formation of peace and war proceeds according to well-defined developmental stages or whether it changes continually and gradually, and according to task salience. The next section deals with conflicts and dilemmas which are essential forces in prompting development. I argue that living in conditions of war and political violence creates unique conflicts, discrepancies, and dilemmas in children's thinking and reasoning. To illustrate these arguments, I will use my research data on children's attitudes toward war, peace, and enmity in the Middle East. For the Israeli and Palestinian children who were studied, concept formation is a highly emotional process which also plays an adaptive role in dealing with painful experiences. Psychoanalytic approaches view concept development as a balance between emotional expression and cognitive structuring. They allow consideration of a wide range of emotional, attachment, and symbolic aspects which are relevant in children's reasoning about war and peace.

Childhood in a Warring Society

Society has traditionally been conceptualized as either a disturbing or safeguarding factor in child development. A violent society interferes with smooth socialization, breaks childhood innocence, and forces children to acquire adult responsibilities too early. A peaceful society, in turn, can play the role of the superego which safeguards maturing children from their inner, often destructive, impulses.

In the same vein, research on the understanding of and attitudes toward peace and war hypothesizes that a violent society is disturbing, impairing and blocking children's capacity for reasoning and concept formation. Cognitive and affective processes of making sense of the world are implicitly regarded as directly reflecting the environmental reality. Researchers describe, for instance, how a pitiless, violent atmosphere and military aggression intrude into family relationships (Garbarino, 1992; Hobfoll et al., 1991) and personality development (Freud & Burlingham, 1943; Punamäki, 1987) and introduce rules for moral reasoning (Fields, 1973). Great concern has been shown over the possibility that political violence damages children's worldviews: they learn to accept violence as a way of solving problems and become habituated to emotional thrills and dim prospects for the future (Arroyo & Eth, 1996; Garbarino, Kostelny, & Dubrow, 1991; Rosenblatt, 1983).

A belligerent atmosphere is thus hypothesized to have its counterpart in children's cognitive-emotional development and external violence somehow to reflect into their thinking. This idea is, however, incorrect in the light of current knowledge about the genesis and progress of cognitive development and about the interactive nature of the association between society and child development. Table 6.1 summarizes the views of cognitive, psychoanalytic, sociocultural, and learning theories about the crucial forces which steer development, functions which concept formation serves in development, and hypotheses about the association between belligerent atmosphere and concept formation.

Most theories indicate that conceptual development emerges from the interaction between the child and his or her social environment, rather than directly reflecting external reality. Only learning theory can be interpreted as advocating a direct link between an aggressive environment and hostile thinking and behavior. Yet the association may be strong or weak, depending on the effectiveness of modeling and reinforcement. According to other theories, conceptualization of peace and war serves children's need to master new experiences, seek novelties and incongruities, and actively reorganize their current understanding. Hence, the question of whether children think in more belligerent terms in wartime than in peace is insufficient. It is more crucial to analyze the ways in which society's atmosphere brings about behavioral transformation and new conceptualizations.

Society "Out There" and Cognitive Development

Societies differ in the acceptance, expression, and control of aggression, and in whether they condemn, ignore, or idealize war. There have been many theoretical attempts to analyze how a society's atmosphere finds its way into child development and concept formation. Empirical researchers, however, know the difficulty of genuinely integrating the social and psychological spheres of life. In sociocultural development theory, child and society are treated as one unit of analysis. This procedure might provide a

Table 6.1. Concept Formation in a Violent Society According to Major Theories.

	Cognitive-Stage	Information-Processing	Psychoanalytic	Sociocultural	Learning
Crucial factors in development	Need for cognitive equilibrium; balance between assimilation and accommodation of relevant knowledge	Expansion of knowledge base and thinking strategies through maturation, motivation, and experience Overcoming limitations in cognitive capacity	Early experience and parental bond Overcoming major conflicts and crises	Guidance in cultural context Discrepancy between potential and actual competencies	Modeling and conditioning through relevant experiences
Function of concept formation	Reconciling new experience with existing understanding Marking developmental shifts such as level of logical thinking	Mastery in terms of retaining old and creating new rules to make sense of environment	Healthy development as a balance between emotion and cognition Internalization of cultural values	Acculturation by active shaping of beliefs, stories, and shared goals Mastery of new capacities	Accurate response to ideas stimulates identification with society

Conceptualization of war and peace in a violent society	Violent atmosphere and war scenes are nonessential; stage of cognitive development determines the conceptualization (Piaget).	Task-salient conceptualization is important; children become experts.	War scenes provide symbolic and metaphoric understanding.	Cultural images of heroism and genocide versus liberation dominate.
	Violent atmosphere and cognitive stage interact and jointly determine the conceptualization (Kohlberg).	Children use multiple strategies and rules.	Violence encourages aggressive impulses and hostile attitudes.	Collectively shared, war-related values are actively shaped.
	There is regression to earlier cognitive stages.	The process of incorporating society's information proceeds by steps: registering stimulus, retaining meaningful experience, and gradually storing information of collective memory.	There is regression into earlier stages of emotional development.	Violence is reflected in the content of thinking and reasoning.

tool for an analysis which concretely integrates societal and developmental characteristics.

According to Vygotsky (1978), a crucial aspect of human mastery is the creation and use of cultural artifacts (tools, like guns and computers, and signs, like heroic war myths and icons). Existing artifacts, in turn, insert humankind's accumulated experiences into developing psychological processes (Engeström, 1987). Cultural images, ideas, values, myths, and collective memories are typical mediating artifacts, and therefore they form the breeding ground for the formation of concepts. The cultural artifacts mediate between a society's violent atmosphere and fighting practices and a child's efforts to make sense of them.

Children incorporate a violent environment into the way they think, remember, and make sense of causal rules through their natural activity, such as playing and learning. Myths and legends are people's construction of their accumulated experience; they provide children with explanations and conceptualizations of issues of war and peace. Fairy tales, fantasies, and play themes further mediate the related collective reasoning of right and wrong and good and bad, and the struggle between light and darkness. In empirical terms, research should examine the particular nature of the "tools and signs" children employ in their concept formation in peaceful and violent environments. For instance, we know little about how the contents of collective memory, mythology, images of heroes and villains, and analogies differ in violent and peaceful societies.

The content and logic of heroic war stories seem, however, rather universal, dealing with dilemmas of justice versus injustice, killing versus mercy, reconciliation versus revenge, courage versus cowardice, fear versus bravery, and victory versus defeat. Characteristically, the warriors are instructed in the rules governing life (such as separation, kinship, and loyalty); they learn to know the secrets of visible and invisible worlds (symbolism) and to realize their individual potential and their responsibility for saving their own people (Campbell, 1949).

Apparently, myths and legends involving universal wisdom are equally available to children living in violent and peaceful societies. Why, then, should their ways of conceptualizing war and peace differ? What makes the difference is the fact that personal traumatization may interfere with the smooth incorporation of the symbolic material into concept development. Some research has provided evidence that symbolic and imaginary processes are especially vulnerable in traumatic conditions. Symbolic, bizarre, condensed, and metaphoric dreams are, for instance, less frequent among traumatized children (Punamäki, 1998a) and adults (Kaminer & Lavie, 1991).

Traumatized children tend to be preoccupied with painful memories and show high vigilance with external visual stimuli. They may also suffer from visual and concrete intrusions of thoughts and memories of the trauma scenes (Terr, 1991). The domination of concrete thinking and the focusing of attention on details is apparently imperative for survival in life-threatening circumstances. These cognitive survival skills may, however, interfere with the smooth incorporation of the symbolic material into concept development.

Some observations of Middle Eastern children indicate that the function of incorporating myths, legends, and fantasies into reasoning varies according to age and developmental task. Concerning the war hero myths, preschool children typically assimilated the role of war hero in their play and expressed omnipotent fantasies of saving their families and nations. In adolescent years, the fantasy of being war heroes played a role in identity formation, and adolescents used the myths to uncover their potential and conflicts concerning their own participation in the ongoing nationalistic war.

Conceptual Progress and Regression

There is some consensus that cognitive development, including concept formation, proceeds through qualitatively different stages. Piaget (1965) and Kohlberg (1969) suggest that higher modes of thought transform, replace, and inhibit lower modes of thought rather than being added to them. Accordingly, older children think about war and peace categorically differently from younger ones, and this difference does not match the increase of some attributes, such as empathy, role taking, and mutuality in concept formation. In other words, children do not think in more sophisticated terms about war and peace with age, but the whole logic of their reasoning changes.

Empirical research on the conceptualizing of peace and war has confirmed that with age children's explanations involve more structural complexity and abstract, universal qualities (Hakvoort, 1996). Young children's reasoning is practical, based on immediate experiences, and accordingly they describe or draw war in the form of concrete war scenes: "In war, houses are destroyed and people are crying." Preschool children start thinking symbolically, but they still reason subjectively: "We have wars because the enemy hates us." School-age children are capable of thinking logically with regard to concrete issues and their own experiences, and their conceptualizations of war and peace involve mutual relationships between nations and people: "We have wars because nations fail to settle their land disputes." Finally, adolescents and adults are able to think abstractly, hypothetically, and universally. Their explanations of the causes of war acknowledge the historical and antagonistic demands of opposing sides. They evaluate the consequences of war in a balanced manner and provide hypothetical solutions for disputes: "Justice is a primary precondition to lasting peace."

The crucial question is how children restructure these types of thoughts as a consequence of the interaction between developmental stages and social-political reality. Another important question is whether and how the transformation of an earlier developmental stage into a new stage differs among children who personally suffer from war violence. According to cognitive and psychoanalytic theories, political violence may disrupt beneficial cognitive-emotional growth and can induce regression to developmentally earlier stages (Freud & Burlingham, 1943).

Along these lines, McLernon and Cairns (1997) hypothesized that personal exposure to violence would lead children to conceptualize peace and war in concrete rather than symbolic, mutual, and universal terms. Fields (1973) hypothesized that living in a belligerent society would hinder the way children progress in their moral development from earlier (obedient and egocentric) to more mature (universal and ethical) stages. In the same vein, Punamäki (1996) assumed that the more children suffered from political violence, the more favorable their attitudes toward war would be; favorable attitudes and idealization of war, in turn, are characteristic of young children's thinking (Cooper, 1965).

Empirical evidence does not unanimously substantiate the idea that violent experience constitutes a risk for regression of developmental achievements (Dawes, 1994; Cairns, 1996). The hypothesis seems to be based on the intuition that war is not healthy for children. More research is needed to reveal the unique ways through which children reconstruct their old understanding and create new concepts when they themselves are victims of political violence. According to Garbarino and Kostelny (1996), healthy progression from earlier developmental stages to new ones is at risk in a violent society because children face challenges in developing a feeling of basic trust, a sense of security, and the ability to control their own aggression. Their observation calls for research showing whether and how the development of basic trust and security, as well as of emotion regulation, would differ among children living in violent as opposed to peaceful societies.

Concept Formation as Information Processing

The idea of specific transition periods where shifts of thinking occur has long been controversial, and information-processing researchers reject it as wrong. They challenge the argument that children's conceptualization differs fundamentally and qualitatively at different developmental stages. They maintain, instead, that thinking strategies change continually and that most changes are gradual rather than sudden (Siegler, 1991).

Siegler (1991) refers to research showing that younger children are just as capable of understanding concepts as older children but do not show any interest in doing so because the reasoning task is irrelevant to them. Other research has substantiated the idea that children use remarkably diverse and complex strategies at all ages and that the acquired skills and strategies may be task-specific and not necessarily generalizable to other situations (Berger & Thomson, 1998). Research on moral development has shown, for instance, that children sometimes demonstrate a more advanced moral reasoning than their cognitive capacity would predict in scenarios which reflect their actual experiences (Berger & Thomson, 1998).

Motivation, present knowledge, experience, and task salience are thus decisive in affecting ways of reasoning. Children's representations and thinking are highly attributable to the task they are performing. By focusing on the step-by-step mechanisms of human thinking, the information-processing approach may contribute to our understanding of how changes in children's thinking and reasoning precisely take place. The emphasis of the target salience of conceptualization rejects the view that children's thinking and reasoning are "deficient" compared with adultlike mature thinking. It contradicts the general hypothesis that political violence disrupts children's conceptual capacity. Hence, the idea of children regressing in their development due to societal violence is meaningless, because development, to begin with, does not proceed through qualitatively immature and mature stages.

One can argue that based on the information-processing theory, a converse hypothesis can also be valid. Political violence forces children to conceptualize moral, political, and human rights issues in truly competent ways, simply because the conflicts embedded in their daily lives are highly complex, thus demanding innovative thinking. Simon (1981) has argued that the more complex and demanding the environment is, the more complex children's thinking and their subsequent cognitive development are.

To substantiate this rather provocative claim, research should, first, focus on tasks and problems which are relevant for children's adjustment and survival in belligerent societies and, second, recognize that significant learning also takes place informally. For example, during the Intifada-related West Bank sieges, young children learned to categorize car registration plates and identity cards with amazing accuracy while they were waiting at checkpoints. The motivation for the non-age-graded classification skills was the security situation, which demanded effective thinking.

In information-processing terms, these children competently orchestrated all three steps of processing information: vigilant sensory registration of a stimulus (the color of the identity card and car plates), retention of meaningful information (detention versus release was related to the characteristics of plates and cards), and utilization of their accumulated knowledge base (the children's own and collective memory of military rules).

According to the information-processing approach, children use a variety of different thinking strategies simultaneously in their attempt to make sense of questions of war, peace, and enmity. Research should focus on analyzing the rules which underlie children's choices of reasoning strategies. Their accumulated knowledge base apparently provides some rules for the conceptualization of war and peace. For instance, Israeli and Palestinian children's understanding of the causes and solutions of their common conflict reveals different underlying rules of reasoning. The dominant rule in Israeli children's thinking was found to be historical-contextual ("The Holocaust must not happen again") but for Palestinian children it was future-oriented ("We fight for our own state") (Punamäki, 1987). It was further found that even if military balance, enemy image, and political opinions greatly changed in the Middle East, children's thinking strategies and the rules governing them were relatively stable. Israeli children continued to emphasize history-oriented and pragmatic aspects of their understanding of war and peace, whereas Palestinians emphasized future-oriented and sentimental aspects (Punamäki, 1993).

Conflict as a Developmental Force

Most theorists agree that the product of development is not as interesting as the processes by which children acquire new, qualitatively different concepts. What are the forces which enable a child to proceed from understanding war as concrete scenes of soldiers and house destruction to understanding it as an increasingly complex, universal, and abstract phenomenon? The shifts marking qualitatively different ways of thinking unveil the essential relationships, contradictions, and potentials of children's conceptualization of peace and war.

Dilemma, conflict, discrepancy, and disequilibrium between present and potential forms of thinking are among the important preconditions of the developmental change. According to psychoanalytic (Erikson, 1950) and sociocultural (Vygotsky, 1978) models, when a child confronts a psychological conflict, solving it successfully predicts developmental mastery. According to Piaget (1965), a state of disequilibrium or imbalance produces confusion initially and then leads to growth as the child modifies old understandings and constructs new concepts to fit the present experience. Finally, according to information-processing theorists, the decisive force in the direction of change is the child's need to overcome the discrepancy between underdeveloped capacity and desire of mastery (Siegler, 1991). Erikson emphasizes the conflict solution in the emotional domain of development, and the others in the cognitive and social domains.

The conflicts, moral dilemmas, and discrepancies may involve unique themes in conditions of war and political violence. Observations among Israeli and Palestinian children showed special kinds of conflicts embedded in their daily experiences. First, a conflict may occur between the early immature and later mature structures of thinking, and between the structure (how a child understands a concept) and the content (what she or he particularly understands) of conceptions related to war and peace. Second, children expressed conflicts between cognitive reasoning and emotional expression in traumatic circumstances. This discrepancy typically involves a dominance of cognitive and rational aspects of reasoning over emotional repertoires.

The dilemma between immature and mature thinking characteristically occurred between abstract, universal, and mutually accepted moral rules (war is bad; all people are brothers) and the concrete, egocentric, and inhuman demands of actual war (our war is good; we should destroy the enemy). Israeli children, for instance, reasoned that war, in general, is bad and harmful and causes suffering, but their own national war was necessary in order to bring security (Punamäki, 1987, 1996). Children applied various ways of solving the dilemma between the basic human values of love and brotherhood and the inhuman demands of a real war. They tried to deny the contradiction, change their worldview to reduce the dissonance, identify the moral dilemma as vital, and reconstruct multiple solutions.

The conflict between the structure and content of thinking refers to the fact that the children's age-graded reasoning ability (how they understand) is more mature than their reasoning about the specific issues related to political violence (what they understand). In peaceful conditions, older children increasingly understand the causes of war in terms of mutuality and can perceive enemy sides as equally guilty and equally deserving of legitimate rights. Older children are able to take the role of opposing sides and feel equal empathy for human suffering (Hakvoort, 1996). In a society at war, the actual dangers hinder children from using logic based on the aspects of mutuality, empathy, and universality in their conceptualization of hostilities and the enemy.

The fact that children are capable of logical reasoning in other spheres of life, but not concerning their own war and enemy, shows the adaptive role of concept formation. First, societies fight over concrete issues, such as land, oil, power, and the right to exist. Children cannot afford to explain their own war in diplomatic terms as a mutual disagreement; instead, they perceive the conflict as an antagonistic "us or them" and as a question of life or death. Second, in war conditions children of all ages perceive the very existence of the enemy as a direct personal threat. They fear and despise the enemy not in abstract terms but because it has the power to destroy their home and deprive them of their parents. Conceptualization of the enemy in terms of mutuality and role taking signifies, in fact, acceptance of one's own vulnerability.

The conflicting conceptualization of war and the enemy is often expressed as an oscillation between extreme views, motivated by fear, as the following example by an Israeli eleven-year-old girl shows: "In general, people should be bound together by friendship, and wise people should gather together and make important discoveries. One should make peace with the enemies, but if they are not willing, we should uproot them from their land and put them all into prison."

Palestinian children, in attempting to cope with and make sense of their violent and dangerous environment, expressed a discrepancy between their cognitive and emotional responses, depicting a psychological conflict between horror and heroism. Typically children employed heroic strategies in explaining and coping with military violence, but they were nevertheless overwhelmed by feelings of horror, fear, and despair (Punamäki, 1990). A similar dilemma was further found in children who expressed courageous activity during the day but whose nighttime dreams incorporated fearful and passive themes. Children who courageously confronted military forces during the day were helpless victims in their dreams (Punamäki, 1998b).

Children used various ways to solve the conflict and to reconcile discrepant cognitions and emotions. One example was their repetitive playing of war, Intifada, and prison games. Through make-believe confrontations between enemy soldiers and their own fighters, children attempted to reorganize their painful experiences and create new conceptual solutions. Play allowed them to integrate feelings of fear and courage, experience both weakness and strength, and feel, for one moment, excitement without danger.

The Adaptive Role of Concept Formation

War and political violence enter into a child's life through loss and injury of family members, destruction of home, and threat to life. In facing trauma, the concept of the world as a safe place is violently shattered, and children attempt to adjust their reasoning to new experiences. They cope by trying to make sense of suffering, explaining its causes and developing cognitive strategies to master it. The reconceptualization of war and peace serves this integrating and control-creating role.

Society at war provides heroic explanations for traumatic events and encourages strong ideological commitment as a solution and as healing. Ideological conceptualization of war helps children to understand why hardships happen, to feel protected, and to ventilate feelings of frustration and aggression. People who suffer personally from war events have been found to express attitudes supportive of war and a willingness to fight (Janis, 1951; Punamäki, 1987, 1996). Apparently ardent patriotism, ideological commitment, and identification with the strength of one's own soldiers serve as shields against fear, despair, and the need to reconceptualize a painful experience.

The concept formation of war and peace is hence an intensely emotional process for children who personally suffer from war and the absence of peace. Empirical research, however, focuses predominantly on the cognitive aspects of concept formation and neglects a wide range of emotional and behavioral aspects (Elbedour, Baker, & Charlesworth, 1997). It might be relevant to examine what emotional and mental health purpose a concept construction serves at various developmental ages and in various security situations.

Contemporary theories integrating affective and cognitive processes provide tools to assess concept formation which include a wider range of relevant elements. Horowitz (1991), for instance, defines person schemes as meaning structures which integrate knowledge and affection about the self, others, and the world. Children's schemes depict developmental changes in organizing thoughts, mood states, self-appraisal, and interpersonal actions. Schemes are considered enduring and slow to change; however, some profound experience, such as grief or trauma, can transform their content.

Creating Concepts in Human Interaction

Both psychoanalytic and sociocultural development theorists emphasize the idea that concept formation takes place in human relationships: in the early years between the child and parents and later between the child and peers, school, media, and other socialization agents. According to Vygotsky (1978), all mental processes, including concept formation, appear twice, first as an interaction between the adult and child and later at the psychological level. In the "zone of proximal development," the seeds of the next development stage are already available, and under the guidance of an adult, a child learns to master them. Early attachments have been found to affect the development of cognitive processes such as memory style and problem-solving and coping strategies (Mikulincer, Florian, & Weller, 1993). Accordingly, we may hypothesize that the influence of the social atmosphere on concept formation is mediated through parental attachments.

In conditions of political violence, parents' guidance for redefining the world in moral and confident terms becomes a complex task (Garbarino & Kostelny, 1996; Punamäki, Qouta, & El Sarraj, 1997). Parents may feel guilty for failing to provide safety and protect their children from shameful war scenes. Witnessing parental helplessness, on its part, forces children to conceptualize war as their own responsibility to defend and fight. The parent-child joint conceptualization of war and peace deals essentially with the question of the parent's ability to protect the child, as this extract from a Palestinian mother's interview reveals: "He is only five years old. He is a sensitive boy, and I am very worried about the effects of the violence on him. When he asked me, 'Mother, why did the soldier rush into our home?' I feel helpless. I do not sound convincing in assuring him that it will not happen again."

Another example presents an eleven-year-old Palestinian girl's conceptualization of peace, as expressed in her essay titled "The Day When Peace Comes." The mother-child relationship is the main organizing principle in her conceptualization of the liaison between war and peace: "I return home from school. There are no soldiers in the streets, and I am home early. My mother comes to kiss me in welcome. I do not know, but her kisses are different. They are like soft roses, but usually when she kisses me I feel the thorns of the roses in her embrace. She is always worried, sad, and afraid of the soldiers. When we have our own state, the food will be less expensive and my mother will be happier."

Conclusion

The importance of the role of the political and historical context in forming cognitive-emotional processes is frequently advocated but seldom realized. Different theories of child development can contribute to our understanding of how children make sense of their world in times of peace and war.

Sociocultural theory allows the translation of such general notions as belligerent atmosphere or militaristic values into concrete signs which mediate the associations between societal and psychological processes. A comprehensive examination of cultural symbols and values contributes to a deeper understanding of concept development. We may hypothesize that while cultural signs, symbols, and metaphors may not differ in peaceful and violent societies, the process by which children incorporate them into their conceptualization of conflicting and painful issues may differ. Apparently children face similar fundamental questions, such as guilt and innocence or punishment and responsibility, in both peaceful and violent societies. The cognitive strategies and underlying rules in reasoning may, however, differ depending on the salience of the experience in question.

Applying cognitive-stage or information-processing models would lead to very different hypotheses about the association between violent society and concept formation. According to information-processing models, living in a belligerent society does not necessarily predict incompetent and disrupted conceptualizations of salient issues of war and peace. Instead, these models provide the controversial notion that a society engaged in a constant struggle with survival and an enemy furnishes children with a complex and acute dilemma, and that children's successful solutions predict mature concept formation. According to cognitive-stage theory, an opposite argument is valid: a violent society can only strip children of the potential to develop healthy patterns of concept formation.

The development of concept formation is understood as proceeding across stages from concrete to abstract or egocentric to universal types of explanations for the causes and consequences of war and ways to attain peace. As far as children in dangerous and violent environments are concerned, the decisive issues seem to be the conflicts or discrepancies between their potential capacity to form concepts and the actual conceptualization of painful and highly personal experiences. The presence of an enemy is one of the highly salient issues in their concept development. With age, children increasingly have the ability to understand people's invisible inner processes and conflicting perspectives. However, to apply these developmental achievements in the conceptualization of an enemy would be life-threatening.

Concept formation, especially symbolic processes, serves a mental health function for children living in a dangerous and violent environment. Children's coping strategies include restructuring of painful experiences, finding imaginary alternative solutions, and "traveling" into imaginary worlds (Punamäki & Puhakka, 1997). This access to fantasy, imagination, and symbolic thinking can be their source of strength and protection (Garbarino & Kostelny, 1996). The difficulty of incorporating symbolic material into thinking presents a "developmental trap," indicating that the more children need symbolic processes, the more they are jeopardized. Hence, I argue that the cognitive and emotional aspects of concept development should be integrated, which is, indeed, in line with contemporary understanding of thinking and reasoning.

REFERENCES

Arroyo, W., & Eth, S. (1996). Post-traumatic stress disorder and other stress reactions. In R. J. Apfel & B. Simon (Eds.), *Minefields in their hearts: The mental health of children in war and communal violence* (pp. 52–74). New Haven: Yale University Press.

Berger, S. K., & Thomson, R. A. (1998). The developing person through the life span. New York: Worth.

Cairns, E. (1996). *Children and political violence.* Oxford, England: Blackwell.

Campbell, J. (1949). *The hero with a thousand faces.* New York: Bollingen.

Cooper, P. (1965). The development of the concept of war. *Journal of Peace Research, 2,* 1–17.

Dawes, A. (1994). The effects of political violence on socio-moral reasoning and conduct. In A. Dawes & D. Donald (Eds.), *Childhood and adversity: Psychological perspectives from South African research* (pp. 200–219). Cape Town & Johannesburg.

Elbedour, S., Baker, A. M., & Charlesworth, W. C. (1997). The impact of political violence on moral reasoning in children. *Child Abuse and Neglect, 21,* 1053–1066.

Engeström, Y. (1987). *Learning by expanding: An activity-theoretical approach to developmental research.* Helsinki, Finland: Orienta Consultants.

Erikson, E. (1950). *Childhood and society.* New York: Norton.

Fields, R. (1973). *Society on the run: A psychology for Northern Ireland.* Harmondsworth, England: Penguin Books.

Freud, A., & Burlingham, D. (1943). *War and children.* Madison, CT: International Universities Press.

Garbarino, J. (1992). Developmental consequences of living in dangerous and unstable environments: The situation of refugee children. In M. McCallin (Ed.), *The psychological well-being of refugee children: Research, practice and policy issues* (pp. 1–23). Geneva: International Catholic Child Bureau.

Garbarino, J., & Kostelny, K. (1996). What we need to know to understand children in war and community violence. In R. J. Apfel & B. Simon (Eds.), *Minefields in their hearts: The mental health of children in war and communal violence* (pp. 33–51). New Haven: Yale University Press.

Garbarino, J., Kostelny, K., & Dubrow, N. (1991). *No place to be a child: Growing up in a war zone.* San Francisco: Jossey-Bass.

Hakvoort, I. (1996). *Conceptualization of peace and war from childhood through adolescence: A social-cognitive developmental approach.* Amsterdam, The Netherlands: University of Amsterdam.

Hobfoll, S., Spielberger, C., Breznitz, S., Figley, C., Folkman, S., Lepper-Green, B., Meichenbaum, D., Milgram, N., Sandler, I., Sarason, I., & van der Kolk, B. (1991). War-related stress: Addressing the stress of war and other traumatic events. *American Psychologist, 46,* 848–855.

Horowitz, M. J. (1991). *Person schemes and maladaptive interpersonal patterns.* Chicago: University of Chicago Press.

Janis, I. (1951). *Air war and emotional stress: Psychological studies of bombing and emotional stress.* Ann Arbor: University of Michigan. (Microfilm copy, 1972)

Kaminer, H., & Lavie, P. (1991). Sleep and dreaming in Holocaust survivors: Dramatic decrease in dream recall in well-adjusted survivors. *Journal of Nervous and Mental Disease, 179,* 664–669.

Kohlberg, L. (1969). Stage and sequence: The cognitive-developmental approach to socialization. In D. A. Goslin (Ed.), *Handbook of socialization theory and research* (pp. 231–259). Skokie, IL: Rand McNally.

McLernon, F., & Cairns, E. (1997). *The impact of political violence on the images of war and peace in the drawing of primary school children.* Manuscript submitted for publication.

Mikulincer, M., Florian, V., & Weller, A. (1993). Attachment styles, coping strategies, and posttraumatic psychological distress: The impact of the Gulf War in Israel. *Journal of Personality and Social Psychology, 64,* 817–826.

Piaget, J. (1965). *Moral judgement of the child.* New York: Free Press. (Originally published 1932).

Punamäki, R.-L. (1987). *Childhood under conflict: The attitudes and emotional life of Israeli and Palestinian children* (Research Report No. 32). Tampere, Finland: Tampere Peace Research Institute.

Punamäki, R.-L. (1990). *Political violence and mental health: A study of Palestinian women, children and ex-prisoners* (Research Report No. 41). Tampere, Finland: Tampere Peace Research Institute.

Punamäki, R.-L. (1993). Mental health function of war attitudes among Palestinian and Israeli children. In L. Van Willigen (Ed.), *Health hazards of organized violence in refugee children* (pp. 44–57). Utrecht, The Netherlands: Pharos Foundation for Refugees Health Care.

Punamäki, R.-L. (1996). Can ideological commitment protect children's psychological well-being in violent conditions? *Child Development, 67,* 55–69.

Punamäki, R.-L. (1998a). The role of dreams in protecting psychological well-being in traumatic conditions. *International Journal of Developmental Behaviour, 22,* 559–588.

Punamäki, R.-L. (1998b). Correspondence between waking-time coping and dream content. *Journal of Mental Imagery, 22,* 109–126.

Punamäki, R.-L., & Puhakka, T. (1997). Determinants and effectiveness of children's coping with traumatic experiences. *International Journal of Developmental Behaviour, 21,* 349–370.

Punamäki, R.-L., Qouta, S., & El Sarraj, E. (1997). Relationships between traumatic events, children's gender, and political activity, and perception of parenting styles. *International Journal of Developmental Behaviour, 21,* 91–109.

Rosenblatt, R. (1983). *Children of war.* New York: Anchor Books.

Siegler, R. S. (1991). *Children's thinking* (2nd ed.). London: Prentice Hall.

Simon, H. A. (1981). *The sciences of the artificial.* Cambridge, MA: MIT Press.

Terr, L. (1991). Childhood traumas: An outline and overview. *American Journal of Psychiatry, 148,* 10–20.

Vygotsky, L. S. (1978). *Mind in society: The development of higher psychological processes* (M. Cole, V. John-Steiner, S. Scribner, & E. Souberman, Eds.). Cambridge, MA: Harvard University Press.

7

CHILDREN, PEACE, AND WAR
IN NORTHERN IRELAND

Frances McLernon and Ed Cairns, University of Ulster

THE MEDIA IMAGE OF NORTHERN IRELAND is that of a war-torn society constantly plagued by gunmen and rioting youths. While this is not
an entirely accurate picture, it is true that Northern Ireland has suffered
some twenty-eight years of continuous political violence. In this chapter
our main aim is to review research in Northern Ireland which has explored
the possibility that emerging from an ongoing political conflict influences
children's and young people's ideas about peace and war. Undoubtedly
children's ideas on these subjects are in part a reflection of their intellectual ability or the level of cognitive development they have reached. The
research reviewed in this chapter provides some insight into the possibility that, in addition to these factors, children's ideas about peace and war
can be altered by their exposure to events in the society in which they live.

Following an overview of some tangential evidence on this topic which
examines children's attitudes toward peace and war in Northern Ireland
and in other war-ridden societies, two recent studies will be reported in
detail. The first of these examines adolescents' ideas about peace and war
before and after the 1994 cease-fire in Northern Ireland. The second study
examines changes over time in a group of elementary school children during the beginning of the current peace negotiations in Northern Ireland.
We will begin, however, by providing a brief background on the history
and politics of the conflict in Northern Ireland in order to provide a context for the research which follows.

Northern Ireland: Background to the Violence

Behind the media headlines about Northern Ireland lies a conflict which is based upon political ideologies and social identities which happen to be divided along religious lines. Protestants generally support unionism, which aims to maintain the link with the United Kingdom, whereas Catholics generally support nationalism, which seeks the reunification of Ireland under a Dublin government.

Following centuries of enmity, the island of Ireland was partitioned, in 1921, into two sections: the predominantly Protestant north, which remained an integral part of the United Kingdom, and the mainly Catholic south, which is now an independent republic. Since that time, spells of serious violence have occurred in Ireland as the Catholic nationalist population in the north attempted to force reunification of Ireland under the Catholic south.

The latest period of violence began in the late 1960s. Although it was mainly concentrated in the Belfast area, the violence also extended into rural areas, touching most towns in Northern Ireland to varying degrees (Poole, 1983; Murray, 1982). Despite its sporadic nature, the violence has resulted in over three thousand deaths, thirty-four thousand shootings, fourteen thousand bombs, and sixteen thousand individuals charged with terrorist offenses. As a result, the impact of "the Troubles" has been marked in an area with a population of only 1.5 million, especially one as closely knit in both urban and rural areas as Northern Ireland (Gallagher, 1992).

The Impact of War on Children's Ideas About War and Peace

Relatively little research has been carried out worldwide into the effects of war on children's ideas about peace. Further, much of the research which does exist in this area has tended to be contradictory and has not explored children's ideas in detail but rather has concentrated on children's attitudes toward war and peace. For example, according to Gillespie and Allport (1950), who found that 60 percent of the college students in their sample expected a third world war within fifteen years, one result of experiencing war is general pessimism about the possibility of achieving peace. Punamäki (1987) was similarly pessimistic about the effects of war on children's ideas about peace. She concluded that the Palestinian and Israeli children in her sample cannot be socialized into peace-loving citizens, and that children who experience violence within their society are more likely to use violence to settle their disputes. In contrast, Bender and Frosch (1942) found that during the Second World War children believed that peace should be sought afterward. Similar views have been expressed by South African children, according to Liddell, Kemp, and Moema (1993), and by Ugandan and Sudanese children during periods of political conflict (Dodge, 1990).

Of particular interest is the distinction drawn by Spielmann (1986) between "active" peace, which involves active contact between groups in conflict, and "passive" peace, which she conceptualizes as involving respite and inactivity. In this context it is interesting that Spielmann reports that children living in Israel were inclined to stress the active factors of peace, such as the changes which peace would bring, including freedom to travel and better social relations. The passive aspects of peace, such as the disappearance of war, fear, and compulsory army service, were less frequently alluded to. Spielmann also observed that "children's vision of peace is always richer and more colourful when the children are in a state of hope, which stimulates imagination" (Spielmann, 1986, p. 64).

Children and the Violence in Northern Ireland

The possibility that the violence during the conflict in Northern Ireland was affecting the children in various ways has attracted a considerable amount of research (see Cairns, 1987, for a review). Of particular interest here is one line of research which has explored the salience of the violence in the lives of children. Perhaps not surprisingly, it has been well documented that children in Northern Ireland are exposed to and retain media information concerning the conflict (Cairns, Hunter, & Herring, 1980; Whyte, 1995). This is important for several reasons. First, it has been suggested (Tolley, 1973) that television and newspapers are the most important sources of knowledge for children concerning issues related to war and peace. This issue is also important because not all children in Northern Ireland have been directly exposed to the political violence. Despite this there is evidence that the vast majority of children in Northern Ireland have been acutely aware of the violence taking place in their society (Jahoda & Harrison, 1975; Cairns, Hunter, & Herring, 1980; Hosin & Cairns, 1984). An important question, therefore, is whether this awareness of the ongoing political violence had any influence on the way children in Northern Ireland think about peace and war?

Northern Irish Children's Ideas About War and Peace

While this question was not assessed directly in Northern Ireland until recently, a small number of studies provide some insight into Northern Irish children's attitudes toward war and peace. For example, McWhirter

(1983) found that when they were asked to write about "violence," two-thirds of a sample of 637 children in Northern Ireland spontaneously censured it. It was suggested, however, that over time, children in Northern Ireland would become habituated to the violence and accept it as normal, thus distorting their ideas about peace. This suggestion was refuted in a study by Hosin, McClenahan, and Cairns (1993), who examined essays entitled "My Country" written by children in Northern Ireland. The participants in the study were 288 twelve-year-olds and 319 fifteen-year-olds, seen in either 1980 ($n = 455$) or 1991 ($n = 152$). All were Protestant children attending religiously segregated schools. Content analysis was carried out on the children's essays, using a number of preset categories. This involved counting the number of children who mentioned such things as loyalty and violence in their essays. The most striking result to be drawn from this study was the finding that irrespective of the period during which they had grown up (the 1970s or the 1980s) or their age (twelve or fifteen), the one feature of Northern Ireland that they were most likely to mention was the political violence.

There were suggestions, however, that the contexts of the violence mentioned differed markedly between 1980 and 1991. In 1980, the children perceived the violence in a more matter-of-fact way, concentrating more on its political aspects. In 1991, it was claimed, the children were more likely to mention the violence in the context of a wish for peace. This suggests that despite the fact that the twelve- and fifteen-year-olds who wrote their essays in 1991 had lived all their lives in the violent climate of Northern Ireland, they had not habituated to the violence, at least not to the extent that they accepted it unconditionally, nor had they lost the wish for peace.

A related study carried out by McClenahan & Cairns (1993) supported this conclusion. In this study, 315 eleven-year-old and 398 fourteen-year-old children in Northern Ireland rank-ordered, in terms of importance to them, the "terminal" values section of the Rokeach Values Survey. All the children, except for boys in the older age group, placed "a world at peace" in first position. Ten years earlier, McKernan (1980) had asked 751 fourteen-year-olds from Northern Ireland to complete the same Rokeach Values Survey. At that time also, "a world at peace" had been the highest-ranked value for both boys and girls. The conclusion was reached, therefore, that children in Northern Ireland overwhelmingly wished for an end to violence and a world at peace.

This wish for peace appeared to be close to fulfillment when, on Wednesday, August 31, 1994, after twenty-five years of violence, the Provisional IRA announced a cease-fire. The immediate reaction to this announcement was widespread hope followed by pessimism and suspicion, especially among Protestants. This uneasy peace lasted from August 1994 until February 1996 (see Exhibit 7.1). One might imagine that to the children of Northern Ireland, the announcement of the cease-fire and the subsequent relaxation of security, the disappearance of the trappings of war, and the ending of bombings and killings must have seemed novel. One might also speculate that the ongoing debate, particularly in the media, about the cease-fire and the peace process could have led children and adolescents in Northern Ireland to think more deeply about peace and war.

Exhibit 7.1. Chronology of Events
Between August 1994 and February 1996.

1994

Aug   _____ Cease-fire begins

Sep   Violent nationalist–Royal Ulster Constabulary clashes

Oct   Further nationalist–Royal Ulster Constabulary clashes

Nov   _____ Interview 1

Nov   IRA murder of postal worker in Newry

Dec

1995

Jan

Feb

Mar   Loyalist riot in Maze prison

Apr   Catholic taxi driver murdered in Lurgan

May   Loyalist rioting

Jun   _____ Interview 2

Jul   Rioting and tension over Orange marches

Aug   Rioting and tension over Orange marches

Sep   Man shot dead in Belfast

Oct   Nationalist rioting

Nov   IRA announces preparations to return to war

Dec   _____ Interview 3

1996

Jan   Irish National Liberation Army leader shot dead in Belfast

Feb   _____ Cease-fire ends

Adolescents' Views of War and Peace: The Impact of the Cease-Fire

The beginning of the cease-fire presented researchers in Northern Ireland with a unique opportunity to study children's ideas about peace and war in a society that had just recently made the first steps toward a transition from war to peace. The first study to take advantage of this compared Northern Irish children's ideas about peace before and after the cease-fire (McLernon, Ferguson, & Cairns, 1997). It was expected that Northern Irish adolescents' views of peace before the cease-fire would emphasize "active" peace and their ideas might thus reflect their society's endeavors to achieve cooperation between groups and to engage in action to bring an end to hostilities. In addition, it was thought that the adolescents' expectations of the changes peace would bring might be unrealistically high. With the announcement of the cease-fire in Northern Ireland, adolescents might, it was suggested, relinquish their emphasis on the primarily active aspects of the concept of peace for a more passive concept typified by tranquility, quietness, or relaxation.

The study by McLernon et al. was based on a study by Hakvoort and Oppenheimer (1993) which found that children's and adolescents' associations with peace tended to be defined predominantly in terms of war—that is, the negation or absence of war, or passive peace. Hakvoort and Oppenheimer found, however, that the reverse was not the case. Children rarely defined war as the absence of peace, suggesting that they perceive peace in a radically different manner from war. In addition, the static and unchangeable nature of war was emphasized by the children in Hakvoort and Oppenheimer's study, in contrast to their perception of peace as a dynamic process. In other words, they understood that a state of peace can give way to a state of war but not necessarily vice versa.

In the light of these findings, McLernon et al. tested three hypotheses:

1. Adolescents in Northern Ireland, like the children in Spielmann's Israeli study (1986), would have pre-cease-fire ideas which emphasized the active aspects of peace, which would give way to more passive ideas about peace following the cease-fire.

2. Before the cease-fire, participants' ideas about strategies to attain and maintain peace would be concentrated on the need to find strategies to bring about peace. After the cease-fire, the emphasis would shift to the need to maintain peace.

3. Before the cease-fire, adolescents would perceive war as static and unchangeable, but with the ending of violence this would change to a more dynamic concept of war.

The study focused on fifty-one girls and sixty-six boys aged fourteen to fifteen from two towns in Northern Ireland. Both towns were of a similar population size and distribution of religious affiliation; both had a relatively low level of political and sectarian violence. Before the cease-fire, seven schools were visited in these towns; after the cease-fire, three of the schools agreed to return visits by the researchers. Questionnaires were administered to twenty-five girls and thirty-one boys in the first section of the study seven months before the cease-fire; twenty-six girls and thirty-five boys took part in the second section of the study three months after the cease-fire. All participants were asked to complete a pencil-and-paper version of Hakvoort's structured interview (see Hakvoort, 1995) to describe their ideas about peace and war. They were also asked about their perception of the status of Northern Ireland as "at war," "at peace," or "not sure."

Northern Ireland: Peace or War?

After twenty-five years of conflict and attempts at negotiating for peace, culminating in a bilateral cease-fire, it might have been expected that adolescents would now perceive their country to be "at peace." However, according to Bizman and Hoffman's study of responses to the Arab-Israeli conflict (1993), expectations for the future are significantly associated with the perceived stability of the causes of the conflict. Those who perceive the causes to be unchangeable are less likely to have confidence in a peace process. As a result, they should be less likely to report that Northern Ireland is at peace, even though the violence has apparently ended.

In fact, there was a significant ($x^2 = 14.18, p < .001, df = 1$) decrease in the number who perceived their country to be at war after the cease-fire (30 percent) compared with before (62 percent) and a significant ($x^2 = 9.57, p < .05, df = 1$) increase in those who were ambivalent before the cease-fire (7 percent) compared with after it (30 percent). The percentage of those who believed that there was peace in Northern Ireland showed a non-significant rise from 29 percent to 40 percent. In other words, the majority of participants (60 percent) were not unequivocal in their view that Northern Ireland was at peace following the cease-fire.

Ideas About Peace

The first hypothesis, that children living in a violent society are less likely to define peace as the absence of war, was not confirmed (McLernon et al., 1997). Some 66 percent of the responses given before the cease-fire were classified as "negation of war at a global level," and this remained the same after the cease-fire (64 percent).

The prediction in the second hypothesis that adolescents' perceptions of ways to attain peace would change from an emphasis on its active aspects to a more pronounced acknowledgment of the passive aspects of peace was confirmed. The number of children who mentioned actively striving to bring about peace declined significantly after peace had been achieved. At the same time there was a corresponding significant increase in the number of participants who responded in the category of universal rights, which can be viewed as a more passive aspect of peace. One possible explanation is that before the cease-fire, participants were sensitive to the urgency of the need for talks, dialogue, negotiations, and cooperation between the communities. Once peace had been achieved, the media emphasis on these aspects of the peace process slackened, and as a result the participants' more general and less personalized perceptions of peace (like their perceptions of war) may have become dominant and been expressed as universal rights.

Ideas About War

Overall, ideas about war changed from a strong emphasis before the cease-fire on one-sided conflict, instigated by a national leader, to a more generalized view of war in terms of war activities, the negative consequences of war, and mutual conflict between countries. Use of all of these categories increased significantly after the cease-fire, thus confirming the third hypothesis and suggesting that adolescents perceived war as more static and unchangeable before the cease-fire than after. This conclusion was supported by the interaction between the significant decrease in the perception of war as one-sided and the significant increase in emphasis on the mutual aspects of war.

Ålvik (1968) has pointed out that the ability to perceive war as resulting from conflicting interests (reciprocity of conflict) is strongly related to age, with older children more likely to use reciprocal reasoning when considering the concept of war. Since the participants before and after the cease-fire were of similar ages, their levels of reciprocal reasoning are likely to have been similar. The change, therefore, from a perception of the conflict as one-sided to acknowledging its mutuality represented a shift from an embedded view of the causes of the conflict being attributable to one side to a more open view of mutual causes.

This change is important in terms of the perception of the causes of the conflict. According to Bizman and Hoffman (1993), attribution of the causes of the conflict to one's own group is associated with increased feelings of shame and guilt, reduced anger toward the members of the other group, and a preference for negotiated concessions. Adolescents' perception of the conflict as mutual is likely to have included at least some element of acknowledgment of the responsibility of their own group and a consequent willingness to consider negotiation and resolution. A significant decrease in the proportion who perceived war as conflict between national leaders suggested that these particular adolescents viewed the cease-fire as the result of cooperation between national leaders rather than the result of conflict between them, as was the case before the cease-fire. This may mean that after the cease-fire the adolescents no longer perceived war strictly in terms of their own environment, but in more general terms.

In other words, these Northern Irish adolescents' conception of war became more like that of adolescents generally, who tend to perceive war in terms of negative consequences and war activities (see Cooper, 1965). Therefore, after the cease-fire, the adolescents in McLernon et al.'s study (1997) displayed more of the age-appropriate concepts of war and fewer results of the influence of their societal experiences.

One unexpected result, however, was the significant increase in the number of adolescents mentioning aspects of war activities and the negative consequences of war following the cease-fire. A possible explanation for this may be related to the claim (Schwebel, 1982) that children are more likely to deal with anxiety by trying, by one means or another, to deny the existence of threat. It is possible, therefore, that before the cease-fire, adolescents felt unable to deal with the anxiety inspired by daily reports of killings and maimings and so denied the existence of the threat. Once the threat was removed, they became able to associate more freely when verbalizing their responses to war, which resulted in the higher level of associations connected with war activities, the negative consequences of war, and negative emotions.

McLernon et al. (1997) concluded that despite the fact that the majority of these adolescents (60 percent) appear not to have accepted the reality of peace when they were asked to express it in concrete terms, they nevertheless were influence by the moves toward peace which were going on. This was evident from their responses to the peace and war questions and, in particular, from the fact that they were now less likely to see war as static and unchanging and the consequence of a struggle between national leaders.

Elementary School Children's Views of War and Peace: The Impact of the Peace Process

As we have noted, the period following the cease-fire brought to Northern Irish society a public debate concerned with, for example, what peace really means and the best ways to achieve it. McLernon and Cairns (1997) attempted to trace the impact of this debate on children in Northern Ireland. To do this they undertook a time-sequential study involving interviews at three times with fifty-three children—thirty girls and twenty-three boys aged eight to eleven—from a Protestant primary school in Belfast (at the second interview, the numbers were reduced to forty-seven and by the third interview to thirty-two). The interviews recorded the children's ideas about peace and war and their perceptions of the peaceful status of Northern Ireland. No particular hypotheses were entertained; therefore, the analyses tended to focus on the changes which occurred over time.

The children were interviewed at three different times at approximately six-month intervals in December 1994, June 1995, and January 1996 (see Exhibit 7.1). Again the questions used were those devised by Hakvoort and Oppenheimer (1993), adapted for use in Northern Ireland. The children were asked a number of questions, of which responses only to the following are reported here:

1. What do you think of when you hear the word "peace"?
2. If someone in your class asked you to explain peace, what would you tell him or her?
3. What do you think of when you hear the word "war"?
4. If someone in your class asked you to explain war, what would you tell him or her?
5. Is there peace in Northern Ireland?

For the purpose of analysis, answers to questions 1 and 2 (ideas about peace) and questions 3 and 4 (ideas about war) were combined to give overall assessments of the children's concepts of peace and war. Results showed that statistically significant changes ($p < .05$: McNemar test) did occur during the period of the cease-fire in the children's ideas about peace and war and that these are probably best understood by first considering the children's perceptions of the peaceful status of Northern Ireland.

Is There Peace in Northern Ireland?

Between times 1 and 2, the children's perceptions of the state of peace in Northern Ireland showed marked changes. At the first interview, a majority of the children (62 percent) were ambivalent about the state of peace in their country; that is, they felt that "there is sometimes peace, but not always" (female, ten years old). This number fell dramatically to 6 percent at time 2 and remained low at time 3 (6 percent). A smaller group at time 1 thought that there was peace (28 percent), and only 10 percent said that there was no peace. By the second interview, however, the children were equally divided between those who thought that there was peace (47 percent) and those who thought there was not (47 percent), with only a very small number of children remaining undecided. At the third interview, again, approximately half of the children (53 percent) thought that there was peace, while most of the remainder (41 percent) thought there was not.

This meant that statistically significant changes occurred between times 1 and 2, that is, between December 1994 and June 1995, when the number of children who thought that there was *not* peace in Northern Ireland rose from 10 percent at time 1 to 47 percent at time 2. Correspondingly, the number of children who thought that there *was* peace in Northern Ireland rose from 28 percent at time 1 to 47 percent at time 2, again a statistically significant difference.

Ideas About Peace

One thing that remained constant was that the most frequent image of peace was the global negation of war, which was mentioned by at least 60 percent of the children at all three times: "Peace I shouldn't think has any war or fighting in it; it should be all just calm and quiet, and I would say that peace isn't war, it is keeping the war down" (female, eleven years old). The second most frequently mentioned category changed, however, across the three times, with "war-related images" the second most frequent at time 1, "positive emotions on an individual level" in second place at time 2, and "individual negation of war" in second place at time 3. These changes were brought about in two ways. The first was a statistically significant decline in the use of "war-related images" between time 1 (23 percent) and time 2 (12 percent). This raises the possibility that the change from talk about peace in security terms to talk about peace in terms of cease-fires and negotiations did indeed have an impact on at least a small number of children.

More puzzling was an increase from time 1 (14 percent) to time 2 (30 percent) in the number of children mentioning "positive emotions at an individual level," followed by a fall in the numbers mentioning this aspect of peace at time 3 (13 percent). One possible explanation is that these children, once they had taken on board the reality of a cease-fire, thought it would lead to "everybody being friends with each other and everybody getting on with each other" (female, ten years old). Subsequent events (see Exhibit 7.1) may have led to a reassessment of this aspect of the peace process on the part of some children.

Ideas About War

The children were consistent in their ideas about war, mentioning "war activities" most frequently at all three times (68 percent, 69 percent, and 61 percent): "people fighting and bombing each other and killing" (male, ten years old). However, "negative consequences of war," which was the second most frequently used category, "people dying and families crying with grief" (female, eleven years of age), increased significantly in frequency at time 2, followed by a significant fall at time 3 (30 percent, 56 percent, and 41 percent). Likewise, mentioning weapons and soldiers rose between time 1 (19 percent) and time 2 (43 percent), followed by a significant fall at time 3 (12 percent): "It makes me think about tanks . . . and the soldiers walking around in their camouflage and the guns with the holes all up the sides" (female, eleven years old).

A quite different pattern emerged where negative evaluation of war was concerned. There was a decline in the use of this category over the three interviews which was statistically significant from time 1 (19 percent) to time 3 (8 percent). It is possible that without the constant media condemnation and revulsion which accompanied each new terrorist atrocity before the cease-fire, the children might have felt increasingly less compulsion to condemn war.

Overall, therefore, living through the period of the cease-fire and the ongoing peace process did apparently bring changes to these Protestant children's ideas about peace and war in general. More specifically, there were alterations over time in their ideas about whether Northern Ireland was at war or not. Ambivalence on this latter question at the first interview gave way to more definite opinions during the second and third interviews. As a result, at times 2 and 3, half the children believed that there was peace while half did not.

At all three times, the majority of children thought of peace primarily in terms of the negation of war and thought of war primarily in terms of war activities. In addition, there were changes in the children's ideas about peace and war in which a U-shaped trend emerged. This was caused by a statistically significant increase between time 1 and time 2 in the use of three categories—one related to peace ("positive emotions") and the other two to war ("weapons and soldiers," "negative consequences"). This was followed by a statistically significant decrease in the use of the same three categories between time 2 and time 3. Given the U-shaped nature of the results, it appears more likely that changes in Northern Irish society are reflected in the subtle but important changes detected here.

Conclusions

Both of the studies reported here can be thought of as providing evidence that in Northern Ireland children and young people's ideas about war and peace have been influenced by the current cease-fire and the subsequent peace process. Although the proportion of adolescents who said that the country was at peace did not change significantly after the cease-fire, the percentage who expressed ambivalent feelings about the status of Northern Ireland in terms of peace increased significantly. It appears, therefore, that many young people had not fully accepted the reality of the peace process. Despite this, their ideas about war were different after the cease-fire. In particular, fewer people thought of war as unchanging and as a struggle between national leaders. Instead war was no more likely to be thought of in terms of war activities and their negative consequences. Ideas about peace also tended to become more abstract and now more participants were more likely to provide strategies to attain peace.

Of course, the fact that ongoing political developments, particularly developments as dramatic as a cease-fire, had an impact on these fourteen- to fifteen-year-olds is hardly surprising. What could not have been predicted as confidently were the results obtained from the interview data with primary school children. Here there was also evidence that the children's ideas about peace and war were being influenced by political events. This result was less predictable for two reasons. To begin with, one might have imagined that younger children would have been relatively sheltered from the debate about peace and how to achieve it which dominated the news during the year in which this study was conducted. Second, during this year no major event like the cease-fire took place. Instead, especially for primary school children, the debate concerning peace was couched in relatively abstract terms.

With this in mind it is, of course, important not to exaggerate the changes detected in the primary school children's thinking about peace and war. Over the three times at which they were studied, the most conspicuous feature of the results for these young children was their stability. The majority of children saw peace as the negation of war, while their concept of war was dominated by war activities. There were, however, changes over time. Had these changes been simple linear increases or decreases, they might have been attributable to the results of age-related cognitive development. Instead, the possibility that these changes are the product of environmental influences was strengthened by the fact that an increase in the frequency of use of three categories, from time 1 to time 2, was then followed by a decrease in their use from time 2 to time 3.

Finally, it is of interest to note that at both age levels it could be argued that the onset of the cease-fire and peace process resulted in rather more changes in the way the children and adolescents thought about war rather than how they thought about peace. In some ways this is counterintuitive. One might have imagined that the arrival of peace (of a sort) in Northern Ireland for the first time in the lives of these young people would have had more impact on their ideas about peace than their ideas about war.

Of course, all of these conclusions are tentative. It goes without saying that we urgently need further research of this kind, particularly in other societies. It is to be hoped that other societies will soon also be taking their first tentative steps along the path of peace, thus allowing the work reported here to be replicated and more young people to come to terms with the ending of war and the beginning of peace.

REFERENCES

Ålvik, T. (1968). The development of views on conflict, war and peace among school children. *Journal of Peace Research, 5* (2), 171–195.

Bender, L., & Frosch, J. (1942). Children's reactions to the war. *American Journal of Orthopsychiatry, 22,* 571–586.

Bizman, A., & Hoffman, M. (1993). Expectations, emotions and preferred responses regarding the Arab-Israeli conflict. *Journal of Conflict Resolution, 37* (1), 139–159.

Cairns, E. (1987). *Caught in cross-fire.* Belfast, Northern Ireland: Appletree Press.

Cairns, E., Hunter, D., & Herring, L. (1980). Young children's awareness of violence in Northern Ireland: The influence of television. *British Journal of Social Psychology, 19,* 3–6.

Cooper, P. (1965). The development of the concept of war. *Journal of Peace Research, 2* (1), 1–17.

Dodge, C. P. (1990). Health implications of war in Uganda and Sudan. *Social Sciences and Medicine, 31* (6), 691–698.

Gallagher, A. M. (1992). Education in a divided society. *The Psychologist, 5,* 353–356.

Gillespie, J. M., & Allport, G. M. (1950). *Youth's outlook on the future: A cross-national study.* New York: Doubleday.

Hakvoort, I. (1995). Children's conceptions of peace and war: A longitudinal study. *Peace and Conflict: Journal of Peace Psychology, 2,* 1–15.

Hakvoort, I., & Oppenheimer, L. (1993). Children and adolescents' conceptions of peace, war and strategies to attain peace: A Dutch case study. *Journal of Peace Research, 30* (1), 65–77.

Hosin, A., & Cairns, E. (1984). The impact of conflict on children's ideas about their country. *Journal of Psychology, 118* (2), 161–168.

Hosin, A., McClenahan, C., & Cairns, E. (1993). *The impact of political violence in Northern Ireland on children's ideas about their country in 1980 and 1981.* Unpublished paper. Ulster, Northern Ireland: Centre for Study of Conflict, University of Ulster.

Jahoda, G., & Harrison, S. (1975). Belfast children: Some effects of a conflict environment. *Irish Journal of Psychology, 3* (1), 1–19.

Liddell, C., Kemp, J., & Moema, M. (1993). The young lions: South African children and youth in political struggle. In L. Leavitt & N. Fox (Eds.), *The psychological effects of war and violence on children.* Hillsdale, NJ: Erlbaum.

McClenahan, C., & Cairns, E. (1993). *Children's values in Northern Ireland: 1980–1990.* Unpublished paper. Ulster, Northern Ireland: Centre for Study of Conflict, University of Ulster.

McKernan, J. (1980). Pupil values as indicators of intergroup differences in Northern Ireland. In J. Harbison & J. Harbison (Eds.), *A society under stress: Children and young people in Northern Ireland.* London: Open Books.

McLernon, F., & Cairns, E. (1997). *Children's ideas about peace and war in Northern Ireland.* Unpublished paper. Ulster, Northern Ireland: Psychology Department, University of Ulster

McLernon, F., Ferguson, N., & Cairns, E. (1997). Comparison of Northern Irish children's attitudes to war and peace before and after the paramilitary ceasefires. *International Journal of Behavioural Development, 20* (4), 715–730.

McWhirter, L. (1983). Looking back and looking forward: An inside perspective. In J. Harbison & J. Harbison (Eds.), *Children of the Troubles: Children in Northern Ireland.* Belfast, Northern Ireland: Learning Resources Unit, Stranmillis College.

Murray, R. (1982). Political violence in Northern Ireland, 1969–1977. In F. W. Boal & J. N. Douglas (Eds.), *Integration and division: Geographical perspectives on the Northern Ireland problem.* London: Academic Press.

Poole, M. (1983). The demography of violence. In J. Darby (Ed.), *Northern Ireland: The background to the conflict.* Belfast, Northern Ireland: Appletree Press.

Punamäki, R.-L. (1987). *Childhood under conflict: The attitudes and emotional life of Israeli and Palestinian children* (Research Report No. 32). Tamere, Finland: Tamere Peace Research Institute.

Schwebel, M. (1982, February). *Effects of the nuclear war threat on children and teenagers: Implications for professionals.* Paper presented at a symposium of Physicians for Social Responsibility, New York, NY.

Spielmann, M. (1986). If peace comes . . . Future expectations of Israeli children and youth. *Journal of Peace Research, 23* (1), 51–67.

Tolley, H. (1973). Children and war: Political socialization to international conflict. New York: Teachers College Press.

Whyte, J. (1995). *Changing times: Challenges to identity.* Aldershot, England: Ashgate.

8

BELIEFS ABOUT WAR, CONFLICT, AND PEACE IN ISRAEL AS A FUNCTION OF DEVELOPMENTAL, CULTURAL, AND SITUATIONAL FACTORS

Amiram Raviv, Tel Aviv University;
Daniel Bar-Tal, Tel Aviv University;
Leah Koren-Silvershatz, Israeli Ministry of Health;
and Alona Raviv, Tel Aviv University

THE QUESTION OF HOW CHILDREN AND ADOLESCENTS understand conceptions of war, conflict, and peace has become a central one in the research about the development of social knowledge. This line of research has mainly focused on the developmental changes in the understanding of these concepts through childhood and adolescence (e.g., Ålvik, 1968; Cooper, 1965; Covell, Rose-Krasnor, & Fletcher, 1994; Hägglund, Hakvoort, & Oppenheimer, 1996; Hakvoort, 1996; Rosell, 1968; Tolley, 1973).

In recent years the interest in this area of research has come to include cultural and situational influences on the acquisition of conceptions and beliefs about war, conflict, and peace (e.g., Cairns, McClenahan, & Hosin, 1996; Hägglund et al., 1996; Spielmann, 1986; see also Chapters Five, Six, and Seven of this volume). Individuals acquire conceptions and beliefs

This study was supported by a grant from NCJW Research Institute for Innovation in Education, School of Education, The Hebrew University of Jerusalem.

related to the domains of social knowledge, such as concepts of war, conflict, and peace, as members of a particular society who live under particular conditions and form a particular culture. Also, as members of a particular society, they experience particular situations which have both short- and long-term effects on their view of the social world.

This chapter describes a particular example of how cultural and situational factors in Israel shape children's and adolescents' beliefs about war, conflict, and peace. The first section presents a general conceptual framework about social knowledge and its acquisition. The second section describes a study done in 1986 which examined beliefs about war, conflict, and peace held by Israeli children and adolescents. That study assumed that these beliefs reflected the cultural social knowledge prevailing in Israeli society at that time. The third section describes a replication of the first study which was carried out with a similar sample a few days after the 1991 Gulf War came to an end, assuming that children's and adolescents' beliefs would have been affected by the recent war experience. The last section of the chapter discusses the conclusions of the two studies.

The Nature and Formation of Social Knowledge

Beliefs about war, conflict, and peace are part of what is commonly called social knowledge. The social characteristic of knowledge refers to specific contents and indicates the way (that is, the process) by which it was formed (Bar-Tal & Kruglanski, 1988; McGuire, 1986). As a category of contents, social knowledge encompasses topics and subjects which refer to people (individuals and groups) and their products, as well as events involving human beings. In terms of processes, social knowledge implies that human beings are influential in the formation and change of these contents. This could be done either directly, through the agency of people or their products (for example, books and paintings), or as a result of events involving other people, such as war.

Individuals store social knowledge in the form of beliefs, which have been defined as propositions to which a person attributes at least a minimal degree of confidence (Bar-Tal, 1990; Bem, 1970; Kruglanski, 1989). Beliefs thus are units of social knowledge which social scientists identify when they study how people understand specific concepts or what they think about particular issues.

After introducing the concept of social knowledge, we will turn to the main objective of this chapter—the analysis of factors which have a determinative influence on the formation of social knowledge. The analysis will omit individual factors, although it recognizes their importance (see Chapter

Nine), and will focus on three common factors which influence collectives: the developmental, cultural, and situational factors.

Developmental Factors

The formation of social knowledge is related to human developmental processes: with age, people develop their cognitive capacities, which, among other things, afford them an understanding of the social world. Children of different ages differ in their cognitive capacities and therefore also in their understanding of the social world (Bar-Tal & Saxe, 1991; Damon, 1977; Inhelder & Piaget, 1958; Neisser, 1987; Piaget, 1950, 1970; Shantz, 1975; Turiel, 1983). Specifically, in the early stages of cognitive development, children think about the world solely from their own point of view. They think intuitively, use images, and refer to concrete objects rather than relying on abstract concepts. This concrete thinking is dominated by those features of the world which are revealed and perceived at the present moment. Also characteristic of this stage is a primitive understanding of causality, an inability to consider a variety of alternatives, and an inability to synthesize several items of information. With age children become able to form complex categories and abstract concepts, to understand metaphoric meaning, and to integrate various details of information. They also become able to focus on several features of a situation and to understand complex causalities. They become able to ponder not only actual experienced or observed events and relationships but also hypothetical ones.

These principles of cognitive development also apply to children's understanding of the notions of war, conflict, and peace. Young children think about war, conflict, and peace in concrete terms which refer to objects, participants, or activities. They also tend to apply these concepts to their own interpersonal experiences. Only with age do adolescents begin to understand the complexity of these concepts: they refer to them in abstract terms, mentioning various international processes and causes which are not immediately observable and which have hypothetical consequences (e.g., Cooper, 1965; Covell et al., 1994; see also Chapters One and Two of this volume).

Cultural Factors

Members of a particular society tend to shape their view of the world on the basis of their society's culture. The culture of any society, which encompasses the shared expressive terms of human behavior, objects, and ideas in a particular society (Griswold, 1994), also includes the particular social knowledge which society members form as a result of their unique history, conditions, and experiences (Bar-Tal, in press; D'Andrade, 1984; Dougherty, 1985). This knowledge is very resistant to change and may survive for generations. Roberts (1964) even pointed out that "it is possible to regard all culture as information and to view any single culture as an 'information economy in which information is received or created, stored, retrieved, transmitted, utilized, and even lost. . . .' In any culture information is stored in the minds of its members and, to a greater or lesser extent, in artifacts" (pp. 438–439). D'Andrade (1984) similarly suggested that "from the representational point of view, culture consists of knowledge and beliefs about the world" (p. 96).

The social knowledge of a culture encompasses a wide scope of concepts and beliefs which pertain also to events such as war, conflict, and peace. This is so because the history of each society includes these events and because they were almost always powerful experiences which had a critical effect on the culture. But different cultures have different concepts of war, conflict, and peace and form different beliefs about them as a result of their different experiences.

Every society will make a special effort to impart cultural beliefs to its members through a long process of socialization. Agents such as families, schools, mass media, and peer groups transmit social knowledge and shape the worldview of new generations (Dawson & Prewitt, 1969; Easton & Dennis, 1969; Ehman, 1980; Hess & Torney, 1967; Renshon, 1977). An example of special interest is a study by Cooper (1965), who compared English and Japanese children's and adolescents' associations regarding concepts of war and peace. He found that British children—compared with their Japanese peers—used the concrete category of weapons more to describe a war and less to describe the category of fighting, killing, and dying. The Japanese adolescents had a greater tendency to use a category referring to contemporary events, people, and countries than the English adolescents. They also presented more protest and antiwar associations. With regard to peace, the English children used more personal categories. The Japanese children referred more to reconciliation and respite and the Japanese adolescents used more peace symbols. In general, the Japanese adolescents were more vehement in their protests against war and more preoccupied with international peace movements than English adolescents. Cooper assumed that these findings reflected cultural differences and the different experiences of the Japanese and English children.

Recently, a study by Hakvoort, Hägglund, and Oppenheimer (in press) compared Dutch and Swedish adolescents' understanding of peace and war and found differences in their orientation toward peace. While Swedish adolescents demonstrated an orientation focusing on peace attainment, Dutch adolescents showed an orientation which emphasized peacekeeping. The researchers suggested that the difference could be explained by a cultural factor which is determined by sociohistorical processes. Adolescents in Sweden, which has not experienced war for centuries, talked about international collaboration to stop the war "out there." In contrast, Dutch adolescents focused on the societal conditions which can secure peace, since for them war and threats of war were real because of the Dutch experiences in this century.

Situational Factors

In addition to cultural factors, which provide a lasting framework for society members' social knowledge, situational factors may powerfully affect society members' understanding of particular conceptions. The extent of such effects depends on the relevance of the particular situation to the life of the society's members. That is, situations influence individuals' view of the world to various extents depending on the intensity of their impact on the lives of those involved. The concrete situational experience of violent conflict and war obviously influences how individuals understand war, conflict, and peace. Even short outbreaks of violence provide important information on what conflicts and wars are. If the situation is of limited duration, the influence may dissipate with time, but during the outbreak of war or for a short time after it, this influence is intact.

Of course, it is not only war or conflict situations which affect conceptions of war, conflict, and peace; situations which instigate hopes for peace may do so too. In this vein, of special interest is a study by Spielmann (1986) which demonstrates the effects of situational factors. She asked Jewish Israeli children and adolescents, ages nine to ten, thirteen to fourteen, and seventeen to eighteen to write an essay titled "Thoughts About Peace" immediately prior to and following the historic visit of Egyptian president Anwar Sadat to Jerusalem in 1977. The results clearly showed the effect of this dramatic event on children's and adolescents' conceptualization of peace. Prior to the visit, nine- to ten-year-old and thirteen- to fourteen-year-old children and adolescents were optimistic and even utopian, referring to peace in terms of justice, equality, and brotherhood. Following the visit, the two younger age groups changed their perceptions to more realistic views. The essays expressed a realization that peace would require a high price, which caused them to wonder if peace was worthwhile. In contrast, the oldest group of adolescents (seventeen- to eighteen-year-olds) demonstrated an opposite shift, from pessimism and an inability to see a way out of the threatening situation to more optimism and hope and even utopian visions of peace. These results suggest that the Egyptian president's visit to Israel was an important situational factor which affected Israeli youth's beliefs about peace.

It is the purpose of the present research to investigate the effects of the elaborated factors—developmental, cultural, and situational—on the beliefs about war, conflict, and peace of Israeli children and adolescents. The research consists of two studies: while the former study focuses on an examination of the developmental and cultural factors, the latter study focuses on an investigation of the situational factor. In the next section, the first study will be described. Since the developmental factor has already been outlined, an attempt is made to describe the cultural factor, which has a determinative influence on the formation of social knowledge.

Israeli Children's and Adolescents' Beliefs About War, Conflict, and Peace

Children and adolescents participating in the first study reported their beliefs about war, conflict, and peace in May and June 1986: nine years after the historic visit of Egyptian president Anwar Sadat to Jerusalem which led to the peace agreement with Egypt signed in 1979; two years after the partial withdrawal of the Israeli army from Lebanon in 1984; one year before the onset of the Intifada, the Palestinian uprising, against Israeli occupation; and five years before the Madrid conference, which began the current peace process in the Middle East. This makes it quite clear that the study was carried out during a period of active conflict between Israel and the Arab world. Although the peace agreement with Egypt dramatically changed the strategic conditions in the Middle East, the Palestinians and many Arab countries still expressed hostile and anti-Israel views. The Israeli-Arab conflict was at that time still perceived as intractable by the majority of Israelis. That is, it was viewed as irreconcilable, total, and of zero-sum nature; it involved violence and was protracted, and the parties involved had an interest in its continuation (Azar, Jureidini, & McLaurin, 1978; Bar-Tal, 1998; Kriesberg, 1993).

At that time, much like today, Israeli culture was marked by the events of war, conflict, and peace. In this society, ridden by continuous conflict which has lasted many decades and has involved five major wars, cultural beliefs about war, conflict, and peace were profoundly shaped by this experience. It can also be assumed that the dramatic peace with Egypt left its mark on those beliefs. Jewish Israelis believed, as many still do, that the security of Israel and its Jewish citizens was under serious threat (Bar-Tal, 1991; Stein & Brecher, 1976; Stone, 1982). Security became a cultural master symbol in the Jewish Israeli ethos (Bar-Tal, Jacobson, & Klieman, in press; Horowitz, 1984). One of the fundamental shared beliefs in Israel concerns the right and duty to cope with the threat by means of the country's own armed might (Horowitz, 1993). Therefore, all the wars, including those which Israel started, were perceived as having been forced on the Israelis and, therefore, as being justified (with the exception of the Lebanon war of 1982). Wars were thus perceived as necessary defensive acts.

All cultural channels nourished a heritage of wars and battles and glorified heroism. Military heroes received special attention and the society commemorated those who fell in military service (Lissak, 1984). This approach was extended to the treatment of Jewish history. Wars for freedom, heroic battles, fights for survival such as the Maccabean revolt in antiquity, the refusal to surrender to the Romans at Masada, Bar Kochba's rebellion during the Roman era, and, much later, the uprising of the Warsaw ghetto were presented as models for identification and admiration (Liebman & Don-Yehiya, 1983; Zerubavel, 1995). Arabs were presented as aggressors whose objective was to annihilate Israel. They were blamed for the continuation of the conflict and were presented as intransigent, refusing a peaceful resolution of the conflict (e.g., Harkabi, 1977; Landau, 1971). In contrast, the Israelis presented themselves as peace-loving people who were forced by circumstances to engage in violent conflict. Peace was always viewed as the ultimate aspiration and hope, described as a dream in utopian and idyllic images. The peace agreement with Egypt showed that peaceful conflict resolution was possible, even if the negotiations were lengthy and Israeli compromises were painful. These are the general outlines of the cultural ethos disseminated by political, social, educational, and cultural channels and institutions. Language, symbols, myths, collective memories, goals, and values were constructed on its basis (e.g., Bar-Tal, 1998; Kimmerling, 1984; Liebman & Don-Yehiya, 1983; Lissak, 1984).

This was the sociocultural environment in which the children and adolescents who participated in our study grew up. In this ethos beliefs about war, conflict, and peace had a significant place. They related directly to the experiences of the society and were embedded into the culture. Though it is hard to hypothesize the particular beliefs held by these children and adolescents, it seems reasonable to assume that in this cultural context, in which war, conflict, and peace play an important role, a complex understanding of these concepts will emerge.

Ichilov, Mazawi, and Dor (1994) collected data with closed-ended scales about perceptions of peace and war in 1988 (the beginning of the Intifada, the Palestinian uprising) among Jewish adolescents twelve to thirteen, fourteen to fifteen, and sixteen to seventeen years old. On the basis of written essays, the researchers constructed six scales to study the causes of war, preoccupation with a war's consequences, justifications to begin a war, the consequences of peace, the chances of peace, and obstacles to peace. The results showed that these Jewish adolescents were especially preoccupied with the human suffering resulting from war; they believed that lack of security is an especially justifiable reason to start a war, and with age they tended less to accept either national-religious or moral-legal causes of war. These respondents thought that wars broke out primarily because of military and political reasons; they believed that it was better to compromise than to win a new war, but they became more pessimistic with age. They had given much consideration to the military, international, personal, and social consequences of war. The present study, which uses open-ended questions, affords a comprehensive view of how Israeli children and adolescents define the concepts of war and peace and how they understand various issues related to war, conflict, and peace.

The first study, in 1986, included 293 upper-middle-class children and adolescents, 92 aged eight to nine (45 boys and 47 girls), 100 aged twelve to thirteen (54 boys and 46 girls), and 101 aged sixteen to seventeen (48 boys and 53 girls). These participants were asked to fill out a questionnaire administered in their classroom during schooltime. The questionnaire consisted of the following six open-ended questions:

1. Imagine that there is a person who does not know the word *war*. How would you explain or define it to him or her?

2. Imagine that there is a person who does not know the word *peace*. How would you explain or define it to him or her?

3. What are the things that states should do in order to secure the peace between them, so that they will continue to live in peace?

4. What are the ways to prevent a war in situations of conflict and hostility between states?

5. What are the events that can take place between states which can lead to the outbreak of war?

6. In what cases do you consider a war to be just?

The responses of the children and adolescents to each of the open-ended questions were classified into categories. A category was formed only when at least 15 percent of one age group's responses were classified into one category. Tables 8.1 and 8.2 report the percentage of the responses to the six questions according to the categories collected in 1986 and in the later study done in 1991, which will be described in the third section of this chapter. For the study done in 1986, only the percentages of the categories used in 1986 should be referred to. A response was scored in a particular category only once, but it could be classified in more than one category if it related to different content. Thus, participants received one of two possible scores in the analyses of the categories: "1" if his or her answer was included in the particular category and "0" if it was not included. Each category was analyzed using logistic regression on gender and age. The analyses showed significant age differences across almost all the categories for all the questions. Few significant gender differences were detected.

Definitions of War and Peace

In Table 8.1, the first column shows that in 1986, children eight to nine years old used in their definition of war mostly the following categories: (1) "Weapons, soldiers, and battles," which includes concrete references to conventional weapons, fighting, soldiers, and battlefields; (6) "Violent international conflict," which includes references to conflict, war, or violence between nations; (2) "Battle injury," which includes concrete descriptions of bloody fighting and injuries; (5) "Opposite of peace," which describes war as the opposite of peace or as the absence of peace; and (4) "Negative interpersonal interactions," which concretizes war in terms of interpersonal conflict, quarrels, or fights. The older group, children twelve to thirteen years old, used in their definition of war mostly the following categories: (6) "Violent international conflict"; (7) "War's causes," which describes various causes and motives for wars; (3) "Killing and death," which refers to the fact that in wars people are killed; (2) "Battle injury"; and (8) "Negative emotions and evaluations," which includes negative valuing and evaluation of war together with the expression of negative emotions such as anger, fear, sadness, or stress. Adolescents sixteen to seventeen years old predominantly used the following categories: (7) "War's causes" and (6) "Violent international conflict." They also used categories (3) "Killing and death" and (8) "Negative emotions and evaluations."

The results of the logistic regressions performed on the 1986 data indicated that the use of the following categories for the definition of war

Table 8.1. Percentage of Used Categories Classifying War Definitions, Peace Definitions, and Ways of Keeping Peace, by Age and Time.

War Definitions

	8–9	12–13	16–17
1. Weapons, soldiers, and battles			
1986	39.1	19.8	11.8
1991	41.8	39.1	20.6
2. Battle injury			
1986	26.1	30.7	8.8
1991	10.1	13.8	14.7
3. Killing and death			
1986	18.5	40.6	38.2
1991	13.9	40.2	43.1
4. Negative interpersonal interactions			
1986	20.7	19.8	4.9
1991	26.6	18.4	14.7
5. Opposite of peace			
1986	20.7	9.9	11.8
1991	7.6	9.2	9.8

Peace Definitions

	8–9	12–13	16–17
1. A greeting word (shalom)			
1986	35.9	5.0	3.9
1991	21.5	1.1	1.0
2. Situation of no war			
1986	53.3	37.6	34.3
1991	32.8	40.2	19.6
3. Interpersonal friendship			
1986	15.2	34.7	18.6
1991	19.0	32.2	22.5
4. Security and calmness			
1986	8.7	25.7	45.1
1991	19.0	32.2	34.3
5. Absence of conflict			
1986	20.7	15.8	7.8
1991	5.1	10.3	11.8

Ways of Keeping Peace

	8–9	12–13	16–17
1. Avoidance of provocations and harm			
1986	47.8	32.7	23.5
1991	29.1	14.9	15.7
2. Positive international relations			
1986	4.3	10.9	4.9
1991	10.1	17.2	22.5
3. Peace education			
1986	1.1	5.0	16.7
1991	5.1	3.4	8.8
4. Positive interpersonal behaviors			
1986	31.5	10.9	3.9
1991	13.9	9.2	9.8
5. Formal international cooperation			
1986	1.1	11.9	29.4
1991	5.1	9.2	23.5

6. Violent international conflict

1986	29.3	44.6	56.9
1991	22.8	35.6	16.7

7. War's causes

1986	12.0	44.6	79.4
1991	11.4	34.5	70.6

8. Negative emotions and evaluations

1986	18.5	28.7	25.5
1991	24.1	40.2	31.4

9. Israel and Israeli-Arab conflict

1986	16.3	2.0	0.0
1991	7.6	3.4	0.0

6. International friendship

1986	7.6	34.7	50.0
1991	13.9	36.8	42.2

7. Process of conflict resolution

1986	8.7	26.7	55.9
1991	7.6	19.5	37.3

8. Positive evaluation of peace

1986	7.6	14.9	12.7
1991	15.2	18.4	14.7

9. Positive consequences of peace

1986	4.3	16.8	18.6
1991	0.0	5.7	7.8

6. Contact between peoples

1986	3.3	23.8	34.3
1991	5.1	21.8	23.5

7. Problem solving with negotiation

1986	8.7	7.9	13.7
1991	6.3	11.5	11.8

8. Compromising and flexible political approach

1986	13.0	21.8	23.5
1991	15.2	24.1	17.6

9. Formal international agreements

1986	17.4	18.8	5.9
1991	27.8	26.4	22.5

10. Observance of agreements

1986	3.3	23.8	30.4
1991	1.3	26.4	29.4

Table 8.2. Percentage of Used Categories Classifying War Prevention in Times of Conflict, Causes of War, and Cases of Just War, by Age and Time.

War Prevention in Times of Conflict

	8–9	12–13	16–17
1. Avoidance of provocations and harm			
1986	22.8	4.0	3.9
1991	12.7	3.4	5.9
2. Actions for peace and friendship			
1986	17.4	12.9	10.8
1991	11.4	12.6	10.8
3. Concessions and positive initiatives			
1986	43.5	22.8	25.5
1991	31.6	19.5	19.6
4. Mutual compromises			
1986	10.9	36.6	40.2
1991	3.8	37.9	44.1

Causes of War

	8–9	12–13	16–17
1. Concrete harmful acts			
1986	28.3	14.9	13.7
1991	19.0	18.4	4.9
2. Terrorism			
1986	4.3	15.8	17.6
1991	11.4	12.6	10.8
3. Interpersonal conflict			
1986	27.2 17.8	1.0	14.1
1991	31.6	34.5	16.7
4. Invasion and occupation			
1986	29.3	38.6	75.5
1991	16.5	48.4	72.5

Cases of Just War

	8–9	12–13	16–17
1. There is no just war			
1986	9.8	24.8	20.6
1991	19.0	25.3	22.5
2. Important reasons and breach of agreements			
1986	16.3	36.6	26.5
1991	16.5	29.9	34.3
3. Defense in response to attack			
1986	11.9	36.3	38.2
1991	22.8	18.4	
4. Reaction to an ongoing harmful situation			
1986	25.0	32.7	22.5
1991	1.3	10.3	6.9

	1986	1991
5. Negotiations and talks	21.7 44.6 68.6	10.1 26.4 30.4
6. Peace agreement	14.1 15.8 27.5	10.1 26.4 30.4
7. Steps of peacemaking	16.3 7.9 1.0	27.8 8.0 0.0
8. Third-party intervention	1.1 14.9 36.3	0.0 11.5 18.6

	1986	1991	**5. Preventive war**
5. International conflict	38.0 54.5 46.1	19.0 35.6 42.2	1.1 3.0 22.5 / 3.8 4.6 11.8
6. Emotional causes	13.0 34.7 29.4	12.7 28.7 25.5	
7. Ideological causes	0.0 16.8 22.5	1.3 13.8 38.2	
8. Economic causes	1.1 11.9 26.5	7.6 29.9 37.3	
9. Rigidity and stupidity	3.3 9.9 15.7	7.6 14.9 24.5	
10. Espionage and provocations	14.1 15.8 4.9	8.9 6.9 2.9	

decreased with age: (1) "Weapons, soldiers, and battles," (2) "Battle injury," (4) "Negative interpersonal interactions," and (9) "Israel and Israeli-Arab conflict." In contrast, the use of the following categories for the definition of war increased with age: (3) "Killing and death," (6) "Violent international conflict," and (7) "War's causes." It was also found that girls tended to use the categories of "Killing and death" and "Israel and Israeli-Arab conflict" more than boys.

With regard to definitions of peace, the second column of Table 8.1 shows that in 1986 the youngest group mostly used the following categories in their definitions of peace: (2) "Situation of no war," which referred to the opposite of war, no war, end of war, cease-fire, and absence of violent acts; (1) "A greeting word," which defined peace in terms of a greeting word, "Shalom" (peace), which the Israelis use in Hebrew; and (5) "Absence of conflict," which included descriptions of no conflict, resolving conflict, and absence of negative feelings. The group of twelve- to thirteen-year-old adolescents most frequently used the following categories: (2) "Situation of no war"; (3) "Interpersonal friendship," which included descriptions of peace in interpersonal relations such as friendship; (6) "International friendship," which consisted of references to international coexistence, friendship, comradeship, and mutual recognition, understanding, and consideration; (7) "Process of conflict resolution," which described various processes and necessary conditions of conflict resolution to achieve peace; and (4) "Security and calmness," which referred to descriptions of a situation in which there is security, routine, calmness, and tranquility. The oldest group of adolescents predominantly used the following categories: (7) "Process of conflict resolution," (6) "International friendship," (4) "Security and calmness," and (2) "Situation of no war."

The analyses of logistic regressions indicated that the following categories were used decreasingly with age: (1) "A greeting word," (2) "Situation of no war," and (5) "Absence of conflict." In contrast, the use of the following categories for the definition of peace increased with age: (4) "Security and calmness," (6) "International friendship," (7) "Process of conflict resolution," and (9) "Positive consequences of peace." It was also found that the girls used the categories of "Interpersonal friendship" and "Security and calmness" more than boys.

Ways of Keeping Peace

In regard to the question about ways to keep peaceful relations between states, the third column of Table 8.1 shows that in 1986 the youngest children most frequently used the following categories: (1) "Avoidance of provocations and harm," which includes avoidance of concrete violent acts, spying, belligerent intentions, or other harmful behaviors; (4) "Positive interpersonal behaviors," which consists of positive interpersonal behaviors between leaders as well as between other members of the two nations, for example, visits, exchange of presents, or mutual respect; and (9) "Formal international agreements," which includes treaties, pacts, alliances, and recognition. The twelve- to thirteen-year-old adolescents mostly used (1) "Avoidance of provocations and harm"; (6) "Contact between peoples," which refers to normal relations between nations such as tourism, contacts, or visits; (10) "Observance of agreements," which refers to the need to observe signed agreements and treaties, keep promises, avoid betrayal, and fulfill commitments; and (8) "Compromising and flexible political approach," which includes concessions, flexibility, persuasion, yielding to requests, and avoiding pettiness. The oldest adolescents mostly used (6) "Contact between peoples"; (10) "Observance of agreements"; (5) "Formal international cooperation," which includes trading, cooperative ventures, various cultural and economic agreements, and cultural and information exchanges; (1) "Avoidance of provocations and harm"; and (8) "Compromising and flexible political approach."

Analyses of logistic regressions of the 1986 responses yielded the following results: the use of (1) "Avoidance of provocations and harm" and (4) "Positive interpersonal behaviors" decreased with age, while (3) "Peace education," (5) "Formal international cooperation," (6) "Contact between peoples," and (10) "Observance of agreements" increased with age. Also, the analyses showed that girls used "Avoidance of provocations and harm" more than boys, while boys used "Contact between peoples" more than girls.

War Prevention in Times of Conflict

As shown in Table 8.2, column 1, the youngest age group, when asked about ways to prevent a war in times of conflict in 1986, showed mostly use of (3) "Concessions and positive initiatives," which includes one-sided acts of concession and symbolic acts which indicated friendship and a will to avoid war; (1) "Avoidance of provocations and harm"; and (5) "Negotiations and talks," which consists of various ways of communicating with the aim to prevent war. The older age group, twelve- to thirteen-year-olds, mostly used the following categories: (5) "Negotiations and talks"; (4) "Mutual compromises," which refers to mutual concessions and compromise; and (3) "Concessions and positive initiatives." The oldest age group mostly used the following categories: (5) "Negotiations and talks"; (4) "Mutual compromises"; (8) "Third-party intervention," which includes various types of third-party interventions such as mediation or arbitration; (6) "Peace agreement," which refers to the need for a formal peace agreement in order to prevent a war; and (3) "Concessions and positive initiatives."

The results of the logistic regressions carried out on the 1986 data showed that with age there is a decrease in the use of (1) "Avoidance of provocations and harm," (3) "Concessions and positive initiatives," and (7) "Steps of peacemaking," as well as an increase in the use of (4) "Mutual compromises," (5) "Negotiations and talks," (6) "Peace agreement," and (8) "Third-party intervention." The results also showed that girls used "Mutual compromises" more than boys.

Causes of War

In 1986, the youngest children mostly used the following categories in response to the question about causes of war (Table 8.2, column 2): (5) "International conflict," which describes references to various conflicts or disagreements between states; (4) "Invasion and occupation," which refers to acts which involve taking a territory from a state, conquering it, or occupying it; (1) "Concrete harmful acts," which includes a long list of concrete harmful acts such as killing, destruction, theft, and assassination of a leader; and (3) "Interpersonal conflict," which includes terms describing interpersonal quarrels and rivalry. The young adolescents, twelve to thirteen years old, most frequently used (5) "International conflict," (4) "Invasion and occupation," and (6) "Emotional causes," which includes references to anger, hatred, jealousy, mistrust, or stress. The older group of adolescents, sixteen to seventeen years old, tended to use the following categories most often: (4) "Invasion and occupation"; (5) "International conflict"; (6) "Emotional causes"; (8) "Economic causes," a category which refers to the will to improve the economic situation or to prevent harm to economic interests; and (7) "Ideological causes," which includes various principles and ideas such as prevention of racism, religious conviction, ideological conflict, and achievement of independence.

Logistic regression analyses on the 1986 data show that with age there is a decrease in the use of the following categories: (1) "Concrete harmful acts," (3) "Interpersonal conflict," and (10) "Espionage and provocations." Also, with age, the use of (2) "Terrorism," (4) "Invasion and occupation," (5) "International conflict," (6) "Emotional causes," (7) "Ideological causes," (8) "Economic causes," and (9) "Rigidity and stupidity" increases. It was, moreover, found that girls used "International conflict" more and "Economic causes" less than boys did.

Cases of Just War

Table 8.2, column 3, shows the categories associated with participants' responses to the question "In what cases do you consider a war to be just?" It shows that the youngest group of children mostly used the category (4) "Reaction to an ongoing harmful situation," which describes various situations in which one state inflicts continuous harm on citizens of another state as, for example, in acts of terror or military action. The older age group mostly used the three following categories: (2) "Important reasons and breach of agreements," which refers to major hostile events, unbridgeable conflicts, or breach of agreements; (4) "Reaction to an ongoing harmful situation"; and (1) "There is no just war," which includes all the responses which did not recognize the possibility of a just war under any circumstances. The oldest adolescent group primarily used the following categories: (3) "Defense in response to attack," which describes a situation of defense against aggression by another state; (2) "Important reasons and breach of agreements"; (4) "Reaction to an ongoing harmful situation"; and (5) "Preventive war," which refers to motives to prevent possible future attacks.

Logistic regression analyses on the 1986 data indicated that with age there is an increase in the use of the following categories: (1) "There is no just war," (3) "Defense in response to attack," and (5) "Preventive war." The use of the category (2) "Important reasons and breach of agreements" initially increases and then decreases. Also, while girls used "Important reasons and breach of agreements" more than boys, boys used "Defense in response to attack" more than girls.

Discussion

The findings presented in this section describe the particular scope of contents of the beliefs about war, conflict, and peace held by Israeli children and adolescents. Within this scope of contents, the present study replicated the age differences found in almost every study done in other parts of the world, as well as several gender differences. The effect of age was a powerful factor which influenced the responses to all the questions. With regard to the definition of war, the youngest children mainly used concrete descriptive terms like *weapons, soldiers,* and *battles* and concrete consequential terms like *injuries,* whereas adolescents' answers pertained to the causes of war, its nature, and its tragic consequences. The definitions of the adolescents were well elaborated, included a number of categories, and provided a clear picture of what war is and why it breaks out. The definitions showed that the adolescents were very familiar with the concept and, on the basis of particular wars, were able to construct general definitions which encompassed the specific cases. The answers show that in line with the Israeli ethos, wars were seen as possible and concrete experiences which were part of international conflict—in this particular case, the Israeli-Arab conflict. This was an unavoidable event, in view of the aggressive intentions of the Arabs. The wars were perceived as negative events which had serious negative and concrete outcomes. But they were also viewed in terms of heroism, since their fighters and battles were glorified.

Our Israeli respondents suggested ten principal causes to explain the outbreak of a war. The youngest group was inclined to suggest causes pertaining to concrete harmful acts or international conflict and tended to view wars in the context of interpersonal relations. In contrast, the oldest group of adolescents overwhelmingly referred to invasion and occupation and to international conflict as causes of a war. Many of them provided specific examples. They revealed their familiarity with the different causes of the Israeli-Arab wars as presented in Israel (for example, terrorism, ideological causes, and even rigidity and stupidity). But their repertoire was surprisingly broad: they also referred to economic causes, which are very seldom used to explain wars between Israel and the Arabs.

The question of a just war is of special importance because Israel started some of the wars with the Arab nations (for example, the Sinai campaign in 1956, the Six-Day War in 1967, and the Lebanese war in 1982) and considered them to be justified. While the youngest children provided relatively few responses and had difficulty finding reasons for a just war, the oldest group saw various situations which would justify a war, especially a defensive war, but also other varieties of reasons such as a justified conflict, lack of recognition by one side, or a situation in which one side strives for peace and the other does not. The review of responses indicates that many of them are borrowed from the repertoire of the official justifications used by Israel in the past for starting wars.

In spite of the fact that Israeli children and adolescents live with the continuing and violent Middle Eastern conflict, the older age groups provided elaborate definitions of peace and suggested various methods for peacekeeping and preventing a war in times of conflict. The great majority of the adolescents' responses referred to positive peace in terms of friendship, cooperation, formal agreement, or contact (Galtung, 1985). The youngest children tended to view peace in negative terms as the absence of war or the opposite of conflict. They also tended to interpret peace in terms of interpersonal relations, either as a (Hebrew) greeting term or as referring to interpersonal friendships. But with age, the definitions became more complex and knowledgeable: adolescents mentioned international processes of conflict resolution, peace processes, the consequences of peace, and positive international relations—all elements found in the strong aspiration for peace expressed in the Israeli ethos. The Israeli adolescents possessed a vivid example of how to make peace and how to keep it: the peace accord with Egypt and ways to maintain it in spite of various disagreements were two subjects often discussed in the public debates in the 1980s. The adolescents of the present study, and especially the oldest group, proposed a number of well-accepted ways to keep a peace and to prevent a war. They proposed contacts between people, formal cooperation, observance of agreements, mutual compromises and negotiations, and talks; all these have a powerfully reciprocal component which dominates the Israeli approach to peace.

The results of the present study regarding gender differences are in line with previous findings which show that girls tend to focus more than boys on human costs in their definition of war (Cooper, 1965; Hakvoort, 1996). They also emphasize interpersonal friendship and security and calmness in their definition of peace more than boys do (Hakvoort & Oppenheimer, 1993; Hall, 1993). The responses showed, moreover, that girls mentioned more than boys avoidance of provocations as a way of peacekeeping, mutual compromises as a way of preventing war in times of conflict, international conflict as a cause of war, and breach of agreement as a justification for a war. In contrast, boys referred more than girls to contact between nations as a way of peacekeeping, economic conflict as a cause of war, and self-defense in response to attack as a justification for war.

In sum, the responses of the Israeli children and adolescents to various questions pertaining to issues of war, conflict, and peace indicate the richness of their cognitive repertoire. The responses reflected the scope of contents prevailing in the Israeli culture. Only rarely did a respondent give just one answer. Many responses related to two or more different categories which illuminated different aspects of the issue. These results indicate familiarity with the investigated concepts and issues, which play such a central role in Israeli culture.

The Effect of the Gulf War on the Understanding of Concepts of War, Conflict, and Peace

The second study sheds light on the influence of situational factors on the understanding of war, conflict, and peace. On January 17, 1991, the Gulf War broke out after Iraq failed to comply with the United Nations' ultimatum to evacuate its troops from Kuwait by January 15, 1991. The allies started the war with massive attacks on Iraq and Kuwait, and Iraq reacted by launching Scud missiles against Israel and Saudi Arabia. Thirty-nine missiles were launched against Israel, most of them falling in the densely populated area of Tel Aviv. It was the first time in Israel's history that its entire civilian population came under the threat of a chemical missile attack. Directly and indirectly, the fired missiles left nine dead, hundreds injured, and extensive property damage (over ten thousand private dwellings and shops were damaged). Also, over 100,000 people left their homes in the targeted area of metropolitan Tel Aviv for safe havens in other parts of the country. The war was continuously televised and families watched events closely. Needless to say, the Gulf War, like all other wars, had dramatic effects on Israeli children (see reviews by Klingman, Sagi, & Raviv, 1993; Milgram, 1993, 1994).

When the war ended and schools reopened their gates, we collected a new set of data about children's and adolescents' understanding of the concepts of war, conflict, and peace with the questionnaire described earlier. We returned to the same schools and grade levels which took part in the 1986 study, on the assumption that the socioeconomic characteristics of the new sample would be similar to those of the earlier sample of children and adolescents. In the second study, 257 children and adolescents participated: 77 aged eight to nine (39 boys and 38 girls), 82 aged twelve to thirteen (43 boys and 39 girls), and 98 aged sixteen to seventeen (32 boys and 66 girls). Their responses were classified into the same categories as those used in the first study and according to the same principles.

The participating children and adolescents lived in the area targeted by the Scud missiles, which allowed an examination of the effect of the situational factor: the Gulf War. The overall conditions had not changed as yet in 1991; Israel was still engaged in conflict with Arab states and the Palestinians. The Madrid conference, which opened the peace process, was to take place later, at the end of 1991, and therefore it was assumed that the basic cultural beliefs of society in 1986 were still prevailing in 1991. Indeed, the wide scope analysis of the Israeli beliefs about peace and war shows that very minor changes took place between 1986 and 1991 (Arian, 1995).

Results

The percentages of used categories for the 1991 sample are also presented in Tables 8.1 and 8.2. Logistic regressions were conducted on the data, consisting of the two samples (1986 and 1991), with age, gender, and time as independent variables. The percentages and analyses show that in general, children's and adolescents' responses in 1991 replicated the age differences found in 1986. The trends of the responses are similar in both samples. Most of the second-stage analyses done on the two samples yielded significant age and gender effects for the same categories and in the same directions as those of the first stage with the 1986 sample described earlier.

Of special interest would be any significant differences between the responses of children and adolescents in 1986 and the responses given in 1991. The results showed that after the Gulf War more children and adolescents defined the war by using the categories of "Weapons, soldiers, and battles" and "Negative emotions and evaluations" than in 1986 (see Table 8.1, column 1). Also, after the Gulf War there was less use of the category of "Violent international conflict" than in 1986. In addition, the results show three interaction effects. Two interactions are of age by time. One shows that while the two younger age groups used the category of "Battle injury" more in 1986 than in 1991, the oldest age group used this category less in 1986 than in 1991. The other interaction shows that while in 1986 there is a considerable and steady increase in the use of the category "Violent international conflict" with age, in 1991 this increase occurs initially and up to the twelve- to thirteen-year-old group, after which the use of this category drops again. An interaction of gender by time shows that while in 1986 more girls than boys selected the category "Killing and death" to define a war, in 1991 there was no difference between these two groups.

With regard to the definition of peace, Table 8.1, column 2, shows that in 1991 the categories "A greeting word," "Situation of no war," "Absence of conflict," "Process of conflict resolution," and "Positive consequences of peace" were referred to less than in 1986. Two interaction effects of age by time showed that (1) while the two younger groups used the category "Security and calmness" more in 1991 than in 1986, the oldest group used it more in 1986 than in 1991, and (2) while the two younger groups used the category "Absence of conflict" less in 1991 than in 1986, the oldest group used it less in 1986 than in 1991.

The analyses of the responses to the question about ways of keeping peace show that while in 1991 children and adolescents used the category "Avoidance of provocations and harm" less than in 1986, they used the categories "Positive international relations" and "Formal international agreements" more than in 1986 (see Table 8.1, column 3). Also, two interaction effects indicate that (1) while the youngest group used "Peace education" more in 1991 than in 1986, the oldest group used it more in 1986 than in 1991, and (2) while the youngest group used "Positive interpersonal behaviors" less in 1991 than in 1986, the oldest group used it less in 1986 than in 1991.

Only one time effect was found with regard to the question about ways to prevent war in times of conflict (see Table 8.2, column 1). In 1991 children and adolescents referred to the category "Third-party intervention" less than in 1986. An interaction effect of gender by time shows that while in 1986 no gender difference was found with regard to the use of the category "Avoidance of provocations and harm," in 1991 girls used it more than boys. Finally, an interaction effect of age by gender shows that the use of the category "Peace agreement" does not differ among the boys of all age groups, but its use increases with age among girls.

The analyses of responses defining the causes of war showed a number of time-related differences. While in 1986 children and adolescents used the categories "Terrorism," "International conflict," and "Espionage and provocations" more than in 1991, in 1986 they used the categories "Interpersonal conflict," "Economic causes," and "Rigidity and stupidity" less than in 1991 (see Table 8.2, column 2). One interaction effect showed that while the two older groups used the category "Interpersonal conflict" more in 1991 than in 1986, no difference was found for the youngest group.

The analyses of responses to the question about cases of just war yielded one significant time effect (see Table 8.2, column 3). Children and adolescents used the category "Reaction to an ongoing harmful situation" less in 1991 than in 1986. Two interaction effects of gender by time show the following: (1) more girls than boys used the category "Important reasons and breach of agreements" in 1986 and no difference was found in 1991, and (2) more boys than girls used the category "Defense in response to attack" in 1986 and no difference was found in 1991.

Finally, it should be noted that the questions pertaining to conflict and war yielded answers which were based on participants' specific recent experiences of the Gulf War. For example, some answers described experiences in shelters or referred directly to the Gulf War. None of these categories reached use by at least 15 percent of one age group and therefore they were not included in the analyses. Nevertheless, these answers provide evidence that the Gulf War affected children's and adolescents' conceptions of war and conflict.

Discussion

Comparisons of responses given in 1986 with responses given in 1991 show several differences. The latter show clear traces of the experience of the Gulf War, although we must state this with some reservation, since different children responded to the same questions at different points in time. But since the respondents' samples were similar with regard to their background, since the general age trends were well replicated in 1991, and since we assumed that the respondents' cultural background did not change significantly between 1986 and 1991, it is possible to attribute the found differences to the effects of the Gulf War. That is, in responding to general questions about war, conflict, and peace, children and adolescents used their own experiences of the Gulf War in answering. They generalized their particular perception of the Gulf War to the perception of wars, conflict, and peace in general.

Definitions of war in 1991 included more concrete concepts of weapons, soldiers, and battles, as well as more negative emotions and evaluations, since the 1991 respondents had experienced war themselves. Also, this group saw the war on television, which covered it extensively. Because of the nature of this particular war and constraints on the televised reports, battle injuries were frequently shown and therefore the use of this category decreased in 1991, especially by the two younger groups. The definitions of a war in 1991 indicate that the Gulf War was not seen as an international conflict, but more in terms of an interpersonal conflict between leaders (particularly Iraqi president Saddam Hussein), economic causes (especially oil), and rigidity and stupidity (especially that of the Iraqi president), as revealed in the answers to the question about the causes of war. In addition, the answers to this question in 1991, in comparison with the answers given in 1986, showed a decrease in references to international conflict, espionage and provocation, and terrorism. The Gulf War did not involve terrorism or espionage and these categories almost disappeared in 1991. Following the war, adolescents mentioned third-party intervention less when considering how to prevent a war in times of conflict. This decrease may be considered unsurprising in view of the fact that third parties did not succeed in preventing the Gulf War.

Finally, the Gulf War also affected responses about the cases of just war. In 1991, in comparison with 1986, more children and adolescents suggested that a war is justified in the case of an attack by another country, as the Gulf War was justified, and fewer children and adolescents used the category of reaction to an ongoing harmful situation to justify a war. It can be assumed that the Gulf War also affected the understanding of peace. In 1991 peace was seen as involving processes of conflict resolution, as absence of war or conflict, and as related to its consequences less than in 1986. Children and younger adolescents, unsurprisingly, tended to see peace as related to security and calmness. This may well have been an outcome of the experience of the Gulf War. Also, following the Gulf War, the use of categories related to positive international relations and formal international agreements as ways of peacekeeping increased. In contrast, avoidance of provocations and harm was less frequently mentioned. It is possible that the Gulf War clearly demonstrated, especially to the adolescents, the importance of making and observing international agreements, as well as of maintaining positive international relations.

The effects of the Gulf War were not noticeable in all the responses of the participating children and adolescents, however. The tables also show that the use of many of the categories did not change in five years. In fact, no time effect was obtained in the majority of the analyses. This lack of significant differences indicates the stability of the cultural factor over time. The Gulf War had a relatively limited effect on Israelis' social knowledge, which is greatly and continuously influenced by the protracted Middle Eastern conflict.

Conclusion

The two studies which were presented here provide an illustration of how developmental, cultural, and situational factors shape beliefs about war, conflict, and peace. These beliefs are formed on the basis of information provided by external sources or one's own experiences. Few concepts are so important and, at the same time, so charged with meaning as the concepts of war, conflict, and peace. This is so because the events related to them are crucial determinants of individuals' and societies' well-being. Every society is likely to be familiar, to a greater or lesser degree, with such events, which are usually related to major cultural beliefs and expressed in collective memories, rituals, myths, and traditions. These give meaning to the past experiences of the society and provide a framework for understanding the present. Needless to say, societies differ in their past experiences and therefore form different understandings of these concepts and beliefs on the basis of their experiences.

Society members acquire these important concepts and related beliefs from early childhood, first from their parents; then in schools, which provide formal societal knowledge through textbooks and teachers; and also through the media and other cultural products. Children and adolescents thus acquire the particular meaning of the concepts related to war, conflict, and peace as members of a particular society with its particular culture. It is thus not surprising that studies have shown that war, conflict, and peace are understood differently by children and adolescents in different cultures (e.g., Cooper, 1965; Hakvoort, Hägglund, & Oppenheimer, in press).

The relatively stable cultural conceptual framework is not the only factor, however, which determines the understanding of conceptions about war, conflict, and peace. Another important determinant is the situational factor. Thus, when children and adolescents have direct experiences of wars or violent conflicts (viewed as situational factors), these experiences provide direct information about what these events are and affect their meaning. When the experiences are powerful, they can be very influential in the formation of beliefs about war, conflict, and peace. They can sometimes even override previous knowledge and serve as the sole basis for the formation of new beliefs. Research shows that children and adolescents who have direct experience of a war or a violent conflict form a particular understanding of concepts related to this event (e.g., Cairns et al., 1996; Punamäki, 1987; see also Chapters Six and Seven of this volume).

Beyond these cultural and situational factors, the understanding of conceptions related to war, conflict, and peace is also determined by universal developmental limitations; that is, it also depends on the child's cognitive capacities, which develop with age. The results of the present studies show that the youngest children, aged eight to nine, have well-defined ideas about various conceptions related to war, conflict, and peace, but their understanding of these concepts is different from that of the older adolescents. The responses to all six open-ended questions show clear age differences; this replicates findings in other countries. With age, the responses are less concrete, are more sophisticated and differentiated, refer less to interpersonal relations and more to international relations, and mention more consequences and underlying reasons and more emotions and evaluations. These findings are in line with the results of other studies which have investigated the development of an understanding of conceptions related to war, conflict, and peace (Ålvik, 1968; Cooper, 1965; Covell et al., 1994; Hägglund et al., 1996; Tolley, 1973). It should be noted that the cultural and situational factors are reflected in the particular contents of beliefs about war, conflict, and peace. Investigation of these beliefs shows how the members of a society understand these concepts. In contrast, the developmental factor is reflected in the general structures of the concepts, which pertain to the level of concreteness, sophistication, differentiation, and so on.

The present conceptual framework focused on three aggregate factors: the developmental factor, the cultural factor, and the situational factor. In doing so, it overlooks individual variables, which also significantly affect individuals' understanding of war, conflict, and peace and which are responsible for individual differences in these notions. Future research should investigate these variables. The research on the formation of beliefs of children, adolescents, and adults about war, conflict, and peace is still at its beginning. Wars, conflicts, and peace are initiated, carried out, and ended by human beings. Given the fact that individuals and societies act on the basis of their beliefs, the importance of research into the nature and formation of these beliefs should be self-evident.

REFERENCES

Ålvik, T. (1968). The development of views on conflict, war and peace among school children. *Journal of Peace Research, 5,* 171–195.

Arian, A. (1995). *Security threatened: Surveying Israeli opinion on peace and war.* Cambridge: Cambridge University Press.

Azar, E. E., Jureidini, P., & McLaurin, R. (1978). Protracted social conflict: Theory and practice in the Middle East. *Journal of Palestine Studies, 8* (1), 41–60.

Bar-Tal, D. (1990). *Group beliefs: A conception for analyzing group structure, processes and behavior.* New York: Springer-Verlag.

Bar-Tal, D. (1991). Contents and origins of the Israelis' beliefs about security. *International Journal of Group Tensions, 21,* 237–261.

Bar-Tal, D. (1998). Societal beliefs in times of intractable conflict: The Israeli case. *International Journal of Conflict Management, 9,* 22–50.

Bar-Tal, D. (in press). *Societal beliefs of ethos: A social psychological analysis of a society.* Thousand Oaks, CA: Sage.

Bar-Tal, D., Jacobson, D., & Klieman, A. (Eds.). (in press). *Security concerns: Insights from Israel's experience.* Greenwich, CT: JAI Press.

Bar-Tal, D., & Kruglanski, A. W. (1988). The social psychology of knowledge: Its scope and meaning. In D. Bar-Tal & A. W. Kruglanski (Eds.), *The social psychology of knowledge* (pp. 1–14). Cambridge: Cambridge University Press.

Bar-Tal, D., & Saxe, L. (1991). Acquisition of political knowledge: A social psychological analysis. In O. Ichilov (Ed.), *Political socialization, citizenship education and democracy* (pp. 116–133). New York: Teachers College Press.

Bem, D. J. (1970). Beliefs, attitudes and human affairs. Pacific Grove, CA: Brooks/Cole.

Cairns, E., McClenahan, C., & Hosin, A. (1996). The impact of political violence on children's ideas about peace: Evidence from Northern Ireland. In S. Hägglund, I. Hakvoort, & L. Oppenheimer (Eds.), *Research on children and peace: International perspective* (pp. 30–39) (Reports from the Department of Education and Educational Research, Report No. 1996:04). Göteborg, Sweden: Göteborg University.

Cooper, P. (1965). The development of the concept of war. *Journal of Peace Research, 2,* 1–17.

Covell, K., Rose-Krasnor, L., & Fletcher, K. (1994). Age differences in understanding peace, war, and conflict resolution. *International Journal of Behavioral Development, 17,* 717–737.

Damon, W. (1977). *The social world of the child.* San Francisco: Jossey-Bass.

D'Andrade, B. G. (1984). Cultural meaning systems. In R. A. Shweder & R. A. LeVine (Eds.), *Culture theory* (pp. 88–119). Cambridge: Cambridge University Press.

Dawson, R. E., & Prewitt, K. (1969). *Political socialization.* New York: Little, Brown.

Dougherty, J. W. D. (Ed.). (1985). *Directions in cognitive anthropology.* Urbana: University of Illinois Press.

Easton, D., & Dennis, J. (1969). *Children in the political system.* New York: McGraw-Hill.

Ehman, L. H. (1980). The American school in the political socialization process. *Review of Educational Research, 50,* 99–119.

Galtung, J. (1985). Twenty-five years of peace research: Ten challenges and some responses. *Journal of Peace Research, 22,* 145–157.

Griswold, W. (1994). *Cultures and societies in a changing world.* Newbury Park, CA: Pine Forge Press.

Hägglund, S., Hakvoort, I., & Oppenheimer, L. (Eds.). (1996). *Research on children and peace: International perspectives.* Göteborg, Sweden: Göteborg University, Department of Education and Educational Research.

Hakvoort, I. (1996). *Conceptualization of peace and war from childhood through adolescence: A social-cognitive developmental approach.* Unpublished doctoral dissertation, University of Amsterdam, Amsterdam, The Netherlands.

Hakvoort, I., Hägglund, S., & Oppenheimer, L. (in press). Dutch and Swedish adolescents' understanding of peace and war. In J. E. Nurmi (Ed.), *Adolescents, cultures and conflicts: Growing up in contemporary Europe.* New York: Garland.

Hakvoort, I., & Oppenheimer, L. (1993). Children and adolescents' conceptions of peace, war and strategies to attain peace: A Dutch case study. *Journal of Peace Research, 30,* 65–77.

Hall, R. (1993). How children think and feel about war and peace: An Australian study. *Journal of Peace Research, 30,* 181–196.

Harkabi, Y. (1977). *Arab strategies and Israel's response.* New York: Free Press.

Hess, R. D., & Torney, J. V. (1967). *The development of political attitudes in children.* Hawthorne, NY: Aldine de Gruyter.

Horowitz, D. (1984). Israeli perception of national security (1948–1972). In B. Neuberger (Ed.), *Diplomacy and confrontation: Selected issues in Israel's foreign relations, 1948–1978* (pp. 104–148). Tel Aviv: Everyman's University. (In Hebrew)

Horowitz, D. (1993). The Israeli concept of national security. In A. Yaniv (Ed.), *National security and democracy in Israel* (pp. 11–53). Boulder, CO: Lynne Rienner.

Ichilov, O., Mazawi, A., & Dor, O. (1994). *Perception of peace and war by Jewish and Arab adolescents in Israel.* (Research Report). Tel Aviv, Israel: Tel Aviv University, Unit of Sociology of Education and Community, School of Education. (In Hebrew)

Inhelder, B., & Piaget, J. (1958). *The growth of logical thinking from childhood to adolescence.* New York: Basic Books.

Kimmerling, B. (1984). Making conflict a routine: A cumulative effect of the Arab-Jewish conflict upon Israeli society. In M. Lissack (Ed.), *Israeli society and its defense establishment* (pp. 13–45). London: Frank Cass.

Klingman, A., Sagi, A., & Raviv, A. (1993). The effect of war on Israeli children. In L. A. Leavitt & N. A. Fox (Eds.), *Psychological effects of war and violence on children* (pp. 75–92). Hillsdale, NJ: Erlbaum.

Kriesberg, L. (1993). Intractable conflicts. *Peace Review, 5* (4), 17–421.

Kruglanski, A. W. (1989). *Lay epistemics and human knowledge.* New York: Plenum.

Landau, J. J. (1971). *Israel and the Arabs.* Jerusalem: Israel Communication.

Liebman, C. S., & Don-Yehiya, E. (1983). *Civil religion in Israel: Traditional Judaism and political culture in the Jewish state.* Berkeley: University of California Press.

Lissak, M. (Ed.). (1984). *Israeli society and its defense establishment.* London: Frank Cass.

McGuire, W. J. (1986). The vicissitudes of attitudes and similar representational constructs in twentieth century psychology. *European Journal of Social Psychology, 16,* 89–130.

Milgram, N. (1993). Stress and coping in Israel during the Gulf War. *Journal of Social Issues, 49,* 103–123.

Milgram, N. (1994). Israel and the Gulf War: The major events and selected studies. *Anxiety, Stress, and Coping, 7,* 205–215.

Neisser, U. (Ed.). (1987). *Concepts and conceptual development: Ecological and intellectual factors in categorization.* Cambridge: Cambridge University Press.

Piaget, J. (1950). *Psychology of intelligence.* Orlando: Harcourt Brace.

Piaget, J. (1970). Piaget's theory. In P. Mussen (Ed.), *Carmichael's manual of child psychology* (3rd ed., Vol. 1, pp. 703–732). New York: Wiley.

Punamäki, R.-L. (1987). *Childhood under conflict: The attitudes and emotional life of Israeli and Palestinian children.* Tampere: Tampere Peace Research Institute.

Renshon, S. A. (Ed.). (1977). *Handbook of political socialization.* New York: Free Press.

Roberts, J. M. (1964). The self-management of cultures. In W. H. Goodenough (Ed.), *Explorations in cultural anthropology* (pp. 433–454). New York: McGraw-Hill.

Rosell, L. (1968). Children's views of war and peace. *Journal of Peace Research, 5,* 268–276.

Shantz, C. (1975). The development of social cognition. In E. M. Hetherington (Ed.), *Review of child development research* (Vol. 5, pp. 257–323). Chicago: University of Chicago Press.

Spielmann, M. (1986). If peace comes . . . Future expectations of Israeli children and youth. *Journal of Peace Research, 23,* 51–67.

Stein, J. B., & Brecher, M. (1976). Image, advocacy and the analysis of conflict: An Israeli case study. *Jerusalem Journal of International Relations, 1,* 33–58.

Stone, R. A. (1982). *Social change in Israel.* New York: Praeger.

Tolley, H. (1973). *Children and war.* New York: Teachers College Press.

Turiel, E. (1983). *The development of social knowledge.* Cambridge: Cambridge University Press.

Zerubavel, Y. (1995). *Recovered roots: Collective memory and the making of Israeli national tradition.* Chicago: University of Chicago Press.

9

PEER RELATIONSHIPS AND CHILDREN'S UNDERSTANDING OF PEACE AND WAR

A SOCIOCULTURAL PERSPECTIVE

Solveig Hägglund, Göteborg University

EMPIRICAL STUDIES SHOW that children, when asked to describe what peace is, tend to refer to negation of war. It has also been reported that when peace is given a meaning without reference to war, small children talk about qualities in personal relationships such as friendship, cooperation, trust, loyalty, and social responsibility. And although they mention negation of war and interpersonal relationships, older children and adolescents also refer to qualities in societal structures such as democracy, equality, and justice (Hakvoort, 1996). Furthermore, similar concepts to those referred to by older children and adolescents when talking about peace also occur when young people are asked to explain or define concepts such as democracy (Moodie, Marková, & Plichtová, 1995) and human rights (Macek, Oseká, & Kostron, 1997). Children's and adolescents' tendency to relate peace to war (and more rarely the opposite), and to link other concepts to these two, illustrates that when we study the understanding of peace and war, we are dealing with multidimensional and complex constructs that cannot easily be separated from each other. It seems a likely assumption that peace and war belong to a set of concepts that represent ideological and normative aspects of the social world.

Looking more closely at the content in children's and adolescents' views of peace and war as reported in the literature, two dimensions are discerned that are recognized as elements in social knowledge (Bennett, 1993). One concerns sociomoral norms for human interaction; the other is related to knowledge of social structures and power relations. Normative rules for human relationships, such as trust and social concern, and qualities in societal structures, such as distribution of power and social justice, constitute elements of the cultural fabric into which a child is born. Any child in any society learns what is socially expected and accepted when interacting with others. Children also reach insights about social, political, and economic hierarchies and their meaning in relation to their own and the group's position.

According to sociocultural theoretical perspectives, development, learning, and socialization are interwoven with the particular cultural contexts in which they take place (Bronfenbrenner, 1979; Winegar & Valsiner, 1992). If the understanding of peace and war is regarded as an element in children's social knowledge of their sociocultural environment, then peace and war will be perceived by the child as both social phenomena and representations, as concrete events and as communication *about* such events. Undoubtedly, conditions for experiencing peace and war as "real" differ. It goes without saying that a child born in a society in which war and violence are experienced daily faces a different reality for learning to understand the meaning of peace and war than a child who meets war primarily on television.

The development of social knowledge is not only an affair between the sociocultural environment in general and the individual child. The importance of the intermediate social level, that is, particular social settings and particular social relationships, has been demonstrated in the literature. For example, intersubjectivity has been shown to influence social cognition (Bruner, 1986; Forman, 1992), and social experience and interaction have been reported to have an impact on the construction of social rules and social knowledge (Emler & Dickinson, 1993; Turiel, 1983; Turiel, Smetana, & Killen, 1991). Furthermore, the influence of peer interaction on socialization, development, and learning has been described and demonstrated with reference to the unique properties of peer interaction compared with adult-child interaction (Corsaro, 1990; Frønes, 1995; Piaget, 1932).

When the conceptualization of peace and war is regarded as part of an ongoing process of learning about social phenomena, social symbols, and social meaning that takes place in the child's close social environment, a description of the child's understanding of peace and war is not complete without taking this environment into consideration. In addition, if social experience and social interaction constitute the contextual frames within which children's interpretations and understanding of peace and war are elaborated, then the interpersonal level constitutes an obvious unit for description and analysis of the social construction of peace and war.

This chapter focuses on children's understanding of peace and war in the light of such a perspective on development. The theme was originally inspired by the observation that children, particularly during middle childhood, refer to various aspects of peer relationships when they are asked to verbalize their understanding of peace and war. In one way or another, norms and rules for interaction with peers seem to be relevant for children's ideas of peace and war. Stating that there seems to be a link between peer relationships and children's understanding of peace and war is in itself rather trivial. The ambition here, however, is to take one step away from the trivial by discussing sociocultural theoretical approaches that allow for a deeper elaboration of the relation between peer relationships and children's understanding of peace and war. As an introduction to this discussion, the two sections that follow present some empirical accounts of children's and adolescents' understanding of peace and war and a brief review of research on peer relationships and friendship. Then three theoretical approaches are discussed. The conclusion of this discussion points to the necessity to broaden the theoretical scope in empirical research by embracing the social level in our models of analysis of children's understanding of peace and war. The chapter ends with some final comments.

Conceptualization of Peace and War

What do we know about children's and adolescents' ideas about peace and war? In her review of empirical studies conducted between 1965 and 1992, Hakvoort concludes that some common observations are discernible (Hakvoort, 1996). Although researchers have used different theoretical and methodological approaches, there is empirical support for stating that children can formulate their understanding of peace and war around the age of six or seven. There are exceptions that indicate a somewhat higher age for the understanding of peace.

Age-related patterns of variation have been observed, although they are not totally consistent. Younger children refer to peace as friendship and the absence of quarrels, while war is described in terms of concrete war activities and war objects. With increasing age, children express their ideas in more complex and abstract terms (Haavelsrud, 1970; Hall 1993; Spielmann, 1986). Older children and adolescents are more inclined to connect peace with international cooperation, reconciliation, and equality, while they refer to war in terms of its negative consequences. In her own longitudinal investigation, Hakvoort (1996) confirmed some of the earlier findings concerning age-related variations in the conceptualization of peace. Of particular interest here is the fact that an increased tendency to perceive peace as a positive interpersonal relationship (for example, being friends and playing) was found between the ages of six and ten. Hakvoort also showed that when they were asked about how to attain peace, the younger children emphasized the importance of being and making friends, while the adolescents referred to strategies involving disarmament, caring for nature and people, sharing, and universal rights.

Apart from age, gender is also a source of variation. Even if the overall picture of the influence of gender in children's and adolescents' conceptions of peace and war is far from consistent, there is a general tendency for girls to express their views and attitudes in more social, emotional, and personal terms, while boys are more oriented toward objects, actions, and international aspects (Cooper, 1965; Falk & Selg, 1982; Haavelsrud, 1970; Hakvoort & Oppenheimer, 1993; Hall, 1993; Von Jacob & Schmidt, 1988; Rosell, 1968). This confirms a well-known picture of gender differences in sociomoral orientation (Bem, 1993; Hägglund, 1986; Gilligan, Ward, Taylor, & Bardige, 1988) and in friendship patterns (Berndt, 1982; Pitcher & Hickey Schultz, 1983; Lever, 1978; Youniss & Smollar, 1985).

Some studies indicate that sociocultural factors, such as political ideologies, institutional practice, social conventions, norms, and traditions, contribute to variations in the content of concepts of peace and war (Cairns, McClenahan, & Hosin, 1996; Dinklage & Ziller, 1989; Hakvoort, 1996; Oppenheimer, 1996; Spielmann, 1986; Tolley, 1973). However, investigations explicitly designed for systematic assessments of the influence of defined sociocultural variables on the content in children's ideas of peace and war have not been conducted.

Although this summary is very brief, it distinguishes a general (and well-known) developmental pattern: younger children tend to express their ideas in concrete terms, while older children and adolescents refer more often to abstract values and ideologies. It is interesting to note that "concrete peace" in this sense seems to mean friends, while "concrete war" seems to mean war objects and war activities. The friendship theme was also present in Hakvoort's study when children were asked how peace can be attained. According to the younger children, good strategies would be to be friends, to make friends, and to refrain from fights and quarrels (Hakvoort, 1996).

There are reasons to believe that the increased use of references to friendship during early and middle childhood corresponds to something in the children's lives. It may be reasonable to assume that children of this age are busy forming friendship relations, and that they are occupied in finding out about norms, conventions, rules, and values that are linked to social relationships, particularly with peers. In order to look more closely at this issue, the following section presents a brief review of research on peer relationships and friendship patterns during childhood.

Peer Relationships and Friendship

A large number of studies have been conducted on peer relationships and their role in development and socialization, and it is not possible to present a fair picture of the entire field of research here. In order to limit the excursion into the literature, I will focus on three major questions related to the major theme of this chapter. The first one concerns developmental patterns of peer relationships and friendship. Does the literature confirm the notion made in the preceding section that children during early and middle childhood are particularly intensive in their formation of peer relationships? The second question concerns children's perceptions of friendship. Are there empirical results in this area of research that correspond to those that have been found in research on the conceptualization of peace and war? The third question concerns the influence of peer relationships on development. Are there any empirical data that may support an assumption that peer relationships influence the development of social knowledge?

Several studies show that stable relationships among children develop in early childhood. Infants and toddlers have been observed to manage social skills in dyadic relationships, indicating close and established relationships (Foot, Chapman, & Smith, 1980; Hartup, 1982, 1989; Howes, 1983). According to Hartup, it has been shown that with increasing age, a more differentiated pattern appears in terms of time spent with other children and interaction styles. Reviewing studies of children's friendships, he concludes that cooperation, reciprocity, competition, and conflict can serve as descriptors of characteristics of interaction with relevance for development. While cooperation and reciprocity seem to be important ingredients in younger children's friendship relationships, competition and conflict may even strengthen friendship bonds in middle childhood and adolescence (Hartup, 1989).

Gender differences have been observed in peer-group formation. Girls tend to establish dyadic, reciprocal relationships, while boys form larger peer groups with less exclusiveness in regard to newcomers (Whiting & Edwards, 1988). However, Hartup argues for more complex research designs in order to reveal the complexity in children's development of friendship relationships. According to him, it is particularly urgent to take contextual factors and sex differences into account (Hartup, 1989).

Children's growing understanding of friendship has been the subject of several investigations. Some authors argue that the concept of friendship is developed in hierarchical stages (Bigelow, 1977), while others suggest that the emerging differentiation occurs in a cumulative manner (Berndt, 1981). Children have been observed to use the word *friend* starting in the early preschool years. Gradually, the concept of friendship becomes more differentiated and elaborated, including not only play and mutual association but also aspects of social reciprocity such as mutual understanding and loyalty. Older children refer to friendship as a relationship with a certain commitment: a friend is someone you defend in threatening situations (Hartup, 1989). Cooperation and conflict have been examined in behavioral manifestations as well as in children's verbalization of friendship. Of particular interest for the present discussion is the observation that during middle childhood, conflicts seem to be more common among friends than among nonfriends, although this is not as clear for preschoolers and adolescents (Hartup, French, Laursen, Johnston, & Ogawa, 1993).

A large number of studies demonstrate the role of peer interaction in various aspects of development such as personality, social behavior, and academic achievement (Berndt, 1989). However, it is emphasized that peer groups only make up a part of children's lives. Interaction with parents, siblings, teachers, and others also play a significant role in development. In addition, particularly during adolescence, several peer groups with various functions contribute to experiences and development. According to Berndt (1989), "Specifying the position of peer relationships in regard to [the] multitude of influences is likely to be more rewarding, in the long run, than a single-minded focus on peer relationships themselves" (p. 415). The functions of peer groups have been suggested to include "the development of social identity, the sharing of norms of social behaviour, the practice of social skills and the establishment of social structures" (Durkin, 1995, p. 143). Consequently, the issue of peer interaction and development includes individual development as well as interpersonal thought and action.

In sum, peer relationships and friendship constitute an important part of a child's social context. The difference between friends and nonfriends is a question of stability and mutuality. It seems as if middle childhood constitutes a period when conflicts are as common as cooperation among friends. With regard to gender differences, girls tend to be more oriented toward dyadic relationships than boys are. The conceptualization of friendship starts at an early age and becomes more differentiated by age, including affective aspects as well as normative ones. The influence of peer interaction on development appears to be important but complex.

Comparing the studies discussed here with what was reported earlier on the conceptualization of peace and war, we can now comment on the three questions that were formulated in the beginning of this section. Reported developmental patterns confirm that middle childhood is a socially intensive period when it comes to establishing and elaborating peer relationships. An increasing tendency to refer to friendship and interpersonal interactions when asked about peace thus corresponds to children's social reality during this age period. Concerning the second question, research on children's conceptualization of friendship shows a similar pattern of increasing abstraction, complexity, and differentiation in children's ideas, as has been demonstrated in research on the conceptualization of peace and war.

The third question is whether any empirical data support the assumption that peer relationships influence social knowledge in general and children's understanding of peace and war in particular. Although some studies indicate that peer relationships do influence developmental outcomes, the results are often questioned because of the difficulty in separating the unique contribution of peer relationships. It can be argued that studies aimed at assessing the influence of complex independent variables, such as peer relationships, on multidimensional dependent variables, such as the concepts of peace and war, are likely to end up with results that are blurred and questionable. Compared, for example, with studying the influence of peer tutoring in classrooms on specified academic skills, our problem is more difficult in terms of assessment procedures and definitions of variables.

What kind of research design is needed, then, in order to build in and handle complexity? The majority of the studies referred to in the empirical reviews were designed according to theoretical paradigms and models based on developmental psychology. Most investigations were aimed at describing, analyzing, and/or explaining developmental patterns in cognition, social cognition, or behavioral manifestations; their variations; and the causes of these variations. When the purpose is to describe and analyze children's understanding of social concepts as they are developed within particular social settings, traditional cause-and-effect models need to be completed with models based on theoretical approaches that emphasize content issues rather than outcomes. Or, more explicitly expressed, in order to find out the nature of the link between children's ideas about peace and war and their experiences with peer relationships, it is probably less meaningful to look for the one-way influence of peer relationships on conceptions than to look for processes with mutual influences in both directions, that is, those in which experiences in the peer group influence children's ideas and vice versa. In the next section I will suggest theoretical models that allow for such an approach.

Sociocultural Theoretical Perspectives

The theoretical perspectives that are introduced in this section share a similar paradigm for the meaning of the sociocultural context in development. One by one, they are far more complex and contain more depth than it is possible to present here. However, a summary of their main features will serve as a framework for my further discussion of the relation between peer relationships and the conceptualization of peace. The three perspectives are represented by Bronfenbrenner's ecological model for human development (Bronfenbrenner, 1979, 1989), Cole's cultural model for cognitive development (Cole, 1988, 1992), and Moscovici's theory of social representations (Moscovici, 1976, 1988, 1993). In the ecological and cultural models, the social context is viewed from the perspective of the child. In the social representation approach, the social context, including the child, is in focus for description and analysis.

The Ecological Model

According to the ecology of human development (Bronfenbrenner, 1979, 1989; see also Chapter Five of this volume), development takes place within a context of nested environmental systems. These systems are located at four interrelated levels, ranging from settings close to the child (the microsystem) to more distant contexts (the meso-, exo-, and macrosystems). Although the developing child is not directly involved in the distant systems, they are assumed to have an indirect influence on the developmental conditions through the settings in the microsystem, such as the family, the school, and the peer group. A commonly used metaphor for the structure of the ecological system is an image of embedded circles, with the outermost representing the macrosystem and the innermost representing the microsystem.

The scope of the ecological model includes historical, cultural, and societal factors and their manifestation in the child's close environment. For example, a decision by the government to build more day-care institutions will indirectly influence children's possibilities for developing friendship relations with other children. The UN declaration of children's rights is another example of an event at a macro level with implications for children's lives at a micro level. However, even if this particular action may have a global impact on children's developmental conditions, the "concrete" version of the declaration varies in thousands of micro settings all over the world. In other words, there is no direct line between the macro and micro levels in ecological systems. A number of interpretations and redefinitions process the original message on its way to a particular child.

One of the key characteristics of the ecological model is that development is defined as a mutual process; not only is the child influenced by the environment but the environment is also influenced by the growing child. These mutual processes are assumed to be connected through the activities, roles, and relations in which the child is engaged. A child's behavior, knowledge, and personality are regarded as the outcome of development at the same time as they are seen as conditions for future development.

The ecological model would imply that children's conceptualization of peace and war is developed within a system of structured, interrelated ecological levels. The formation of peer relationships takes place in various micro settings. Experiences of peer relationships in different micro settings may involve additional and even antagonistic norms and rules, depending on how the macro messages are translated and interpreted in the daily practice of a particular micro setting (Hägglund & Öhrn, 1992). In order to define the experiential foundation for developing an understanding of peace and war, the content in cultural messages, as interpreted at a micro-setting level, is of major concern.

The Cultural Model

While the ecological model stresses the environmental aspects of development, the cultural model focuses more explicitly on cognitive processes (Cole, 1988, 1992). However, both models regard the interaction between the child and the cultural context as crucial. Cole (1995, p. 35) defines culture as "a medium constituted of historically cumulated artefacts which are organised to accomplish human growth." This model assumes that cognitive development is mediated by the aggregated cultural activities in the history of humankind. The mediating function of culture implies a cultural continuity in terms of the reproduction of norms, values, beliefs, and knowledge.

Cole suggests structured time as a key for understanding the dynamics in the interaction between cultural context and cognitive development. The emphasis on time is related to a general paradigm of the uniqueness of human beings as possessing the cognitive tools to communicate the past and the future in the present. When the child interacts with the close environment, he or she encounters messages from yesterday as well as expectations for tomorrow. The content in these cultural messages, transmitted to the child by parents, teachers, and peers, can be regarded as a representation of cultural memories from the past and visions for the future.

Developing the notion of structured time in a historical, evolutionary perspective, Cole, in a way similar to that of the ecological model, stresses that developmental processes are influenced by factors within a broader scope than the immediate environment. In using a garden metaphor for culture, he argues that "if what one is interested in is more than a short-run demonstration of the possibility of creating a development-promoting system, but rather the creation of conditions which sustain the needed properties of the artificial environment, . . . then it is as important to attend to the system in which the garden is embedded as the properties of the 'garden itself' " (Cole, 1995, p. 35).

Drawing on the ecological and cultural perspectives, we would anticipate that children's ideas of peace and war would be initiated, transformed, and practiced in social interactions in the close environment. But we would also assume that cultural traditions, beliefs, norms, values, and knowledge, based in history and displayed in this environment, would have an impact on conditions for creating peer relationships. Play, educational practices, and child-rearing patterns are examples of institutionally based activities that mediate cultural messages.

In the two models presented so far, the mutual processes that link cognitive activities with the cultural context are assumed to take place in social interactions between the child and the environment. The theoretical project in both the ecological and cultural models is to describe aspects of the sociocultural environment as it encounters the individual child in a developmental context. We now turn to a somewhat different theoretical model.

Social Representations

While the first two models are formulated from the perspective of the individual child, the third model advocates a social psychological focus. The unit of analysis is the social group and its members' shared knowledge of the social reality. The theory of social representations as introduced by

Moscovici about three decades ago (Moscovici, 1976) implies "a particular theory of the collective forms of thought and belief and of the communications produced under the constraint of society" (Moscovici, 1993, p. 161). Social representations constitute discursive complexes of norms, values, beliefs, and knowledge, adhered to various phenomena in human beings' lives. The processes in which social representations are developed can be understood as social constructions of meaning. Social representations serve as anchors for new information by making unfamiliar objects, events, or people familiar. Furthermore, they facilitate communication between people by implying normative and conventional rules and serving as standards for the classification, explanation, and comparison of social behavior and social objects. Social representations are constructed, transmitted, confirmed, and reconstructed in social interactions, and they mediate social action.

Although it is rarely applied in developmental research, the theory of social representations implies a developmental perspective. According to Farr and Moscovici (1984), "Our representations of our bodies, of our relations with other people or justice, of the world, etc., evolve from childhood to maturity. A detailed study of their development might be envisaged which would explore the way a society is conceived and experienced simultaneously by different groups and generations" (p. 69). Durkin (1995) argues that the studies that have been conducted in this tradition "appear promising in that they help uncover the social nature of thought about social relations: a *social* social cognition" (p. 387). Durkin also refers to the theory of social representations as responding to a need for a *"social* theory of *social* knowledge. . . . Clearly, developing such a theory is especially challenging, since it requires attention simultaneously to the processes of development, to the complex nature of the phenomena that are being acquired, and to the interaction between these" (p. 381).

Empirical studies within this tradition have shown, for example, that young children develop their understanding of mental illness by anchoring the concept in social representations of deviant and dangerous people. In older children's representations, drugs or accidents were referred to as causing mental illness. Among adolescents, more psychologically oriented explanations to mental illness were observed (De Rosa, 1987). In another study, the social dynamics involved in children's development of social representations of gender in classroom settings were described and analyzed (Duveen, 1993; Lloyd & Duveen, 1992). Systematic observations of classroom interactions during the first year in British primary schools showed that social representations of gender mediated individual children's actions and served as shared social scripts for collective actions of confirmation or negative sanctions of behavior. Norms and rules for gender relations, known by the children from other settings such as preschool and family, were tested and reacted upon by concerted individual and collective actions.

Corsaro (1985, 1990, 1993) argues that children's ways of organizing play and interaction (that is, their construction of a peer culture) serves as a fundamental base for learning and acquiring social knowledge about the adult world. According to Corsaro, social representations facilitate development by allowing elaboration, testing, and even protesting against the adult world. By anchoring adult rules and concepts in the more familiar peer culture, the children reconstruct and make sense of a sometimes incomprehensible adult world. Corsaro emphasizes the importance of investigating the particular conditions for the development of social knowledge offered in peer cultures, especially social rules for friendship, social status, roles, and norms: "If we are to understand the socialisation process, that is, how children acquire adult knowledge and skills and eventually reproduce the adult world, we must study this process as it occurs in children's worlds" (Corsaro, 1985, p. 279).

In what way would the theory of social representations promote models for studying the nature of the connection between peer relationships and children's understanding of peace and war? The most obvious contribution is the focus on the social dynamics in the content of discourses at a group level. However, this requires that meanings of peace and war be communicated and negotiated. Since social representations are likely to occur when the phenomenon to be represented constitutes something that is perceived as important or problematic for the group, it may be that social representations of peace and war are not always at hand. One interesting question here is whether children talk about and play at peace and war to the same extent, and if they act in ways that indicate that peace and/or war are socially significant in their peer interactions. Compared, for example, with the concept of gender, which is crucial for all children, in all societies, and in all times because it is unavoidably connected with social identity, peace may not be as important for all children. In societies where war, political conflicts, and/or explicit peace strivings are "hot" political or military issues, social representations of peace may be more likely to be socially elaborated. By investigating social representations of peace and war in peer groups, we should be able to define content dimensions and their relative importance in the concepts as shared by the members of a particular group or category of children.

It was suggested in the first section of this chapter that concrete peace during middle childhood is expressed by referring to aspects of friendship and that concrete war during the same age period is conceptualized in terms of war objects and war activities. Even if social representations of peace and war are not always present, it is likely that peace-related phenomena occur as objects for social elaboration in peer groups. Concepts such as friendship, justice, loyalty, and sharing—that is, concepts representing the sociomoral aspects of interpersonal interaction—probably are tested and elaborated in play and other spontaneous group activities. In this way, children develop a collective understanding of the meaning of these concepts in their construction of social representations. Since these concepts correspond to what children refer to when they are asked about peace, we may anticipate that social representations of, for example, friendship and justice mediate children's interpretations of the peace concept. By analyzing the content in social representations of "neighbor concepts," it should be possible to study children's understanding of peace in a "conceptual ecology"; that is, its relation to other concepts such as friendship or democracy may be discerned.

In the theoretical models presented here, the common theme is that children's understanding of the social world takes place in a complex social context. The ecological model emphasizes the structured and systemic character of this context. It also highlights the fact that cultural traditions, values, and norms that are located in the macrosystem find their way to the microsystems, where they reach the child and are interpreted and transformed into institutional practices. The child in this model is regarded as an active respondent and learner, mostly in dyadic relationships. The cultural model regards culture as a mediator for learning and development, stressing historical artifacts as the core of the information that is passed on to every new generation. Development is described as an ongoing dialogue between the child and the culture. The social representation model adds a level between the child and the culture, focusing on the social group. According to this model, *children,* not the *child,* are regarded as the actors in the developmental drama. The social knowledge of the world is seen as mediated by and mediating social knowledge.

Described in this way, it seems difficult to exclude any of these models if one strives for a deeper understanding of the role of peer relationships in children's understanding of peace. Although peer groups are formed within ecological systems and constitute parts of the child's microsystem, they also represent the culture and communicate cultural content to the child. Finally, and in line with the theory of social representations, not only do peer groups constitute a social context for development; in a sense, they *are* development.

Conclusion

In this chapter, I have shown that research on children's understanding of peace and war and research on peer relationships and friendship have certain features in common. Similar developmental patterns in cognition are revealed in empirical data on the conceptualization of peace and war and on friendship. Middle childhood has been identified as a particularly interesting age period because it contains an "overlap" between contents in social behavior and social cognition, with relevance for the construction of concepts of peace and war. However, it has not been possible to examine the core question in this chapter—the nature of the connection between children's peer relationships and their understanding of peace and war—by drawing on existing empirical data. The reason for this is that the studies in the reviewed literature do not explicitly focus on problems that call for contextual information with relevance for the conceptualization of peace and war. In other words, my question was different from the questions on which most of the studies were based. In some studies, comments were made on the necessity of developing theoretical and analytic approaches that allow for more detailed descriptions of sociocultural conditions for conceptualizations of peace and war (Hakvoort, 1996; Hartup, 1989). In a way, the major theme of this chapter can be considered to be an argument for such a research strategy.

According to my view, two major lines of reasoning can be used in order to theoretically elaborate the link between ideas of peer relationships and conceptions of peace and war. On one hand, we may ask in what way experiences of peer relationship influence individual children's understanding of peace and war. This question assumes that views of peace and war are the outcome of developmental processes in which different kinds of social experiences cause different content in ideas of peace and war. It also assumes that the child is the receiver and interpreter of the messages that may come about in a peer group. On the other hand, we may ask in what way children's experiences of peer relationship and conceptions of peace and war mutually constitute each other. This question assumes that views of peace and war are socially constructed, confirmed, and reconstructed at a group level. It also assumes that not only the child, but also the peer group, receives and interprets messages and events that are relevant for the understanding of peace. In this chapter the second approach for future research on children's understanding of peace and war has been illustrated by three theoretical models based on a sociocultural perspective on development.

HOW CHILDREN UNDERSTAND WAR AND PEACE

There is a lot more to say about the topic of this chapter. For example, throughout the chapter I have been discussing children's concepts of peace *and* war as if they were one concept. This is not true. Peace and war constitute two very different concepts that are linked to each other in a complex way in children's minds. Particularly when the concepts are related to peer relationships, as has been done in this chapter, their different characteristics are relevant. However, the details around and behind this statement are another story.

REFERENCES

Bennett, M. (1993). (Ed). *The child as a psychologist: An introduction to the development of social cognition.* New York: Harvester Wheatsheaf.

Bem, S. L. (1993). *The lenses of gender: Transforming the debate on sexual inequality.* New Haven, CT: Yale University Press.

Berndt, T. J. (1981). Relations between social cognition, nonsocial cognition, and social behaviour: The case of friendship. In J. H. Flavell & L. Ross (Eds.), *Social cognitive development* (pp. 176–199). Cambridge: Cambridge University Press.

Berndt, T. J. (1982). The features and effects of friendship in early adolescence. *Child Development, 53,* 1447–1460.

Berndt, T. J. (1989). Contributions of peer relationships to children's development. In T. J. Berndt & G. W. Ladd, *Peer relationships in child development* (pp. 407–416). New York: Wiley.

Bigelow, B. J. (1977). Children's friendship expectations: A cognitive-developmental study. *Child Development, 48,* 246–253.

Bronfenbrenner, U. (1979). *The ecology of human development: Experiments by nature and design.* Cambridge, MA: Harvard University Press.

Bronfenbrenner, U. (1989). Ecological systems theory. In R. Vasta (Ed.), *Six theories of child development: Revised formulations and current issues* (pp. 85–146). Greenwich, CT: JAI Press.

Bruner, J. (1986). *Actual minds, possible worlds.* Cambridge, MA: Harvard University Press.

Cairns, E., McClenahan, C., & Hosin, A. (1996). The impact of political violence on children's ideas about peace: Evidence from Northern Ireland. In S. Hägglund, I. Hakvoort, & L. Oppenheimer (Eds.), *Research on children and peace: International perspectives* (pp. 28–38). (Reports from the Department of Education and Educational Research, Report No. 1996:04). Göteborg, Sweden: Göteborg University.

Cole, M. (1988). Cross-cultural research in the socio-historic tradition. *Human Development, 31,* 137–157.

Cole, M. (1992). Context, modularity, and the cultural constitution of development. In L. T. Winegar & J. Valsiner (Eds.), *Children's development within social context: Vol. 2. Research and methodology* (pp. 5–32). Hillsdale, NJ: Erlbaum.

Cole, M. (1995). Culture and cognitive development: From cross-cultural research to creating systems of cultural mediation. *Culture and Psychology, 1,* 25–54.

Cooper, P. (1965). The development of the concept of war. *Journal of Peace Research, 2,* 1–17.

Corsaro, W. A. (1985). *Friendship and peer culture in the early years.* Norwood, NJ: Ablex.

Corsaro, W. A. (1990). The underlife of the nursery school: Young children's social representations of adult roles. In G. Duveen & B. Lloyd (Eds.), *Social representations and the development of knowledge.* Cambridge: Cambridge University Press.

Corsaro, W. A. (1993). Interpretative reproduction in the "scuola materna." *European Journal of Psychology of Education, 8,* 357–374.

De Rosa, A. S. (1987). The social representations of mental illness in children and adults. In W. Doise & S. Moscovici (Eds.), *Current issues in social psychology* (Vol. 2, pp. 47–138). Cambridge: Cambridge University Press.

Dinklage, R. I., & Ziller, R. C. (1989). Explicating conflict through photocommunication. *Journal of Conflict Resolution, 33,* 309–317.

Durkin, K. (1995). *Developmental social psychology: From infancy to old age.* Cambridge, MA: Blackwell.

Duveen, G. (1993). The development of social representations of gender. *Papers on Social Representations: Threads of Discussion, 2,* 171–177.

Emler, E., & Dickinson, J. (1993). The child as sociologist: The childhood development of implicit theories of role categories and social organization. In M. Bennet (Ed.), *The child as a psychologist: An introduction to the development of social cognition* (pp. 168–190). Hempstead Hertfordshire, U.K.: Harvester Wheatsheaf.

Falk, A., & Selg, H. (1982). Die Begriffe "Krieg" und "Frieden" in der Vorstellung von Kindern und Jugenlichen [The concept of war and peace in the minds of children and youths]. *Psychologie in Erziehung und Unterricht, 29,* 353–358.

Farr, R., & Moscovici, S. (1984). (Eds.). *Social representations.* Cambridge: Cambridge University Press.

Foot, H. C., Chapman, A. J., & Smith, J. R. (1980). *Friendship and social relations in children.* New York: Wiley.

Forman, E. A. (1992). Discourse, intersubjectivity, and the development of peer collaboration: A Vygotskian approach. In L. T. Winegar & J. Valsiner (Eds.), *Children's development within social context: Vol. 1. Metatheory and theory* (pp. 143–159). Hillsdale, NJ: Erlbaum.

Frønes, I. (1995). *Among peers: On the meaning of peers in the process of socialisation.* Oslo, Norway: Scandinavian University Press.

Gilligan, C., Ward, J. V., Taylor, J. M., & Bardige, B. (1988). (Eds.). *Mapping the moral domain: A contribution of women's thinking to psychological theory and education.* Cambridge, MA: Harvard University Press.

Haavelsrud, M. (1970). Views on war and peace among students in West Berlin public schools. *Journal of Peace Research, 7,* 99–120.

Hägglund, S. (1986). *Sex-typing and development in an ecological perspective.* Göteborg, Sweden: Acta Universitatis Gothoburgensis.

Hägglund, S., & Öhrn, E. (1992). *Kön, utbildningsmiljö och prosocial utveckling* [Gender, educational settings and prosocial development] (Reports from the Department of Education and Educational Research, Report No. 1992:02). Göteborg, Sweden: Göteborg University.

Hakvoort, I. (1996). *Conceptualizations of peace and war from childhood through adolescence.* Unpublished doctoral dissertation, University of Amsterdam, Amsterdam, The Netherlands.

Hakvoort, I., & Oppenheimer, L. (1993). Children's and adolescents' conceptions of peace, war and strategies to attain peace: A Dutch case study. *Journal of Peace Research, 30,* 65–77.

Hall, R. (1993). How children think and feel about war and peace: An Australian study. *Journal of Peace Research, 30,* 181–196.

Hartup, W. (1982). Peer relations. In C. Kopp & J. Krakow (Eds.), *The child.* Reading, MA: Addison-Wesley.

Hartup, W. (1989). Behavioral manifestations of children's friendships. In T. J. Berndt & G. W. Ladd (Eds.), *Peer relationships in child development* (pp. 46–70). New York: Wiley.

Hartup, W., French, D. C., Laursen, B., Johnston, K. M., & Ogawa, J. R. (1993). Conflict and friendship relations in middle childhood: Behavior in a closed-field situation. *Child Development, 64,* 445–454.

Howes, C. (1983). Patterns of friendship. *Child Development, 54,* 1041–1052.

Lever, J. (1978). Sex differences in the complexity of children's play and games. *American Sociological Review, 43,* 471–483.

Lloyd, B., & Duveen, G. (1992). *Gender identities and education: The impact of starting school.* London: Harvester Wheatsheaf.

Macek, P., Oseká, L., & Kostron, L. (1997). Social representations of human rights amongst Czech university students. *Journal of Community and Applied Social Psychology, 7,* 65–76.

Moodie, E., Marková, I., & Plichtová, J. (1995). Lay representations of democracy: A study in two cultures. *Culture and Psychology, 1,* 423–453.

Moscovici, S. (1976). *La psychanalyse, son image et son public* (2nd ed.). Paris: Presses Universitaire de France.

Moscovici, S. (1988). Notes towards a description of social representations. *European Journal of Social Psychology, 18,* 211–250.

Moscovici, S. (1993). Introductory address given at the First International Conference on Social Representations, Ravello, Italy, 1992. *Papers on Social Representations: Threads of Discussion, 2,* 160–170.

Oppenheimer, L. (1996). War as an institution, but what about peace? Developmental perspectives. *International Journal of Behavioural Development, 19,* 201–218.

Piaget, J. (1932). *The moral judgement of the child.* London: Routledge.

Pitcher, E. G., & Hickey Schultz, L. (1983). *Boys and girls at play: The development of sex roles.* New York: Praeger.

Rosell, L. (1968). Children's view of war and peace. *Journal of Peace Research, 5,* 268–276.

Spielmann, M. (1986). If peace comes . . . Future expectations of Israeli children and youth. *Journal of Peace Research, 28,* 231–235.

Tolley, H., Jr. (1973). *Children and war: Political socialisation to international conflict.* New York: Teachers College Press.

Turiel, E. (1983). *The development of social knowledge: Morality and convention.* Cambridge: Cambridge University Press.

Turiel. E., Smetana, J. G., & Killen, M. (1991). Social contexts in social cognitive development. In J. L. Gewirtz & W. M. Kurtines (Eds.), *Handbook of moral behaviour and development* (pp. 307–332). Hillsdale, NJ: Erlbaum.

Von Jacob, A., & Schmidt, H.-D. (1988). Die Konzeptualisierung von "Krieg" und "Frieden" bei sechs—bis zwölf-järigen Kindern in der DDR [Conceptualization of "war" and "peace": Six- to twelve-year-old children in the DDR]. *Zeitschrift für Psychologie, 196,* 265–277.

Whiting, B. B., & Edwards, C. P. (1988). *Children of different worlds: The formation of social behavior.* Cambridge, MA: Harvard University Press.

Winegar, L. T., & Valsiner, J. (1992). *Children's development within social context: Vol. 2. Research and methodology.* Hillsdale, NJ: Erlbaum.

Youniss, J., & Smollar, J. (1985). *Adolescent relations with mothers, fathers and friends.* Chicago: University of Chicago Press.

10

ADOLESCENTS' BELIEFS ABOUT THEIR CONFLICT BEHAVIOR

CORRELATES, CONSEQUENCES, AND CROSS-CULTURAL ISSUES

---

*Michael R. Van Slyck, Research Institute for Dispute Resolution
and State University of New York, Albany;
Marilyn Stern, State University of New York, Albany;
and Salman Elbedour, Ben Gurion University at Negev*

THIS CHAPTER IS ORGANIZED in the context of three interrelated goals. The first goal is to present a review and summary of the results from a series of five studies which examined the relationship between adolescents' beliefs about their conflict behaviors with peers or parents, operationalized as self-reported use of various conflict management strategies, and, respectively, various aspects of their experience with conflict and a variety of indexes of psychosocial adjustment. The use of samples varying in both cultural background and level of at-risk status provides the basis for examining the relationship of these two factors to the delineated sets of variables. The results of this program of research demonstrate consistent general patterns of

The research reported in this chapter was supported in part by a Faculty Research Award Program grant from the Research Foundation of the University at Albany, State University of New York, to the first two authors. Portions of this manuscript were presented to the meetings of the International Association for Conflict Management, College Park, MD, June 1998.

relationships between beliefs about conflict behavior and the other variables as well as specific patterns related to the cultural and at-risk factors.

A second goal of the chapter is to elaborate a theoretical model which provides a framework for interpreting the results of this research and guiding the direction of future research. Our basic tenet is that the beliefs adolescents hold about their conflict behaviors, which we argue are most usefully thought of as part of a conflict attitude system, have implications not only for the dynamics of their conflict experience but also for the quality of their psychosocial adjustment. This contention suggests the need to understand both the nature of adolescents' beliefs about their conflict behavior and the impact of these beliefs on psychosocial adjustment as a basis for developing interventions designed to promote beliefs about conflict behavior which enhance good psychosocial adjustment.

The third goal is to consider the implications of our data and model for adolescents' understanding of peace, conflict, and war in the context of international relations. We argue that our model, which we believe is supported by our data, is especially useful for understanding these issues because it provides a unitary, intrapsychic construct which not only allows, but may account for, the impact of culture on adolescents' understanding of these concepts, thus facilitating cross-cultural comparisons. This argument is in line with recent thinking about cultural conflict which suggests the need for conflict resolution principles which may be applicable across cultures and conflict situations (Bjorkqvist & Fry, 1997).

We next provide a brief overview of the empirical and theoretical context for our program of research. We then will provide a necessarily limited explication of the conflict attitude system construct which guides our research in this area, followed by a review of the findings of each of the five studies and an integrated summary of the results. We will conclude by discussing our findings concerning how adolescents' beliefs about conflict relate to their conflict experiences and their psychosocial adjustment, as well as the implications of these findings for understanding cross-cultural conflict involving children and adolescents.

Empirical and Theoretical Background

In previous research, we examined conflict resolution interventions designed to ameliorate adolescents' conflict with their peers in school and parents at home through the use of mediation (Van Slyck & Stern, 1991; Van Slyck, Stern, & Newland, 1992). This and other research on the use of mediation with adolescents has demonstrated that this intervention can be an effective alternative to such standard approaches as the juvenile justice system, counseling, and normative school-based disciplinary procedures for resolving such conflicts (e.g., Hall, 1996). In addition, some of the research on these conflict resolution interventions has found broader and unanticipated effects, for example, improvements in self-esteem in adolescents who have been trained to be peer mediators (see Van Slyck & Stern, 1991; Hall, 1996). In the context of these findings, it has been suggested that conflict resolution interventions have a potential value which goes beyond their intended effects (such as reductions in disciplinary incidents).

This body of research provided the basis for the development of an initial theoretical framework (Van Slyck, Stern, & Zak-Place, 1996) to explain the unanticipated positive effects of adolescent participation in these interventions. This model postulates that the fundamental effect of these interventions is to alter the adolescent's beliefs, attitudes, and behaviors in relation to conflict. This contention is in line with the ideas of others (e.g., Harris, 1996) who have suggested that a major goal of peace education is to move children from negative to positive attitudes toward conflict as a basis for preventing violence, and it is supported by a recent review of the research on peer mediation (Hall, 1996).

The model accounts for the beneficial effects of these interventions by arguing that the acquisition of "positive" (that is, prosocial) beliefs, attitudes, and behaviors in relation to conflict is developmentally appropriate to the adolescent period (Van Slyck et al., 1996). Specifically, the model suggests that such interventions promote the acquisition and use of problem-solving coping skills which are associated with optimal developmental outcomes (Van Slyck & Stern, in press). The acquisition of such problem-solving coping skills can be viewed as enhancing what is referred to as youths' "resilience" in meeting the challenges of the major stressors associated with the adolescent developmental period. Thus, this model suggests that children's and adolescents' beliefs, attitudes, and behaviors in relation to conflict have implications for the quality of their development and adjustment.

This theoretical analysis finds support in the developmental literature on adolescent conflict, which also suggests a relationship between how conflict is conceptualized and dealt with by adolescents and their adjustment. Specifically, based on a review of this literature, Laursen and Collins (1994) conclude that "the cumulative effects of contentiousness are detrimental" (p. 201). Among the effects found are a negative impact on adolescents' attitudes toward parents. In addition, they conclude that frequent contentious conflict has adverse implications for developmental outcomes and that high rates of contentious conflict have been found to be associated with greater rates of adolescent delinquency, behavioral disorders, and runaway and suicide attempts.

In contrast, they note that although it is limited in quantity, the research literature suggests that engaging in prosocial conflict resolution strategies has a positive impact on adolescent development (Laursen & Collins, 1994). For example, the finding of a relationship between greater levels of the use of compromise in conflicts with peers and positive self-esteem (Cooper & Cooper, 1992) suggests that conflict behaviors may in fact be related to aspects of adolescent adjustment. However, other research on adolescent conflict (Laursen & Collins, 1994) indicates that while adolescents tend to endorse the use of compromise at a high rate in hypothetical disagreements, they manifest a much lower rate of its use in actual conflicts, thus demonstrating a disparity between their beliefs and attitudes about conflict and their conflict-related behaviors.

An Attitude System Approach to Adolescent Conflict

To further explore this topic, we have embraced an orientation which can be labeled an attitude system approach (Zimbardo & Leippe, 1991). Given the arguments concerning the impact on attitudes and behaviors of conflict resolution interventions and the apparent relationship of conflict attitudes and behaviors to aspects of adjustment, we believe that the attitude system approach is appropriate to considering issues related to adolescent conflict. Such an approach seems particularly relevant to understanding issues of conflict on an international cross-cultural level, given the argument made by some (Bjorkqvist & Fry, 1997) who state unequivocally their belief that the road to lasting peace is through attitude change. When an attitude system approach is embraced, the extensive theory and research on attitudes becomes available for application to the understanding of issues related to child and adolescent conflict. For example, this literature provides insight into the relationship of attitudes and behavior, the impact of behavior on attitudes, and the best ways to change attitudes.

The attitude construct has, at least in principle, provided the basis for some recent research examining the impact of culture on youths' understanding of peace, war, and conflict (Hall, 1993; Covell, 1996). However, this research has not examined the relationship of these attitudes to behavior or other aspects of the youths' lives. We believe that this limitation mitigates the usefulness of the attitude system construct, which includes associated cognitive, affective, and behavioral aspects, thus allowing for a consideration of the role and interrelationship of all three of these factors in the context of a single integrating concept.

Beliefs and Attitudes About Conflict Resolution

Attitude Systems

The attitude construct has been subject to extensive research and theoretical consideration, a full discussion of which is well beyond the scope of this chapter. Instead, we will offer a brief review of some of the definitions which have been postulated, concluding with a description of an attitude system approach. As Zanna and Rempel (1988) note, the original conceptualization of attitude was that it consists of how we feel, what we think, and what we are inclined to do about the object of the attitude. In contrast, the sine qua non of what has been labeled the current modal approach to the attitude construct (Anderson & Armstrong, 1989) is its definition as a psychological tendency to respond to an object or entity with a favorable or unfavorable evaluation (Eagly & Chaiken, 1993). Central to this definition is the distinction between evaluation and the affective, cognitive, or behavioral response to the object. Indeed, from this perspective, attitude is equated with evaluation, with the affect, cognition, and behavior relevant to the object not being viewed as part of the attitude proper but rather as "response modalities" through which the attitude can be expressed.

However, this approach to defining the attitude construct is not universally accepted. Zanna and Rempel (1988) argue strongly that associated affect, cognition, and behavior not only are response modalities but also constitute the ways in which the attitude is formed and experienced. Taking even greater exception to the emphasis on attitude as evaluation is the work of Anderson and Armstrong (1989), who argue that evaluation is only one narrow class of attitudinal response, indicating a preference for a broader definition of attitude as a knowledge structure which includes an affective component. Further, recent work by Tesser and Martin (1996) examining what they label the "psychology of evaluation" does not equate evaluation with attitude, which by implication must be regarded as a broader construct. Indeed, it can be suggested that this new approach to evaluation puts those who equate attitude with evaluation at risk of defining themselves out of a construct.

Thus we believe that a definition of the attitude construct which is limited to evaluation is indeed "limited" and, although it is perhaps "modal," it is not universally accepted; even more important, it is not as useful as a more broadly defined attitude construct. One answer to this issue which we find useful is the concept of the attitude system (Zimbardo & Leippe, 1991), which maintains attitude as a central evaluation component but includes explicitly associated affective, cognitive, and behavioral components (with the behavioral aspect including both behavioral inclination and actual behavior); all of these, taken together, constitute the attitude system.

In the context of this overarching framework, we have attempted to examine how one aspect of adolescents' conflict attitude system—their self-reported behavioral inclinations toward interpersonal conflict with their peers or parents—relates to their overt conflict behavior as well as to aspects of their psychosocial adjustment. By implementing this research in diverse or multicultural settings, we established the potential to elucidate some of the influence of culture on such inclinations. This approach is in line with recent thinking on understanding issues of cultural conflict as expressed by Bjorkqvist and Fry (1997), who contend that "more attention should be directed towards the understanding of world views, internalization of normative beliefs and the particular scripts for dealing with conflicts, provided within cultures" (p. 247).

Conflict Attitudes and Behaviors: A Cognitively Oriented Definition of Conflict

We believe that the attitude system construct is also useful in considering issues of adolescent conflict because it is compatible with one of the major definitions of conflict. Two major approaches to defining conflict have evolved in the literature. One school of thought takes a behavioral perspective, defining conflict as "behavioral opposition," which suggests that conflict does not exist unless one can see overt and negative interactions between two parties (Laursen & Collins, 1994). We prefer the cognitive approach offered by Rubin, Pruitt, and Kim (1994), who define conflict as a perceived divergence of interest.

This cognitively based definition suggests a distinction between the perception by the individual of the existence of conflict, based on a belief that his or her needs and interests are divergent from those of another person, and the behavioral response to that perception. In this orientation, responses to the perception of conflict include, in addition to behavioral opposition as one strategy for resolving the conflict (referred to variously as coercing, competing, contending, or dominating), such other responses as yielding (also labeled as accommodating or obliging), compromising, collaborating (also referred to as integrating or problem solving), and avoiding (also referred to as denial or withdrawal).

In this theoretical context, a primary concern becomes the determinants of the behavioral response to conflict (that is, one of the five response strategies delineated earlier). One explanation, referred to as the dual concern model, suggests a choice of strategy based on an interaction between the level of concern for the interests of the self and others; for example, high concern for self-interest and low concern for others' interests would result in a contentious strategy (Rubin et al., 1994). A cultural perspective suggests that the way in which conflict is responded to is largely culturally determined, with different cultures emphasizing responses which are consistent with some overarching societal value, such as maintaining or repairing relationships (Fry & Fry, 1997). Developmentally oriented research on adolescent conflict suggests that such situational determinants as the specific relationship (with parents, peers, or others) determine the nature of the response (Laursen & Collins, 1994).

Alternatively, we suggest that although all of these factors may influence the choice of a response strategy, in a fashion similar to the development of coping styles (Carver & Scheier, 1994), individuals develop preferences for the use of specific styles. This brings us back to the notion of a conflict attitude system, which by our definition includes a behavioral inclination as an underlying mechanism which may influence the choice of an individual's response style to conflict. We note here that another and growing approach to explaining the basis for responding to conflict is cognitively based and looks to the schema or script construct (Guerra, Eron, Huesmann, Tolan, & Van Acker, 1997). We regard this approach as simultaneously compatible with and subsumed within the attitude system approach, in which cognitive and behavioral inclinations would be represented in schematic or script structure. However, we argue that a "pure" cognitive approach leaves out both the issue of evaluation and, perhaps more important, the issue of affect, which research on interethnic conflict has demonstrated to be an important issue (Glazer, 1997).

Thus we argue here for an attitude system approach to understanding adolescent conflict, based on a cognitively oriented definition of conflict which distinguishes between the perception of the existence of conflict and the behavioral response to it, which may in part be determined or at least influenced by the individual's conflict attitude system. Such an approach offers the opportunity to examine not only the antecedents (for example, the underlying attitude components) of specific responses to conflict but also the impact on the antecedents of the response of engaging in specific behaviors in response to conflict. Finally, such an approach also allows for an examination of the source (for example, culture) and the impact of having specific attitudes toward conflict (especially "negative" attitudes) on other aspects of the adolescent's life.

Development of a Negative Conflict Attitude System

In sketching out one possible conflict attitude system, we must keep in mind some of the issues related to the definition of attitude delineated earlier. Most relevant here is the issue of the source of an attitude, which from a "technical" perspective may derive variously from or through an affective, behavioral, or cognitive modality. In turn, culture will play a critical role in shaping the manner in which children perceive, evaluate, and choose options for dealing with conflict (Bjorkqvist & Fry, 1997). Finally, as Zanna and Rempel (1988) note, for some attitudes, the initiation may be early in development and may therefore be unknown (unconscious) to the individual. Thus the scenario which follows is only one of a variety of sequences which may produce a given conflict attitude system for a child.

We begin with the issue of the evaluative component, which consists of whether the individual "judges" conflict as good or bad, or perhaps as positive or negative. We believe that conflict is an area in which attitude systems are likely to be developed very early and perhaps without direct experience, but rather through a socialization process whereby the prevailing cultural view is embraced (Guerra et al., 1997). The work of Bar-Tal (in press) on the development of a negative Arab stereotype in Israeli children by the age of four supports this contention. We argue here that the most common evaluation of conflict is that it is "bad," a negative thing. However, the evaluation of conflict as bad does not necessarily provide a basis for predicting behavior in response to a conflict situation. For that we would need to have an understanding of the other components of the attitude system: the individual's beliefs about the meaning and nature of conflict, affective response to being in conflict, and behavioral inclinations, perhaps based on previous successful or unsuccessful responses to conflict.

Culture will clearly play a critical role in this regard, shaping the manner in which children perceive, evaluate, and choose options for dealing with conflict (Bjorkqvist & Fry, 1997), thus providing the basis for specific conflict attitude systems. Here we will turn to the general literature on social conflict (e.g., Rubin et al., 1994) as the basis for understanding one possible generic cognitive component of a conflict attitude system. The literature suggests that conflict is commonly viewed as being unidimensional in nature, that is, a zero-sum situation in which one party's gain is the other party's loss. Such a belief would be consistent with an evaluation of conflict as bad or would produce such an evaluation if it did not already exist. It might also have implications for behavior by suggesting the need for a contentious response to achieve one's interests.

Part of the "conflict as a zero sum" belief system would be the logical corollary belief that conflict puts individuals at risk of not having their needs and interests met and therefore represents a threat to their welfare. Such a belief is likely to result in or be associated with a state of negative arousal such as anxiety or fear in response to being in a state of conflict; this would constitute the affective component of a conflict attitude system. In the context of a set of beliefs about the nature and meaning of conflict and an associated affective reaction to these beliefs, a behavioral inclination might develop. In the case of a negative belief system and a threatening affective component, behavioral inclinations might typically conform to the classic fight, flight, or freeze scenario. In terms of the strategies outlined earlier, a contentious, yielding, or avoiding response depends on such other factors as cultural norms, behavioral models, and experience.

Assessing Conflict Attitude Systems: The Conflict Management Inventory as a Measure of Beliefs About Behavioral Inclinations

On a theoretical level, the preceding analysis of the structure and development of a negative (that is, contentious) conflict attitude system suggests that a useful approach to furthering our understanding of youths' concepts of conflict, war, and peace is to assess the content of their conflict attitude systems, including their beliefs about conflict, their affective reactions to conflict, and their behavioral inclinations. In turn, we believe that it is important to investigate the relationship of this content to such conflict-related factors as overt conflict behavior and expectations about others' conflict behaviors, as well as psychosocial adjustment. In addition to helping us understand these issues, such an approach can serve a methodological function by providing the basis for developing assessment techniques which can be used in testing the impact and effectiveness of programs designed to change conflict attitude systems and conflict behaviors through educationally based interventions such as peer mediation programs.

An example of one such measure is the Rahim Organizational Conflict Inventory (ROCI) (Rahim, 1983). The ROCI is a theoretically derived assessment tool designed to measure individuals' tendencies to use one of five conflict styles (Van de Vliert & Kabanoff, 1990). Specifically, the twenty-eight items of the ROCI ask individuals to indicate how they usually respond to conflict with specified others, with the results indicating the degree to which each of the five response styles is used. The five conflict response styles have been described by differing but roughly equivalent sets of labels. Those adopted by Rahim (1983) are as follows: accommodating, avoiding, compromising, dominating, and integrating.

Several efforts have been made to examine and establish the reliability and validity of the ROCI and a similar measure (Thomas & Kilmann, 1974). This research indicates that of these two instruments, the ROCI is the superior one, meeting conventional psychometric standards (e.g., Van de Vliert & Kabanoff, 1990). In addition, and central to our research program, the ROCI has been shown to have moderately good construct validity (Van de Vliert & Kabanoff, 1990) as well as good discriminant and divergent validity (e.g., Rahim, 1983). Because of its psychometric superiority, we have made use of the ROCI in our research on adolescent conflict as a measure of one component of adolescents' conflict attitude system: their beliefs about their behavioral inclination or, as we have come to refer to it, their conflict response tendency (CRT).

Specifically, we have conducted a multistudy program of research which has examined the relationship between adolescents' beliefs about their CRT and such other factors as conflict-related behaviors and experience, beliefs about other adolescents' CRTs, and other aspects of the adolescents' lives related to psychosocial adjustment and developmental sequelae. The program includes a study on the effectiveness of a parent-child mediation project in the United States and a series of studies which were specifically designed to assess adolescents' beliefs about their CRT and the correlates of these beliefs in, respectively, high schools in the Middle East, an educational facility in a U.S. prison, and a middle school and high school setting in the United States. The key results for the ROCI from each of these studies are reported in the next section.

Beliefs About Conflict Resolution Tendencies: A Program of Research

Study 1: Adolescents' Beliefs About Their CRT and the Resolution of Parent-Child Conflict

Research in upstate New York examined the use of parent-child mediation as an alternative to the standard interventions of probation and counseling for cases brought to the juvenile justice system (Stern & Van Slyck, 1993). The design of the study was a preintervention-postintervention assessment (probation versus mediation versus counseling). The majority of the sample (72.08 percent) was of European American background, with a little over one-fourth (26.4 percent) being of African American background. The majority of the youth ranged from thirteen to fifteen years of age, evenly split on gender. In addition to the ROCI, the pre-assessment battery measured the quality of family functioning (Family Environment Scale [FES]; Moos & Moos, 1986) and self-esteem (Coopersmith Self-Esteem Inventory; Coopersmith, 1981). Author-designed questionnaires were administered at intake to assess the characteristics of the precipitating conflict and three months subsequent to intervention to assess perceptions of the effectiveness of the intervention process and satisfaction with the outcome.

The results revealed a relationship between the ROCI and such factors as level of family conflict, aspects of the dispute which brought the youths into contact with the juvenile justice system, and amenability to intervention. Greater reported use of integrating, compromising, and accommodating by the adolescents was significantly associated with perceptions of their family as more cohesive and less conflicted as measured by the FES, with ratings of the incident as less serious and with lower levels of hostility in the family. These adolescents were also more likely to report that they were interested in resolving the problem, they wanted to see their family stay together, they were satisfied with the way decisions were made in the family, they were satisfied with who made the decisions in the family, and they were satisfied with the way decisions were made about them.

In contrast, self-reported use of a dominating style of resolving conflicts was significantly related to a perception of greater family conflict on the FES. In addition, the ROCI score was also found to be correlated with levels of self-esteem, with higher reported use of integrating, compromising, and accommodating being associated with higher levels of self-esteem. No gender or ethnic differences were found.

Study 2: Assessing Adolescents' Beliefs About Their CRT in a High-Conflict, Cross-Cultural Setting

Research in the state of Israel and the Gaza autonomous region (Stern, Van Slyck, & Elbedour, 1995) was designed to generate baseline data on cross-cultural differences in adolescents' beliefs about their CRT and such possible correlates as self-esteem, mental health status (Symptom Checklist 90–Revised [SCL 90-R]; Derogatis, 1983), and aspects of personality (SYMLOG; Hare, 1989). Participants consisted of a total of 331 tenth- and eleventh-grade male and female Jewish, Bedouin, and Palestinian high school students sampled from schools in the Negev region of Israel and Gaza.

Differences as a function of cultural group were found on the ROCI, with Israeli Jewish youth indicating a greater use of integrating, and both

Israeli Bedouin and Gaza youth indicating a greater use of dominating, with no differences between the latter two groups. Across the three groups, beliefs about CRT were found to be a significant correlate of emotional distress. Higher levels of reported use of integrating, compromising, and avoiding were associated with lower levels of overall emotional distress as well as significantly lower scores on a majority of the individual subscales of the SCL 90-R. In contrast, a higher score on the dominating subscale of the ROCI was associated with higher levels on two of the SCL 90-R subscales: phobic ideation and obsessive compulsiveness.

Correlations between the ROCI and the personality measure indicated that the Israeli Jewish youth who reported a greater use of integrating or compromising were more likely to endorse positive characteristics about themselves, whereas the Jewish youth who reported a greater use of dominating were more likely to acknowledge negative personality characteristics. Bedouin and Palestinian youth, however, showed an opposite pattern of relationships: those who reported a greater use of integrating or compromising were less likely to acknowledge possession of positive personality characteristics, while Arab youth who indicated higher levels of dominating were more likely to acknowledge positive personality characteristics. Similarly, reported use of integrating and compromising was found to have a positive relationship with self-esteem for Jewish youth, while for Palestinian youth, greater reported use of integrating or compromising was found to be inversely related to self-esteem, with no significant relationship between these variables for Bedouin youth. We note finally that some limited gender differences, which were decidedly nonsystematic and not easily interpreted, were found on the ROCI.

Study 3: Assessing Expectations of Others' CRTs in a High-Conflict, Cross-Cultural Setting

This study (Van Slyck & Stern, 1996) was designed to extend the findings of study 2 by assessing the expectations held by adolescents concerning the CRTs of members of their own group as well as those of other cultures. To accomplish this, a revised version of the ROCI was used. The nature of expectations was assessed by asking adolescents from each cultural group to rate how they believed a typical member of their own group and a typical member of the other two groups would respond to conflict. Once again, approximately three hundred male and female Israeli Jewish, Bedouin, and Palestinian tenth- and eleventh-grade students from high schools in the Negev region of Israel and Gaza participated in the study.

Analyses of the data comparing self-reported CRT and expectations of their own group and members of the other two groups are worth noting. Specifically, for Jewish adolescents the higher the self-reported integrative style, the more likely they were to report the average Jewish and Bedouin adolescent as using integrating as a preferred style. Similarly, the higher the self-reported dominating style by the Jewish adolescents, the more likely they were to expect the average Jewish and Bedouin adolescent to be dominating. No similar relationships were found for Jewish adolescents' expectations for the Palestinian group.

Similar patterns were found for Bedouin adolescents. The higher their integrating score, the more likely they were to expect other Bedouin and Jewish, but not Palestinian, adolescents to use integrating as a preferred style of conflict management. However, the higher the dominating score, the more likely they were to expect Palestinian, but not Jewish or other Bedouin, adolescents to be dominating. Palestinian adolescents from Gaza who had higher integrating scores also expected the average Jewish, Bedouin, and Palestinian adolescent to use integrating as a preferred style. Similarly, Palestinian adolescents with higher dominating scores expected the average Jewish and Palestinian, but not Bedouin, adolescent to use a dominating style.

Study 4: Beliefs About CRT Among Incarcerated Adolescents

Research designed to further test the relationships found in the Middle Eastern setting was conducted in the prison system of New York State (Van Slyck, Pitts, & Van Brammer, 1998). It must be noted that although the prison is a standard adult, medium-security facility, it is a designated "youth facility" based on an average inmate age of less than twenty, a situation resulting from a policy aimed at congregating incarcerated youth in specific facilities. Inmates without high school diplomas are required to obtain one, and because of the high rate of such individuals within this facility's population, a large educational establishment is housed within it—in effect, a high school within a medium-security prison. Approximately four hundred of these incarcerated adolescents were the subjects of this research. The majority of participants were of African American or Latin American backgrounds, of distinctly lower socioeconomic status, and from disadvantaged backgrounds—that is, from poverty areas within New York City.

Adolescents who had committed a violent offense were significantly more likely to report using a dominating style than nonviolent offenders.

A relationship between reported use of a dominating style and more emotional distress as measured by the SCL 90-R was also found. This relationship held more strongly for adolescents who had been incarcerated for nonviolent offenses than for those incarcerated for violent offenses. In addition, for adolescents who had been incarcerated for violent offenses, higher reported rates of the use of integrating were related to lower levels of self-esteem. This pattern also was found for nonviolent offenders, but the relationship did not reach significance.

Study 5: Adolescents' Beliefs About Their CRT and Psychoactive Drug Use

Our most recent research was conducted at a middle school and high school in an essentially middle-class environment in upstate New York (Van Slyck, Stern, & Wulfert, 1998). In addition to examining the relationship between self-reported CRT, conflict behavior, and indexes of adjustment, self-reported attitudes and behaviors concerning substance use and abuse were also assessed. Approximately two hundred high school and two hundred middle school boys and girls were the subjects.

In areas of behavior related to conflict, students reporting a greater use of integrating or compromising were less likely to report having witnessed or participated in a physical fight. In addition, greater reported use of integrating was associated with a greater likelihood of reporting that they got along with their primary caretaker. For girls, reporting a greater use of integrating was associated with reports of experiencing less stress at home, greater satisfaction with home life, and a general sense of feeling happy.

Students reporting a greater tendency to use integrating and compromising reported less interest in and less actual use of psychoactive substances, for example, binge drinking, marijuana use, and use of drugs in general. This pattern of findings held more strongly for middle school boys than middle school girls and held more strongly for high school students than middle school students. Students reporting a greater use of integrating were also more likely to report having friends who would disapprove of their using any type of drugs.

Summary of Results: Consistencies and Patterns

The results from the five studies are highly consistent, with self-reported CRT as measured by the ROCI being regularly associated with conflict-related experiences and/or a variety of indexes of psychosocial adjustment.

Even more striking is the consistency across several studies with decidedly different populations of rather complex but orderly patterns of relationships among these factors.

Adolescents' beliefs about their CRT were associated with their self-reported likelihood of witnessing or engaging in physical violence in a middle-class school setting, with the general level of conflict and hostility in the family, with the seriousness of the precipitating incident for those intersecting with the juvenile justice system for the first time, and with the level of violence of the offense for those actually incarcerated. In all cases, greater reported use of a prosocial conflict resolution style (accommodating, compromising, or integrating) was related to reports of less contentious conflict experience, whereas greater reported use of a dominating conflict response style was related to greater levels of contentious conflict experiences such as hostility and violence. On a more global level, beliefs about their CRT were related to the adolescents' general relationships with their parents and their overall life satisfaction. Specifically, in the United States, both middle-class adolescents and those intersecting with the juvenile justice system for the first time who reported using prosocial conflict resolution styles reported greater satisfaction with their relationship with their parents and with the quality of their lives on a variety of dimensions.

Adolescents' beliefs about their CRT were consistently found to be related to indexes of psychosocial adjustment such as self-esteem, emotional distress, personality traits, and attitudes and behaviors toward substance use. Interestingly, and perhaps most important, two specific and decidedly different patterns emerged among these factors. For U.S. adolescents experiencing their first intersection with the justice system, greater reported use of prosocial conflict response styles was positively related to self-esteem. This same relationship obtained for Israeli Jewish youth. In addition, for this latter group, greater reported use of prosocial conflict resolution styles was related to positive personality traits and less emotional distress, while greater reported use of dominating was associated with lower self-esteem and negative personality traits. For middle-class adolescent females in upstate New York, reported use of prosocial conflict response styles was related to experiencing less stress, greater home life satisfaction, and a general sense of happiness; for both boys and girls, it was related to reports of less interest in or actual use of psychoactive drugs or associations with those who used drugs.

In contrast, the samples of Palestinians, Bedouins, and incarcerated youth in the United States all tended to report greater use of a dominating conflict response style. For all of these samples, greater reported use of a dominating conflict response style was associated with greater emotional distress. However, for the Palestinian and Bedouin adolescents, greater reported use of dominating was associated with greater endorsement of positive personality traits, while greater reported use of an integrating style was associated with lower levels of endorsement of positive personality traits. In a parallel trend, for both our Palestinian sample and our sample of incarcerated adolescents in the United States, greater reported use of an integrating style was associated with lower self-esteem.

Adolescents' beliefs about their CRT were found to vary as a function of culture and ethnicity in some settings but not others. Israeli Jewish adolescents reported distinctly different responses to conflict than Arab adolescents, that is, greater use of integrating for the former and greater use of dominating for the latter. In contrast, in both U.S. settings where such comparisons were possible (the juvenile justice system and the prison setting), no cultural or ethnic differences were found between African American, European American, and Latin American adolescents. Finally, adolescents' beliefs about their CRT were related to their expectations for other adolescents' CRTs in the Middle Eastern setting, with a tendency to expect others to respond to conflict in a fashion similar to theirs.

Conclusions and Implications

Beliefs About Conflict Behavior and Psychosocial Adjustment

The fundamental premise of our program of research is that the attitude system construct provides a good working model for understanding the nature and dynamics of adolescent conflict. The findings from the series of studies reviewed here support this proposition. On the most basic level, the results provide support for the concept of a behavioral inclination component of the conflict attitude system. Specifically, the finding of a logical relationship between CRT and conflict-related experiences supports its construct validity. The findings of differential content for this component of a conflict attitude system from samples of different populations of adolescents supports its discriminant validity. These results also support the definition of conflict used here, which emphasizes a cognitive orientation and distinguishes between the perception of conflict and the overt behavioral response to it, a response which is not limited to behavioral opposition but includes the full range of the five response styles measured by the ROCI.

The broader premise, that components of the conflict attitude system would be related to the adolescent's psychosocial adjustment, was also strongly supported. The results of these studies are in line with the limited research on this topic and both support and extend the previous findings of relationships between children's and adolescents' beliefs, attitudes, and behaviors in regard to conflict and psychosocial adjustment. Based on their review of the developmental research on adolescent conflict, Laursen and Collins (1994) suggest the existence of a "two-track" pattern concerning this relationship. Specifically, they found positive developmental effects resulting from prosocial conflict resolution styles, including higher self-esteem, and adverse developmental consequences resulting from involvement in chronically contentious conflict.

With the exception of an intriguing variation, this basic normative pattern emerges in our series of studies. Specifically, the endorsement of a prosocial conflict management style was associated with positive conflict-related experiences and factors shown to be related to the optimal development of the adolescent, such as higher self-esteem. In contrast, the endorsement of a negative conflict management style was correlated with negative conflict-related experiences and adverse developmental sequelae. The exception to the general pattern is the finding of some relationship between reports of a contentious CRT and positive indexes of psychosocial adjustment, as well as some relationship between reports of a prosocial CRT and negative indexes of psychosocial adjustment. However, these variations from the normative pattern are themselves consistent, suggesting an underlying source for this difference in the conflict attitude system and its impact.

The Development and Impact of Conflict Attitude Systems

The variation from the normative pattern seems to be consistent with the nature of risk within the particular populations examined. With the exception of our middle-class sample in our study of attitudes and behaviors toward substance abuse, all of our samples came from stressful environments, although to greater or lesser degrees, resulting in a situation in which most of the youth can be characterized as at risk. Within this context, a distinction can be made between samples which came from environments which could be characterized as potentially the least damaging and which therefore put the adolescents at minimal or, at worst, moderate risk and samples which came from environments which could be characterized as potentially maximally damaging to the adolescents, putting them at high risk for adverse developmental consequences.

The former group of samples includes our U.S. middle-class sample, the Israeli Jewish sample, and our U.S. juvenile justice sample (note that this was the first intersection of these youth with the juvenile justice system).

The latter group of samples includes Palestinian youth from Gaza, who live under warlike conditions; Bedouin youth, a minority group in Israel who live under conditions of extreme social change; and incarcerated U.S. adolescents, who were raised in high-crime and high-poverty communities. In this latter group of samples, the conditions which these adolescents live under have produced a situation in which many have already suffered the consequences of their negative environment (for example, extreme emotional distress among the Palestinians and incarceration in the U.S. sample), thus putting them "beyond risk."

The low-risk samples adhere in a straightforward fashion to the normative pattern noted in the literature (Laursen & Collins, 1994). Specifically, adolescents who manifest a conflict attitude system characterized by the endorsement of prosocial conflict management styles report positive experiences concerning conflict and, perhaps more important, manifest positive developmental outcomes, such as higher self-esteem, positive personality traits, better parental relationships, higher global life satisfaction, and resistance to substance use. For this group, endorsement of a dominating conflict management style is related to negative conflict experience and poor developmental outcomes, such as lower self-esteem.

The pattern which emerges for our high-risk and beyond-risk adolescents from adverse environments (consisting of violence and/or poverty) is more complex. Adolescents in this group of samples tend to manifest a conflict attitude system characterized by a dominating CRT which, in line with the normative pattern, is associated with negative conflict experiences and poor psychosocial adjustment, including greater levels of emotional distress. However, for these samples, a dominating CRT is also associated with such factors as the acknowledgment of positive personality traits, while a prosocial CRT is associated with negative personality traits and lower self-esteem.

Apparently these environments foster the development of negative conflict attitude systems as manifested by endorsement of a dominating conflict management style. This endorsement is related to some negative developmental outcomes, such as emotional distress. However, because such negative conflict attitude systems may be normative within these environments, possibly because they are adaptive, they are also associated with positive characteristics. This analysis suggests that interventions with adolescents who manifest this pattern will be particularly difficult because they are complicated by social endorsement of negative components of the conflict attitude system.

This contention is in line with arguments made by others (Guerra et al., 1997) who have suggested that children develop conflict-related scripts which are adaptive for their environmental context and that for children from difficult environments, such as the inner city, complex environmental factors both promote belief systems which justify aggression and impede efforts to change these attitudes and behaviors. Recent research supports this argument, suggesting that children and youth cope with exposure to violence by employing strategies which include acting out and substance use, strategies which are likely to have a negative impact on their ability to function in socially acceptable ways (Duckworth et al., 1997).

Conflict Attitudes, Culture, and Peace

An alternative but not dichotomous way to view the apparent environmental impact on the development of conflict attitude systems is to consider the cultural context. In our series of studies, cultural differences were found in the Middle Eastern setting, but not in the United States. The finding of cultural differences in the former setting was not surprising given the common perception of the existence of at least two cultures which might be expected to have distinct culturally based beliefs and attitudes about conflict and appropriate ways to respond to it. In addition, children in this region have been demonstrated to have inherently similar attitudes about the other culture, defining it as the enemy (e.g., Bar-Tal, in press), which would be expected to influence the conflict attitude system. Indeed, our research suggests that in conditions in which members of one culture view members of another culture as enemies, expectations concerning the other culture's CRT may influence the conflict attitude system, at least with regard to members of the "enemy" culture.

In contrast, the failure to find cultural differences in CRT in the U.S. settings was somewhat surprising. It was presumed that differences were likely to be found between African Americans, European Americans, and Latin Americans, based on the general assumption that they came from different cultural backgrounds. The lack of differences suggests that definitions of culture may need to be clarified. It is possible that while these adolescents came from different ethnic backgrounds, their primary influence was a generic "American" culture which overrode ethnic differences. However, in line with our previous argument regarding the potential impact of negative environments, perhaps such factors as the common experience of violence, poverty, and involvement in the justice system were responsible for the lack of differences based on the ethnic factor; that is, all the subjects shared the values of a poor, disadvantaged, or criminal "environmental culture." This explanation might also apply to the differences found in the Middle East, where the Israeli Jewish sample can be distinguished from the two Arab samples in terms of positive and negative environment as well as on a cultural basis.

Awareness of the impact of culture is clearly important because it allows for consideration of how individuals may be limited in their approach to conflict by culture-based beliefs and norms. Indeed, it has been argued that societies may in fact establish "cultures of conflict," consisting of a network of scripts or schemata which provide models for dealing with conflict situations (Bjorkqvist & Fry, 1997). Thus attention should be directed toward understanding views, beliefs, and scripts from the culture. However, part of this consideration should include an effort to distinguish between what can be referred to as specific ethnically or religiously based cultures of conflict and those which can be referred to as generic, environmentally based cultures of conflict (for example, those formed through exposure to violence).

To address this issue, future research should attempt to elucidate the differences between culture and environment as the sources of conflict attitude systems. While it may be the case that different cultures embrace different values as the basis for their orientations to conflict (for example, maintaining face versus maintaining relationships), such general environmental factors as exposure to violence may be as or more important in developing conflict attitude systems. This type of information has implications for intervention with children in settings of cross-cultural conflict. It would provide a basis for determining whether such interventions would need to be sensitive to inherent cultural differences in responding to a conflict which might not be amenable to change or to environmental factors, such as violence and poverty, which might be as much a target of intervention as the specific conflict. This important distinction which must be made in designing interventions has recently been recognized in the literature on cultural conflict. Bjorkqvist and Fry (1997) argue for culture-specific intervention in the context of inherent ethnically or religiously based cultural orientations toward conflict, while Guerra et al. (1997) argue for the need to explicitly address and attempt to change environmental factors where they can be judged to be the dominant influence in the cultural orientation toward conflict.

Finally, we also believe that it is important for future research to attempt to measure the different components (affect, cognition, and behavioral inclination) of the proposed conflict attitude system simultaneously in order to examine their interrelationships as well as their respective relationships to conflict experience and psychosocial adjustment. Such research, which we are currently initiating, holds promise for furthering our understanding of the development and impact of conflict attitude systems as well as for providing a basis for designing interventions with the goal of altering negative conflict attitude systems.

REFERENCES

Anderson, N. H., & Armstrong, M. A. (1989). Cognitive theory and methodology for studying marital interaction. In D. Brinberg & J. Jaccard (Eds.), *Dyadic decision making* (pp. 3–43). New York: Springer-Verlag.

Bar-Tal, D. (in press). Development of social categories and stereotypes in early childhood: The case of "the Arab" concept formation, stereotype and attitudes by Jewish children in Israel. *International Journal of Intercultural Relations.*

Bjorkqvist, K., & Fry, P. (1997). Conclusions: Alternatives to violence. In D. P. Fry & K. Bjorkqvist (Eds.), *Cultural variation in conflict resolution: Alternatives to violence* (pp. 243–254). Hillsdale, NJ: Erlbaum.

Carver, C. S., & Scheier, M. F. (1994). Situational coping and coping dispositions in a stressful transaction. *Journal of Personality and Social Psychology, 66,* 184–195.

Cooper, C. R., & Cooper, R. G. (1992). Links between adolescents' relationships with their parents and peers: Models, evidence, and mechanisms. In R. D. Parke & G. W. Ladd (Eds.), *Family-peer relationships: Modes of linkage* (pp. 135–158). Hillsdale, NJ: Erlbaum.

Coopersmith, S. (1981). *The Self-Esteem Inventory (SEI).* Palo Alto, CA: Consulting Psychologists Press.

Covell, K. (1996). National and gender differences in adolescents' war attitudes. *International Journal of Behavioral Development, 19,* 871–883.

Derogatis, L. R. (1983). *SCL 90-R, Administration, Scoring and Procedures manual* (2nd ed.). Towson, MD: Clinical Psychometric Research.

Duckworth, M. P., Moody-Thomas, S., Fick, A. C., Hayden, J., Nguyen, L. T., & Hale, D. D. (1997). *The impact of violence exposure on coping responses of children and adolescents.* Paper presented to the meetings of the Society for Research in Child Development, Washington, DC.

Eagly, A., & Chaiken, S. (1993). *The psychology of attitudes.* Orlando: Harcourt Brace.

Fry, D. P., & Fry, C. B. (1997). Culture and conflict resolution models: Exploring alternatives to violence. In D. P. Fry & K. Bjorkqvist (Eds.), *Cultural variation in conflict resolution: Alternatives to violence* (pp. 9–23). Hillsdale, NJ: Erlbaum.

Glazer, I. M. (1997). Beyond the competition of tears: Black-Jewish conflict containment in New York neighborhood. In D. P. Fry & K. Bjorkqvist (Eds.),

Cultural variation in conflict resolution: Alternatives to violence (pp. 137–144). Hillsdale, NJ: Erlbaum.

Guerra, N. G., Eron, L., Huesmann, L. R., Tolan, P., & Van Acker, R. (1997). A cognitive-ecological approach to the prevention and mitigation of violence and aggression in inner-city youth. In D. P. Fry & K. Bjorkqvist (Eds.), *Cultural variation in conflict resolution: Alternatives to violence* (pp. 199–213). Hillsdale, NJ: Erlbaum.

Hall, R. (1993). How children think and feel about war and peace: An Australian study. *Journal of Peace Research, 30,* 181–196.

Hall, R. (1996). *Peer mediation in schools: A review and bibliography.* Bathurst, Australia: Charles Sturt University, School of Teacher Education. (Mimeo, 44 pp.)

Hare, P. (1989). New field of theory: SYMLOG research, 1960–1988. *Advances in Group Processes, 6,* 229–257.

Harris, I. M. (1996). From world peace to peace in the "hood." *Journal for a Just and Caring Education, 2,* 378–395.

Laursen, B., & Collins, W. A. (1994). Interpersonal conflict during adolescence. *Psychological Bulletin, 15,* 197–209.

Moos, R., & Moos, B. (1986). *Family Environment Scale manual* (2nd ed.). Palo Alto, CA: Consulting Psychologists Press.

Rahim, M. A. (1983). *Rahim Organizational Conflict Inventories.* Palo Alto, CA: Consulting Psychologists Press.

Rubin, J., Pruitt, D. G., & Kim, S. H. (1994). *Social conflict:* Escalation, stalemate, and settlement. New York: McGraw-Hill.

Stern, M., & Van Slyck, M. (1993). *PINS Diversion Research Project: Final report.* Washington, DC: Fund for Research in Dispute Resolution.

Stern, M., Van Slyck, M., & Elbedour, S. (1995, March). *Relationship between conflict management style and emotional status among Israeli Bedouins, Israeli Jewish and Gaza Palestinian adolescents.* Paper presented to the meetings of the Society for Research in Child Development, Indianapolis, IN.

Tesser, A., & Martin, L. (1996). The psychology of evaluation. In E. T. Higgins & A. W. Kruglanski (Eds.), *Social psychology: Handbook of basic principles* (pp. 400–432). New York: Guilford Press.

Thomas, K. W., & Kilmann, R. H. (1974). *The Thomas-Kilmann Conflict Mode Instrument.* Tuxedo, NY: Xicom.

Van de Vliert, E. V., & Kabanoff, B. (1990). Towards theory-based measures of conflict management. *Academy of Management Journal, 33,* 199–209.

Van Slyck, M., Pitts, J., & Van Brammer, R. (1998, August). *Incarcerated adolescents' conflict attitudes: Relationship with offense and dispositional factors.* Paper presented to the meetings of the American Psychological Association, San Francisco.

Van Slyck, M., & Stern, M. (1991). Conflict resolution in educational settings: Assessing the impact of peer mediation programs. In K. Duffy, P. Olczak, & J. Grosch (Eds.), *The art and science of community mediation: A handbook for practitioners and researchers* (pp. 257–274). New York: Guilford Press.

Van Slyck, M., & Stern, M. (1996, August). Assessing conflict attitudes: Pre-intervention strategy for enhancing conflict resolution intervention. In L. Nelson (Chair), *Conflict in political and cultural context: Psychological and educational approaches.* Invited symposium presented to the meetings of the American Psychological Association, Toronto.

Van Slyck, M., & Stern, M. (in press). Developmental issues in the use of conflict resolution interventions with adolescents. In I. Harris & L. Forcey (Eds.), *Peacebuilding for adolescents: Strategies for teachers and community leaders.*

Van Slyck, M., Stern, M., & Newland, L. (1992). Parent-child mediation: An empirical assessment. *Mediation Quarterly, 10,* 75–88.

Van Slyck, M., Stern, M., & Wulfert, E. (1998, August). *Understanding, enhancing and assessing peace education: An attitude change approach.* Paper presented to the meetings of the American Psychological Association, San Francisco.

Van Slyck, M., Stern, M., & Zak-Place, J. (1996). Promoting optimal development through conflict resolution education, training, and intervention: An innovative approach for counseling psychologists. *The Counseling Psychologist, 24,* 433–461.

Zanna, M. P., & Rempel, J. K. (1988). Attitudes: A new look at an old concept. In D. Bar-Tal & A. W. Kruglanski (Eds.), *The social psychology of knowledge* (pp. 315–334). Cambridge: Cambridge University Press.

Zimbardo, P. G., & Leippe, M. R. (1991). *The psychology of attitude change and social influence.* New York: McGraw-Hill

PART THREE

LEARNING
IN SCHOOLS

TEACHING CONFLICT AND CONFLICT RESOLUTION IN SCHOOL

(EXTRA-)CURRICULAR CONSIDERATIONS

Kathy Bickmore, Ontario Institute for Studies in Education, University of Toronto

> *The power of democracy rests in its capacity to transform the individual as teacher, trader, corporate executive, child, sibling, worker, artist, friend or mother into a special sort of political being, a citizen among citizens.*

—Mary Dietz 1989, p. 14

AS YOUNG PEOPLE develop and learn about the intersecting social systems of which they are a part, conflict is all around them. Inescapably, as children grow they develop understandings about interpersonal and social conflict, about procedures for handling it, and about the violence and war that may emerge when conflicts are not resolved. In school, official curricula

Presented at Connections '97 International Social Studies Conference, Sydney, New South Wales, Australia, July 1997.

guide children's and adolescents' development of understanding about war, conflict, and peace. At least as powerfully, young people also learn about conflict from the implicit curricula of student activities, teacher and peer responses to political events, school governance, and discipline practices. This chapter discusses the school factors that influence young people's developing understanding of war, conflict, and peace.

Two concerns motivate this research: first, the apparent inescapability of individual and group violence that results in children's entanglement as bystanders, victims, and perpetrators of wartime and peacetime injury (Merelman, 1990; Prothrow-Stith, 1994) and second, the spread of apathy and political cynicism that results in low citizen involvement in democratic activities (Klaassen, 1996; Lasch, 1995). These are really the twin horns of one dilemma: young citizens are often less involved in the institutionalized processes that are designed to manage social conflict and increasingly involved in the violence that is a consequence of the escalation of such conflict. Ironically, many young people are involved in violent activity without necessarily understanding themselves as social actors who make choices that influence the course of that activity. Peace appears to be an abstraction, while war and violent conflict carry vivid images into every developing mind. Children often don't understand peace as a dynamic equilibrium that depends on citizens' participation in (learned) processes for handling conflict.

Schools can play an important part in handling this dilemma by helping diverse young people to "see themselves in the definition of citizen" (Adler, 1994, p. 35) and therefore to internalize skills, norms, and roles for managing personal and social conflict. Clearly educators do not agree on the importance of such citizenship education for peace, never mind on how to do it. Powerful absences and silences in school activities leave certain matters unquestioned and certain citizens uninvolved and unheard. In this chapter, I examine a broad range of school-based learning opportunities that influence young people's development of knowledge and inclinations for handling conflict. I argue for more systematic and careful inclusion of conflict education in school: if peace requires nonviolent management of conflict, then education for peace requires *practice* with conflict.

Conflict—perceived incompatible objectives between two or more people or groups—occurs in every social system. It is part of being alive. The evolution and successful management of a conflict depends upon these factors (Deutsch, 1973; Kriesberg, 1982)

- The parties' awareness of problems and potential solutions
- The degree of interdependence (relationship) among the parties

- The degree of equilibrium (balance and stability) among the parties
- The existence of predictable (understood) procedures for handling problems

The ingredients for conflict resolution, in relation to each of these factors, can be taught. Like violence, nonviolence is learned behavior. School classrooms and school activities are important settings in which children and youth develop

- An understanding of conflict and its consequences
- Skills in recognizing and nurturing healthy relationships with people like and unlike themselves
- Knowledge of (and the capacity to navigate) the workings of power in social and political systems
- The skills and inclinations to use a broad repertoire of conflict resolution (peacemaking) processes (Deutsch, 1993)

Paradoxically, peacemaking requires confrontation with conflict. Without carefully balanced opportunities to practice making informed decisions, particularly in public schools, the prevalent cultural models of social fragmentation, alienation, and violence are bound to carry tremendous weight in young people's socialization. In societies with contested political regimes, children may learn a great deal about managing conflict and violence, but meanwhile they may be developing rigid, fearful notions of themselves and others that impede efforts at conflict resolution (Merelman, 1990). In regimes that are largely peaceful or uncontested, children may learn to fear conflict and to regard dissenters as abnormal, thus undercutting positive possibilities for social integration and democratization. This paradox can put schools in an awkward position because of the political nature of public education. However, the alternative to confronting conflict in school is to have young citizens learn about conflict idiosyncratically and accidentally, thus allowing the spiral of violence to persist.

How do schools teach about conflict and peace? As public concern over violence increases, school leaders often respond with what has been called "negative peacemaking," the premature use of bargaining or settlement procedures, before underlying problems have been solved or understood (Curle & Dugan, 1982; see also Bettman & Moore, 1994; Fennimore 1997). The goal of negative peacemaking is avoidance, not problem solving. For example, educators may take short-term safety measures that emphasize control, exclusion or segregation of disruptive students, and avoidance of sensitive topics. From these models, students may learn to hide their true feelings, to blame others for problems, and to censor uncomfortable topics or viewpoints. In contrast, feminist political science identifies "positive liberty"—procedures and encouragement for broad involvement in handling community concerns and conflicts—as a guiding principle of democracy (Dietz, 1989). Positive liberty involves the practice of active democratic participation. For example, students are engaging in positive liberty when:

- They learn about conflict resolution by serving on a student government committee.
- They learn about power and problem solving by contributing to a service project.
- They learn about peacemaking by serving as peer facilitators or conflict mediators.
- They learn about analyzing multiple perspectives on public questions by studying problems of war, peace, or controversial issues.

With the good intention of protecting political neutrality and safety, public education—even education intended to teach conflict resolution—may be "co-opted" by the "powerful logic" of hierarchical school management and thus reduced to mere "violence prevention" (Deutsch, 1993).

The notions of negative peacemaking and positive liberty are contrasting emphases in education for citizenship that provide a conceptual framework for organizing this chapter. First, I will examine some prevailing practices in school discipline, in particular negative peacemaking efforts to minimize disruption and overt violence. Second, I will review the research on a range of school-based conflict resolution training programs in order to examine the relative space that may be given to negative peacemaking and positive liberty in such efforts. Third, I will discuss a range of programs, including student governance and academic classroom work, that show promise for infusing positive liberty into school practices. In particular, I will focus on the infusion of controversial material and peace concerns into the academic curriculum and instructional processes. I will conclude by assessing the possibilities for citizenship education that would develop young people's understanding of conflict and peace.

School Discipline and Violence Prevention

Discipline, the management of student behavior, is at the heart of school-based socialization. Repeated modeling and consistent practice are powerful influences on learning (whether or not they are consciously planned):

deeds speak more loudly than words. Thus the processes of developing and enforcing school rules, and of grouping and sorting students for the delivery of the curriculum, are powerful contributors to young people's understanding of themselves as members of society (Clifton & Roberts, 1993; Epp & Watkinson, 1996; Ingersoll, 1996). Young citizens learn about conflict and violence by observing the ways conflictual or violent incidents are handled (and by whom), and by practicing and internalizing particular norms and roles in relation to conflict management. This implicit curriculum regarding conflict, violence, and peace varies widely from place to place and from teacher to teacher. Educators wield different types and degrees of authority in relation to students and their conflicts, sometimes in ways that facilitate students' development of their own autonomous strategies for handling conflict and preventing violence and sometimes (unfortunately) in ways that insist upon dumb obedience. Freire comments: "[While a young teacher of Portuguese] I began to see that the authority of the teacher is absolutely necessary for the development of the students, but if the authority of the teacher goes beyond the limits authority has to have in relation to the students' freedom, then we no longer have authority. We no longer have freedom. We have authoritarianism" (Horton & Freire, 1990, pp. 61–62).

Classroom conflicts matter to students. Young people learn a great deal about conflict from the ways they and their peers are treated in school. Discipline practices sometimes ignore what educators know about good teaching, for example, the importance of clear explanations, positive feedback, and guided practice to help students improve their skills (Schimmel, 1997). This negative peacemaking undermines young people's opportunities to develop *self*-discipline and an understanding of democratic citizenship. If classroom rules are negative, restrictive, unexplained, or delivered in a rigid legalistic manner, then students may be provoked to subvert or ignore the teacher's goals, especially when they are not under direct surveillance. Thus students develop understandings of conflict and power that the teacher may not have intended. Furthermore, *constructive* resistance (for example, clarifying procedures, correcting misinformation, or assisting peers) is sometimes tarred with the same brush as other forms of perceived "misbehavior" (Kearney & Plax, 1992). As a result, students may cease to think of such teachers as legitimate guides or may internalize implicit values that marginalize conflict, blame particular individuals for confronting problems, or assume that conflict must be managed by powerful authorities rather than by ordinary citizens.

Schools have custodial (control and safety) responsibilities, for which negative peacemaking is a necessary though not sufficient condition.

However, schools also carry humanistic (democratic and child development) responsibilities, for which positive liberty is essential (Larson, 1991). Positive liberty (democratic) experiences in school can make a difference in students' capacity and willingness to engage in democratic citizenship activities, including conflict resolution (Hahn, 1996; Hepburn, 1983). Children learn to make decisions and to solve problems only by participating in—practicing—making decisions and solving problems (Carlsson-Paige & Levin, 1992; Kamii, 1991). It is possible for schools to protect students' safety without asserting authoritarian control that would deny the students opportunities to learn about positive conflict resolution and peacemaking.

It can be a challenge to broaden the range of student involvement in nonpunitive learning opportunities so that democratic experiences are not limited to an elite group of students. When particular students' liberty to participate in positive ways is curtailed, their opportunities to learn conflict resolution and peacemaking are thereby limited. School disciplinary policies often implicitly focus on males, especially minority males, because data on visible school violence, vandalism, and suspension highlight the involvement of these populations (Slee, 1995). Lower-status and minority youth are disproportionately blamed and labeled "difficult" by educators; they often suffer the most severe negative consequences of the negative peacemaking embodied in traditional disciplinary practices (Butchart & McEwan, 1998; Leal, 1994). The kinds of student resistance that are less disruptive, such as absence from school or nonparticipation in activities, are more commonly associated with female students: these behaviors are often relatively ignored (Bergsgaard, 1997; Slee, 1995). Similarly, less visible violence that contributes to girls' absence or alienation, such as sexual harassment, is often not attended to by school personnel (Stein, 1995). In either case, certain students may be denied positive liberty by being implicitly or explicitly excluded from the more autonomous democratic opportunities. Thus, these students learn roles and skills for handling conflict that are different from those of their more privileged peers.

Violence prevention and antibullying programs generally involve narrowly focused "training" in social skills and anger management, supplemented by counseling, stricter punishment, physical plant remodeling, and/or increased staff monitoring responsibilities (Pepler & Craig, 1994; Smith & Sharp, 1994). For example, many schools in North America have recently implemented "zero-tolerance" policies built around negative peacemaking—blaming and excluding from school the identified "perpetrators" of violence. Many of these interventions single out particular populations—disproportionately, ethnic minority males—that are considered by educational leaders to be at risk (Guliano, 1994; Prothrow-Stith, 1994). Critics point out that control-oriented and culturally imposed violence prevention efforts may backfire by reinforcing mutual distrust among members of school communities, thus escalating conflict and breeding additional resistance (Lederach, 1991; Noguera, 1995; Soriano, Soriano, & Jimenez, 1994). The unintended consequence of negative peacemaking programs may be to marginalize people who have engaged in violence, rather than to educate the broad population of students regarding nonviolent alternatives. Some violence prevention efforts do build in prejudice reduction lessons or problem-solving strategies (Girard & Koch, 1996; Greenberg, 1995; Metis Associates, 1990; Schwartz, 1994). However, when such programs are limited to the margins of schools, they are ill prepared to address problems of social conflict or violence. This is the dilemma of negative peacemaking: it is understandable that school leaders would wish to put a lid on school violence, but premature imposition of surface-level remedies can exacerbate underlying tensions and resolve nothing.

Peer Conflict Resolution Programs

School-based conflict resolution programs are spreading rapidly and are persisting, in part because the public demands that school administrators "do something" about school violence (Posner, 1994). Many participants in programs strongly believe in the positive effects they have experienced (Cameron & Dupuis, 1991; Davis, 1994; Lawton, 1994). Increasingly, there is firm evidence of those effects (Jones, 1998; Roderick, 1998). Not surprisingly, the strongest well-documented effects of peer conflict resolution programs have been on the most direct and frequent participants, especially the student leaders selected to be leaders and conflict managers (Bickmore, 1997; Lam, 1988; Shulman, 1996). It has been difficult to substantiate the influence of these programs on whole-school climates. Surveys of attitudes toward interpersonal conflict, for example, are difficult to attribute to any one educational experience. Changes in rates of suspension for fighting (Koch, 1988; Stichter, 1986) can be attributed to many factors, including administrative policy, not merely to conflict resolution programs. Some of the most convincing assessments of student conflict resolution programs are closely tied to conflict resolution theory, showing, for example, how many peer conflicts were successfully resolved, how many integrative (win-win) rather than distributive (win-lose) settlements were proposed (in real or hypothetical scenarios), and/or to what degree particular skills and conflict management procedures were retained and used spontaneously (Johnson & Johnson, 1996). The evidence indicates that intensive instruction and practice in conflict resolution processes can have a profoundly positive effect on those with the positive liberty to participate directly and for a significant period of time.

Many of the earliest, and still common, school conflict resolution programs have been cadre peer mediation programs, in which a few students are identified and pulled out of regular classes for special conflict resolution training (see Chapter Thirteen of this volume). Most such programs are based on the assumption that only students, not adults, need to learn conflict resolution skills (Maxwell, 1989; Stomfay-Stitz, 1994). Typically, twenty to thirty students per school are pulled out of regular classes for twelve to twenty hours of skill-building workshops. Thus trained, the peer mediators help their schoolmates to voluntarily negotiate resolutions to their own conflicts, generally following a prescribed series of steps. Often, peer mediators serve on the playground at recess or in special mediation areas during free periods. Some programs choose "model" students (predominantly girls who are already doing well in school) to be mediators. This elite approach can limit the influence of a program and the willingness of many students to self-refer conflicts to mediation, compared with programs that choose a broader range of students who are identified as having both "positive" and "negative" leadership potential (Bickmore, 1993b; Bodine & Crawford, 1997; Day-Vines, 1996). In any case, the vast majority of students in these schools encounter alternative dispute resolution only as observers of an introductory presentation or as clients. Most school-based conflict education programs have not been sufficiently large, well funded, or well integrated into the business of schooling to offer such an experience to the majority of students, much less to the adult members of these school communities.

Recently, there has been an increasing trend toward moving conflict resolution in from the extracurricular margins. There are many examples of social skills and conflict resolution curriculum materials that are designed to be used by teachers in regular classrooms (Bickmore, with Looney & Goldthwait, 1984; Carruthers, Carruthers, Day-Vines, Bostick, & Watson, 1996; Glass, 1994; Opffer, 1997). The goal has been to offer conflict resolution education to more students in each school over a sustained period of time. These programs guide students to develop knowledge, inclinations, and skills in what might be called the "basics" of conflict resolution, whether or not any students' roles are actually changed to include negotiation or mediation of actual peer conflicts in school. One of the most venerable and influential of such programs, more than twenty years old and still flourishing, is the Children's Creative Response to Conflict (CCRC) program (Prutzman, Burger, Bodenhamer, & Stern, 1978). CCRC's materials build student-centered activities around four intersecting themes that increase students' capacity for handling conflict: affirmation (appreciating oneself and others), communication (sending and interpreting verbal and nonverbal cues), cooperation (working and playing together to do things one could not do alone), and conflict resolution (developing a repertoire of skills for handling problems and creating win-win solutions). CCRC's recent work adds a fifth theme, bias awareness, that intersects with all the others (Prutzman & Johnson, 1997).

A contrasting program that infused conflict resolution into regular classroom activity was designed, based on cognitive development theory, and implemented in several Icelandic elementary classrooms (Adalbjarnadóttir, 1992). This program emphasized "activating children's reasoning processes for the promotion of their social development" (p. 400). Teachers led groups of students through discussions, using open-ended questions, in order to model and have students practice cognitive strategies for autonomously working out problems. The students' ability to generate solutions to various hypothetical dilemmas was assessed before and after the program. It was interesting that girls generally improved more in their reasoning about conflicts with peers whereas boys, on average, improved most in reasoning about conflicts with the teacher. One possible explanation is that many boys received more of the teacher's attention: thus, during the conflict resolution lessons, these assertive children had more practice with cognitive skills that require self-confidence in dealing with authority.

In common with a negative peacemaking emphasis, many conflict resolution education materials emphasize teaching students to be polite and nondisruptive, rather than assertive and active in handling conflict. On the other hand, conflict skills can be powerful tools for positive liberty; with these skills students become more able to solve their own problems and to express their interests in ways that can be effectively heard. A few conflict education programs, which I will discuss in more detail, begin to transcend the weight of school tradition and to broaden the positive liberty that provides students with opportunities to learn about conflict and peace.

Implicit Curriculum About Conflict: Diverse Students' Citizenship in School

Conflict management and school governance are important aspects of the implicit curriculum that is embedded in the regular valuing and sanctioning of particular behaviors. Young people learn from what they practice, in particular, from the responsibilities they fulfill in their communities, schools, and classrooms. For example, they learn about interpersonal and social conflict from the roles they play (or are excluded from playing) in handling school community questions and problems. How do educators help diverse students to see themselves as potential actors, not merely pawns, in peacemaking and conflict management efforts? Close and Lechman (1997, p. 11) discuss some of the problems:

> Violence prevention programming, safe and peaceful schools, and school reform are all issues that are discussed and debated without the students. . . . Yet, when there are successful programs that have embraced these young people, encouraged them, cried with them, and shared power with them, our educational institutions are slow to accept these models and respect the young people's knowledge and abilities. We must examine these attitudes and how they [affect] the conflict resolution work we do. . . . It is imperative that we examine the issue of power, who has it, and how it is being used.

If people learn to handle conflict by participating in making decisions, then leadership responsibilities provide particularly good opportunities for conflict learning. Student leadership and student governance have been elements in many school programs for at least the last fifty years, but with widely fluctuating scope and purposes (Danielson, 1989; Goodman, 1992; Smith, 1951). Adults, including educators, are not necessarily disposed toward sharing power with young people. Some student government programs embody educators' notions of "good citizens" but involve very little autonomous decision making. For example, classroom management tasks or community service responsibilities are sometimes delegated to students without allowing them much voice in decisions affecting the activities (Cole & Proctor, 1994; Heath & Vik, 1994; Lewis, 1996). Student input may be limited to planning relatively marginal special occasions or publications (Howard & Kenny, 1992, Mueller & Perris, 1996). Only rarely do student organizations engage in significant decision making regarding essential school or community issues, which would provide opportunities to develop participants' understanding of conflict.

Students learn to manage increasingly complex conflicts when their decisions carry tangible authority—for example, when student leaders fulfill executive and judicial as well as legislative roles, when they have the power to override an administrative veto, or when any student can participate without prior adult approval (Blight, 1996; Dreyfuss, 1990; Koskinen, Shadden, & Steffan, 1972). Young people may learn contradictory lessons about conflict if their student newspapers are censored by administrators (Oettinger, 1995). However, even limited forms of student leadership or governance, especially when they involve skilled facilitation by adult advocates, give participating students opportunities to develop an understanding of conflict and peacemaking. For example, student leaders develop proficiency in effective communication, recognition of differing viewpoints, persuasion, identification of shared interests, and invention of problem-solving procedures (Hepburn, 1983; Leatt, 1987). In class or school community meetings, students can apply their concepts of justice to conflicts among their peers: "They practice creating the rules by which they want to live" (Angell, 1996, p. 24; see also Sadowsky, 1992).

In common with most adult political systems, student governance efforts persistently run into the challenges of inclusivity and unequal status. It is common to view the noninvolvement of some individuals as evidence of apathy, rather than as evidence of an implicitly exclusionary system (Keith, 1971). People tend to get involved in activities that embody the concerns they feel are important. The population of student leaders, and the matters they take on, thus influence which of their peers will be interested in becoming involved in those activities. Just as teachers sometimes allow only "good" students to be peer mediators, students with below-average grades are commonly excluded from student council participation (Keith, 1971; Koskinen et al., 1972). Even among students deemed eligible by the school staff, only a few students are sufficiently popular among their peers to be elected to leadership positions. Girls and other lower-status students may have little representation in student governance if they have limited opportunities to develop the prerequisite skills and self-confidence; however, compensatory leadership training can reduce such barriers (Stiles, 1986). Bringing student governance activities into the mainstream of school life (for example, by making them part of classroom activity or scheduling governance meetings into regular slots during the school day) gives proportionately more students the opportunity to participate in democratic decision making, and thus to develop a practiced understanding of conflict and its resolution.

In earlier generations, young people often did carry significant responsibilities for handling social problems and conflicts simply because of the ways their communities were organized. Now, many youth have the luxury of remaining children (carrying little responsibility) for more years (Conrad & Hedin, 1977; Postman, 1982). Everyday life outside of school, especially in socially marginalized areas or in communities at war, is unlikely to facilitate young people's natural development of democratic strategies for handling conflict and violence (Merelman, 1990). Therefore, today educators create new avenues for young people to experiment with (and reason about) community participation, in order to help them learn to manage the conflicts inherent in citizenship. Schools sometimes encourage or require students to practice with many types of citizen action, including social involvement such as recycling or peer mediation, direct service such as helping in hospitals or soup kitchens, advocacy such as persuading local governments to change toxic dumping regulations, and electoral participation such as analyzing the positions of candidates for the school board (Avery, 1994). In contrast, many other schools limit student participation, implicitly teaching students that "problems should be solved by the unilateral decision of authorities rather than by more democratic means" (Hepburn, 1983, p. 12). Students develop their understanding of conflict, violence, and peacemaking through participation in communities' and schools' patterns of decision making and conflict management: wider opportunities for active involvement yield broader gains in understanding.

Explicit Curriculum About Conflict: Handling Diverse Viewpoints in the Classroom

The unknown, the controversial, and the problematic are the fuel for good conversation and the sparks that motivate inquiry for learning (Britzman, 1992; Engle & Ochoa, 1988, esp. pp. 28–48; Graff, 1992; Hooks, 1994). Democratic peacemaking depends on citizens' development of capacity and respect for independent critical thought (Edwards, 1998; Simmons, 1994). Critical thinking (conflict management) skills cannot be developed without critique. War, conflict, and peace are core concepts, prominent in human imagination and action, yet treatment of these ideas remains remarkably muted in most schools' curricula. Avoidance of conflict in school subject matter distances the curriculum from life, rendering it meaningless. Comprehensive infusion of cooperation and conflict resolution into *both* school processes *and* the core curriculum is more likely to yield significant and lasting learning than more limited interventions (Carruthers et al., 1996; Deutsch, 1993; Johnson & Johnson, 1996).

Conflict education may be infused directly into academic lessons. Confronting conflicting perspectives in the protected world of the classroom provides students with opportunities to learn strategies for handling conflict and for avoiding violence in their lives (Duryea, 1992; Newmann & Oliver, 1970; Soley, 1996). For example, students may analyze and respond to the conflicts in literature while learning to read, learn processes for managing political controversies in social studies, or discuss problems concerning the application of technology in science lessons. Open discussion of controversial matters in the classroom has been shown to help students to develop an interest in the social and political world, the capacity for reflective analytic and evaluative thinking, and a sense of efficacy as actors in their own lives (Hahn, 1996; Harwood, 1992; Mellor, 1996).

It is important to note, however, that conflict-centered instruction involves more than putting controversial topics on the agenda. Virtually all history curricula deal with immense human conflicts involving war and peace, yet commonly they manage to give the impression that these momentous events occurred almost *without* conflict. Curriculum and text-book materials chronicle military exploits and even the outcomes of war from such a distance that the events appear inevitable and nearly blood-less. The underlying conflicts over which wars were waged, and the dis-agreements at the time over how countries, communities, and individuals should handle those conflicts, have been erased from public school inter-pretations of history. Students develop understanding by engaging in the "conflictuality" of conflictual topics: that is, conflict education involves not only content but also the *processes* of asking critical questions and confronting contrasting viewpoints in relation to those topics.

A curriculum that at first appears to present human problems may, by avoiding conflict, actually marginalize some viewpoints and mold others into oversimplified "correct" answers or formulas (Ennis, 1996; Foster, 1996). For example, feminist movements have caused the inclusion of a few women's names in school history books. However, many texts still avoid really examining the *points of view* of these newly included char-acters, in particular their disagreements with the military and political leaders around whom the narratives are organized. This serves to trivial-ize women's (or other low-status citizens') contributions to society. Ignor-ing the perspectives of women such as Nobel Peace Prize–winner Emily Greene Balch leaves certain kinds of human endeavors, such as peace-making, unrecognized (Noddings, 1992). This is a major challenge to prevailing curriculum models: young people will not develop an under-standing of war, conflict, and peace by "covering" certain information, but only by grappling with the messy business of human disagreement. Conflict education weaves the *process* of engaging diverse students inex-tricably into the curricular content.

Introduction of conflictual questions can bring previously silenced young people into the pedagogical conversation, giving them the means, the opportunity, and the motivation to learn. For example, a seventh- to eighth-grade social studies and English class practiced research methods by conducting an observational study to see whether boys talked or inter-rupted more than girls in other classrooms in their school. It was inter-esting that the students found wide variations among classrooms, but what was tremendous was the impact of having opened this question at all: "The effect on the girls of actually conducting this study was immeasurable. They spoke up passionately throughout our discussions—some for the first time" (Schur, 1995, p. 147).

A caution: there is perhaps no such thing as a climate that is equally open and safe for all members of the class. Participants' diverse histories, relationships, and prior knowledge affect the degree to which they feel safe and respected, even in an apparently open classroom climate (Ellsworth, 1989). Paradoxically, opening the floor to diverse viewpoints can include some students and at the same time silence others (Bickmore, 1993a). Considerable planning and listening are involved in facilitating the human processes that make openness real for the widest possible variety of students (Kreidler, 1990; Rossi, 1996).

In order to learn, young people need a balance between "dissonance" (conflict that stimulates cognitive development) and "emotional safety" (negative peacemaking that enables them to learn in a certain environment) (Houser, 1996; Hydrick, 1994). This balance is often skewed away from dissonance, especially in elementary classrooms: when educators emphasize safety at all costs, they create comfortable but unstimulating environments that, ironically, slow down or narrow students' learning. Furthermore, classroom climates that are closed to dissent, or that assign passive roles to students, can have a decidedly negative effect on young people's willingness and capacity to engage in further discussion regarding social and political issues (Ehman, 1969). Controversial subject matter, if it is presented with careful attention to inclusive and respectful instructional processes, can develop diverse students' understanding of social conflict and confidence in responding to it (Hahn, 1996).

Since conflict resolution requires communication skills, language and literature classes are natural places for conflict education. Conflict is intrinsically interesting; thus a curriculum that embraces conflict gives students reasons to talk and read together, whether in a first or second language (Iino, 1994). For example, many children's books highlight questions about conflict and its consequences. Some young people's literature provides insight into concepts of justice and practice in understanding the perspectives of others (Easley, 1993; Luke & Myers, 1994; Stevahn, Johnson, & Johnson, 1996). Literature that touches upon unresolved human conflicts and unpopular viewpoints risks provoking fear and even calls for censorship (Herzog, 1994). However, if a teacher has a clear rationale to explain why the risks are worthwhile (that is, what students are expected to learn) and how diverse students with minority views will be protected, then such lessons can be defended effectively (Worthington,

1985). Students themselves can *create* texts that handle conflict. For example, a summer literacy program guided adolescents to develop persuasion skills by producing a public document regarding the dangers of drugs (Long, Flower, Fleming, & Wojahn, 1995). Guided opportunities for managing conflict can stimulate the development of language, an essential ingredient of nonviolent conflict resolution.

Conflict and its resolution are also important in mathematical and scientific education. Peer disagreements can help students to articulate their understandings, to clarify underlying concepts, and to translate ideas into language that helps peers to understand (Crumbaugh, 1996). Furthermore, application of math or science to real-life problems (in which there inevitably are disagreements) can help young people to take a measure of control over some of the powerful influences in their lives: "Both the (apparent) complexities of technology and the (superficially) wonderful concrete changes it has made in daily life, from washing machines to word processors, convince people that control over our high-tech society must be left to 'experts.' Critical education in the United States, therefore, must counter this belief by showing people that they can understand how technology works, and in whose interest" (Frankenstein, 1987, p. 185). Application of science and technology to "real life" connects it with the social context, as, for example, when students examine legal cases involving conflicts over fundamental scientific beliefs (Morishita, 1991). Another approach, in keeping with the work of adult scientists, is to engage students in testing alternative theories for explaining physical phenomena—either as these theories have evolved in the history of science or inductively, based on concrete experimentation and observation (Settlage & Sabik, 1997). Any human endeavor worth learning about involves some conflict.

Perhaps the most common way teachers present conflict as a learning opportunity, in history and the social sciences, is by initiating debates. These are no doubt motivating, especially for the most confident and aggressive students, but it takes considerable planning to make debates a real opportunity for a wide range of students to learn to manage social conflict. For example, an integrated social studies and language arts Debating Society program in an Ontario public school focused on controversial events in Canadian society (McGeown, 1995). In this program, high school students led preparatory discussions with younger students (grades three through eight), so that they all had opportunities to participate and to develop understanding over time. If debates are organized around thoughtful preparation and mutual response, not simply winning, then students who participate actively may learn to listen for big ideas and points of view, to respect opposing opinions, and to communicate persuasively. In order for students to learn the skills and understanding for integrative rather than competitive management of conflict, lessons that begin with debate may require the students to switch roles and eventually to negotiate a mutually acceptable solution (see Chapter Twelve of this volume).

A way to handle conflictual topics that is more oriented toward broad participation and conflict *resolution* is the simulation activity. This strategy encourages students to develop a more complex understanding of problems such as war, as well as to handle more localized problem solving or peacemaking. Students may play the roles of historical characters, for example in a simulation of negotiations regarding Canada's role in the conflict that became the deadly World War II battle of Dieppe (Morton, 1986). Alternatively, students take the perspectives of various interest groups in relation to conflict scenarios such as the control and use of resources or choices in energy development (Borad & Fagerstrom, 1985; Curow, 1985). Lessons may also introduce students to the challenges faced by global and local institutions, such as nongovernmental organizations, the United Nations, and international treaties, in attempting to prevent violence and its causes (Angell & Hahn, 1996; Boulding, 1988). Simulation-type activities highlight the *interdependent* relationships between conflicting parties; thus students practice cooperation and the creation of integrative solutions, not simply winning or losing.

Oddly enough, peace is one of the more controversial matters to teach about, especially if this involves examining the causes and consequences of particular episodes of political violence. The careful examination of "human-initiated, catastrophic events whose legacy we still live" can help young people to understand the dangers of thoughtlessness and to develop understandings that can be applied to preventing future wars and injustices (Eppert et al., 1996, p. 19; see also Avery, Sullivan, & Wood, 1997; Strom, Sleeper, & Johnson, 1992). Peace education requires connection of the interpersonal to the cross-cultural and international in order to develop transferrable (useful) understandings regarding the management of conflict (Harris, 1996; Hicks, 1988; Tabachnick, 1990).

Value-laden international material is particularly well suited to helping students develop their capacity for flexible and independent thought because it highlights and demystifies multiple perspectives (Bottery, 1992; Merryfield & Remy, 1995). A few critics have argued that multiple loyalties to the nation and the world, inherent in a global perspective, are unworkable (Fullinwider, 1994). However, loyalty without understanding would fly in the face of democracy and human development, especially in today's era of multiple and particularistic identities (Elkind, 1995).

Children develop allegiances and patterns of conflict management from the political realities in which they live (Merelman, 1990): public education is generally intended to *broaden* their horizons, to help them to view the conflicts of their lives with new eyes. Problem posing and peace education extend to students the positive liberty to engage in handling social conflict, first by developing an awareness of particular instances of conflict and second by creating and practicing mechanisms for developing peaceful and balanced relationships, thus countering the primary causes of violence (Curle & Dugan, 1982).

Conclusion

It is tempting to respond to educational problems with quick fixes, and thus to respond to the problem of violence with negative peacemaking strategies that put the lid on the symptoms of the problem. If we were content to live under a dictatorship, perhaps it would suffice to prevent overtly violent behavior by means of coercion and manipulation. However, stable peace and democratic development require a more open approach to education. Short-run problem reduction strategies tend to enhance hierarchical control and breed dependence without enhancing the students' capacity to resolve problems autonomously. Many important opportunities for long-term conflict management learning exist, not when people are hurt and angry (whether in wars or schoolyard scuffles) but in the everyday process of learning and living in a school community. Paradoxically, this means that just at the times when conflict *can* be avoided in school, it often *shouldn't* be. If students have the positive liberty to practice managing conflict in the protected environment of their school, then they will develop the skills and understandings to participate in the nonviolent management of conflict as citizens.

The pursuit of peace and justice is not embodied in any particular curricular or extracurricular program. Instead, every realm of school life is involved in teaching young people about war and violence, conflict and peace. Behavior management patterns and the core academic curriculum, by virtue of being most of what happens in school, are the most pervasive organizers of student learning about conflict, and also the most difficult to change. Smaller-scale and pilot programs in conflict resolution education provide spaces for innovation and experimentation, in the hope that they will eventually influence the core subject matter and the regularized processes of schooling.

What is getting in the way of systemic implementation of positive liberty in schools and the consequent development of students' capacity for nonviolent peacemaking? Beliefs about which relational processes and knowledge count as "real school" are deeply embedded in the norms of our cultures (Metz, 1990). Deeply entrenched habits of schooling reinforce

- Avoidance of conflict rather than development of students' awareness of problems and solutions
- Sorting and ethnocentric-nationalistic content rather than an understanding of human relationships and interdependence
- Curbing of controversy or student resistance rather than fostering students' capacity to understand and navigate the realms of power and inequality
- Short-term efficiency and safety rather than helping students to develop autonomous skills in conflict resolution or peacemaking processes

Furthermore, the bureaucracies that run many public schools have elevated standardization, summative assessment, and replicability to the status of sacred principles: the indirect, student-centered, and context-bound nature of the kinds of education that nurture peace and democracy sit awkwardly in the prevailing organization of schools (Kahne, 1996). Perhaps true peace education cannot be mandated or fully tested across cultural and political contexts.

However, the same forces of alienation and violence that make peace and conflict education necessary are also challenging these old realities of schooling. It is not merely that schools *should* not limit students' liberty to practice managing conflict; schools demonstrably *cannot* and *will not* go on as they have in the past. The world is simply changing too fast: to their credit, students are already actively resisting the old order (Elkind, 1995). As necessity is the mother of invention, the efforts to broaden students' conflict education opportunities are likely to persist and multiply.

REFERENCES

Adalbjarnadóttir, S. (1992). Fostering children's social conflict resolutions in the classroom: A developmental approach. In F. K. Oser, A. Dick, & J.-L. Patry (Eds.), *Effective and responsible teaching: The new synthesis* (pp. 397–412). San Francisco: Jossey-Bass.

Adler, S. (1994). The future of equity in the social studies. In M. Nelson (Ed.), *The future of the social studies* (pp. 35–40). Boulder, CO: Social Science Education Consortium.

Angell, A. (1996, April). *Nurturing democratic community at school: A qualitative analysis of an elementary class council.* Paper presented at meeting of American Educational Research Association, New York, NY.

Angell, A., & Hahn, C. (1996). Global perspectives. In W. Parker (Ed.), *Educating the democratic mind* (pp. 337–367). Albany: State University of New York Press.

Avery, P. (1994). The future of political participation in civic education. In M. Nelson (Ed.), *The future of the social studies* (pp. 47–52). Boulder, CO: Social Science Education Consortium.

Avery, P., Sullivan, J., & Wood, S. (1997, Winter). Teaching for tolerance of diverse beliefs. *Theory into Practice, 36* (1), 32–38.

Bergsgaard, M. (1997, Fall). Gender issues in the implementation and evaluation of a violence-prevention curriculum. *Canadian Journal of Education, 22* (1), 33–45.

Bettman, E., & Moore, P. (1994, November). Conflict resolution programs and social justice. *Education and Urban Society, 27* (1), 11–21.

Bickmore, K. (1993a, Fall). Learning inclusion/inclusion in learning: Citizenship education for a pluralistic society. *Theory and Research in Social Education, 21* (4), 341–384.

Bickmore, K. (1993b, May). *Teaching youth leaders to be peacemakers.* Unpublished evaluator's report on Alternative Dispute Resolution Project, Cleveland Public Schools, Cleveland, OH.

Bickmore, K. (1997, Winter). Preparation for pluralism: Curricular and extracurricular practice with conflict resolution. *Theory into Practice, 36* (1), 3–10.

Bickmore, K., with Looney, J., & Goldthwait, P. (1984). *Alternatives to violence: A manual for teaching peacemaking to youth and adults.* Cleveland, OH: Cleveland Friends Meeting. (ERIC Document Reproduction Service No. ED 250 254)

Blight, M. (1996, Spring–Summer). The Hanover High School Council. *Democracy and Education, 10* (3), 31–36.

Bodine, R., & Crawford, D. (1997). *The handbook of conflict resolution education: A guide to building quality programs in schools.* San Francisco: Jossey-Bass & NIDR.

Borad, B., & Fagerstrom, R. (1985, July). Environmental decision. *Intercom, 107,* 8–10.

Bottery, M. (1992). Education, dissent, and the internationalisation of schooling. *Westminster Studies in Education, 15,* 69–78.

Boulding, E. (1988). *Building a global civic culture: Education for an interdependent world.* New York: Teachers College Press.

Britzman, D. (1992). Decentering discourses in teacher education: or, the unleashing of unpopular things. In K. Weiler & C. Mitchell (Eds.), *What schools CAN do: Critical pedagogy and practice* (pp. 151–175). Albany: State University of New York Press.

Butchart, R., & McEwan, B. (Eds.). (1998). *Classroom discipline in American schools: Problems and possibilities for democratic education.* Albany: State University of New York Press.

Cameron, J., & Dupuis, A. (1991, Spring). The introduction of school mediation to New Zealand. *Journal of Research and Development in Education, 24* (3), 1–13.

Carlsson-Paige, N., & Levin, D. (1992, November). A constructivist approach to conflict resolution. *Young Children, 48,* 4–13.

Carruthers, W., Carruthers, B., Day-Vines, N., Bostick, D., & Watson, D. (1996, May). Conflict resolution as curriculum: A definition, description, and process for integration in core curricula. *The School Counselor, 43,* 345–373.

Clifton, R., & Roberts, L. (1993). *Authority in classrooms.* Scarborough, Canada: Prentice Hall Canada.

Close, C., & Lechman, K. (1997, Winter). Fostering youth leadership: Students train students and adults in conflict resolution. *Theory into Practice, 36* (1), 11–16.

Cole, C., & Proctor, V. (1994, March). Action councils: An alternative to student council. *Middle School Journal, 25* (4), 47–49.

Conrad, D., & Hedin, D. (1977). Learning and earning citizenship through participation. In J. Shaver (Ed.), *Building rationales for citizenship education* (pp. 48–73). Washington, DC: National Council for the Social Studies.

Crumbaugh, C. (1996, April). *From harmony to cacophony: A study of student disagreement in a fourth grade math classroom.* Poster session presented at American Educational Research Association, New York, NY.

Curle, A., & Dugan, M. (1982, Summer). Peacemaking: Stages and sequence. *Peace and Change, 8* (2–3), 19–28.

Curow, F. (1985, July). Energy policy. *Intercom, 107,* 18–21.

Danielson, N. (1989). Helping pupils to help themselves: Pupils' councils and participation. In K. Jenson & S. Walker (Eds.), *Toward democratic schooling: European experiences* (pp. 151–156). Milton Keynes, U.K.: Open University Press.

Davis, G. (1994, Summer). Don't fight, mediate. *Journal of Invitational Theory and Practice, 3* (2), 85–94.

Day-Vines, N. (1996, May). Conflict resolution: The value of diversity in the recruitment, selection, and training of peer mediators. *School Counselor, 43* (5), 392–410.

Deutsch, M. (1973). *The resolution of conflict*. New Haven, CT: Yale University Press.

Deutsch, M. (1993, May). Educating for a peaceful world. *American Psychologist, 48* (5), 510–517.

Dietz, M. (1989). Context is all: Feminism and theories of citizenship. In J. Conway, S. Bourque, & J. Scott (Eds.), *Learning about women: Gender, politics and power* (pp. 1–24). Ann Arbor: University of Michigan Press.

Dreyfuss, E. (1990, Spring). Learning ethics in school-based mediation programs. *Update on Law-Related Education, 14* (2), 22–27.

Duryea, M. L. (1992). *Conflict and culture: A literature review and bibliography*. Victoria, British Columbia: University of Victoria Institute for Dispute Resolution.

Easley, S.-D. (1993, June–September). Conflict study through children's literature. *Green Teacher, 34,* 18–19.

Edwards, J. (1998). *Opposing censorship in the public schools: Religion, morality, and literature*. Hillsdale, NJ: Erlbaum.

Ehman, L. (1969). An analysis of the relationships of selected educational variables with the political socialization of high school students. *American Educational Research Journal, 6* (4), 559–580.

Elkind, D. (1995, September). School and family in the postmodern world. *Phi Delta Kappan, 77* (1), 8–14.

Ellsworth, E. (1989, Fall). Why doesn't this feel empowering? Working through the repressive myths of critical pedagogy. *Harvard Educational Review, 59* (3), 297–324.

Engle, S., & Ochoa, A. (1988). *Education for democratic citizenship: Decision making in the social studies*. New York: Teachers College Press.

Ennis, C. (1996, Winter). When avoiding confrontation leads to avoiding content: Disruptive students' impact on curriculum. *Journal of Curriculum and Supervision, 11* (2), 145–162.

Epp, J. R., & Watkinson, A. M. (Eds.). (1996). *Systemic violence: How schools hurt children*. London: Falmer Press.

Eppert, C., Hiller, C., Rosenberg, S., Salverson, J., Sicoli, F., & Simon, R. (1996). Historical memory, violence, and civic education. *Orbit, 27* (2), 19–21.

Fennimore, B. (1997, Winter). When mediation and equity are at odds: Potential lessons in democracy. *Theory into Practice, 36* (1), 59–64.

Foster, V. (1996, April). *Gender equity, citizenship education, and inclusive curriculum: Another case of add women and stir?* Paper presented at meeting of American Educational Research Association, New York, NY.

Frankenstein, M. (1987). Critical mathematics education: An application of Paulo Freire's epistemology. In I. Shor (Ed.), *Freire for the classroom:*

A sourcebook for liberatory teaching (pp. 180–210). Portsmouth, NH: Boynton-Cook.

Fullinwider, R. (1994). Global education and controversy: Some observations. In J. Fonté & A. Ryerson (Eds.), *Education for America's role in world affairs* (pp. 23–30). Lantham, MD: University Press of America.

Girard, K., & Koch, S. (1996). *Conflict resolution in the schools: A manual for educators.* San Francisco: Jossey-Bass & NIDR.

Glass, R. (1994, February). Keeping the peace: Conflict resolution training offers hope for countering the violence in our schools and communities. *American Teacher, 78* (5), 6–7, 15.

Goodman, J. (1992). *Elementary schooling for critical democracy.* Albany: State University of New York Press.

Graff, G. (1992). *Beyond the culture wars: How teaching the conflicts can revitalize American education.* New York: Norton.

Greenberg, B. (1995, January). Identifying and resolving conflict in multicultural settings. *NASSP Bulletin, 79* (567), 51–61.

Guliano, J. (1994, March). A peer education program to promote the use of conflict resolution skills among at-risk school age males. *Public Health Reports, 109,* 158–161.

Hahn, C. (1996). Empirical research on issues-centered social studies. In R. Evans & D. Saxe (Eds.), *Handbook on issues-centered social studies* (pp. 25–41). (Bulletin No. 93). Washington, DC: National Council for the Social Studies.

Harris, I. (1996, October). From world peace to peace in the "hood": Peace education in a postmodern world. *Journal for a Just and Caring Education, 2* (4), 378–395.

Harwood, A. (1992, Winter). Classroom climate and civic education in secondary school. *Theory and Research in Social Education, 20* (1), 47–86.

Heath, J., & Vik, P. (1994, September). Elementary school student councils: A statewide survey. *Principal, 74* (1), 31–34.

Hepburn, M. (1983). Can schools, teachers, and administrators make a difference? In M. Hepburn (Ed.), *Democratic education in schools and classrooms* (pp. 5–29). (Bulletin No. 70). Washington, DC: National Council for the Social Studies.

Herzog, M. (1994, Winter). Teachers' stories about their school censorship experiences. *Democracy and Education, 9* (2), 25–28.

Hicks, D. (1988). Peace and conflict. In B. Carrington & B. Troyna (Eds.), *Children and controversial issues* (pp. 172–188). London: Falmer Press.

Hooks, B. (1994). *Teaching to transgress: Education as the practice of freedom.* New York: Routledge.

Horton, M., & Freire, P. (1990). *We make the road by walking.* Philadelphia, PA: Temple University Press.

Houser, N. (1996, Summer). Negotiating dissonance and safety for the common good: Social education in the elementary classroom. *Theory and Research in Social Education, 24* (3), 294–312.

Howard, R., & Kenny, R. (1992). Education for democracy: Promoting citizenship and critical reasoning through school governance. In A. Garrod (Ed.), *Learning for life: Moral education theory and practice* (pp. 210–227). New York: Praeger.

Hydrick, J. (1994). The elementary school: Censorship within and without. In J. Simmons (Ed.), *Censorship* (pp. 95–106). Newark, DE: International Reading Association.

Iino, A. (1994, November–December). Teaching about the United Nations through the hunger issue in an English as a Foreign Language class. *Social Education, 58* (7), 438–439.

Ingersoll, R. (1996, April). Teachers' decision-making power and school conflict. *Sociology of Education, 69* (2), 159–176.

Johnson, D., & Johnson, R. (1996, Winter). Conflict resolution and peer mediation programs in elementary and secondary schools: A review of the research. *Review of Educational Research, 66* (4), 459–506.

Jones, T. (1998, March–April). Research supports effectiveness of peer mediation. *The Fourth R* (CREnet), *82,* 1, 10–12, 18, 21, 25, 27.

Kahne, J. (1996). The eight-year study: Evaluating progressive education. In J. Kahne, *Reframing educational policy: Democracy, community and the individual* (pp. 119–146). New York: Teachers College Press.

Kamii, C. (1991). Toward autonomy: The importance of critical thinking and choice making. *School Psychology Review, 20* (3), 382–388.

Kearney, P., & Plax, T. (1992). Student resistance to control. In V. Richmond & J. McCroskey (Eds.), *Power in the classroom: Communication, control, and concern* (pp. 85–100). Hillsdale, NJ: Erlbaum.

Keith, K. (1971). *The silent majority: The problem of apathy and the student council.* Washington, DC: National Association of Secondary School Principals.

Klaassen, C. (1996, Autumn). Education and citizenship in a post-welfare state. *Curriculum, 17* (2), 62–73.

Koch, M. (1988, January). Mediated dispute resolution–resolving disputes: Students can do it better. *NASSP Bulletin, 72* (504), 16–18.

Koskinen, J., Shadden, R., & Steffan, S. (1972). Toward a democratic student government. In L. Cuban (Ed.), *Youth as a minority: An anatomy of student rights* (pp. 128–129). Washington, DC: National Council for the Social Studies.

Kreidler, W. (1990). Teaching controversial issues to elementary children. In W. Kreidler, *Elementary perspectives: Teaching concepts of peace and conflict* (pp. 229–236). Cambridge, MA: Educators for Social Responsibility.

Kriesberg, L. (1982, Summer). Social conflict theories and conflict resolution. *Peace and Change, 8* (2–3), 3–17.

Lam, J. (1988, January). *The impact of conflict resolution programs on schools: A review and synthesis of the evidence* (Research Report). Amherst, MA: National Association for Mediation in Education.

Larson, M. (1991, Winter). Intergroup relations and school discipline. *Equity Coalition, 2* (1), 13–18.

Lasch, C. (1995). The lost art of argument. In C. Lasch, *The revolt of the elites and the betrayal of democracy* (pp. 161–178). New York: Norton.

Lawton, M. (1994, November 9). Violence-prevention curricula: What works best? *Education Week,* pp. 1, 10–11.

Leal, R. (1994, November). Conflicting views of discipline in San Antonio schools. *Education and Urban Society, 27* (1), 35–44.

Leatt, D. (1987, December). Developing student leaders: Exemplary school activity programs. *Oregon School Study Council Bulletin, 31* (4), 1–38. (ERIC Document Reproduction Service No. ED 291 151)

Lederach, J. P. (1991). *Beyond prescription: New lenses for conflict resolution training across cultures.* Waterloo Inter-Racial and Cross-Cultural Conflict Resolution Project. (Monograph, distributed by The Network)

Lewis, C. (1996, Fall). Beyond conflict resolution skills: How do children develop the will to solve conflicts at school? *New Directions for Child Development, 73,* 91–106.

Long, E., Flower, L., Fleming, D., & Wojahn, P. (1995). Negotiating competing voices to construct claims and evidence: Urban American teenagers rivalling anti-drug literature. In P. Costello & S. Mitchell (Eds.), *Competing and consensual voices: The theory and practice of argument* (pp. 172–183). Clevedon, U.K.: Multilingual Matters.

Luke, J., & Myers, C. (1994, Winter). Toward peace: Using literature to aid conflict resolution. *Childhood Education, 71* (2), 66–69.

Maxwell, J. (1989). Mediation in the schools: Self-regulation, self-esteem and self-discipline. *Mediation Quarterly, 7,* 149–155.

McGeown, C. (1995, July–August). The King Edward Debating Society adds current events to elementary and middle-school social studies. *The Social Studies, 86* (4), 183–187.

Mellor, A. (1996, December). *The centrality of an active, experiential pedagogy to learning outcomes in citizenship education.* Paper presented at Culture and Citizenship Conference, Brisbane, Australia. (http://www.gu.edu.au/gwis/akccmp/papers/Mellor.html)

Merelman, R. (1990). The role of conflict in children's political learning. In O. Ichilov (Ed.), *Political socialization, citizenship education, and democracy* (pp. 47–65). New York: Teachers College Press.

Merryfield, M., & Remy, R. (1995). *Teaching about international conflict and peace.* Albany: State University of New York Press.

Metis Associates. (1990). *The Resolving Conflict Creatively Program 1988–89: Summary of significant findings.* (ERIC Document Reproduction Service No. ED 348 422)

Metz, M. (1990). Real school: A universal drama amid disparate experience. In D. Mitchel & M. Goertz (Eds.), *Education politics for a new century* (pp. 75–91). London: Falmer Press.

Morishita, F. (1991, February). Teaching about controversial issues: Resolving conflict between creationism and evolution through law-related education. *American Biology Teacher, 53* (2), 91–93.

Morton, T. (1986, Summer). Decision on Dieppe: A cooperative lesson on conflict resolution. *History and Social Science Teacher, 21* (4), 237–241.

Mueller, V., & Perris, C. (1996, Spring). A shift in power: From teacher to student-directed government. *Social Studies Review, 34* (3), 40–42.

Newmann, F., & Oliver, D. (1970). *Clarifying public controversy: An approach to teaching social studies.* New York: Little, Brown.

Noddings, N. (1992). Social studies and feminism. *Theory and Research in Social Education, 20* (3), 230–241.

Noguera, P. (1995, Summer). Preventing and producing violence: A critical analysis of responses to school violence. *Harvard Educational Review, 65* (2), 189–212.

Oettinger, L. (1995, November). *Censorship and the student press.* Paper presented at meeting of the Speech Communication Association, San Antonio, TX. (ERIC Document Reproduction Service No. ED 390 052)

Opffer, E. (1997, Winter). Toward cultural transformation: Comprehensive approaches to conflict resolution. *Theory into Practice, 36* (1), 46–52.

Pepler, D., & Craig, W. (1994). About bullying: Understanding this underground activity. *Orbit, 25* (3), 32–34.

Posner, M. (1994, August–September). Research raises troubling questions about violence prevention programs. *The Fourth R* (National Association for Mediation in Education), *52,* 4, 12–14.

Postman, N. (1982). *The disappearance of childhood.* New York: Laurel Press.

Prothrow-Stith, D. (1994, April). Building violence prevention into the curriculum. *School Administrator, 51* (4), 8–12.

Prutzman, P., Burger, L., Bodenhamer, G., & Stern, L. (1978). *The friendly classroom for a small planet.* Wayne, NJ: Avery.

Prutzman, P., & Johnson, J. (1997, Winter). Bias awareness and multiple perspectives: Essential aspects of conflict resolution. *Theory into Practice, 36* (1), 26–31.

Roderick, T. (1998, March–April). Evaluating the Resolving Conflict Creatively Program. *The Fourth R* (CREnet), *82,* 3–4, 19–21.

Rossi, J. (1996, January). Creating strategies and conditions for civil discourse about controversial issues. *Social Education, 60* (1), 15–21.

Sadowsky, E. (1992). Taking part: Democracy in the elementary school. In A. Garrod (Ed.), *Learning for life: Moral education theory and practice* (pp. 246–262). New York: Praeger.

Schimmel, D. (1997, February). Traditional rule-making and the subversion of citizenship education. *Social Education, 61* (2), 70–74.

Schur, J. (1995, March). Students as social science researchers: Gender issues in the classroom. *Social Education, 59* (3), 144–147.

Schwartz, W. (1994, May). Anti-bias and conflict resolution curricula: Theory and practice. *ERIC/CUE Digest,* No. 97. (ERIC Document Reproduction Service No. ED 371 085)

Settlage, J., & Sabik, C. (1997, Winter). Harnessing the positive energy of conflict in science teaching. *Theory into Practice, 36* (1), 39–45.

Shulman, H. (1996, February). Using developmental principles in violence prevention. *Elementary School Guidance and Counseling, 30,* 170–175.

Simmons, J. (Ed.). (1994). *Censorship: A threat to reading, learning, thinking.* Newark, DE: International Reading Association.

Slee, R. (1995). Adjusting the aperture: Ways of seeing disruption in school (pp. 93–115). In R. Slee, *Changing theories and practices of discipline.* London: Falmer Press.

Smith, J. (1951). *Student councils for our times: Principles and practices.* New York: Teachers College Bureau of Publications.

Smith, P., & Sharp, S. (Eds.). (1994). *School bullying: Insights and perspectives.* London: Routledge.

Soley, M. (1996, January). If it's controversial, why teach it? *Social Education, 60* (1), 9–14.

Soriano, M., Soriano, F., & Jimenez, E. (1994, January). School violence among culturally diverse populations: Sociocultural and institutional factors. *School Psychology Review, 23,* 216–225.

Stein, N. (1995, Summer). Sexual harassment in school: The public performance of gendered violence. *Harvard Educational Review, 65* (2), 145–162.

Stevahn, L., Johnson, D., & Johnson, R. (1996, April). *Integrating conflict resolution training into academic curriculum units: Results of recent studies.*

Paper presented at meeting of American Educational Research Association, New York, NY.

Stichter, C. (1986, March). When tempers flare, let student mediators put out the flames. *American School Board Journal, 173* (4), 41–42.

Stiles, D. (1986, December). Leadership training for high school girls: An intervention at one school. *Journal of Counseling and Development, 65* (4), 211–212.

Stomfay-Stitz, A. (1994). Conflict resolution and peer mediation: Pathways to safer schools. *Childhood Education,* pp. 279–282.

Strom, M., Sleeper, M., & Johnson, M. (1992). Facing history and ourselves: A synthesis of history and ethics in effective history education. In A. Garrod (Ed.), *Learning for life: Moral education theory and practice* (pp. 131–153). New York: Praeger.

Tabachnick, R. (1990, Spring). Studying peace in elementary schools: Laying a foundation for the Peaceable Kingdom. *Theory and Research in Social Education, 18* (2), 169–173.

Worthington, P. (1985, January). Writing a rationale for a controversial common reading book: Alice Walker's *The Color Purple. English Journal, 74* (1), 48–52.

12

TEACHING AN UNDERSTANDING OF WAR AND PEACE THROUGH STRUCTURED ACADEMIC CONTROVERSIES

*Patricia G. Avery, David W. Johnson, Roger T. Johnson,
and James M. Mitchell, University of Minnesota*

> *Since the general or prevailing opinion on any subject
> is rarely or never the whole truth, it is only by the collision
> of adverse opinion that the remainder of the truth has any
> chance of being supplied.*

—John Stuart Mill

TO SOCIALIZE CHILDREN AND ADOLESCENTS into an understanding of war and peace, (1) curriculum units about war and peace may be presented, (2) students need to internalize conceptual frameworks containing the concepts "war" and "peace," and (3) instructional procedures need to be based on an epistemic process that adds meaning and relevancy to what is being studied. While the nature of children's and adolescents' conceptions of war and peace has been investigated and the relative influences of the sources of knowledge (family, school, media, peers) have been studied, there has been relatively little examination of the instructional processes that create the epistemic curiosity and motivation to understand the nature of war and peace. The foci of this chapter are (1) the instructional process of academic controversy and (2) teacher scripts (expectations based on prior experiences).

War, Peace, and Academic Controversy

If children and adolescents are to develop a complex conceptualization of war and peace, (1) the interrelationships between war, peace, cooperation, and conflict have to be clear; (2) the constructive resolution of conflict and the continuation of cooperative efforts have to pervade daily experience in the school; (3) students must develop enough expertise in cooperating with others and resolving conflicts constructively to take pride in their abilities; and (4) teacher scripts have to change to promote the daily use of cooperative learning and constructive conflict resolution.

First, it should be understood that *war* (a state of open and declared armed combat between states or nations), *peace* (freedom from war, or a state of mutual concord between governments), *cooperation* (working together to achieve mutual goals), and *conflict* (the occurrence of incompatible activities) are all interrelated (Johnson & Johnson, 1989, 1995a, 1995b; Johnson, Johnson, & Holubec, 1998). War and peace are two ends of a single continuum. If there is war, there is no peace, and vice versa. Peace exists when there is cooperation between nations and war ends when cooperation is reestablished. Peace, however, is not an absence of conflict. Peace is a state in which conflicts occur frequently and are resolved constructively (war, in contrast, is a state in which conflicts are managed through the use of large-scale violence). Conflicts should occur frequently, because when they are managed constructively they have many positive outcomes, such as increasing the motivation and energy to solve problems, increasing achievement and productivity, clarifying one's identity and values, and increasing one's understanding of other perspectives (Johnson, 1970; Johnson & Johnson, 1995a, 1995b).

Second, children and adolescents gain a constructive understanding of the nature of war and peace through their daily experiences with cooperation and conflict. Their conceptualizations of war and peace will be different depending on whether they primarily experience competitive, individualistic, or cooperative efforts. Competition assumes that there are limited resources that are distributed in a winner-take-all fashion, so participants need to focus on short-term self-interest and strive to defeat all others. Individualistic experiences assume that other people are irrelevant to one's success or failure, so a person pursues his or her own short-term self-interest with little or no regard for others. Cooperation assumes that there are expandable resources that are distributed on an equal basis, success depends on the joint efforts of all collaborators, and participants should coordinate their efforts and focus on long-term mutual gain. A conflict is constructive, furthermore, when all parties are satisfied with the outcomes, the relationship between the parties has been improved (or at least not damaged), and the participants' ability to resolve conflicts in the future has been improved (Deutsch, 1973; Johnson & Johnson, 1995a, 1995b). Cooperation and conflict (managed constructively) need to pervade classroom life and learning situations in order for children and adolescents to gain the experiences they need in order to understand war and peace. Meaning and relevance arise out of personal experiences that result from the structure of life within the school. In order for war and peace to be meaningful and relevant concepts, students must directly experience cooperation and constructively managed conflicts.

Third, in addition to having cooperation and constructively managed conflict dominate classroom life, students need to gain personal expertise in working effectively with others and resolving conflicts constructively. To do so they must be taught clear procedures and use them frequently enough to perfect their skills. The procedures for cooperation may be found in Johnson et al. (1998); the procedures for resolving conflicts constructively are academic controversy (Johnson & Johnson, 1995a) and conflict resolution training in problem-solving negotiations and peer mediation (Johnson & Johnson, 1995b).

Fourth, in order for students to understand concepts related to war and peace, to experience cooperation and conflict in daily classroom activities, and to develop skills in dealing with conflict, the scripts underlying teachers' behavioral patterns need to be changed. Teachers need new scripts to use academic controversy and highlight the ways in which classroom life clarifies the nature of peace and war. The nature of academic controversy will be discussed next, followed by a discussion of teacher scripts.

Academic Controversy

Have you learned lessons only of
those who admired you, and were tender
with you, and stood aside for you?

Have you not learned great lessons
from those who braced themselves
against you, and disputed the passage
with you?

—Walt Whitman

War and peace are just words until children and adolescents engage in conflict and learn how to resolve it constructively. One type of conflict that ideally would occur frequently each school day is academic controversy. *Academic controversy* exists when one student's ideas, information, conclusions, theories, and opinions are incompatible with those of another, and the two seek to reach an agreement (Johnson & Johnson, 1979, 1989, 1995a). Controversies are resolved by engaging in what Aristotle called *deliberate discourse* (that is, the discussion of the advantages and disadvantages of proposed actions), which is aimed at synthesizing novel solutions (creative problem solving). Structured academic controversies are most often contrasted with *individualistic learning* (students can work independently with their own set of materials at their own pace), *debate* (students present different positions and a judge determines who presented his or her position best), and *concurrence seeking* (students inhibit discussion to avoid any disagreement and compromise quickly to reach a consensus). Concurrence seeking is close to Janis's groupthink concept (1982), in which members of a decision-making group set aside their doubts and misgivings about whatever policy is favored by the emerging consensus so as to be able to concur with the other members. Academic controversy is an instructional procedure that combines cooperative learning (students work together in small groups to develop a report on an assigned topic) with structured intellectual conflict (students argue the pro and con positions on an issue in order to stimulate creative problem solving and reasoned judgment) (Johnson & Johnson, 1995a). In order to understand academic controversy, the procedure for structuring it, the process by which it works, and its outcomes should be discussed.

What Controversy Looks Like in the Classroom

Academic controversy may be used with almost any topic being studied. Since it is the process of controversy that teaches children and adolescents critical lessons about war and peace, the direct study of war and peace is not needed (Johnson & Johnson, 1995a). An example of a structured academic controversy is as follows. In a social studies class, students are considering the issue of civil disobedience. They learn that in the civil rights movement in the United States, individuals broke the law to gain equal rights for minorities. In numerous instances in the civil rights and antiwar movements, individuals wrestled with the issue of breaking the law to redress a social injustice. In the past few years, however, prominent public figures have felt justified in breaking laws for personal or political gain. In order to study the role of civil disobedience in a democracy, students are placed in a cooperative learning group of four members. The group is then divided into two pairs. One pair is given the assignment of making the best case possible for the constructiveness of civil disobedience in a democracy. The other pair is given the assignment of making the best case possible for the destructiveness of civil disobedience in a democracy. In the resulting conflict, students draw from such sources as the Declaration of Independence, by Thomas Jefferson; "Civil Disobedience," by Henry David Thoreau; Abraham Lincoln's Speech at Cooper Union, New York; and "Letter from Birmingham Jail," by Martin Luther King Jr., to challenge each others' reasoning and analyses concerning when civil disobedience is, and is not, constructive.

The teacher guides the students through the following steps (Johnson & Johnson, 1979, 1989, 1995a):

1. *Researching and preparing a position.* Each pair develops the position assigned, learns the relevant information, and plans how to present the best case possible to the other pair. This involves both a cognitive generation and cognitive validation stage. Pairs are encouraged to compare notes with pairs from other groups who represent the same position.

2. *Presenting and advocating their position.* Each pair makes its presentation to the opposing pair. Each member of the pair has to participate in the presentation. Students are to be as persuasive and convincing as possible. Members of the opposing pair are encouraged to take notes, listen carefully to learn the information being presented, and clarify anything they do not understand.

3. *Engaging in an open discussion in which they refute the opposing position and rebut attacks on their own position.* Students argue forcefully and persuasively for their position, presenting as many facts as they can (arranged in a logical order) to support their point of view. The group members analyze and critically evaluate the information, rationale, and inductive and deductive reasoning of

the opposing pair, asking them for the facts that support their point of view. While refuting the arguments of the opposing pair, students rebut attacks on their position. Students keep in mind that the issue is complex and they need to know both sides to write a good report.

4. *Reversing perspectives.* The pairs reverse perspectives and present each other's positions. In arguing for the opposing position, students are forceful and persuasive. They add any new information that the opposing pair did not think to present. They strive to see the issue from both perspectives simultaneously.

5. *Synthesizing and integrating the best evidence and reasoning into a joint position.* The four members of the group drop all advocacy and synthesize and integrate what they know into factual and judgmental conclusions that are summarized into a joint position to which all sides can agree. They (a) finalize the report (the teacher evaluates reports on the quality of the writing, the logical presentation of evidence, and the oral presentation of the report to the class), (b) present their conclusions to the class (all four members of the group are required to participate orally in the presentation), (c) individually take the test covering both sides of the issue (if every member of the group achieves up to the criterion, they all receive bonus points), and (d) process how well they worked together and how they could be even more effective next time.

This procedure is based on the process of controversy and results in predictable instructional outcomes.

The Process of Controversy

> *Conflict is the gadfly of thought. It stirs us to observation*
> *and memory. It instigates invention. It shocks us out of*
> *sheep-like passivity, and sets us at noting and contriving. . . .*
> *Conflict is a "sine qua non" of reflection and ingenuity.*
>
> —John Dewey

A number of developmental (Hunt, 1964; Kohlberg, 1969; Piaget, 1948, 1950), cognitive (Berlyne, 1966; Hammond, 1965), social (Janis, 1982; Johnson, 1970, 1978, 1979; Johnson & Johnson, 1979, 1989, 1995a), and organizational (Maier, 1970) psychologists have theorized about the processes through which conflict leads to positive outcomes. On the basis of their work, we have proposed the following process (Johnson & Johnson, 1979, 1989, 1995a):

1. When individuals are presented with a problem or decision, they have an initial conclusion based on categorizing and organizing incomplete information, their limited experiences, and their specific perspective. They have a high degree of confidence in their conclusions (they freeze the epistemic process).

2. When individuals present their conclusion and its rationale to others, they engage in cognitive rehearsal, deepen their understanding of their position, and discover higher-level reasoning strategies.

3. When individuals are confronted with different conclusions based on other people's information, experiences, and perspectives, they become uncertain as to the correctness of their views, and a state of conceptual conflict or disequilibrium is aroused. They unfreeze their epistemic process.

4. Uncertainty, conceptual conflict, or disequilibrium motivates *epistemic curiosity*, an active search for more information and new experiences (increased specific content) and a more adequate cognitive perspective and reasoning process (increased validity), in hopes of resolving the uncertainty.

5. By adapting their cognitive perspective and reasoning through understanding and accommodating the perspectives and reasoning of others, they derive a new, reconceptualized, and reorganized conclusion. Novel solutions and decisions that, on balance, are qualitatively better are detected. The process may begin again at this point or it may be terminated by freezing the current conclusion and resolving any dissonance by increasing their confidence in the validity of the conclusion.

How Students Benefit

When students interact, conflicts among their ideas, conclusions, theories, information, perspectives, opinions, and preferences are inevitable. Teachers who capitalize on these differences find that academic conflicts can yield highly constructive dividends. Over the past thirty years, Johnson and Johnson (1979, 1989, 1995a) have conducted a systematic series of research studies to discover the consequences of structured controversy. Compared with concurrence seeking, debate, and individualistic efforts, controversy tends to have the following results:

1. *Greater student mastery and retention of the subject matter being studied as well as a greater ability to generalize the principles learned to a wider variety of situations.* In a meta-analysis of the available research, Johnson and Johnson (1989) found that controversy produced higher achievement than did debate (effect size = 0.77), individualistic learning (effect size = 0.65), and concurrence seeking (effect size = 0.42). Students will learn the content of lessons focused on the concepts of war and peace better when the content is presented within an academic controversy.

2. *Higher-quality decisions and solutions to complex problems for which different viewpoints can plausibly be developed.* If students are to become citizens capable of making reasoned judgments about the complex problems facing society, they must learn to use the higher-level reasoning and critical thinking processes involved in effective problem solving, especially with problems for which different viewpoints can plausibly be developed. They must enter empathetically into the arguments on both sides of the issue (ensuring that the strongest possible case is made for each side) and arrive at a synthesis based on rational, probabilistic thought. Participating in structured controversy teaches students how to find high-quality solutions to complex problems. Implicitly, such experiences teach students that peace is possible when conflicts are managed in constructive ways.

3. *More frequent creative insights into the issues being discussed and creative synthesis combining both perspectives.* Controversy increases the number of ideas, the quality of ideas, the creation of original ideas, creative solutions, imaginative solutions, novel solutions, the use of a wider range of ideas, originality of expression in problem solving, and the use of more varied strategies. Creative problem solving may be perceived to be the key for maintaining peace and avoiding war.

4. *More positive attitudes toward conflict.* Students perceive conflict as being more valuable and having more positive outcomes after participating in a controversy. For peace to be maintained, conflict must be valued, sought out, and managed constructively.

5. *More frequent transitions from one stage of cognitive and moral reasoning to another.* Students participating in a controversy more frequently advance to a higher level of cognitive and moral reasoning. Mature conceptualizations of war and peace require higher-level reasoning.

6. *Greater attitude change.* Involvement in a controversy tends to result in changes in attitude and position. If peace is to be maintained, participants must open-mindedly believe that opposing positions are based on legitimate information and logic that, if fully understood, will lead to creative solutions that benefit everyone.

7. *Greater exchange of expertise.* Students often know different information and theories, make different assumptions, and have different opinions. Conflict among their ideas, information, opinions, preferences, theories, conclusions, and perspectives is inevitable. Having the skills to manage the controversies constructively and knowing the procedures for exchanging information and perspectives among individuals with differing expertise are essential for maximal learning and growth.

8. *Greater perspective-taking accuracy.* Students participating in a controversy learn both the opposing perspective and perspective-taking skills more accurately and completely than students participating in debates, concurrence seeking, or individualistic learning. Without the ability to see issues from all points of view, peace will not be maintained.

9. *Greater task involvement.* This is reflected in greater emotional commitment to solving the problem, greater enjoyment of the process, and more feelings of stimulation and enjoyment. Conflicts can be fun!

10. *More positive relationships among participants and greater perceived peer academic support.* Children and adolescents learn that conflicts bring people closer together and create new dimensions in relationships.

11. *Higher academic self-esteem.* Managing conflicts constructively brings pride in and satisfaction with oneself.

12. *Mastery of cognitive and social skills.* Students master the cognitive and social skills involved in researching, presenting, arguing, perspective taking, and synthesizing.

A set of social skills is taught and mastered by participating in the academic controversy procedure. Like the cognitive skills, these skills give children and adolescents the tools they need for resolving complex conflicts constructively and implicitly teach that peace is possible when conflict management skills are present. Following are some of these skills (Johnson & Johnson, 1995a).

1. Emphasize the mutuality of the situation and avoid win-lose dynamics. Focus on coming to the best decision possible, not on winning.

2. Confirm others' competence while disagreeing with their positions and challenging their reasoning.

3. Separate your personal worth from criticism of your ideas.

4. Listen to everyone's ideas, even if you do not agree with them.

5. Define the differences between positions and then integrate the various ideas.

6. Be able to take the opposing perspective in order to understand the opposing position.

7. Change your mind when the evidence clearly indicates that you should.

8. Paraphrase what someone has said if it is not clear.

9. Emphasize rationality in seeking the best possible answer, given the available information.

10. Follow the golden rule of conflict: act toward your opponents as you would have them act toward you.

Key Elements for Making Controversy Constructive

> *He that wrestles with us strengthens our nerves, and*
> *sharpens our skill. Our antagonist is our helper.*
>
> —Edmund Burke, *Reflection on the Revolution in France*

Although controversies can operate in a beneficial way, they will not do so under all conditions (Johnson & Johnson, 1995a). As with all types of conflicts, the potential for either constructive or destructive outcomes is present in a controversy. Whether there are positive or negative consequences depends on the conditions under which controversy occurs and the way in which it is managed. These key elements (Johnson & Johnson, 1979, 1989, 1995a) are (1) a cooperative context, (2) heterogeneous participants, (3) relevant information distributed among participants, (4) social skills, and (5) rational argument.

Concluding Comment

Academic controversy is a procedure for managing intellectual conflicts in a constructive way. It implicitly teaches students how to maintain peace; frequent conflicts encourage them to improve their cooperative efforts to achieve mutual goals. Participating in academic controversies teaches children and adolescents a procedure for resolving conflicts constructively, the skills required to use the procedure effectively, and an understanding that peace and effective cooperation require frequent conflicts managed constructively. In order for the academic controversy procedure to be used, the scripts teachers, students, and society hold for the process of schooling need to be changed.

Exploring Teacher Scripts

Scripts are expected sequences of events based on prior experiences. All people have scripts for the activities in which they engage repeatedly—going to the movies, starting the car, attending church, buying groceries. Many scripts reflect cultural norms (forms of greeting, for example), and others are deeply personal, such as family traditions during the holidays. Regardless of the nature of the script, however, deviations can cause considerable discomfort and uncertainty. The introduction of conflict into class discussions is a violation of powerfully held teacher, student, and societal scripts.

The Teacher's Script

Intellectual conflict may be perceived to contradict some dominant themes of the teacher's script: coverage, recitation, and quietness. World history teachers may "chunk" the academic year into time periods between the cradle of civilization and the present day. Concern about covering as much as possible leaves little time for students to grapple with enduring issues such as the role of government in society, individual rights versus the public good, or competition versus cooperation among nations (Newmann, 1988).

The notion of coverage reveals underlying beliefs about the nature of knowledge. First, if material is to be "covered," it follows that there is a body of relatively static knowledge to be learned that reflects the accumulated wisdom of experts. This conception of knowledge stands in stark contrast to the constructivist view, which states that individuals develop and shape their own knowledge. Second, the development of critical thinking skills may be marginalized by the belief that students must have a solid understanding of the facts before they can engage in critical inquiry. While background knowledge is required in the discussion of controversial issues lest students engage in "opining" (Ehman, 1970), the mastering of background information may relegate critical inquiry into issues to a secondary, if not forgotten, role. Byrnes and Torney-Purta's research (1995) on young people's cognitive approaches to social issues suggests that students can engage in higher-order thinking if they are presented with a historical or contemporary problem and asked to identify its causes and solutions. Similarly, scholars in social studies education have long recommended that instructional units be designed around a "central question" of enduring significance (Engle & Ochoa, 1988; Hunt & Metcalf, 1968; Oliver & Shaver, 1966; Onosko, 1992).

When controversial issues are addressed in the classroom, often the teacher's dominant script tends to be one of recitation rather than discussion. Wilen and White (1991) note that in a recitation format, the teacher asks a student a question, the student responds, the teacher evaluates the response ("Good," "Correct," "Not quite," "That's interesting," and so on) and asks another student a question, and the pattern repeats itself. Most questions are closed-ended and have "correct" answers. In the discussion format, the teacher facilitates (and moderates) a process in which students question and respond to one another. When the teacher poses a question, he or she will often ask the students to elaborate on or explain their views. Questions tend to be more open-ended and value-laden. The second pattern is clearly more conducive to the discussion of controversial issues because they have no "right" answer and often involve value conflicts. What teachers identify as "discussions" are more characteristic of recitations (Alvermann, O'Brien, & Dillon, 1990; Larson & Parker, 1996).

The script for the "good teacher" includes a relatively quiet classroom in which the teacher commands her or his students' attention and respect. Linda McNeil's (1986) outstanding ethnographic study of four midwestern high schools suggests that teachers avoid controversial issues because they fear losing control of the classroom, and thus losing their own sense of being a good teacher. Images of discussions that spill into chaos are particularly associated with lower-socioeconomic-status and lower-achieving students. These students rarely experience issues-centered discussions and inquiry because they "need to cover the basics" and "aren't mature enough to handle discussions" (Page, 1991).

In addition to coverage, recitation, and quietness, teachers may avoid conflict and the discussion of controversial issues because of fear (real or imagined) of reprisals from school administrators or the community and lack of training in conducting academic controversies. Those teachers who do engage students in academic controversy on a consistent basis have succeeded in overcoming formidable obstacles.

The Student Script

Intellectual conflict may be perceived as contradicting several dominant themes of the student's script for classroom learning and interaction: reluctance to express dissenting views, need for peer approval, fear of teacher reprisals for disagreeing, and gender and ethnic definitions of appropriate behavior. Although young people may be intrigued by social and political issues, particularly those that affect them, they are often reluctant to express dissenting views in class. There is a strong concern for peer approval, especially among early adolescents (Savin-Williams & Berndt, 1990). In the student script, offering an opinion risks setting oneself apart from one's peers. Students may envision embarrassment or humiliation if their opinion deviates markedly from the norm. They may also envision reprisals, such as lower grades, from the teacher if they disagree with the teacher's point of view; therefore, they try to figure out what the teacher wants rather than focusing on the issue. Finally, studies suggest that females may be uncomfortable with conflict when discussing higher-level issues, believing that disagreement with a peer may place their friendship at risk (Wilen & White, 1991). Among some ethnic and cultural groups, such as Native Americans, it may be considered impolite to express opposition to another person's point of view (Delpit, 1995). This is particularly true when the interaction is between a young person and an adult in a position of authority, such as a teacher. Student passivity may be the result of these barriers to engaging in spirited discussions of controversial issues or academic controversies.

The Community or Societal Script

The societal script emphasizes the idea that teaching basic reading, writing, and math skills is more important than teaching the habits of good citizenship (Wadsworth, 1997). Most communities do not expect young people to learn to be political activists, to challenge the status quo, or to engage in intense political debate. U.S. textbooks tend to minimize conflict (Carroll et al., 1987). The dynamic sense of government and politics—the fierce debates, colorful characters, triumphs and tragedies—tends not to be covered. Controversies like school prayer and civil rights that have ignited passions at all points along the political spectrum are ignored or barely mentioned. The vitality of political involvement and the essential give-and-take between people and their elected officials is neglected. High school history textbooks tend to minimize the role of dissent in our history, which may threaten the tolerance of disagreement that is funda-mental to democracy (Gottlieb, 1989).

Merelman (1990) argues that the degree of political conflict within a society affects the way in which conflict is perceived. Citizens of relatively uncontested democracies may have a low tolerance for conflict and may overestimate the degree to which violence is a part of political conflict. Adolescents in the United States, for example, imagine that verbal politi-cal conflicts result in physically brutal scenarios (Avery, 1992). Fear of serious conflict may play an important role in reducing tolerance (Sullivan, Piereson, & Marcus, 1982). The literature on political tolerance suggests that perceived threat from a sociopolitical group is an important predic-tor of willingness to extend civil liberties to that group. The higher the level of threat an individual associates with a group, the less likely she or he is to grant the group basic civil liberties. In the societal script, young people's exposure to controversial issues, particularly those that place the United States in a negative light, threatens their attachment to the nation.

Taken together, the teacher, student, and societal scripts for academic conflict in the precollege classroom stand as formidable barriers to young people's serious engagement in academic controversies and examination of controversial issues. If the prevailing scripts mitigate against the dis-cussion of controversial issues, what evidence exists that such discussions are appropriate, valuable, and relevant to a democratic community? The next section explores the developmental appropriateness of discussions of controversial issues and the research on such discussions among young people.

Developmental Appropriateness

Teachers and parents often question whether young people have the cog-nitive maturity to investigate issues related to war, peace, and conflict. As early as the first grade, many children can distinguish between social con-ventions ("Is it okay to eat with one's fingers?"), noncontroversial ques-tions ("Is the earth flat?"), and controversial issues ("Should we spend more money on health care or transportation?"). Further, children expect their teachers to teach these types of knowledge differently. Children can recognize the fact that others hold different perspectives from their own (Selman, Jaquette, & Lavin, 1977). With increasing age, elementary school students expect their teachers to present different viewpoints on questions about which there is little societal consensus (Nicholls & Nelson, 1992). Even if the teacher presents the position the students favor, the majority of students believe that the teacher should discuss opposing viewpoints as well.

It is during adolescence that young people may become capable of taking the generalized perspective of society, a particularly important skill in the discussion of issues relating to war, peace, and conflict. Adolescence is also the time when youth are capable of and interested in issues related to justice, fairness, and equality. In a classic series of studies conducted in the 1960s, Joseph Adelson (1971) interviewed over three hundred young people between the ages of eleven and eighteen in three countries (the United States, Great Britain, and West Germany) about concepts such as law, community, individual rights, and the public good. The young people's reasoning processes were explored as they were confronted with a range of issues (for example, "Should a dissenting religious group be vaccinated?"). About the age of fourteen, a shift in the quality of thought was noted. Social class, gender, and national differences were so muted that Adelson commented, "A twelve-year-old German youngster's ideas of politics are closer to those of a twelve-year-old American than to those of his fifteen-year-old brother" (p. 1050). Unlike their younger counterparts, the older students were beginning to recognize the potential conflict between individual rights and the public good, to connect specific examples of rights with abstract principles, and to consider the long-term consequences of given actions on individuals and communities. Similar findings have been noted in subsequent research (Tapp & Levine, 1974; Miller & Sears, 1986; Owen & Dennis, 1987). These changes in the quality of thought processes have led many to believe that adolescence is an ideal period during which to develop critical thinking skills (Keating, 1990) because young people may be constructing "lay social theories" about public issues (Haste, 1992). Lay social theories are composed of schemata and scenarios of "how the world works and how the individual is located in that world."

In the 1960s and 1970s, research on political socialization found that instruction was dominated by a "structures and functions" approach to government, with only superficial treatment of controversial issues. The effects on students' political attitudes were generally found to be small and insignificant (Ehman, 1980). In an extensive review of the literature on issues-centered social studies, Hahn (1996) concludes that the power of issues discussions is based on an interaction between conflictual content, conflictual pedagogy, and classroom climate. Content is conflictual to the degree that it includes differing viewpoints, perspectives, or interpretations of matters of significance. A teacher engages in conflictual pedagogy when he or she challenges students' lay social theories. Conflictual content can be presented without the use of conflictual pedagogy—that is, without raising the questions that challenge young people's thinking (Bickmore, 1993). Conversely, teachers may raise important issues but not ground those issues in conflicting texts or perspectives.

Conflictual content and pedagogy must take place in an open classroom climate, one that supports and encourages the expression of ideas (Hahn, 1996). An open classroom climate may be created by teachers who model the tentativeness with which they approach complex issues by explaining their thinking processes to students and sharing their rationales, doubts, and concerns (Newmann, 1990). Such teachers tend to explore issues in depth rather than engaging in superficial coverage of a lot of issues and to structure discussions in which the class probes for the reasons and rationale underlying the conclusions. What is perhaps most remarkable about Newmann's work is how infrequently he and his colleagues observed robust issues discussions.

From a developmental perspective, then, most young people, particularly adolescents, are cognitively capable of addressing controversial issues in the classroom. They are potentially capable of identifying areas of public controversy (as opposed to matters of social convention), understanding that others may hold different perspectives on an issue, adopting a societal perspective, and imagining the short- and long-term consequences of alternative positions. But if young people's lay social theories are not addressed, they will likely remain intact. The ability to think critically about social issues does not develop naturally; critical thought about public issues is an evolving skill that may be enhanced through instruction, modeling, and practice. One of the primary ways that students' social explanations become more complex is through classroom instruction and dialogue, such as that created by participation in academic controversies. To understand concepts such as war, peace, and conflict, courses need to include conflictual content, be taught with conflictual pedagogy, and have an open classroom climate that encourages thoughtful discussion and intellectual inquiry.

Conclusion

While curriculum units about war and peace and credible sources of influence are important in children's development of conceptions of war and peace, the most powerful influence may be the process of learning. Children's and adolescents' understanding of and attitudes toward war and peace may be largely based on their personal experiences involving social interdependence (cooperative, competitive, and individualistic efforts) and conflict. Teaching children and adolescents about the nature of war and peace should include (1) teaching about the interrelationships between war, peace, cooperation, and conflict; (2) ensuring that cooperation and constructively managed conflict are pervasive in classrooms; (3) giving students sufficient practice to gain expertise in engaging in the procedures of cooperation and constructive conflict; and (4) reducing the barriers to using academic controversy procedures by changing the scripts underlying teachers' and students' behavioral patterns.

Peace continues as long as nations cooperate effectively and manage their conflicts constructively. War results from the breakdown of cooperation and the destructive management of conflict. War ends when effective cooperation is reestablished among participants. Children and adolescents tend to gain an understanding of the nature of war and peace through their daily experiences with cooperation and conflict. Their conceptualizations of war and peace will be different depending on whether they primarily experience (1) competitive, individualistic, or cooperative efforts and (2) destructive or constructive management of conflict. It is through daily participation in cooperative efforts that an implicit understanding of peace is developed. The heart of effective cooperation is the constructive resolution of conflict. Unless collaborators can face their conflicts and resolve them constructively, cooperative efforts will break down. If children and adolescents are to develop a full understanding of peace, they have to participate daily in conflicts from which they (1) understand that conflict has many positive outcomes and should occur frequently, (2) learn procedures for constructively resolving conflicts, and (3) master the skills required to use the procedures effectively.

Academic controversy is a procedure that combines cooperative learning with engagement in intellectual conflict. Students work together in cooperative groups to develop the best-reasoned judgment possible on the issue being studied. To do so they must research and prepare a position, advocate it, critically analyze challenges by students with opposing positions, see the issue from all perspectives simultaneously, and create a synthesis that incorporates the best information and reasoning advocated by all sides. This procedure is based on a process in which (1) students who have an initial conclusion about an issue present it to others, (2) they are confronted with an opposing point of view that creates uncertainty over the correctness of their conclusion, (3) the uncertainty in turn creates epistemic curiosity (a search for more information and a more adequate perspective), and (4) this leads to a reorganized and rethought conclusion.

This process results in greater mastery and retention of content, higher-quality decisions, more creative problem solving, a greater exchange of expertise, greater perspective-taking accuracy, more positive relationships, and higher self-esteem. In addition, cognitive and social skills are mastered that are essential for the constructive resolution of conflict and the understanding of war and peace. Conflict skills include criticizing ideas while confirming the other person's competence, taking other perspectives, and synthesizing. These outcomes are best achieved in a cooperative context, with heterogeneous participants who have relevant knowledge and skills and who engage in rational argument. As the controversy procedure and required skills become integrated into children's and adolescents' behavior repertoires and become an automatic habit pattern, the children and adolescents are able to capitalize on the powerful positive potential of conflict. Doing so promotes the development of conceptual frameworks in which the interrelationships between war, peace, cooperation, and conflict are clear.

If students are to understand war and peace, teacher and student scripts have to change to include the use of academic controversy. The teacher script needs to change from an emphasis on coverage, recitation, and quietness to a focus on deeper-level understanding, facilitation of the construction of knowledge by students, and active discussion. The student script needs to change from a reluctance to express dissenting views because of gender and ethnicity role definitions and fear of peer disapproval or teacher reprisals to open advocacy of one's conclusions and challenges to classmates' and the teacher's conclusions. The community or societal script needs to change from a focus on teaching basic reading, writing, and math skills to the use of the controversy procedure to foster skills in challenging the status quo and engaging in political discourse. Existing teacher, student, and societal scripts are formidable barriers to the use of academic controversy in teaching students about war and peace.

From a developmental perspective, children and adolescents are cognitively capable of identifying areas of public controversy (as opposed to matters of social convention), understanding that others may hold different perspectives on an issue, adopting a societal perspective, and imagining the short- and long-term consequences of alternative positions. Critical thought about war, peace, and other public issues may not occur unless it is enhanced through instruction, modeling, and practice. To understand concepts such as war, peace, and conflict, courses need to include conflictual content, be taught with conflictual pedagogy, and have an open classroom climate that encourages thoughtful discussion and intellectual inquiry. The use of the controversy procedure to discuss controversial topics provides socialization into political attitudes and processes.

REFERENCES

Adelson, J. (1971). The political imagination of the young adolescent. *Developmental Psychology, 1,* 1031–1051.

Alvermann, D., O'Brien, D., & Dillon, D. (1990). What teachers do when they say they're having discussions of content area reading assignments: A qualitative analysis. *Reading Research Quarterly, 24,* 296–322.

Avery, P. (1992). Political tolerance: How adolescents deal with dissenting groups. In H. Haste & J. Torney-Purta (Eds.), *The development of political understanding: A new perspective* (pp. 39–51). (New Directions for Child Development, CD No. 55). San Francisco: Jossey-Bass.

Berlyne, D. (1966). Notes on intrinsic motivation and intrinsic reward in relation to instruction. In J. Bruner (Ed.), *Learning about learning* (Cooperative Research Monograph No. 15). Washington, DC: U.S. Department of Health, Education, and Welfare, Office of Education.

Bickmore, K. (1993). Learning inclusion/inclusion in learning: Citizenship education for a pluralistic society. *Theory and Research in Social Education, 21* (4), 341–384.

Byrnes, J. P., & Torney-Purta, J. V. (1995). Naive theories and decision making as part of higher thinking in social studies. *Theory and Research in Social Education, 23*(3), 260–277.

Carroll, J., Broadnex, W., Contreras, G., Mann, T., Orenstein, N., & Steihm, J. (1987). *We the people: A review of U.S. government and civics textbooks.* Washington, DC: People for the American Way.

Delpit, L. (1995). *Other people's children: Cultural conflict in the classroom.* New York: New York Press.

Deutsch, M. (1973). *The resolution of conflict.* New Haven, CT: Yale University Press.

Ehman, L. (1970). Normative discourse and attitude change in the social studies classroom. *The High School Journal, 54,* 76–83.

Ehman, L. (1980). The American school in the political socialization process. *Review of Educational Research, 50,* 99–119.

Engle, S., & Ochoa, A. (1988). *Education for democratic citizenship: Decision making in the social studies.* New York: Teachers College Press.

Gottlieb, S. (1989). In the name of patriotism: The constitutionality of "bending" history in public secondary schools. *The History Teacher, 22* (4), 411–495.

Hahn, C. (1996). Research on issues-centered social studies. In R. Evans & D. Saxe (Eds.), *Handbook on teaching social issues* (pp. 25–41). Washington, DC: National Council for the Social Studies.

Hammond, K. (1965). New directions in research on conflict resolution. *Journal of Social Issues, 11,* 44–66.

Haste, H. (1992). Lay social theory: The relation between political, social, and moral understanding. In H. Haste & J. Torney-Purta (Eds.), *The development of political understanding: A new perspective* (pp. 27–38). (New Directions for Child Development, CD No. 55). San Francisco: Jossey-Bass.

Hunt, J. (1964). Introduction: Revisiting Montessori. In M. Montessori (Ed.), *The Montessori method.* New York: Shocken Books.

Hunt, M., & Metcalf, L. (1968). *Teaching high school social studies: Problems in reflective thinking and social understanding.* New York: HarperCollins.

Janis, I. (1982). *Groupthink: Psychological studies of policy decisions and fiascoes.* Boston: Houghton Mifflin.

Johnson, D. W. (1970). *Social psychology of education.* New York: Henry Holt.

Johnson, D. W. (1978). Conflict management in the school and classroom. In D. Bar-Tal & L. Saxe (Eds.), *Social psychology of education: Theory and research* (pp. 199–326). Bristol, PA: Hemisphere.

Johnson, D. W. (1979). *Educational psychology.* Englewood Cliffs, NJ: Prentice Hall.

Johnson, D. W., & Johnson, R. (1979). Conflict in the classroom: Controversy and learning. *Review of Educational Research, 49* (1), 51–70.

Johnson, D. W., & Johnson, R. (1989) *Cooperation and competition: Theory and research.* Edina, MN: Interaction.

Johnson, D. W., & Johnson, R. (1995a). *Creative controversy: Intellectual conflict in the classroom* (3rd ed.). Edina, MN: Interaction.

Johnson, D. W., & Johnson, R. (1995b). *Teaching students to be peacemakers* (3rd ed.). Edina, MN: Interaction.

Johnson, D. W., Johnson, R., & Holubec, E. (1998). *Cooperation in the classroom* (7th ed.). Edina, MN: Interaction.

Keating, D. (1990). Adolescent thinking. In S. Feldman & G. Elliott (Eds.), *At the threshold: The developing adolescent* (pp. 54–92). Cambridge, MA: Harvard University Press.

Kohlberg, L. (1969). Stage and sequence: The cognitive-developmental approach to socialization. In D. Goslin (Ed.), *Handbook of socialization theory and research* (pp. 347– 480). Skokie, IL: Rand McNally.

Larson, B., & Parker, W. (1996). What is classroom discussion? A look at teachers' conceptions. *Journal of Curriculum and Supervision, 11* (2), 110–126.

Maier, N. (1970). *Problem-solving and creativity in individuals and group.* Pacific Grove, CA: Brooks/Cole.

McNeil, L. M. (1986). *Contradictions of control: School structure and school knowledge.* New York: Routledge.

Merelman, R. (1990). The role of conflict in children's political learning. In O. Ichilov (Ed.), *Political socialization, citizenship education, and democracy* (pp. 47–65). New York: Teachers College Press.

Miller, S., & Sears, D. (1986). Stability and change in social tolerance: A test of the persistence hypothesis. *American Journal of Political Science, 30,* 214–236.

Newmann, F. M. (1988). Can depth replace coverage in the high school curriculum? *Phi Delta Kappan, 69,* 345–348.

Newmann, F. M. (1990). Qualities of thoughtful social studies classes: An empirical profile. *Journal of Curriculum Studies, 22*(3), 253–275.

Nicholls, J., & Nelson, J. (1992). Students' conceptions of controversial knowledge. *Journal of Educational Psychology, 84* (2), 224–230.

Oliver, D., & Shaver, J. (1966). *Teaching public issues in the high school.* Boston: Houghton Mifflin.

Onosko, J. (1992). An approach to designing thoughtful units. *The Social Studies,* pp. 193–196.

Owen, D., & Dennis, J. (1987). Preadult development of political tolerance. *Political Psychology, 8,* 547–561.

Page, R. (1991). *Lower-track classrooms: A curricular and cultural perspective.* New York: Teachers College Press.

Piaget, J. (1948). *The moral judgment of the child.* New York: Free Press.

Piaget, J. (1950). *The psychology of intelligence.* Orlando: Harcourt Brace.

Savin-Williams, R., & Berndt, T. (1990). Friendships and peer relations. In S. Feldman & G. Elliott (Eds.), *At the threshold: The developing adolescent* (pp. 277–307). Cambridge, MA: Harvard University Press.

Selman, R. L., Jaquette, D., & Lavin, D. R. (1977). Interpersonal awareness in children: Toward an integration of developmental and clinical child psychology. *American Journal of Orthopsychiatry, 47*(2), 264–274.

Sullivan, J. L., Piereson, J., & Marcus, G. E. (1982). *Political tolerance and American democracy.* Chicago: University of Chicago Press.

Tapp, J., & Levine, F. (1974). Legal socialization: Strategies for an ethical legality. *Stanford Law Review, 27,* 1–72.

Wadsworth, D. (1997). The public's view of public schools. *Educational Leadership, 54,* 44–48.

Wilen, W., & White, J. (1991). Interaction and discourse in social studies classrooms. In J. Shaver (Ed.), *Handbook of research on social studies teaching and learning* (pp. 483–496). New York: MacMillan.

13

LEARNING
CONFLICT MANAGEMENT
THROUGH PEER MEDIATION

Robin Hall, Charles Sturt University

PEER MEDIATION, or variant labels such as student mediation and school-based mediation, is a relatively new phenomenon in Australian schools but has been described as the "fastest growing type of conflict resolution program being implemented in American schools" (Shepherd, 1994, p. 16). This overview of peer mediation studies, focusing on how peer mediation relates to the learning of conflict management, leads off with a discussion of the theoretical background and then examines the types of programs practiced and their effectiveness.

Theoretical Background

Several definitions of mediation exist in the literature; the one preferred here is "a process in which a third party (the mediator) manages the negotiations of the disputing parties to enable them to reach an acceptable solution to their dispute" (Haynes, 1996, p. 119). Peer mediation in schools, then, mainly consists of interpersonal conflict being managed by one or more third-party student mediators. Like other forms of mediation, especially community and family mediation, the process is characterized by the following elements (Haynes, 1996):

1. The mediator plays a facilitative role, helping disputants to reach a solution: the mediator's role is not to arbitrate the conflict or coercively impose a solution on the disputants.

2. Both parties agree to and accept a solution: the agreement is negotiated between the disputants and is resolved in a way that both parties find acceptable.

3. The mediator manages the procedure by which the resolution is reached: mediators adopt a neutral position and establish the ground rules by which the negotiations are conducted.

4. The parties negotiate to reach an agreement; the mediator may provide constructive advice in developing options to pursue, but the weight of responsibility is on the disputants to produce an agreement.

5. The disputants control the content of the negotiation outcome; the mediator manages the process but the disputants provide the precise nature of the agreement.

6. The mediator acts to empower the disputants to control their own futures by helping them to take responsibility for their own actions and make decisions to which they think they can adhere.

Conflict, at least in Western societies, is regarded as a "natural and indispensable part of our everyday life and a corollary of personal and social change" (Bagshaw, 1994, p. 22). Disputes over the sharing of resources, group membership, failure to take turns and observe rules, unkind name-calling, and the rest are commonplace in playgrounds and classrooms. What matters is whether these conflicts are managed constructively or destructively (Deutsch, 1973). Managed constructively, conflict provides an opportunity to enrich relationships between disputants and to establish a more cooperative and collaborative educational environment. Peer mediation is one strategy that may form a part of a school's conflict management repertoire. In a school where disputes are being managed constructively through a peer mediation program, students may become skilled at handling conflict and these skills may be transferred into the home and into society generally.

The aims of peer mediation programs vary considerably. In some cases the rationale is narrow, for example, to reduce fighting, vandalism, and disruptive behavior. In other cases, the intention is to radically change school culture and to create a "peaceable school" and safe community that live by a credo of nonviolence (DeJong, 1994, p. 9). A narrow, unified view of the aims and rationale for peer mediation programs does not exist. There tends to be a range of intentions and objectives for these programs, depending on school context and local need, and it has to be said that sometimes program objectives are only vaguely stated. In broad terms, the aims can be summarized as follows (Davis, 1986, p. 294)

1. Promoting a more receptive and responsive view of conflict as a positive force that can accompany personal growth or institutional change

2. Helping young people, school personnel, and community members to deepen their understanding of themselves and others through improved communication, thereby improving the school and community climate and preparing students to live in a multicultural world

3. Increasing appreciation for the ability of conflict resolution training to enhance the academic and lifetime skills that are considered basic to all learning, such as listening, critical thinking, and problem solving

4. Encouraging a higher level of citizenship activity by sharpening students' knowledge of nonadversarial conflict resolution, its relationship to the legal system, and the role it can play in promoting world peace

5. Recognizing the unique competence of young people to participate in the resolution of their own disputes, while allowing teachers and administrators to concentrate more on teaching and less on discipline

6. Offering a more appropriate and effective school-based dispute resolution method than expulsion, suspension, detention, or court intervention, thus reducing violence, vandalism, and chronic school absences

An important point to note, however, is that the development, implementation, and evaluation of peer mediation programs have generally lacked a coherent theoretical orientation (Johnson & Johnson, 1996; Van Slyck & Stern, 1991). The connections between program practice and the relevant theorizing about conflict management and cognition are tenuous and rarely made explicit. As a result, reports have focused on the behavioral effects of mediation programs, and evaluations of program effectiveness are largely atheoretical and descriptive. Studies that clearly identify independent variables (such as mediation training), dependent variables (such as reduction in violent incidents), and potential mediating variables (such as student commitment) are the exception rather than the rule. The cognitive processes involved in being or using a mediator are understudied; arguably, the most pressing item on the peer mediation research agenda is to understand them better.

The small number of mediation studies that have been set in a theoretical context have drawn on perspectives related to both social learning and cognitive development. In terms of social learning, *self-regulation* has been identified as a dependent variable that may be strengthened by practicing mediation (Johnson, Johnson, Dudley, Ward, & Magnuson, 1995; Lane & McWhirter, 1992; Maxwell, 1989). Self-regulation entails being able to comply with a request; to initiate and cease activities according to situational demands; to modulate the intensity, frequency, and duration of verbal and motor acts in social and educational settings; to postpone acting upon a desired object or goal; and to generate socially approved behavior in the absence of external monitors (Maxwell, 1989). In doing this, students should monitor their own behavior, assess situations, make judgments as to which behaviors are appropriate, and master the procedures and skills required to engage in the desired behavior (Johnson, Johnson, Dudley, et al., 1995).

Developmentally, Van Slyck and Stern (1991, p. 270) suggest that "the prevailing orientation of dispute resolution, as well as its specific approach through mediation, is congruent with the necessary conditions for optimal resolution of the *independence-dependence* developmental task of adolescence" (emphasis added). They also assert that active problem-solving coping skills such as those required during mediation are associated with greater resilience and competence and better adjustment in adolescence, and that they facilitate the development of prosocial skills that are generalizable to other settings encountered over a lifetime (Van Slyck, Stern, & Zak-Place, 1996).

The literature has not been very informative thus far about the significance of cognitive development in learning mediation skills, either as an independent or a mediating variable. Cameron and Dupuis (1989) confidently assert that these skills can be taught at any level of the educational system, but observations from other studies are more equivocal. Johnson, Johnson, Cotten, Harris, and Louison's evaluation of a conflict manager program (1995) concludes that even third-grade students can learn to mediate their schoolmates' most difficult conflicts successfully. In contrast, commenting on the same type of program, Stichter (1986) quotes research indicating that third graders had difficulty in grasping the abstract principles involved, so the selection of mediators was restricted to students in the fourth grade and above. Studies conducted by the University of Minnesota's Cooperative Learning Center have included children as young as first graders (Johnson & Johnson, 1995), with the major conclusion that "the procedures can be learned in a relatively short period of time by academically heterogeneous students as young as second graders" (Johnson, Johnson, Dudley, & Magnuson, 1995, p. 684). However, not all parts of the negotiation sequence in this program were easy for the elementary school children to master (Johnson, Johnson, & Dudley, 1992).

Types of Programs

Peer mediation programs are not uniform but vary according to the boundaries of the disputes to be settled by mediation, the referral or assignment of cases, the selection of students for training as mediators, and the content of the training. Classically, mediation is a short-term, finite process that is task-directed and goal-oriented, aimed at producing an agreement with which disputants can comply, preparing participants to accept the consequences of their decisions, and reducing anxiety and other negative effects associated with the conflict (Folberg & Taylor, 1984). Generally speaking, in peer mediations, student disputants tell their stories and are helped to clarify the issues involved, to understand how each participant feels, and to find a solution on which all disputants can agree (Cameron & Dupuis, 1989).

Most programs focus on student-student disputes, though a small number have experimented with disputes between students and teachers and students and other adults (for example, students and parents), and all exclude conflicts involving physical injury, weapons, and drugs. One model restricts the program to play groups and recess disputes, while other programs extend into classroom time and commuting to and from school. In many respects it seems more logical not to restrict attention to the break sessions, given that unregulated conflict is likely to boil over into other settings. However, empowering students to mediate the more globally occurring conflicts may be perceived by teachers as undermining their authority in the classroom.

Most studies have used basic content analysis to categorize the disputes referred for mediation. These typologies include events such as physical aggression and fighting, verbal disagreements, gossip, name-calling, teasing, harassment, playground incidents, property damage, invasion of privacy (such as giving out phone numbers), boyfriend-girlfriend problems, unreturned borrowed money, turn taking, insults, and disputes over academic work (Araki, 1990; Burrell & Vogl, 1990; Cameron & Dupuis, 1989; Johnson et al., 1992; NSW DOSE, 1994; Van Slyck & Stern, 1991).

There is evidence here of gender differentiation in the use of peer mediations. Though more males tend to be involved in disputes in schools, more females make use of mediation services (Araki, 1990; Johnson, Johnson, Cotten, et al., 1995; Jones & Carlin, 1994). This difference may be due to the perception that mediation is more appropriate for the more verbal, female conflicts rather than the more physical, male disputes. For example, one study (NSW DOSE, 1994) reports that name-calling was the most common cause of disputes among females and property loss or fighting among males. However, it is also worth noting that after mediation training, no difference was found between the genders in the strategies students used to manage conflict or in the resolutions they produced (Johnson, Johnson, Dudley, Ward, et al., 1995).

On a more theoretical level, some use has been made of Deutsch's theory of conflict as a basis for classifying disputes. One study of an inner-city primary school (Johnson, Johnson, Cotten, et al., 1995) found that relationship problems were the most frequent source of conflict (83 percent), whereas another study of a suburban elementary school revealed that control of resources (37 percent) and preferences (31 percent) were the most common types of school disputes, with relationships accounting for a further 20 percent (Johnson, Johnson, Dudley, Ward, et al., 1995).

An unresolved question is whether peer mediation is an appropriate way of dealing with bullying in school. It is generally accepted that mediation works better where the balance of power between the disputants is relatively even and where the mediator can adopt a neutral position. Both of these conditions are likely to be violated in cases of bullying. It would not be acceptable for the mediator to endorse bullying behavior, and there are substantial asymmetries of power between bullies and their victims. On the face of it, peer mediation would not appear to be an appropriate way of managing bullying. However, as Rigby (1996) reports, some schools have adopted a combination of student counseling and mediation to deal with bully-victim problems. In this role, the student counselor–mediator essentially facilitates the negotiation between the bully and victim but does so within carefully circumscribed guidelines. Rigby comments on the maturity and responsiveness of the students adopting this role and on the fact that in their relations with other students, students possess a much greater moral authority than teachers.

In most studies, mediation referrals are reported as being voluntary. For example, one approach to running a playground mediation program is for the co-mediators on duty to wear distinctive clothing and to sit at a designated table or station in the playground. The mediators might be allowed to play around the station, but they would be expected to wait for clients to approach them or for teachers on playground duty to refer disputes to them. The immediacy of this type of mediation and the semipublic context (along with the peer approval and esteem to be gained by making a settlement) are attractive features of the process (Marshall, 1987).

There are two significant variations from this pattern. In secondary schools, disputes may be referred by an executive teacher such as the counselor or year adviser, and designated spaces may be set aside for mediation. However, there may be problems if the program relies on a discipline or welfare manager for referrals, because the disputes may assume some form of formal status. Brown (1995) found that where there was little voluntary involvement, the program did not work. The other variation stems from having mediators play a more interventionist role. Some authors refer to mediators who intervene before problems develop (Cutrona & Guerin, 1994; Roesner, 1995), conflict managers who patrol playgrounds and cafeterias (Black, 1994), or mediators who supervise playground duties, monitor room noise levels, and recommend classmates who deserve recognition cards (Cahoon, 1988). To what extent these "policing" functions interfere with "pure" mediation has not been addressed.

A fundamental distinction can be drawn between mediator selection in whole-school and cadre programs (Johnson & Johnson, 1995; Johnson, Johnson, Cotten, et al., 1995). In the former, *all* students receive some training in conflict resolution and/or mediation, whereas in the latter, training is provided for *a select group* of students. The selection of mediators is mainly decided by the teachers and has been identified as the most difficult part of the whole process (Miller, 1994). The most common selection criteria that emerge are leadership, appropriate interpersonal skills (or more specifically good listening and interviewing or questioning skills), and the ability to work cooperatively. Particular programs specifically mention (1) a sense of commitment to the school ethos (Heuchan & Young, 1994); (2) a nonjudgmental attitude to conflict, the ability to maintain eye contact, and a commitment to training, including ongoing training (Cameron & Dupuis, 1989); (3) the ability to stay neutral, maintain confidentiality, and refrain from giving advice, as well as patience and regular attendance (Cutrona & Guerin, 1994); and (4) a good sense of humor (Burrell & Vogl, 1990). The qualities cited in being a successful mediator include a willingness to learn, good verbal skills, and the respect of peers; a confident and strong character; a good understanding of the process; and the ability to write agreements clearly and to be directive, responsible, and caring (Araki, 1990). The consensus among these authors is that teachers should avoid the tendency to pick the intellectually best and brightest in favor of selecting a cross-sectional representation of the student body in terms of gender, ethnicity, age, non-English-speaking background, and special education requirements.

Making a decision on the number of mediators to train contains an inherent tension. A sufficient number is needed to ensure that the students can handle the public relations, the troubleshooting, and the record keeping without jeopardizing their other responsibilities. At the same time there may be only a limited flow of clients or mediation incidents to deal with. This is not a problem that is restricted to school mediation; it is also apparent in the community mediation literature. Fisher (1996, p. 89) asserts that "there is not the population in Australia to sustain mediation services to the extent needed to keep all 'wannabe' mediators in work," and other research indicates that underutilization is the main reason mediators leave the service (Olczak, Grosch, & Duffy, 1991). Araki (1990) comments that in school mediations, the limited number of cases meant that mediators did not have the opportunity to sharpen their skills; Payne (1993) reports that enthusiasm was low because of the small case flow; and Brown (1995) reports a loss of student interest for the same reason.

In these latter cases, a major factor in the underuse of mediators was the referral process. Teachers lacked commitment to, or awareness of, the program and continued to use the more established disciplinary procedures in the school. In some cases there may also be teacher resistance to the concept; Eisler (1994b, p. 5) quotes one respondent as saying, "They still think that the peer mediation process means coddling the kids and they want immediate punishment." The executive teachers in charge of discipline may be pivotal in this respect because they may act as a filter system, referring cases or not as they think appropriate. If there is a limited flow of mediation cases, then having a large number of mediators will blunt enthusiasm. As a rule of thumb, Miller (1994) recommends that twenty-one mediators be trained (multiples of three are good for role playing) in a school of one thousand.

A particularly interesting question relates to the use of negative as well as positive role models in selecting students. A number of authors report on the successful use of "troublemakers" as mediators (Burrell & Vogl, 1990; Eisler, 1994b; McCormick, 1988; Van Slyck & Stern, 1991). Johnson, Johnson, Cotton, et al. (1995) note that a very small number of students account for a substantial proportion of mediated conflicts, and they suggest that providing this small group with special training would reduce the incidence of aggression and violence in schools. This is a student group whose members Araki (1990) characterizes as being perceived to be nonlisteners, having a history of past conflicts, lacking problem-solving skills, and being less involved with school. However, Miller (1994) asserts that the biggest troublemakers turn out to be the most effective mediators. She further suggests that a good question to ask when selecting students is who will benefit the most from being a mediator. In a similar vein, Bagshaw (1992) asks whether training bullies as mediators and assigning them mediation roles could reduce bullying behavior. This is a slightly different question than asking whether mediation should be used directly in incidences of bullying. Her argument is that bullying stems from pressures such as the need for power or recognition, anger expression, self-protection against fear or low self-esteem, venting of frustration, and exercise of leadership. These pressures might be assuaged by learning a set of skills like assertiveness, anger management, problem solving, teamwork, and negotiation—that is, the skills required to be a mediator.

More discussion is required on this question in terms of the purpose of establishing mediation programs and what actually happens during the mediation process. Much of the research comments favorably on the effects of mediating on the personal development of mediators. If the rationale for establishing a mediation program is that being a mediator is a very effective vehicle for personal development and human relations education, then it would be inequitable to select a cadre of mediators. Equity principles would demand that everyone be trained as a mediator and benefit from the self-improvement that results from practicing mediation. This does not, of course, preclude individualizing training to suit the requirements of particular students, and indeed, much curriculum theory would recommend that training be tailor-made. However, if a whole-school or whole-class approach is taken, questions arise about whether students might fail mediation training (for example, are any minimum skills standards required to practice as a mediator?) and about what to do when negative leaders choose to eschew or even revile the program.

The much broader question is whether the personal development of the mediators is a valid rationale for establishing a program. By and large, mediation training is justified in terms of improving the dispute resolution environment in the school. The personal development argument is more valid when a whole-school approach is taken, rather than a cadre approach, in that it can be reasoned (Johnson & Johnson, 1994) that if all students learn how to mediate, then all students have their personal development and conflict management skills enhanced, resulting in the establishment of a more cooperative educational environment. The other question related to the use of negative leaders is the empirical issue of what actually happens in the mediation process and whether there are significant differences between negative and positive student leaders in the way they conduct mediation sessions. Reference has previously been made to reports of mediator aggressiveness and to mediator roles that border on policing, and Burrell and Vogl (1990) warn against selecting student mediators who perceive themselves as law enforcers or as bouncers who break up fights. We know very little about student mediator styles and whether they vary systematically with behavioral status, age, or gender.

Finally, there is some diversity in the way in which students are trained to be mediators, but making comparisons across training courses is difficult because of the lack of detailed information that is readily available. The essential point of difference between them is the curricular focus. In particular, they vary in the relative emphasis given to general conflict resolution skills, such as active listening and dealing with emotions, and to specific mediation skills such as being impartial, developing a nonjudgmental attitude, and maintaining the mediation process. Some readily available training schedules were compared. (Lack of space prevents a detailed description of the sources and methodology used in this investigation, but I will provide a copy of the analysis on request.) The comparison revealed the following characteristics:

- Almost all of the training schedules develop some broad understanding of the nature of conflict.
- All teach about communication skills, usually active listening but also the use of appropriate assertiveness such as "I" statements.
- Almost all focus on dealing with emotions or understanding feelings, but some focus specifically on anger management.
- Almost all teach the technical skills of establishing ground rules, working through the phases of mediation, and keeping appropriate records.
- All make use of experiential learning in the training.
- Only a small number pay attention to managing power imbalances between disputants or addressing prejudices.

It would be useful to know which parts of these courses students find more and less difficult to master, and how different degrees of mastery affect mediation practices. Apart from the Teaching Students to Be Peacemakers Program (Johnson & Johnson, 1996), these questions have not yet been addressed.

Program Effects and Effectiveness

There has been a general lack of systematic research on the effectiveness of peer mediation programs, and the limited number of evaluations that have been conducted and published are vulnerable to methodological criticisms (Johnson & Johnson, 1996). Many of these criticisms are based on the view that it is outcome evaluation that should be receiving attention, and that the most appropriate design for outcome research is an experimental or quasi-experimental one. Only a small number of evaluations meet the requirements of a valid quasi-experimental design. The evaluation designs have been pragmatic, so it is difficult to make generalizations across studies. Few reports have considered effects on the same variables, and where the same effect has been examined, it has often been defined and measured in different ways (Van Slyck & Stern, 1991). An over-reliance on self-reporting, a focus on attitudes and short-term behavior, and the neglect of factors such as maturation are additional weaknesses in some of these studies. Establishing program effects is also made more difficult by the fact that program goals and objectives are not always fully and clearly articulated (Brewer-Wilson, 1991). Nevertheless, despite these conceptual and methodological limitations, a substantial body of data is being accumulated, and it is possible to categorize this research into the effects of peer mediation programs on discipline events, on mediators and disputants, and on school climate.

Discipline Events

The reported decline in the occurrence of discipline problems after the introduction of mediation services is astonishing. Authors refer to very large reductions in the number of disputes referred to the teacher (Johnson, Johnson, & Dudley, 1992), of discipline events (Lam, 1989), of incidents of fighting and aggression (Araki, 1990; Burrell & Vogl, 1990; Eisler, 1994b; McCormick, 1988; Metis Associates, 1990; Van Slyck & Stern, 1991), and of suspension rates (Umbreit, 1991). Johnson and Johnson (1996) advise caution in interpreting these data because of bias introduced by self-reporting, by the vested interests of some of the respondents, by the lack of clear definitions of concepts such as fighting and referral, and by the use of mediation as a substitute for suspension in some schools. Nevertheless, these studies provide substantial evidence that peer mediation programs do improve the school's social environment.

Effects on Mediators and Disputants

The most striking consequence of introducing mediation programs is the effect on the mediators. Well-conducted mediation training can change negative attitudes toward conflict into positive ones (Johnson & Johnson, 1996), and there is evidence that it transforms students' perception of physical violence as an appropriate conflict management behavior (Jones &

Carlin, 1994). Several studies comment on the effect of being a mediator on the mediators' self-image, especially among males (Eisler, 1994b; Van Slyck & Stern, 1991). Alluding to turning gladiators into mediators, Miller observes that mediators see themselves as performing a valuable service for their classmates and that "their grades go up and they walk taller" (Miller, 1994, p. 2). This is especially the case where student mediators are trainers of other students and adults (Close & Lechman, 1997). In a similar vein, mediators' social skills, such as communicating, respecting differences, and being able to express anger and empathy, improve as a result of practicing mediation (Eisler, 1994a, 1994b; Lam, 1989; Payne, 1993).

There is also a small body of research that suggests that these social skills are transferred into mediators' personal lives (Brown, 1995; Metis Associates, 1990; Payne, 1993). Gentry and Benenson (1992) found that student mediators perceived a significant decline in the frequency and intensity of their conflicts with siblings, and their parents perceived reductions in their interventions in conflicts. Similarly, Johnson, Johnson, and Dudley (1992) and Johnson and Johnson (1995) report anecdotal evidence that mediators used their skills with siblings, friends, grandparents, and parents, and in a separate study (Johnson, Johnson, Dudley, et al., 1995), they found that elementary school students made use of their school mediation training in dealing with home conflicts. In addition, mediators in the evaluations conducted by Eisler (1994a) and Brown (1995) indicated that they used their skills to resolve family conflicts and that parent-student relationships had improved at home.

There are also indications that mastery of mediation skills enhances the development of students' cognitive abilities. It has been reported that classes of high school English students who were taught negotiation procedures in tandem with literature performed better on academic achievement tests than a control group (Stevahn, Johnson, Johnson, Green, & Laginski, 1997; Stevahn, Johnson, Johnson, & Real, 1996). More anecdotally, Araki (1990) recounts the story of a poorly performing student whose grades improved dramatically after becoming a mediator and who attributed the change to the increased self-esteem brought about by helping classmates out of trouble rather than getting them into it. These dramatic effects on the mediators are echoed in the reported effects on disputants who use mediation services (Miller, 1994). Their self-esteem improves, their problem-solving abilities are enhanced, they become empowered to make decisions about their lives, and, because they own the solutions, the rates of agreement are exceptionally high.

The reported success rates for mediations are frequently over 90 percent (Araki, 1990; Crary, 1992; Johnson, Johnson, Cotten, et al., 1995;

Lam, 1989). Most studies simply report the occurrence of an agreement: few data are available on the types of agreements being reached, the longer-term stability of agreements, or the role that mediators play in the process. One study reports that solutions were temporary and non-integrative, with disputants predominantly agreeing to avoid each other (77 percent), and the researchers doubted that any long-term reduction in the use of coercive resolution strategies was achieved (Johnson, Johnson, Cotten, et al., 1995). There may also be a superficiality about the process. For example, Roush and Hall (1993) found that often young children simply wanted to narrate their dispute to someone; they then ran off before a fuller process could be initiated. In addition, Marshall (1987) notes that the public context of playground mediation could increase the agreement rate but adds the rider that the lack of adult intervention in these mediations is seldom likely to produce a lasting solution.

These very high success rates actually beg questions about the mediation process being practiced. Research in family mediation indicates that very high success rates reflect a more coercive mediator style (Kelly, 1996). This could be a factor in accounting for the high success rates in student mediation. In one program, disputants' criticisms of the process included aggressiveness on the part of the mediators, the fact that nonagreement led to detention, and a fear of records of nonagreements being kept in school files (Araki, Takeshita, & Kadomoto, 1989). There are also reports of mediators being overly critical of their peers and disdainful of disputants' trite arguments and inability to solve conflicts (Burrell & Vogl, 1990).

School Climate

A substantial amount of attention has been devoted to the effect of mediation programs on school climate, especially when the goal is to change school culture (DeJong, 1994). The results so far are equivocal. Research that explicitly addresses this question has not produced data confirming that significant changes do occur (Araki et al., 1989; Crary, 1992). The counterevidence is more anecdotal and comes from evaluations of the larger violence prevention programs. Eisler (1994b) reports that changes in the overall school climate did occur in the Schools Teaching Options for Peace study. In addition, participants in the Comprehensive Conflict Resolution Program believed that it had a positive impact on personal relations and school climate, and the Metis Associates (1990) evaluation of the Resolving Conflict Creatively Program found that 60 percent of respondents had observed positive changes in school climate attributable to the program. The Metis study also noted that respondents observed positive changes in classroom climate, and Lam (1989) cites three programs that had a positive effect on the amount of instructional time in class.

Other teacher benefits that are reported in the literature include changed teacher attitudes toward conflict, acquisition of new teaching skills, and an increased understanding of students' needs (Eisler, 1994a; Lam, 1989). However, a distinction needs to be made between the reactions of teachers who were closely involved with these programs and those who were not. Brown (1995) reports that among "uninvolved" teachers, the Toronto Board of Education's program had limited credibility and was seen as a political exercise in diverting resources rather than as making existing arrangements more effective.

Conclusion

Student mediation programs have gathered considerable momentum over the past ten years and have been implemented in countries such as New Zealand, Australia, the United States, Canada, and the United Kingdom. Published systematic evaluations of these programs are few, and some of those have been criticized for methodological weaknesses. Nevertheless, the overall tenor of these evaluations is positive, with particular emphasis being placed on the educational value to the mediators of practicing mediation, the very high success rates for mediating agreements, and the positive impact of reducing discipline events in the school at large.

We know little, however, about the cognitive processes involved when students are learning and practicing mediation skills. In particular, there has been no published work on the connections between learning about mediation at the interpersonal level and students' understanding of conflict management and peacemaking at the regional or international levels. Development and testing of models that make these cognitive links explicit will be a pressing challenge for peer mediation research.

REFERENCES

Araki, C. T. (1990). Dispute management in the schools. *Mediation Quarterly,*
    8, 51–62.
Araki, C. T., Takeshita, C., & Kadomoto, L. (1989). *Research results and final*
    report for the Dispute Management in the Schools Project. Honolulu, HI:
    Program on Conflict Resolution, University of Hawaii. (ERIC Document
    Reproduction Service No. ED 312 750)

Bagshaw, D. (1992). *Teaching conflict resolution skills to bullies.* Paper presented at the seminar "Understanding and Countering Bullying in Schools," University of South Australia, Institute of Social Research and the Children's Interest Bureau, Adelaide.

Bagshaw, D. (1994). Peer mediation strategies in schools. In K. Oxenberry, K. Rigby, &. P. Slee (Eds.), *Proceedings of the Conference on Cooperation and Conflict* (pp. 22–30). University of South Australia, Institute of Social Research, Adelaide.

Black, S. (1994). Handling anger. *Executive Educator, 16,* 27–30.

Brewer-Wilson, R. (1991). *Violence prevention for young adolescents: A survey of the state of the art and guidelines for future program evaluation.* Newton, MA: Education Development Centre. (ERIC Document Reproduction Service No. ED 356 442)

Brown, R. S. (1995). *An evaluation of the conflict resolution programs at the secondary level at the Toronto Board of Education 1993–94.* Toronto: Board of Education. (ERIC Document Reproduction Service No. ED 380 730)

Burrell, N. A., & Vogl, S. M. (1990). Turf-side conflict mediation for students. *Mediation Quarterly, 7,* 237–250.

Cahoon, P. (1988). Mediator magic. *Educational Leadership, 45,* 92–94.

Cameron, J., & Dupuis, A. (1989). *Dealing with conflict: Mediation programmes in schools* (Set #2, Item 8). Wellington, New Zealand: New Zealand Council for Educational Research.

Close, C. L., & Lechman, K. (1997). Fostering youth leadership: Students train students and adults in conflict resolution. *Theory into Practice, 36,* 11–16.

Crary, D. R. (1992). Community benefits from mediation: A test of the "peace virus" hypothesis. *Mediation Quarterly, 9,* 241–252.

Cutrona, C., & Guerin, D. (1994). Confronting conflict peacefully. *Educational Horizons, 72,* 95–104.

Davis, A. M. (1986, July). Dispute resolution at an early age. *Negotiation Journal,* pp. 287–297.

DeJong, W. (1994). School-based violence prevention: From the peaceable school to the peaceable neighborhood. *NIDR Forum, 25,* 8–14.

Deutsch, M. (1973). *The resolution of conflict.* New Haven, CT: Yale University Press.

Eisler, J. (1994a). *The Comprehensive Conflict Resolution Training Program 1993–94* (OER Report). New York: Office of Educational Research. (ERIC Document Reproduction Service No. ED 780 747)

Eisler, J. (1994b). *Project Schools Teaching Options for Peace (STOP) teen mediation project 1993–94.* New York: Office of Educational Research. (ERIC Document Reproduction Service No. ED 380 750)

Fisher, L. (1996). The selection, training and education of mediators. In
    D. Bagshaw (Ed.), *Proceedings of the Second International Mediation
    Conference: Mediation and Cultural Diversity* (pp. 78–92). University of
    South Australia, Institute of Social Research, Adelaide.

Folberg, J., & Taylor, A. (1984). *Mediation: A comprehensive guide to resolving
    conflicts without litigation.* San Francisco: Jossey-Bass.

Gentry, D. B., & Benenson, W. A. (1992). School-age peer mediators transfer
    knowledge and skills to home setting. *Mediation Quarterly, 10,* 101–109.

Haynes, J. (1996). Beyond diversity: Practicing mediation. In D. Bagshaw (Ed.),
    *Proceedings of the Second International Mediation Conference: Mediation
    and Cultural Diversity* (pp. 119–128). University of South Australia, Insti-
    tute of Social Research, Adelaide.

Heuchan, A., & Young, G. (1994). Peer mediation in a primary school. In
    M. Tainsch & J. Izard (Eds.), *Widening horizons: New challenges, direc-
    tions and achievements. Papers from the 1994 National Conference on
    Behaviour Management and Behaviour Change of Children and Youth
    with Emotional and/or Behaviour Problems.* Adelaide: Australian Council
    for Educational Research.

Johnson, D. W., & Johnson, R. T. (1994). Constructive conflict in the schools.
    Journal of Social Issues, 50, 117–137.

Johnson, D. W., & Johnson, R. T. (1995). Teaching students to be peacemakers:
    Results of five years of research. *Peace and Conflict: Journal of Peace Psy-
    chology, 1,* 417–438.

Johnson, D. W., & Johnson, R. T. (1996). Conflict resolution and peer media-
    tion programs in elementary and secondary schools: A review of the
    research. *Review of Educational Research, 66,* 459–506.

Johnson, D. W., Johnson, R., Cotten, B., Harris, D., & Louison, S. (1995).
    Using conflict managers to mediate conflicts in an inner-city elementary
    school. *Mediation Quarterly, 12,* 379–390.

Johnson, D. W., Johnson, R., & Dudley, B. (1992). Effects of peer mediation
    training on elementary school students. *Mediation Quarterly, 10,*
    89–99.

Johnson, D. W., Johnson, R., Dudley, B., & Magnuson, D. (1995). Training ele-
    mentary school students to manage conflict. *Journal of Social Psychology,
    135,* 673–686.

Johnson, D. W., Johnson, R. T., Dudley, D., Ward, M., & Magnuson, D.
    (1995). Impact of peer mediation training on the management of school
    and home conflicts. *American Educational Research Journal, 32,*
    829–844.

Jones, T. S., & Carlin, D. (1994). *Philadelphia peer mediation program: Report
    for 1992–1994 period.* Philadelphia: Good Shepherd Neighbourhood

House and Office of Desegregation of the Philadelphia Public School District.

Kelly, J. B. (1996). A decade of family mediation research: Some answers and questions. In D. Bagshaw (Ed.), *Proceedings of the Second International Mediation Conference: Mediation and Cultural Diversity* (pp. 149–156). University of South Australia, Institute of Social Research, Adelaide.

Lam, J. (1989). *The impact of conflict resolution programs on schools: A review and synthesis of the evidence.* Amherst, MA: National Association for Mediation in Education. (ERIC Document Reproduction Service No. ED 358 535)

Lane, P. S., & McWhirter, J. J. (1992). A peer mediation model: Conflict resolution for elementary and middle school children. *Elementary School Guidance and Counselling, 27,* 15–24.

Marshall, T. F. (1987). Mediation: A new mode of establishing order in schools. *Howard Journal of Criminal Justice, 26,* 33–46.

Maxwell, J. P. (1989). Mediation in the schools: Self-regulation, self-esteem, and self-discipline. *Mediation Quarterly, 7,* 149–155.

McCormick, M. (1988). Evaluation of the Wakefield Pilot Peer-Mediation program: Summary report. In P. Kestner, V. Kim, & J. Devonshire (Eds.), *Education and mediation: Exploring the alternatives* (pp. 263–274). Washington, DC: American Bar Association, Standing Committee on Dispute Resolution, Government Affairs and Public Services Group.

Metis Associates. (1990). *The Resolving Conflict Creatively Program 1988–89.* New York: Metis Associates. (ERIC Document Reproduction Service No. ED 348 422)

Miller, S. (1994). Kids learn about justice by mediating the disputes of other kids. In J. Wolowiec (Ed.), *Everybody wins: Mediation in the schools* (pp. 2–5). Chicago: American Bar Association. (ERIC Document Reproduction Service No. ED 375 046)

NSW DOSE (New South Wales Department of School Education). (1994). *Peer mediation: The Dispute Resolution Pilot Project report.* Sydney, N.S.W., Australia: Department of School Education.

Olczak, P. V., Grosch, J. W., & Duffy, K. G. (1991). Toward a synthesis: The art with the science of community education. In K. G. Duffy, J. W. Grosch, & P. V. Olczak (Eds.), *Community mediation: A handbook for practitioners and researchers* (pp. 329–343). New York: Guilford Press.

Payne, M. (1993). *Project S.T.O.P.: Final evaluation report 1991–92.* New York: Office of Research, Evaluation and Assessment. (ERIC Document Reproduction Service No. ED 364 816).

Rigby, K. (1996). *Bullying in schools, and what to do about it.* Melbourne: Australian Council for Educational Research.

Roesner, L. (1995). Changing the culture at Beacon Hill. *Educational Leadership, 52,* 28–32.

Roush, G., & Hall, E. (1993). Teaching peaceful conflict resolution. *Mediation Quarterly, 11,* 185–191.

Shepherd, K. S. (1994). Stemming conflict through peer mediation. *School Administrator, 51,* 14–17.

Stevahn, L., Johnson, D. W., Johnson, R. T., Green, K., & Laginski, A. (1997). Effects on high school students of conflict resolution training integrated into English literature. *Journal of Social Psychology, 137,* 302–315.

Stevahn, L., Johnson, D. W., Johnson, R. T., & Real, R. (1996). The impact of a cooperative or individualistic context on the effectiveness of conflict resolution training. *American Educational Research Journal, 33,* 801–823.

Stichter, C. (1986). When tempers flare, let student mediation put out the flames. *American School Board Journal, 173,* 41–42.

Umbreit, M. S. (1991). Mediation of youth conflict: A multi-system perspective. *Child and Adolescent Social Work, 8,* 141–153.

Van Slyck, M., & Stern, M. (1991). Conflict resolution in educational settings: Assessing the impact of peer mediation programs. In K. G. Duffy, J. W. Grosch, & P. V. Olczak (Eds.), *Community mediation: A handbook for practitioners and researchers* (pp. 257–274). New York: Guilford Press.

Van Slyck, M., Stern, M., & Zak-Place, J. (1996). Promoting optimal adolescent development through conflict resolution education, training, and practice: An innovative approach for counseling psychologists. *The Counseling Psychologist, 24,* 433–461.

14

TYPES OF PEACE EDUCATION

Ian M. Harris, University of Wisconsin at Milwaukee

*I still have a dream today that one day war will come to an end,
that men will beat their swords into plowshares, and their
spears into hooks, that nations will no longer rise against
nations, neither will they study war no more.*

—Martin Luther King Jr.

PEACE EDUCATION PROVIDES SUBSTANCE for Dr. King's dream. It has had a long and glorious history (Stomfay-Stitz, 1993). Since the middle of the nineteenth century, teachers and professors have hoped that by teaching about peace, they would educate children in such a way that human beings would avoid the scourges of war. Peace education at the end of the nineteenth century was concerned about the terror of modern warfare. Responding to the fear that mechanized weaponry would wipe out huge numbers of civilians, educators of young children as well as adults promoted international understanding as a way of avoiding war.

As we end the twentieth century, peace education is taking on new directions. Earlier in this century, Maria Montessori (1939/1972) argued that peace education was the best way to counteract fascism's hatred. Her educational methods taught young children to think for themselves so that they wouldn't fall prey to dictatorial authorities. In the 1970s in the West, peace education was heralded as a response to the war in Vietnam, and educators provided information to counteract government propaganda that favored the war. During the 1980s, a decade that saw considerable growth in peace education, teachers at all levels started to address the threat of a nuclear holocaust and expressed concern about the relationship between structural violence, cultural violence, and interpersonal violence. They become more concerned about internal security, whereas previously peace educators had addressed threats to international security. Peace educators at the end of this century address all aspects of violence and the trauma that violence causes to ordinary citizens, children, and the communities they inhabit.

At the end of the twentieth century, children and women are most often brutalized by wars. In war-torn areas of the Middle East, Central America, inner-city areas of the United States, the former Yugoslavia, Northern Africa, and elsewhere, children who are exposed to violence have both visible and invisible scars that lead to post-traumatic stress disorders. The adults in their lives, parents and teachers, need to address their fears, for research shows that adult denial of the trauma in children's lives contributes to making the children feel crazy as they struggle to handle the powerful emotions triggered by violence (Garbarino, Dubrow, Kostelny, & Pardo, 1992). Peace education can give children exposed to violence positive images of alternatives to violence: "Research indicates that children are most reassured when adults attempt to do something about children's fears. Children have many different reactions to violence. Possessing a minimum of information, young people are likely to ask difficult questions of teachers, parents, and government leaders. Adults who respond to these questions in ways that respect human growth and maturation can reassure young people growing up in a violent world" (Harris, 1988, p. 141). To help youth counteract despair about large-scale destruction in human communities, promoters of peace education draw upon peace theory to teach them the skills to construct a peaceful world and the motivation to live their lives based upon nonviolent principles.

Peace theory states that there are three ways to achieve peace: peacekeeping, peacemaking, and peace building. Peacekeeping, also known as peace through strength, depends upon using force to deter aggression. Peacemaking uses conflict resolution techniques so that the warring parties can resolve their differences once they have stopped fighting. Peace building attempts to create a desire for peace in students' minds. Peace educators have both short- and long-term goals. In the short term, school personnel use peacekeeping strategies to stop violence. In the long term, they want children to acquire peacemaking skills and to be motivated to build a more peaceful world.

Studies on young children have shown that teaching young people peaceful ways to respond to conflict can help lay an important foundation for helping them to become more peaceful as adults (Bernat, 1993; Carlsson-Paige & Levin, 1985). Research on college students has shown that they can experience a change in value orientation as a result of peace education classes (Eckhardt, 1984). Other studies have demonstrated cognitive changes as a result of peace education efforts (Feltman, 1986; French, 1984; Lyou, 1987). Harris (1992) has shown that college students most often are more interested in changing their own behavior after such instruction than in trying to work on the external circumstances that cause violence. Evaluations of peer mediation programs have shown that young people can learn peacekeeping skills in school and even apply these skills to their own lives (Johnson, Johnson, & Dudley, 1992).

Although these studies, done in school classroom settings, lack longitudinal follow-ups to see how well the pupils retain their learning about peace over time, they have demonstrated that young people can benefit from peace education. Teachers involved in the Resolving Conflicts Creatively Project in New York City public schools teach cooperation, communication skills, responsible decision making, conflict resolution, and cultural competence. Research on this project shows that students' in-school behavior changed positively as a result of peacemaking training: "Fully 71 percent [of the teachers] reported moderate or great decreases in physical violence in the classroom, while 66 percent observed less name calling and fewer verbal put-downs. Teachers reported that they had changed, too. Fully 84 percent said their own listening skills had improved. Many also noted that they had applied their increased knowledge of conflict resolution techniques in their own lives" (Lantieri & Patti, 1996, p. 208). Buoyed by these positive findings and feeling an urgency to reach out to children who are struggling to deal with the painful effects of violence, teachers all over the world are turning to peace education to create peaceful learning environments in their schools and to help young people deal with the stresses caused by violence.

This chapter will describe five different types of peace education used at the end of the twentieth century and explain how educators are applying them to school settings in terms of curricular instruction, classroom climate, and school climate.

Five Types of Peace Education

Throughout this century, peace education has been interpreted in different ways by teachers in unique cultures who are facing various forms of violence specific to their region. For example, during the decade of the 1980s, educators in countries in Africa and South America did not worry about nuclear issues, a concern that promoted peace education reforms in Europe, North America, and Japan, where it is known as A-bomb education (Fujita & Ito, 1992). Peace educators in poorer countries are more concerned about structural violence and have been promoting a variety of peace education called development education (Toh & Floresca-Cawagas, 1996), where students learn about human rights and alternative strategies for economic development. In Scandinavian countries, peace educators have developed disarmament studies, questioning why poor countries spend so much of their precious capital on upgrading their armed forces. In Japan, peace educators focus on human rights. In Africa, they are concerned with problems of underdevelopment. In North America, violence prevention and conflict resolution programs are spreading through the schools. These different peace education strategies can be broken down into five different types: global peace education, conflict resolution programs, violence prevention programs, development education, and nonviolence education.

Global Peace Education

Global peace education is closely allied to international studies, where educators inform their pupils about an international system that promotes wars. This form of peace education provides an understanding of security systems and cultural awareness. Followers of this peace-building strategy try to get students to think of themselves as compassionate global citizens who identify with people throughout the world who are struggling for peace. They hope that through the study of security systems, they can teach their pupils how to construct laws and institutions, like the United Nations, that will help humans avoid the terrors of war.

Within the diverse field of international studies, some teachers discuss the pros and cons of a federal world state, with laws and courts that can adjudicate conflicts between nations so that they don't go to war to settle their disagreements. Others look to alternative ways to structure the global economy, so that debt does not further impoverish developing nations that are struggling with the difficult conditions of structural violence. Peace educators provide their students with an awareness of problems around the planet. The assumption behind global education programs is that learning about the humanity of an enemy will reduce hostilities between opposing forces.

Problems associated with war occur at many different levels on this planet. Every country with the exception of Costa Rica and Iceland employs armed forces to provide security for its citizens. These armies promote a militaristic culture that diverts resources away from education, development, and other alternative means to provide security. Young people in different parts of the world face ethnic wars based upon long-standing hatreds. Civil wars often fail to provide social stability. At the end of the millennium, wars have shifted from those between countries to those within countries, with the vast majority of killing occurring between ethnic groups rivaling for control of contested areas. Education about these issues attempts to break down enemy images and seeks reconciliation of long-standing feuds. Such programs, however, often do not challenge the structures that cause enmity in the first place. Therefore, they may not be very effective in changing state policies that promote aggressive behavior. Since global education programs have long-term effects in regard to changing attitudes, it is hard to evaluate their effectiveness.

Conflict Resolution Programs

Conflict resolution training helps children to resolve interpersonal conflicts constructively. Recently, peer mediation has become an important part of peace education. Whereas global educators are concerned with international forms of violence, school personnel are bringing conflict resolution programs into schools to address aspects of interpersonal violence, teaching peacemaking skills such as mediation, empathy, and alternative dispute resolution methods. (Chapter Thirteen of this volume spells out in some detail the strengths and weaknesses of these programs.)

Studies show that children who learn negotiation procedures in school apply these skills to conflict situations they face in their own lives (Johnson et al., 1992). Furthermore, children who receive training have more positive attitudes about conflict (Stevahn, Johnson, Johnson, & Real, 1996). They are less likely to avoid conflicts and more likely to seek nonviolent remedies for conflicts in their lives. These results are even stronger when there is whole-school involvement in conflict resolution activities and academic integration of peacemaking themes into school content. A groundbreaking study on conflict resolution programs in New York City schools showed that as a result of this training children increased their use of supportive comments, were more cooperative, and exhibited more caring behavior and a greater understanding of other points of view (Metis Associates, 1990).

Violence Prevention Programs

Promoters of violence prevention education programs are concerned with the violent behaviors some children exhibit in school, hostile acts that make it hard for students to learn the cognitive lessons they are supposed to master. Their goal is to create safe school climates. In the United States, more than 400,000 crimes are reported in U.S. schools each year and 270,000 guns are brought to school on a typical day (Kimball, 1997). Peace educators pursuing a violence prevention strategy are often concerned with fights, street crime, unruly students in school settings, and sexual assaults. They have children examine how prejudices and stereotypes contribute to enemy images. Teaching anger management techniques helps students to avoid fights. The prime generator of these programs, Deborah Prothrow-Stith (1991), describes them in the following way: "The point of the violence prevention course is to provide these young people with alternatives to fighting. The first three lessons of the ten-session curriculum provide adolescents with information about violence and homicide" (p. 176).

An example of such a program is "squash it," which began in Kansas, City, Missouri, in 1994, organized by the Partnership for Children: "When a confrontation arises, youths say 'squash it' and make a time-out hand gesture placing a flat hand onto a vertical fist" (Kimball, 1997, p. 32). New York City schools have implemented comprehensive violence prevention programs that emphasize student rights, responsibilities, and discipline.

Evaluations of violence prevention programs show that they help to reduce aggressive physical acts and increase prosocial behavior (Grossman, Neckerman, & Koepsell, 1997). There are many risk factors for violent behavior—family patterns of behavior, violent social environments, negative cultural models, peers, alcohol and/or drug abuse, and availability of weapons. Addressing some of these factors directly in school can provide children with positive ideas about how to respond to conflict. Such programs do not solve all the problems of violence, but studies show that they have an additive affect. Each new behavior that helps an individual who might otherwise be violent to resolve conflict in constructive ways helps in overcoming destructive behaviors.

Development Education

Peace educators use development studies to provide their students with insights into the various aspects of structural violence, focusing on social institutions with their hierarchies and their propensity for dominance and oppression. Human rights education falls into this category, as do environmental studies, in which children learn about the negative consequences of environmental destruction and about how to live sustainably on this planet. In this form of education, which has often been referred to as development education, students learn about the plight of the poor and about different strategies to address the problems of poverty. The goal is to build peaceful communities by promoting an active democratic citizenry that is interested in equitably sharing the world's resources.

Peace educators question the dominant patterns of development that have preoccupied the West for the past millennium. They give more emphasis to ecologically sound folk practices than to cultures of unlimited consumerism based upon exploitation of natural resources and human capital. They teach about appropriate technology and sustainable development. Development educators are concerned about the rush to modernity and its impact upon human communities. Rather than promoting elitist, top-down strategies imposed by bureaucrats and politicians who see ordinary people as ignorant, peace educators promote poor people's involvement in planning, implementing, and controlling development schemes. They would like to see resources controlled equitably rather than monopolized by elites. They teach a critical consciousness that challenges injustice and undemocratic policymaking. They call for urgent attention to the environment and the need to live in harmony with natural forces. These peace educators look for more appropriate forms of technology that are not as destructive for natural ecosystems.

The field of development education lacks rigorous evaluation. It has been most successful in socialist countries like Tanzania and Nicaragua. Environmental education itself, which in this typology belongs to development education, is too new a field for its effectiveness to be evaluated, although the environmental movement as a whole has had an impact upon some elements of consumer behavior in Western countries, where citizens recycle and buy "green" products.

Nonviolence Education

Nonviolence education attempts to put positive images of peace in children's minds. To create a peaceful society those images must be so attractive that humans will choose to behave nonviolently when confronting conflict. This type of peace education draws heavily upon the great nonviolent thinkers like Mohandas Gandhi, Martin Luther King Jr., and Jiddu Krishnamurti, as well as on the ideas of many outstanding religious leaders. Students interested in learning more about nonviolence can study the lives of the winners of the Nobel Peace Prize to learn to develop the positive images of peace that can give them the desire to create what Martin Luther King Jr. called "beloved communities." In India this type of education includes Gandhian studies.

Teaching young people about nonviolence provides them with an image of "shalom," a world where human beings work together to resolve their differences and live sustainably on the planet. An example of a peace education program that takes this approach is Voices of Love and Freedom, a K–12 curriculum being implemented in the Boston public schools that uses multicultural literature in English and Spanish to address three goals: (1) to promote the development of the students' social skills and values, (2) to improve the literacy skills of students, and (3) to prevent violence and the use of alcohol and other drugs by students and their families.

Education about nonviolence can help to counter the culture of violence that reverberates throughout the media, the entertainment industry, politics, national policy, the schools, the community, and the family. Nonviolence in education provides an image of positive peace where human needs are met and there is no overt violence. Solutions to problems are sought in a win-win perspective. Ralph Summy (1995) has argued that the best way to achieve positive peace is to overcome the distrust in the human psyche that says that nonviolence is not possible. Students in classes where teachers are promoting nonviolence become motivated to work for peace.

A research study has shown that teenagers exposed to nonviolence benefit in many positive ways (Harris, Jeffries, & Opels, 1997). Parents of adolescents who participated in a summer institute on nonviolence noted that their children were taking more responsibility for their actions: they were keeping out of fights more, having fewer emotional outbursts, and applying fairness rules more often.

The five different forms of peace education are highlighted in Table 14.1. Using educational strategies to address the various forms of violence provides a challenge. Often children feel hopeless in the face of ethnic conflict, destruction of the ozone layer, and seemingly intractable conflicts like those in the Middle East. Young people have strong emotions about these conflicts, fears that often distract them from the cognitive lessons they are supposed to master in school. Despairing, they can feel that there is nothing they can do to alleviate their suffering and misery. Throughout the planet, teachers are turning to these different types of peace education to provide children with understanding about the sources of violence in their lives and with a positive sense of how they can contribute to constructing a more peaceful future. Peace education is a holistic approach to the complex forms of violence experienced in diverse communities. Teachers are using these different types of peace education to heal wounds in children who have been violated by wars, terrorism, domestic abuse, street crime, bullies, or sexual harassment. Teachers find many dynamic ways to incorporate these different types of peace education into their daily practice.

Applying Peace Education in Schools

In order to give students an appreciation of the power of peace, school personnel apply peace theory to all different levels of educational enterprises. They can teach about peace (curriculum) to pupils of all ages. At the micro level, they can use peace techniques to run their classes (classroom climate). At the macro level, they can run schools peacefully (school climate). Infusing an awareness of peace into all levels of schooling gives children hope about creating a better world.

Curriculum

Peace educators do not just want to stop violence and reduce conflict in schools. They want to build in young people's minds the foundations for positive peace. Curricular approaches to peace education provide concrete examples of how peace works, helping students to understand what escalates and what de-escalates violence. When young people watch the news, they see acts of violence being committed all around the world. They are subjected to violence on television, in movies, and in video games. To counteract such violent cultural images, teachers teach about the various nonviolent cultures that have existed throughout history. Children can learn in school how nonviolent strategies have been used to address injustice by studying the activities of peace heroes and heroines who have been active in peace movements but who are often overlooked in traditional history classes. Peace education encourages students to express their wishes for peace by involving them in peace projects such as planting trees or volunteering in a refugee camp. Peace educators provide peace resources—books, posters, movies, and videos—that have peace themes. They connect students with community-based organizations that promote peace—women's shelters, programs for violent men, refugee camps, peace groups, and anger management support groups. Such projects motivate pupils to value peace. Children can learn about the humanity of their enemies through exchange programs, like the various Arab-Jewish reconciliation programs carried out in Israel (Chetkow-Yanoov, 1996).

Peace educators are committed to building democracy, because a democracy allows all points of view to be heard in the promotion of the truth. Such an approach to education has been heralded in recent school

Table 14.1. Types of Peace Education.

	Violence Addressed	Goals	Peace Type (Strategy)	Curriculum
Global Peace Education International studies Security studies Holocaust studies Nuclear education A-bomb education	Interstate rivalry War Human rights education Ethnic conflicts Terrorism Tribal warfare	Understanding of international system Cultural knowledge Appreciation of national differences Multicultural awareness Study of nationalism	Prevent hostilities Build security systems Disarmament Exchange of scholars Global identity Reduce ethnic tensions Treaties	International relations Peace movements Different cultures Historical perspectives of wars Comparative social structures Principles for collective responsibility Political differences Problems of refugees
Conflict Resolution Programs Peer mediation	Interpersonal Personal	Mediation and communication skills Promote empathy Manage conflict Understand conflict style	Problem-solving skills Mediation Peace agreements Sustaining relationships Transformation	Gender studies Communication skills Anthropology of conflict Sociology of conflict styles Enemy imaging Family differences
Violence Prevention Programs Multicultural education	Street crime Domestic violence Parent education Sexual assault Anger management Peer pressure Hate crimes Drug and alcohol abuse	Anti-bias Educate about prejudice and stereotypes Understand depth of violence problem Learn about causes of violence Personal responsibility Socioemotional literacy Understand cost of violence	Self-control Support groups Meditation Counseling Anger management Personal transformation Win-win relationships Addressing fears Parent education	Alternatives to violence Dispute resolution mechanisms Causes of domestic violence and crime Punitive responses Judicial system Laws Block club organizing Gangs Consequences of violence

Development Education				
Environmental studies Future studies Human rights education	Inequalities of health and wealth Structural violence Lack of freedoms Positive peace Environmental destruction	Ecological security Equitable models of development Promote democracies Critical thinking Strategic planning	Elimination of pollution Building for the future Sharing resources Self-help Empowerment Community development Disarmament	Imperialism Economic development Social development Strategies for change Ecology Conservation skills Environmental issues Recycling Economic conversion
Nonviolence Education				
Gandhian studies	All forms of violence Enemy stereotyping Popular media images of violence Despair about possibilities for peace	Understand power of peace Appreciate peace Learn about power of nonviolence Help students discover their own truth Appreciate truths of others	Maintain beloved community Forgiveness Positive peace Nonviolence Elimination of ego Visualize peaceful world Caring Empathy	Nonviolence Love Great peacemakers Philosophy of humanness Study of human nature Ethics Challenge of being a peace-maker Interdependence Barriers to peace History of peace movement

reforms through the promotion of a multicultural approach to knowledge (Nieto, 1992) that teaches that all different cultures have important insights into the truth. In order to appreciate the diversity of life on this planet, students need to learn to value different cultures so that they can live with people who are different from themselves in a "global village."

Children in classes where teachers are promoting peace acquire theoretical concepts about the dangers of violence and the possibilities of peace as well as practical skills about how to live nonviolently. Becoming committed to peace requires more than a theoretical understanding of the problems of violence and knowledge of conflict resolution strategies. Young people need to learn social skills and become emotionally literate. Peace educators attempt to stimulate the human heart to be charitable and provide children with skills they can use to demonstrate their feelings of compassion for all forms of life. They believe that "there must be love in our hearts, not mere learning or knowledge. The greater our love, the deeper will be its influence on society. But we are all brains and no heart; we cultivate the intellect and despise humanity" (Krishnamurti, 1954/ 1981, p. 78).

A challenge provided by a commitment to peace education is to figure out how to teach content that develops compassion and caring within the hearts of the world's citizens. Peace educators teach communication skills so that students will know about alternatives to dysfunctional, violent behaviors. They teach listening, caring, tolerance, cooperation, impulse control, anger management, perspective taking, and problem-solving skills. They also try to make students aware of their own biases, the ways in which they stereotype others by gender, nationality, sexual preference, religious belief, or skin color. They teach children about racial differences and gender identity formation to help them avoid discriminatory behavior. The goal of these instructional activities is to provide students with peaceful communication skills and to help them to be empathic. Peer mediation techniques provide students with conflict resolution skills that help them to move beyond hate and become more loving.

At the feeling level, teachers instruct students about the power of generative love, care, and justice to build the beloved community. Trauma circles, peer counseling, and support groups can help young children to deal with some of the grief, fear, and anger caused by violent events in their lives. Anger management groups in secondary schools help adolescents who come from abusive and/or dysfunctional homes to deal with some of their deep-seated rage. Some urban school districts in the United States even have curricula on death and dying to help young people deal with the trauma of losing their friends to suicide, accidental death, or homicide (Ulin, 1977). Such activities can help to improve the academic performance of children who are so distracted by violence that they cannot focus on cognitive lessons. Adults who listen and show concern about the problems caused by violence in young people's lives can help to heal some of the wounds that often lead youth to hostile, antisocial behaviors.

Classroom Climate

Peace education does not just mean a peaceful classroom. It suggests a learning environment in which students are acting to resolve problems, working with others, and taking on challenging tasks. The hidden curriculum in peaceful classrooms should promote peace. Students learn to be peaceful by following the model set by the adult teacher. A research study has shown that this kind of modeling of peaceful behavior is the most effective way to teach young people about peace (Harris, 1995). In a peaceful classroom, students assist each other in discovering their own truths. A teacher committed to nonviolence in education uses a dialogue method to help children share insights into how to resolve conflicts. In such a classroom children are encouraged to think critically, a skill badly needed for young people who are to challenge the violent cultures that surround them.

Teachers who promote nonviolent learning structures in their classrooms draw upon the principles of cooperative learning (Johnson, Johnson, Holubec, & Roy, 1984). They set up democratic learning communities in their classes where students provide each other with feedback and support so that they become proficient in group process techniques. In cooperative learning situations, students challenge each other to find the best solution to problems, learning how human beings benefit from cooperative relationships. Such classes, based upon positive interdependence among group members, teach individuals to care for other group members.

Teachers who are interested in peace have a unique approach to discipline. They give their students guidelines about how to behave through positive affirmations rather than through punishment and use of authoritarian power to control behavior. They use democratic boundary-setting principles that help students to understand the importance of respecting different people's boundaries (Harris, 1973). Instead of threatening to punish children, a peaceful teacher seeks their input.

Teachers in peaceful classrooms study their students carefully. They watch them develop and understand their strengths and weaknesses. To know something is to understand its nature. Rather than responding to students mechanically, assuming that all students are learning at the same rate, peaceful teachers respond to the uniqueness in each individual. In a peaceful class, listening and watching are more important instructional activities than lecturing and commanding.

School Climate

A peaceful school is administered democratically. Children have rights that must be respected within nonviolent schools. Such schools are like loving families. They provide sanctuaries where children feel good and safe. Nonviolent schools have an inclusive atmosphere where everyone contributes to keeping the peace; they are run on the principle of site-based management, where the staff has the authority to make personnel choices and decisions about resources. The staff at the New Mexico Center for Dispute Resolution, which has been running community-based mediations for over ten years, has concluded that "school-based conflict resolution programs must change the culture of the schools, not just the students. School staff must be committed to model and reinforce the skills for students and create a school community that adheres to the positive expression and resolution of conflict" (Smith, 1996, p. 254). It is hard for teachers to commit themselves to the principles of peace education unless they have a supportive school climate. The administration needs to develop a commitment to peace in order to reinforce the efforts of teachers and students to promote nonviolence.

Principals of such schools need to create structures that are less extreme than traditional authority punishments like suspensions or expulsions. Such structures, such as time-out rooms for students who are acting aggressively, peer mediation programs, and programs that teach anger management skills, prepare students to face difficulties in a rational, constructive, and compassionate way. They help everyone on a school staff to develop creative solutions to problems that reduce tension, anger, aggression, and violence. Administrators of peaceful schools practice nonviolence in thought, word, and deed. A balance of consequences and empathy replaces punishment wherever possible.

The principal can create school-wide events that motivate students to seek peace. Pep rallies for peace and school assemblies can inspire youth to seek nonviolent ways to resolve their conflicts. Awards for peacemakers, such as peacemaker badges, can be passed out to all students individually or through a school assembly where each class nominates a student who has excelled at peacemaking. Such recognition helps young people to understand the importance of nonviolent behavior.

Principals concerned about creating a nonviolent school climate can educate parents about the importance of not hitting their children. Physical means of disciplining children provide bad role models of conflict resolution, lower children's self-esteem, and make it difficult for children to trust adults—all of which are counterproductive to school success, which depends upon rational ways of learning, high levels of self-esteem, and an atmosphere in which young people trust adults, including their teachers. Many parents teach their children to stand up and fight when they are challenged. Such pugilistic behavior, when it is carried into a classroom, can create chaos. Parents need to be told that fighting has no place in a school setting. Principals can sponsor workshops for parents in positive parenting skills at their schools and send home newsletters with tips about nurturing.

Administrators can also establish school planning and management teams to help involve community members in resolving conflicts. Since so much violence comes from the neighborhoods surrounding schools, some administrators seek to involve police, parents, and community members in school-based attempts to manage disputes. These important resources help school personnel to deal with problems of substance abuse, teen pregnancy, dropout rates, and gang involvement. Violence prevention programs, in order to be successful, must carry over into the community so that the alternatives to violence that young people are learning in school are reinforced when they leave school.

Climbing a Mountain to Peace

Martin Luther King Jr. used the imagery of going to the mountaintop, where he viewed a world built upon the principles of nonviolence in which people use alternative dispute mechanisms to resolve their conflicts and nurture social organizations based upon positive peace principles. Peace education is idealistic. It strives to give children dynamic images of nonviolence and the skills to create beloved communities wherever they live. Throughout this century, interest in peace education has grown as teachers respond to various forms of violence by teaching about global issues, nonviolent resolution of conflicts, and environmental sustainability. However, in spite of this interest, peace education has not yet entered the mainstream of educational reform efforts. Although many schools have implemented conflict resolution programs, peace education has not been widely adopted in countries where education reformers are trying to raise standards in order to promote higher levels of academic achievement.

Teachers attempting to teach about peace at the end of the twentieth century live in countries that use peacekeeping strategies to promote security. Nations prefer to spend money on arms rather than to invest in development strategies that will address some of the sources of structural violence that are creating so much violence (and school failure) throughout the world. As politicians play upon people's fears, citizens' need to feel secure escalates. When people perceive their world to be full of enemies and hostile forces, attempts at peace education challenge their sense of reality. In most societies violence is an acceptable way of solving conflicts. Teachers who promote peacemaking and peace-building strategies are bucking strong cultural pressures that rely on peace through strength to create social order.

One of the problems teachers face in their attempts to promote positive peace is that they cannot show immediate results. A citizenry frightened by violence wants generals to wipe out aggressors and prisons to lock up criminals. It demands immediate results and votes for politicians who promote get-tough policies. Peace education provides a long-term strategy for dealing with problems of violence. Peace educators try to create healthy children who are emotionally aware and spiritually attuned to the incredible levels of suffering on this planet caused by violence. They hope that in the future these young people will grow up into citizens who will use their knowledge of the different alternatives to violence to promote peacemaking structures that will help reduce levels of violence. Because such a preventive strategy does not receive support from scared citizens who want immediate protection, teachers involved in peace education resemble Sisyphus, pushing a rock up an endless hill; they struggle to teach alternatives to violence in a climate where most people champion the principles of peace through strength.

Peace educators have not been able to convince their colleagues of the value of the different types of peace education mentioned in this chapter. Most educators who are faced with escalating levels of violence in the modern world resort to get-tough peacekeeping policies that provide children neither with an understanding of the problems of violence nor with strategies to avoid violence. Such get-tough policies mirror the punitive strategies used in the international arena, where political states use their armed forces to dominate their enemies, and in criminal justice systems that deal with juvenile crime by locking up youth. History books continue to celebrate the victories of warriors, and science textbooks encourage the exploitation of natural systems. Teachers continue to prefer to act like authorities, rather than climbing up the lofty slopes of peace to provide children with alternatives to the violence that surrounds them. Peace education will not become a dominant force in school reform efforts until a powerful cultural shift moves humans away from a fear-based response to conflict and toward a compassionate response to interpersonal, social, and political problems.

Peace educators have been trying to promote such a paradigm shift. They understand that school failure often comes from the negative reaction young people have to the various forms of violence in their lives. Youth who are frightened cannot focus on their lessons. Children will learn better when their teachers use some of these different types of peace education to directly address the many forms of violence that scare them. Those few teachers who are committed to the lofty ideals of peace education play a proactive role in relation to the problems of violence, rather than responding to at-risk students with threats of retribution. Supporters of peace education realize that the failure of some children in school does not happen because they are stupid. Instead, some young people are at risk in school because of the problematic nature of the modern world, which is so deeply steeped in violence. Many children come to school suffering from post-traumatic stress disorders that are ignored by teachers who are focused solely on imparting subject matter. In order to improve the academic performance of those youth who are doing poorly in school, teachers need to use the peace education strategies discussed in this chapter to promote a vision of "shalom" in a violent world.

REFERENCES

Bernat, V. (1993). Teaching peace. *Young Children, 48* (3), 36–39.

Carlsson-Paige, N., & Levin, D. (1985). *Helping young children understand peace, war, and the nuclear threat.* Washington, DC: National Association for the Education of Young Children.

Chetkow-Yanoov, B. (1996). Conflict resolution can be taught. *Peabody Journal of Education, 71* (3), 12–28.

Eckhardt, W. (1984). Peace studies and attitude change: A value theory of peace studies. *Peace and Change, 4* (1), 79–85.

Feltman, R. (1986). Change in peace attitude: A controlled attitude change study of internationalism. *Peace Research, 18* (1), 66–71.

French, P. (1984, September). Preventive medicine for nuclear war. *Psychology Today,* p. 70.

Fujita, H., & Ito, T. (1992). Peace education in Japanese universities. In A. Bjerstedt (Ed.), *Education for peace: A conference report from Kyoto* (pp. 15–30). Malmö, Sweden: Lund University, School of Education.

Garbarino, J., Dubrow, N., Kostelny, K., & Pardo, C. (1992). *Children in danger: Coping with the consequences of community violence*. San Francisco: Jossey-Bass.

Grossman, D. C., Neckerman, J. J., & Koepsell, T. D. (1997). The effectiveness of a violence prevention curriculum among children in elementary school: A randomized controlled trial. *Journal of the American Medical Association, 277* (20), 1605–1611.

Harris, I. M. (1973). Boundaries, limits, and set theory: An alternative way to structure the classroom. *Education, 93* (3), 285–292.

Harris, I. M. (1988). *Peace education*. Jefferson, NC: McFarland.

Harris, I. M. (1992). The challenge of peace education: Do our efforts make a difference? *Educational Foundations, 6* (4), 75–98.

Harris, I. M. (1995). Teachers' response to conflict in selected Milwaukee schools. In H. Lofgren (Ed.), *Peace education and human development* (pp. 197–219). Malmö, Sweden: Lund University, School of Education.

Harris, I. M., Jeffries, R., & Opels, R. (1997). Assessing the effectiveness of the University of Wisconsin–Milwaukee Summer Institute on Nonviolence. *Viewpoints on War, Peace, and Global Cooperation*, pp. 26–41.

Johnson, D. W., Johnson, R. T., & Dudley, B. (1992). Effects of peer mediation training on elementary students. *Mediation Quarterly, 10* (1), 89–99.

Johnson, D. W., Johnson, R. T., Holubec, E. J., & Roy, P. (1984). *Circles of learning*. Washington, DC: Association for Supervision and Curriculum Development.

Kimball, G. (1997). *The teen trip: The complete resource guide*. Chico, CA: Equity Press.

Krishnamurti, J. (1981). *Education and the significance of life*. New York: HarperCollins. (Original work published 1954)

Lantieri, L., & Patti, J. (1996). *Waging peace in our schools*. Boston: Beacon Press.

Lyou, J. K. (1987). Studying nuclear weapons: The effect on students. *Peace Research, 19* (1), 11–18.

Metis Associates. (1990). *The Resolving Conflict Creatively Program, 1988–1989: A summary of recent findings*. New York: Author.

Montessori, M. (1972). *Education for peace*. Washington, DC: Regnery. (Original work published 1939)

Nieto, S. (1992). *Affirming diversity*. White Plains, NY: Longman.

Prothrow-Stith, D. (1991). *Deadly consequences*. New York: HarperCollins

Smith, M. (1996). Strategies to reduce school violence: The New Mexico Center for Dispute Resolution. In A. Hoffman (Ed.), *Schools, violence and society* (pp. 253–264). New York: Praeger.

Stevahn, L., Johnson, D., Johnson, R., & Real, R. (1996). The impact of a cooperative or individualistic context on the effectiveness of conflict resolution training. *American Education Research Journal, 33* (4), 801–824.

Stomfay-Stitz, A. (1993). *Peace education in America, 1828–1990.* Metuchen, NJ: Scarecrow Press.

Summy, R. (1995). Vision of a nonviolent society. In M. Salla, W. Tonetto, & E. Martinez (Eds.), *Essays on peace: Paradigms for global order* (pp. 63–69). Queensland, Australia: Central Queensland University Press.

Toh, S. H., & Floresca-Cawagas, V. (1996). Toward a better world? A paradigmatic analysis of development education resources from the World Bank. In R. J. Burns & R. Aspeslagh (Eds.), *Three decades of peace education around the world: An anthology* (pp. 175–210). New York: Garland.

Ulin, M. L. (1977). *Death and dying education.* Washington, DC: National Education Association.

ABOUT THE EDITORS

DANIEL BAR-TAL (Ph.D., University of Pittsburgh, 1974) is a professor of social psychology at the School of Education and Department of Psychology, Tel Aviv University. His major areas of interest and research are in political and social psychology, studying societal beliefs regarding conflict, delegitimization, security, patriotism, and the siege mentality. Presently he is serving as president of the International Society of Political Psychology (1999–2000). He is the author of *Group Beliefs* (Springer-Verlag, 1990) and *Societal Beliefs of Ethos* (Sage, in press) and is coeditor of *Social Psychology of Knowledge* (Cambridge University Press, 1988), *Social Psychology of Intergroup Relations* (Springer-Verlag, 1988), *Stereotyping and Prejudice* (Springer-Verlag, 1989), *Patriotism in the Lives of Individuals and Nations* (Nelson Hall, 1997), and *Security Concerns* (JAI Press, 1998).

LOUIS OPPENHEIMER (Ph.D. in social sciences, University of Nijmegen, 1978) is a professor of developmental psychology in the Department of Psychology, University of Amsterdam, and codirector of the Cross-Cultural Research Programme on Children and Peace. He received his training in experimental and developmental psychology at the Universities of Tel Aviv, Groningen, and Nijmegen. His research interests focus on social cognitive development and concern a wide range of topics, such as social competence, social status, the self-concept and self-system, understanding peace and war, and humor. Self-concept and self-system research resulted in two publications, *The Self-Concept: European Perspectives on Its Development, Aspects, and Applications* (Springer-Verlag, 1990) and, with Annerieke Oosterwegel, *The Self-System: Developmental Changes Between and Within Self-Concepts* (Erlbaum, 1993). His peace research has also resulted in various publications, such as the coedited report *Research on Children and Peace: International Perspectives* (Göteborg University, 1996). He has published 100 articles and chapters in developmental, social, and political journals and books.

AMIRAM RAVIV (Ph.D. in psychology, Hebrew University, Jerusalem, 1974) is an associate professor in the Psychology Department at Tel Aviv

University and is also a school and children's clinical psychologist. His major research interests are the formation of social knowledge, school psychology, and the development of children's thinking. In recent years he has studied the influence of stress and crisis situations on children and adolescents. He is presently involved in a research project that examines the effects of children's exposure to violence. Through the years, he has published over sixty articles and chapters in leading psychological journals and professional books.

ABOUT THE CONTRIBUTORS

PATRICIA G. AVERY (Ph.D. in educational leadership, Emory University, 1987) is an associate professor at the University of Minnesota. Her areas of interest are political socialization and civic education. She has written articles in *The American Educational Research Journal, Social Education, Theory and Research in Social Education, Theory into Practice, The Social Studies,* and other journals.

KATHY BICKMORE (Ph.D., Stanford University, 1991) is an assistant professor in Curriculum, Teaching and Learning and Sociology and Equity Studies in Education at the Ontario Institute for Studies in Education at the University of Toronto. She teaches in the graduate and teacher education program at OISE/UT and received an Exemplary Dissertation Award from the U.S. National Council for the Social Studies in 1993. Her research emphasizes school-based conflict resolution and education for democratic citizenship. Her recent publications include *Alternatives to Violence: A Manual for Teaching Peacemaking to Youth and Adults* (Cleveland Friends Meeting, 1984) and "Teaching Conflict Resolution: Preparation for Pluralism" (Special issue of *Theory into Practice, 36,* 1997).

ED CAIRNS (Ph.D. in psychology, Queen's University, Belfast, Northern Ireland, 1968) is a professor of psychology in the School of Behavioral and Communication Sciences at the University of Ulster in Coleraine, Northern Ireland. Much of his work has been conducted through the Centre for the Study of Conflict at the University of Ulster and, more recently, through INCORE, the joint United Nations University/University of Ulster program on conflict resolution and ethnicity. He is a fellow of the British Psychological Society and is also associated with the Division of Peace Psychology of the American Psychological Association. He has written some seventy books, chapters in books, and articles in this area. His most recent book is *Children and Political Violence* (Blackwell, 1995).

KATHERINE COVELL (Ph.D., University of Toronto, 1986) is an associate professor of psychology and director of the Children's Rights Center at the University College of Cape Breton, Nova Scotia, Canada. She won a teaching award at the University of Toronto in 1988. Covell's work reflects her interest in policy-related issues. She has published a number of research articles and book chapters that focus on family and community influences on child and adolescent development. She also is editor of *Readings in Child Development: A Canadian Perspective* (Nelson, 1995). Covell is active in the local community, where she is working on the design and implementation of a children's rights curriculum for elementary school children in Nova Scotia, and the international community, where she is working on child labor issues with the Office of the North American Agreement on Labour Cooperation.

SALMAN ELBEDOUR (Ph.D. in school psychology, University of Minnesota, 1992) is a lecturer in the School of Education, Ben-Gurion University of the Negev, Israel. He is also a school psychologist in the Israeli/Bedouin school system. His primary professional focus is in the area of the psychopathology of adolescence. His major research focus has been on the impact of war and violent conditions on the emotional status of the adolescent. Within this context, he has a special focus on the effect of such factors as social change on developmental issues of Bedouin adolescents.

SOLVEIG HÄGGLUND (Ph.D. in education, Göteborg University, Sweden, 1986) is an associate professor of education in the Department of Education and Educational Research, Göteborg University, Sweden. Her research focuses on socialization, development, and learning in different settings. She has conducted studies on gender socialization, prosocial development, and social responsibility in preschool and school settings. Recent research projects concern social exclusion and social inclusion in formal educational settings and national and European identity. She is codirector of the Cross-Cultural Research Program on Children and Peace.

ILSE HAKVOORT (Ph.D. in developmental psychology, University of Amsterdam, 1996) is a research fellow in the Department of Education and Educational Research at Göteborg University, Sweden. She is currently also program coordinator of the Cross-Cultural Research Programme on Children and Peace. The core of her research work is presented in her doctoral thesis, "Conceptualizations of Peace and War from Childhood Through Adolescence: A Social-Cognitive Developmental Approach." In recent years, her research activities have included studies of the conceptualization of peace and war in different cultural contexts.

ROBIN HALL (Ph.D. in education, Macquarie University, Australia, 1994) is a senior lecturer in social education in the School of Teacher Education, Charles Sturt University, Bathurst, Australia. His fields of interest include peace studies at both the international and interpersonal levels. He has published research on children's conceptions of peace in the *Journal of Peace Research* and has also written about the postwar situation in Eritrea, North Africa. He is currently preparing a primary school text on global education. As a teacher educator, he teaches a course in conflict management and is engaged in researching the effectiveness of peer mediation programs in Australian schools.

IAN HARRIS (Ed.D. in urban education, Temple University, 1975) is a professor of educational policy and community studies at the University of Wisconsin–Milwaukee, where he directs the Peace Studies Program. He is the author of *Peace Education, Messages Men Hear* and coauthor of *Experiential Education for Community Development* and *Peacebuilding for Adolescents*.

DAVID W. JOHNSON (Ed.D., Columbia University, 1967) is a professor and codirector of the Cooperative Learning Center, University of Minnesota. He has written many books, including *Reaching Out: Interpersonal Effectiveness and Self Actualization; Joining Together: Group Theory and Group Skills* (with Frank P. Johnson); *Circles of Learning: Cooperation in the Classroom* (with Roger T. Johnson and Edythe J. Holubec); and *Teaching Students to Be Peacemakers*.

ROGER T. JOHNSON (Ed.D., University of California at Berkeley, 1969) is a professor and codirector of the Cooperative Learning Center, University of Minnesota. He is coauthor with David W. Johnson of *Circles of Learning; Leading the Cooperative School; Active Learning: Cooperation in the College Classroom;* and *Creative Controversy in the Classroom*.

LEAH KOREN-SILVERSHATZ (M.A. in clinical psychology, Tel Aviv University, 1992) is a senior research associate for the study of the development of concepts of war and peace at Tel Aviv University. Her research interests focus on the development of political concepts in children and adolescents in Israel, and specifically on the development of concepts of war and peace. She works as a clinical psychologist at the Ministry of Health Mental Health Center, Beer Yaakov, and in private practice. She conducts both individual and group analytically oriented psychotherapy.

ORLANDO LOURENÇO (Ph.D. in developmental psychology, Lisbon University, 1986), is a professor of developmental psychology in the Department of Psychology, University of Lisbon, Portugal. His research interests span a broad range of topics in developmental psychology and educational psychology (prosocial reasoning and behavior; moral reasoning; cognitive development; and children's ideas about peace and war. He is the author of several books and of more than sixty articles in journals including *Psychological Review, International Journal of Behavioral Development, Human Development, British Journal of Developmental Psychology,* and *Archives de Psychologie.* He is a member of several scientific societies, including the Jean Piaget Society, the International Society for the Study of Behavioral Development, and the Association for Moral Education.

FRANCES MCLERNON is a research officer in psychology at the University of Ulster, Northern Ireland. She is currently working on a three-year research project that investigates the role of intergroup contact in the processes of forgiveness and reconciliation in Northern Ireland. Her Ph.D. research was based on Northern Irish children's attitudes to war and peace before and after the paramilitary cease-fires and was published in the *International Journal of Behavioural Development,* 1997.

JAMES M. MITCHELL (Ph.D. in educational psychology, University of Minnesota, 1997) is a lecturer at the University of Minnesota. His areas of interest include conflict resolution, cooperative learning, AIDS education, and inner-city youth.

DAHLIE S. MORIARTY is a doctoral candidate and research assistant at the University of Florida, Gainesville. She has focused her research interests on the impact of social behaviors on health. Increasingly, she has come to see that conflict with others, whether directed toward groups or individuals, has an invidious influence on physical well-being.

STEPHEN PHILLIPS (Ph.D. in social psychology, University of Florida, 1985) is an assistant professor at Broward College, Ft. Lauderdale, Florida. He is presently coauthoring the book *The Tolerant Personality.*

RAIJA-LEENA PUNAMÄKI (Ph.D. in psychology, University of Helsinki, 1990) is senior researcher of the Academy of Finland in the Department of Psychology, University of Helsinki. Her main research interest relates to children's emotional and cognitive development in traumatic conditions. She has authored a number of articles on coping strategies, child-parent relationships, and dreaming as an integrating process in trauma. She is a founding member of the Finnish Psychologists for Social Responsibility and was awarded the title of Psychologist of the Year in 1991 for developing peace psychology.

ALONA RAVIV (Ph.D. in statistics, Hebrew University, Jerusalem, 1976) is a senior teacher in the Department of Statistics and Operation Research, Tel Aviv University. Her major research interests are nonparametric statistics and applied statistics. She has coauthored *An Introduction to Statistics: Probability* (Amichai, 1994) and *An Introduction to Statistics: Statistical Inference* (Amichai, 1995).

MARILYN STERN (Ph.D. in counseling psychology, University at Buffalo, State University of New York, 1984) is an associate professor in the Department of Educational and Counseling Psychology, University at Albany, State University of New York, with a joint appointment in the Department of Health Policy, Management, and Behavior in the School of Public Health. She is also a former recipient of a Fulbright Scholarship for research in Israel. Her primary professional focus is as a counseling health psychologist whose work includes an examination of issues related to the impact of stereotyping processes and adolescent coping with stress and conflict. Her work in the area of dispute resolution includes research on parent-child and peer mediation. Her other professional activities include serving on the editorial boards of the *Journal of Counseling Psychology* and *The Counseling Psychologist*. She also serves as the chair of the Section of Health Psychology and as the international liaison to Israel for the Division of Counseling Psychology of the American Psychological Association.

MICHAEL R. VAN SLÝCK (Ph.D. in social psychology, University at Buffalo, State University of New York, 1992) is the founder of the Research Institute for Dispute Resolution, Albany, New York, a consulting organization providing comprehensive dispute resolution services, including research, training, and intervention; he also is currently a lecturer in the Department of Educational and Counseling Psychology at the University at Albany. His primary research focus for the last ten years has been on the resolution of conflicts involving adolescents and their peers and parents through mediation. Among his other professional activities, he serves on the editorial board of *Mediation Quarterly* and is currently co-chair of the Peace Education committee of the Division of Peace Psychology of the American Psychological Association.

LENNART VRIENS (Ph.D., Utrecht University, 1987) is a professor in and Special Chair for Peace Education at Utrecht University, The Netherlands. His field of interest and research is pedagogy and educational psychology. His most recent publications include the chapters "Peace and War in the Child's Perception of Its Environment," in *Ombudswork for Children: A Way of Improving the Position of Children in Society* (Leuven/Amersfoort,

1989); "Peace Education in the Nineties: A Reappraisal of Values and Options," in *Peace, Environment and Education* (1990); "Coping with Violence in the Schools: The Challenge of Limited Possibilities," in *Thresholds in Education* (1995); "Postmodernism, Peace Culture and Peace Education," in *Three Decades of Peace Education Around the World: An Anthology* (Garland, 1996); and "Peace Education: Cooperative Building of a Humane Future," in *Pastoral Care in Education* (1997).

ROBERT C. ZILLER (Ph.D., University of Michigan, 1956) is a professor of psychology at the University of Florida. He has written 100 articles on the topics of individual-group conflict, group decision making, long-term groups, the self-concept, and photo-observation. Earlier books include *The Social Self* (1972) and *Photographing the Self* (1990). He is working with Stephen Phillips on *The Tolerant Personality* and a measure of the meaning of life. He served in the United States Army during World War II as a medical corpsman.

NAME INDEX

SUBJECT INDEX

Academic controversy, 260–277; benefits to students of, 266–269; defined, 263, 276; developmental appropriateness of, 273–275; elements of constructive, 269; example of structured, 263–265; steps in process of, 265–266; traditional avoidance of, 270–273; war/peace and conflict/cooperation related to, 261–262. *See also* Conflict

Active peace, 147

Age. *See* Development

Alltagserfahrungen (everyday experiences), 40

Amnesty International, 45

Assemblée Internationale pour le Pensement des Blessures de Guerre, 49

Attitude systems, 212–213; as approach to adolescent conflict, 211, 214. *See also* Conflict attitude systems

Beliefs, 184–186; about conflict resolution, 212–223; Gulf War's effect on, in Israel, 179–184; of Israeli children and adolescents, 166–179; as units of social knowledge, 162. *See also* Attitude systems

Canada: gender role socialization in, and attitudes toward war, 119–122; information from television in, 116–119; political culture in, 114; political socialization in, 113–122; values transmitted in schools of, 114–116

Care, Gilligan's ethic of, 94–95

Central Commission on Children and War, 32

Children's Creative Response to Conflict (CCRC), 240–241

Cognitive theory: on concept formation, 130–131, 133–134, 141; conflict definition based on, 213–214

Cognitive-developmental theory: on social knowledge development, 6, 9, 163. *See also* Cognitive theory; Developmental theory

Cold War, 28–29, 33, 40

Collier's Encyclopedia, 96

Committee for the Psychological Study of Peace, 94

Community, academic controversy avoidance by, 272–273

Comprehensive Conflict Resolution Program, 293

Concept formation, 127–142; adaptive role of, 138–139; cognitive theory on, 130–131, 133–134, 141; conflict as developmental force in, 136–138; human relationships as context for, 139–140; information-processing theory on, 130–131, 134–136, 141; major theories on, 129, 130–131; sociocultural theory on, 129–133, 140–141; in violent societies, 128–129, 141

Conflict: attitude system approach to, 211, 214; cooperation related to, 261–262, 276; defined, 213–214, 261; as developmental force, 136–138; in school curriculum, 244–249; schools as opportunity